# THE ORIGINS OF CONCRETE CONSTRUCTION IN ROMAN ARCHITECTURE

In this study, Marcello Mogetta examines the origins and early dissemination of concrete technology in Roman Republican architecture. Framing the genesis of innovative building processes and techniques within the context of Rome's early expansion, he traces technological change in monumental construction in long-established urban centers and new Roman colonial cites founded in the 2nd century BCE in central Italy. Mogetta weaves together excavation data from both public monuments and private domestic architecture that previously have been studied in isolation. Highlighting the organization of the building industry, he also explores the political motivations and cultural aspirations of patrons of monumental architecture, reconstructing how they negotiated economic and logistical constraints by drawing from both local traditions and long-distance networks. By incorporating the available scientific evidence into the development of concrete technology, Mogetta also demonstrates the contributions of anonymous builders and contractors, shining a light on their ability to exploit locally available resources.

MARCELLO MOGETTA is a Mediterranean archaeologist whose research focuses on early Roman urbanism in Italy. He conducts primary fieldwork at the sites of Gabii (Gabii Project) and Pompeii (Venus Pompeiana Project), for which he has received multiple grants from the National Endowment for the Humanities, the Loeb Classical Library Foundation, the AIA, and the Social Sciences and Humanities Research Council. He coordinates the CaLC-Rome Project, an international collaboration that applies 3D modeling and surface analysis to the life cycle of ceramic vessels from the Esquiline necropolis in Rome. He is the editor of *Élite Burial Practices and Processes of Urbanization at Gabii* (JRA Suppl. 108, 2020), and coeditor of *A Mid-Republican House from Gabii* (2016) and *Domitian's Rome and the Augustan Legacy* (forthcoming).

# THE ORIGINS OF CONCRETE CONSTRUCTION IN ROMAN ARCHITECTURE

## TECHNOLOGY AND SOCIETY IN REPUBLICAN ITALY

### MARCELLO MOGETTA

University of Missouri, Columbia

CAMBRIDGE
UNIVERSITY PRESS

# CAMBRIDGE
## UNIVERSITY PRESS

University Printing House, Cambridge CB2 8BS, United Kingdom

One Liberty Plaza, 20th Floor, New York, NY 10006, USA

477 Williamstown Road, Port Melbourne, VIC 3207, Australia

314–321, 3rd Floor, Plot 3, Splendor Forum, Jasola District Centre,
New Delhi – 110025, India

79 Anson Road, #06–04/06, Singapore 079906

Cambridge University Press is part of the University of Cambridge.

It furthers the University's mission by disseminating knowledge in the pursuit of
education, learning, and research at the highest international levels of excellence.

www.cambridge.org
Information on this title: www.cambridge.org/9781108845687
DOI: 10.1017/9781108990516

First published 2021

*A catalogue record for this publication is available from the British Library.*

*Library of Congress Cataloging-in-Publication Data*
NAMES: Mogetta, Marcello, author.
TITLE: The origins of concrete construction in Roman architecture : technology and society in
Republican Italy / Marcello Mogetta, University of Missouri, Columbia.
DESCRIPTION: Cambridge ; New York : Cambridge University Press, 2021. | Includes
bibliographical references and index.
IDENTIFIERS: LCCN 2021000600 (print) | LCCN 2021000601 (ebook) | ISBN 9781108845687
(hardback) | ISBN 9781108964852 (paperback) | ISBN 9781108990516 (ebook)
SUBJECTS: LCSH: Building – Rome. | Concrete construction – Rome. | Architecture, Roman. |
Architecture and society – Rome.
CLASSIFICATION: LCC TH16 .M64 2021 (print) | LCC TH16 (ebook) | DDC 624.1/8340937–dc23
LC record available at https://lccn.loc.gov/2021000600
LC ebook record available at https://lccn.loc.gov/2021000601

ISBN 978-1-108-84568-7 Hardback

Publication of this book has been aided by a grant from the von Bothmer Publication Fund of the
Archaeological Institute of America.

# CONTENTS

The color plate section will be found between pages xiv and 1.

# PLATES

# FIGURES

# TABLES

# ACKNOWLEDGMENTS

This book began to take shape from dissertation research completed at the University of Michigan between 2010 and 2013. Several people and institutions have enabled me to develop the project in the intervening years. The groundwork was laid during a postdoctoral fellowship I held at the Kelsey Museum of Archaeology in 2013–14, in the context of the *Architectural Revolutions from the Roman Empire to the Digital Age* initiative, an interdisciplinary collaboration spearheaded by Chris Ratté, Nic Terrenato, and Steven Mankouche. Most of the thinking for my article *A New Date for Concrete in Rome*, which appeared in the *Journal of Roman Studies* in 2015, and whose content is reproduced with revisions and integrations in Chapter 3 under the same title, occurred then. Further research on the domestic architecture of Pompeii was facilitated by a research fellowship carried out at the Freie Universität Berlin in 2014–15, kindly hosted by Monika Trümper and the Institut für Klassische Archäologie. The results, originally published as "The Early Development of Concrete in the Domestic Architecture of Pre-Roman Pompeii" in the *Journal of Roman Archaeology* in 2016, have been incorporated in Chapter 5. The opportunity for an in-depth study of the evidence from Cosa was prompted by my participation in the international workshop Size Matters – Understanding Monumentality across Ancient Civilizations, organized by the Exzellenzcluster Topoi in Berlin in 2017. The relevant chapter from the published proceedings, titled *Monumentality, Technological Innovation, and Identity Construction in Roman Republican Architecture: The Remaking of Cosa, post-197 BCE*, forms the core of Chapter 6. Access to the marvelous collections of the Classics Library at the University of Cincinnati when I was Tytus Visiting Scholar in Fall 2018 allowed me to gather additional data for Chapters 1, 4, and 6 and provided the needed quiet time to bring everything together. I thank Steven Ellis for making that happen.

Many others have given valuable assistance and research contributions to parts of the book, knowingly or not: Ilaria Battiloro, Seth Bernard, Jacopo Bonetto, Francesco Maria Cifarelli, Alessandro D'Alessio, Penelope Davies, Andrea De Giorgi, Janet DeLaine, Hélène Dessales, Dan Diffendale, John Dobbins, Lisa Fentress, Mikho Flohr, Anna Gallone, Elaine Gazda, Marco Giglio, Ivo van der Graaff, John Humphrey, Marie Jackson, Lynne Lancaster,

Sue Langdon, Paolo Lupino, Fabrizio Marra, Dominik Maschek, Marden Nichols, Jeremia Pelgrom, Fabrizio Pesando, Eric Poehler, Caterina Previato, Marcus Rautman, Jamie Sewell, Tesse Stek, Martin Tombrägel, Mario Torelli, as well as two anonymous reviewers for the press. Any errors, of course, are mine.

The manuscript was written mostly at the University of Missouri, Columbia during 2019–20 thanks to the support of the College of Arts & Science Research Leave Program. Several graduate students have shared their feedback over the course of the project, especially Matt Harder and Stephen Czujko, who also helped me with the final illustration and copyediting program. Funding for it was provided by the von Bothmer Publication Fund of the Archaeological Institute of America. I am grateful to Beatrice Rehl for guiding me through the various stages of the process, and to Gráinne and the kids for everything else.

I dedicate the book to the memory of my grandfather, Salvatore Lupino (1913–93), and to his own achievements with concrete construction.

Plate I.A Rome, Nuovo Mercato di Testaccio excavations. On-site workstation for the fabrication of reticulate facing pieces employed for the construction of a *horreum* (mid 2nd cent. CE). View from the side (archival photo courtesy of R. Sebastiani, Soprintendenza Speciale Archeologia Belle Arti e Paesaggio di Roma).

Plate I.B Rome, Nuovo Mercato di Testaccio excavations. On-site workstation for the fabrication of reticulate facing pieces employed for the construction of a *horreum* (mid 2nd cent. CE). View from the top (archival photo courtesy of R. Sebastiani, Soprintendenza Speciale Archeologia Belle Arti e Paesaggio di Roma).

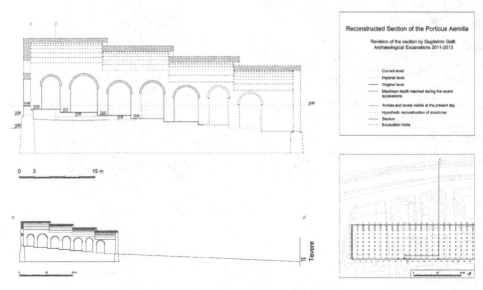

Plate II  Rome, Testaccio Building. Restored cross section of the complex according to Burgers *et al.* (2018: 5, fig. 5; by kind concession of the Soprintendenza Speciale Archeologia Belle Arti e Paesaggio di Roma).

Plate III.A  Rome, Testaccio Building. View of the exterior side of the back wall of the complex. Note the *opus incertum* foundations (Burgers *et al.* 2018: 5, fig. 4a; by kind concession of the Soprintendenza Speciale Archeologia Belle Arti e Paesaggio di Roma).

Plate III.B  Rome, Testaccio Building. Section of the *opus incertum* foundation exposed below one of the arches that open into the side wall of aisle XV (Burgers *et al.* 2018: 5, fig. 4b; by kind concession of the Soprintendenza Speciale Archeologia Belle Arti e Paesaggio di Roma).

Plate IV.A  Rome, east side of the Forum Romanum. Temple of Castor and Pollux (Phase IA). View of the cemented-rubble mass overlaying the original ashlar podium, later encased by the concrete grid of the Metellan temple (Nielsen and Poulsen 1992b: 81 fig. 58; Accademia di Danimarca - Digital Collection; used by permission).

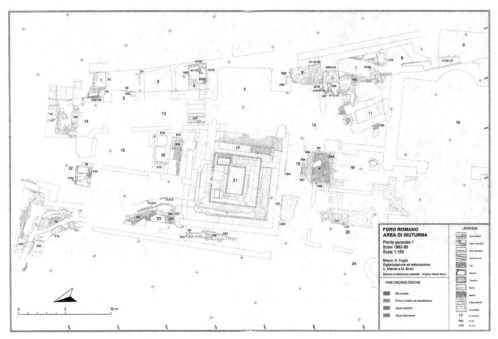

Plate IV.B Rome, east side of the Forum Romanum. Composite map of the Lacus Iuturnae and annexed features (Steinby 2012b : tav. XLVI; used by permission)

**Legend**

- – – Excavation Limit    Walls    Ceramic Object    Floors

     Drains and Cisterns    Hypocaust/Praefurnium    Pavement

Plate V.A Gabii. Phase plans of the Area F Building excavated by the Gabii Project. Left: ashlar architecture, *c.* 250 BCE; right: cemented-rubble and *opus incertum* modifications, *c.* 100 BCE (© Gabii Project). Drawing: M. Mogetta and M. Naglak.

Plate V.B  Gabii. Area F Building, upper terrace. View of the east side wall featuring polygonal masonry made with pieces of *lapis Gabinus* of small module bedded in clay mortar (© Gabii Project).

Plate VI.A  Pompeii, Stabian Baths. View of the "earth mortar" fill below a compact lava *opus incertum* wall in the eastern service tract, Room L16a (Trümper *et al.* 2019: 141, fig. 23; used by permission)

Plate VI.B  Pompeii. Republican Baths (VIII.5.28). View of the *praefurnium* showing the original compact lava structures and later modifications (Trümper 2018: 98, fig. 3; used by permission).

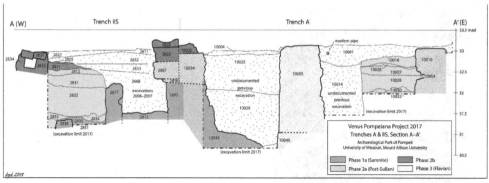

Plate VII.A  Pompeii, area of the Sanctuary of Venus. Composite cross section of the stratigraphy excavated in 2017 below the east court and portico of the Roman temple (Trenches IIS and A) showing the relationship between the Samnite-era features and the Roman structures (© Venus Pompeiana Project). Drawing: D. Diffendale.

Plate VII.B  Pompeii, area of the Sanctuary of Venus. Composite photomodel of the cemented-rubble wall (SU 2677 in Plate VII.A) and sidewalk (SU 2836 in Plate VII.A) delimiting the east side of the Samnite-era alley found below the east court and portico. (© Venus Pompeiana Project). Drawing: D. Diffendale.

Plate VIII.A   Aquileia. View of the southeast corner of the Republican fortifications. The arrow indicates the position of a concrete fill abutting the brick foundation (Bonetto and Previato 2018: 311, fig. 14.2; used by permission).

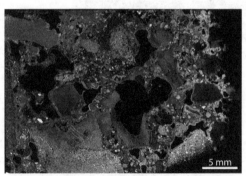

Plate VIII.B   Thin section of a mortar sample from the Republican fortifications of Aquileia analyzed with Polarized Light Microscopy (PLM) using Nicol prism and analyzer. Note the presence of ghosts and relicts of chert clasts and lime nodules almost completely dissolved into amorphous C–S–H phases (photo courtesy of J. Bonetto).

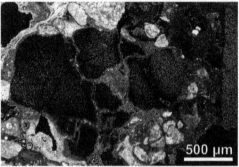

Plate VIII.C   High-resolution PLM observation of the thin section shown in Plate VIII.B. Note the ghosts of chert almost completely dissolved into amorphous C–S–H phases (photo courtesy of J. Bonetto).

# ONE

# INTRODUCTION

## AIMS AND METHODS

Concrete construction represents Rome's major contribution to the history of
ancient architecture and engineering. Scholars have touted the modern character
of this man-made material, which gave planners the ability to cast structures
wherever they were needed, emphasizing the inextricable link between building
medium and building forms.[1] Observation of the durability and longevity of
concrete features, and particularly their survival in hostile environments such as
seawater, has stimulated the scientific study of the material in order to identify the
constituent elements and to describe the mechanical, chemical, and physical
characteristics for possible reproduction.[2] As a result, the systematic testing of
ancient samples has greatly improved our understanding of how Roman builders
of the Late Republican and Imperial periods exploited raw materials.[3] Moreover,
the approach has shifted to concentrate on the step-by-step examination of the
construction process, and standardized procedures have been developed to
quantify the costs of construction, thus allowing for a contextualization of the
building industry within the broader Roman economy.[4] As current scholarship
shows, by teasing out the actual choices made by patrons and builders from the

---

[1] On the concept of Rome's architectural revolution: Lechtman and Hobbs 1987. On the
relationship between Roman concrete and vaulted architecture see Ward-Perkins 1981 (first
published in 1970) and MacDonald 1982: 3–19; Yegül and Favro 2019: 134–37.
[2] Lamprecht 1987: 41–69.
[3] Brandon *et al.* 2014; Jackson 2014.
[4] DeLaine 1995; 1997; 2001.

range of technological options available to them at any one time and place, it has been possible to recognize that innovative techniques emerged independently in the provinces, in response to local environmental circumstances and sociopolitical conditions.[5] Thanks to these seminal methodological advances, the issue of originality in the architectural manifestations of the Roman imperial period has been fundamentally reoriented, moving the debate away from the old perspective that privileged the center over the periphery. Such an investigation, however, has not been undertaken yet for the formative phases of Roman architecture.

The advent of concrete construction has attracted far less attention than its large-scale adoption in imperially sponsored programs. The general consensus is that the building technology was first developed in central Italy during the Mid-Republican period. Partly because of the scattered nature of the dataset, previous studies have discussed the initial dissemination of the building medium only in anecdotal fashion.[6] A common idea has been that it was the outcome of slow and incremental accumulation of experience from trial-and-error starting as early as the middle of the 4th century BCE.[7] Based on this assumption, architectural historians have avoided assigning hard dates to the origins and significant advances in concrete technology, claiming among other things that early experiments would not have survived due to their presumed inferior quality.[8] Excavations and architectural surveys of relevant sites, however, have continued to yield new information, radically changing the nature of the archaeological evidence available from Rome, the core regions of Latium and Campania, and beyond. Traces of ephemeral Archaic hut architecture have been uncovered in the deeper levels of the monumental center of Rome and elsewhere in the *suburbium*,[9] thus undermining that theory. Despite the recent wave of fieldwork, however, the record for the Mid-Republican period has generally remained elusive throughout central Italy. Beyond fortifications and temples, many urban entities – Cosa and Pompeii being the most thoroughly explored and published besides Rome – have very little civic architecture that

---

[5] For this perspective, see Lancaster 2015: 5–7, following Greene 1992 and 2008. On the diversity of construction techniques in the Roman provinces, see also Yegül and Favro 2019: 145.

[6] E.g., Adam 1994: 79–80; Billig 1944; Boëthius 1978: 128–29; Coarelli 1977; Lugli 1956; Rakob 1983. Peterse 1999 represents a notable exception, though narrowly focused on the Pompeian phenomenon (*infra*, ch. 5).

[7] Giuliani 1998: 50.

[8] E.g., Ward-Perkins 1981: 98, "Such slow, empirical advances are in the nature of things hard to document. It is the successes that survives, the failures that are swept away." See also Adam 1994: 73, "In reality, the only buildings with concrete masonry [. . .] that have survived above ground in a good condition are those that were constructed with great care, using a high-quality lime [. . .] It is not possible to discuss the innumerable inferior buildings since those remaining in the open air have disappeared due to their vulnerability."

[9] Cifani 2008. Evans *et al.* 2019 presents an example of hut architecture from Gabii.

predates the 2nd century BCE.[10] Similarly, the sample size of domestic architecture is surprisingly smaller when compared to that of previous or later periods.[11] This book attempts a first synthesis of the new data.

By investigating how the innovation of concrete came about and spread within Roman society, I explore the relevance of the material to answer questions about the cultural implications of Rome's expansion. Pushing the date for the emergence of the technology forward by a few generations, the chronological scope of my project spans from the aftermath of the Second Punic War to the age of Sulla (200–80 BCE), a period that encompasses a fundamental moment of change for Roman urbanism and its physical topography. By the early 2nd century BCE Rome had already morphed from prominent regional polity to capital of a Mediterranean empire.[12] Throughout the middle and second half of the 2nd century BCE, a disproportionate amount of public funds were earmarked for the maintenance of urban infrastructure and for construction projects – in 179 BCE the entire *vectigal* (i.e., the revenue derived from public land and state property) was spent on public building according to Livy (40.46.16) – culminating in the introduction of new building types such as the *basilica* and *porticus*.[13] This phase was also characterized by a revival of Rome's colonization program, which resulted in a number of ex novo foundations and the redevelopment of colonial sites. Moreover, elites from allied city-states in central Italy became increasingly engaged in Rome's imperialistic agenda, earning economic and social capital that could be reinvested in urban beautification programs at an unprecedented scale, in both the private and communal spheres.[14] As is argued here, this complex historical context sparked those social and cultural dynamics out of which early experiments with concrete construction eventually materialized.

The possibility of identifying precisely by whom, when, and where it was originally discovered how concrete could be used for structural purposes is probably beyond our reach. Rather, this work aims to elucidate the pattern of implementation of that discovery across the constellation of higher-order settlements in the Italian peninsula.[15] Technological change is often brought

---

[10] On Mid-Republican Rome, see Bernard 2018a. For Roman Italy, see Lackner 2008; Sewell 2010. For Pompeii: Ball and Dobbins 2013.

[11] Bentz and Reusser 2010; Jolivet 2011 (atrium houses); Sewell 2010: 169–71 discusses the scarcity of house construction at other colonial sites for most of the 3rd century BCE (Fregellae, Alba Fucens, Paestum). Cf. Pesando 1999.

[12] For the internal periodization of the phase, see Flower 2011.

[13] Cf. Nünnerich-Asmus 1994; Davies 2014. For a comprehensive overview of public building, see Davies 2017: 78–182.

[14] Cébeillac-Gervasoni 1983. Monumental building has played a central role in accounts of the diffusion of Hellenistic art and architecture in Italy: Zanker 1976; Wallace-Hadrill 2008: 103–43. On economic growth after the period of the Second Punic War, see Kay 2014. On the agency of the Italians in the process, see Roselaar 2019: 61–120.

[15] On the structural characters of Mid-Republican urbanism in Italy, see Sewell 2016.

about as a result of everyday use and experience of something that already existed rather than abstract thought. Thus, innovation happens with relation to an existing tradition, to which it contributes something "new." It is precisely the focus on contrasts and differences observed at the local level that reveals the variety of technological solutions accessible to sponsors, planners, and masons, thereby making the study of the "new" possible. Expanding on this idea, I pursue a set of research problems to define the context of innovation and disentangle the web of social, cultural, and environmental factors that influenced the sudden shift from previous practice.[16] By drawing from studies that present individual techniques at particularly representative urban centers, my intention is to show that key steps in the switch from ashlar to concrete construction were achieved simultaneously yet differently at different places for different (mostly local) reasons. As we see, the lack of any discernible common thread from the broader scale of analysis suggests that concrete construction did not emerge as part of a centralized process. The results, therefore, will provide an opportunity to test ideas about the relationship between Roman hegemony and the mechanisms of technological transfer, and to reassess the contribution of both Roman and non-Roman patrons and builders.

## GROUND RULES: THE BUILDING INDUSTRY OF REPUBLICAN ROME AND ITALY

At the core of my argument is the idea that the built environment of Roman Italy was not shaped by impersonal forces or processes, but by patrons and builders who had agency, especially in periods of sociopolitical crisis or change. In order to write a history of early concrete construction it is, therefore, necessary to take into account relevant aspects of the organization and administration of public building, identifying which stresses on the system may have triggered technological innovation.[17] Unfortunately, the loss of Livy's text for the period after 167 BCE means that we lack a crucial source of data to reconstruct the full scope and extent of the phenomenon throughout the critical phase analyzed in this book. The surviving literary evidence is sparse, but it does provide some valuable information on the functioning of Rome's building industry. In addition, building inscriptions from urban sites across the study area outline the procedures involved in funding and executing monumentalization programs and other civic benefactions.[18] Collectively, the

---

[16] For a survey of building techniques used in earlier periods in Rome, see Jackson and Marra 2006; Cifani 2008.

[17] E.g., Bernard 2018a: 193–227 links advances in Mid-Republican Rome's stone masonry with urban labor migration and high demand for builders and contractors.

[18] For Latium and Campania, see Cébeillac-Gervasoni 1998: 66–79; Panciera 1997.

available details shed enough light on the overarching economic and legal conditions under which the early development of concrete technology was actually negotiated, revealing significant overlaps between the public and private spheres.

By the 2nd century BCE, architectural projects were undertaken on the basis of legally binding contracts formed between a landowner who commissioned the construction of a building on their property and a builder who possessed or could provide the required expertise, labor, and materials. The most common framework regulating such transactions, generally referred to as *locatio conductio operis* (after the term for contracts involving hire and lease), originated in the building period dominated by ashlar construction.[19] In its basic form, the *locatio conductio operis* holds the contractor who has agreed to organize the job on a fixed price (*conductor*) accountable for the correct execution of the work until final inspection and approval (*probatio*), normally by the same individual who let out the contract (*locator*). The system applied to both the private and public domains, though in public building only elected magistrates duly authorized by local councils could discharge those duties (in public contracts the *conductor* is replaced by the *redemptor*, but in legal terms they represent the same party). Given the time constraints imposed on public officials tasked with the oversight of building projects by municipal constitutions based on yearly appointments,[20] it is not uncommon to find cases in which construction work lasted longer than a single term of office. This is demonstrated by building inscriptions such as the one associated with the Temple of Castor and Pollux at Cora, one of the *priscae coloniae latinae* in Latium. The document (*CIL* $1^2$.1506; early 1st century BCE) records one pair of magistrates supervising the letting of the contract and most of the construction, and another pair giving final approval and dedicating the building in the following year; different members of the local *gens Caluia*, however, were involved through the various stages.[21] Thus, there were ways to maintain control over the project, and the prestige that derived from it, within the same extended family.

The explicit nature of the obligations and liabilities under the *locatio conductio operis* served primarily to protect the patrons, explaining why the system came to be preferred over older contract forms such as the *stipulatio*, which were

---

[19] On the origins of the system, see Biscardi 1960. The earliest document mentioning a *probatio* in the context of public building in Rome refers to the construction of a mosaic floor in the Temple of Apollo Medicus (*CIL* $1^2$.2675; first half of the 2nd century BCE. Davies 2017: 88 and 91, fig. 3.11). On the nature of pre-2nd century BCE contracts, see Anderson 1997: 79–82, and the discussion in Bernard 2018a: 153–57.

[20] For Rome see Davies 2017: 1–5. Steinby 2012a emphasizes the prerogatives of the Senate in allocating tasks and controlling expenditures.

[21] *[- – -] Caluius P(ubli) f(ilius) P(ubli) n(epos) C(aius) Geminius C(ai) f(ilius) Mateiclus aed[em] | Castoris Pollucis de s(enatus) s(ententia) faciendam pequn(ia) sac(ra) coeraver[e] | [M(arcus)] Caluius M(arci) f(ilius) P(ubli) n(epos) C(aius) Crassicius P(ubli) f(ilius) C(ai) n(epos) Verris d(e) s(enatus) s(ententia) prob[auer(unt)] d]edicar(unt)q(ue).*

based on verbal agreements.[22] Cato's prescriptions on how to establish and equip a rural residence from scratch (*Agr.* 14.1–5) seem to relate to this generalized pattern, although the literary nature of the work means that the evidence can only be used with caution: His list specifies almost obsessively all the activities and items that were supposed to be the sole responsibility of the builder – among which a round table, three benches, and five chairs! Cicero's letters suggest that for certain small-scale private projects the *conductor* could serve also as architect and supervising mason (e.g., *Att.* 12.18.1 on the *fanum* in memory of his daughter Tullia), but in most cases the primary roles were divided more specifically, with the property owner performing the *probatio*.

The *Lex Puteolana parieti faciendo* (*CIL* 1².698 = 10.1781; 105 BCE), a building inscription from the Roman colony of Puteoli, is the best surviving example to show the degree of detail that could be incorporated in public building contracts.[23] The text spells out the terms for the *locatio* of minor structural modifications in the public area in front of the Temple of Serapis, which were part of a larger project begun earlier (l. 4: *operum lex* II). From it we learn that, besides providing sureties, the *redemptor* C. Blossius was required to follow sets of design instructions for each aspect of the construction (walling, carpentry, and roofing), supplying building materials that met certain specifications. The payment was to be rendered in two installments, one half paid as an advance at the time of signing and the remainder disbursed after work had successfully passed the *probatio* (ll. 54–57). In all likelihood the technical requirements were issued by the panel of ex-magistrates (ll. 48–50: *duouirales qui in consilio esse solent Puteolis*) who assisted the sitting *duouiri* in judging the conformity of the works throughout the building process. Vitruvius' description of his own project at Fanum (*De arch.* 5.1.6–10) seems to imply that architects in charge of the design and planning of public buildings could be expected to serve as general organizer of the entire building process, and therefore to play their part in arranging for the contracts to be let.[24] Thus, the provisions set out in the *Lex Puteolana* may also reflect the advice and input of the architect at the time of the initial decision about what sorts of materials were to be used (cf. Vitr., *De arch.* 6.8.1). There are, however, other cases in which the task of selecting the appropriate building materials was left entirely to the *redemptor*, as was generically stated in the contract for the restoration of the Temple of Castor and Pollux in the Forum Romanum in 73 BCE (Cic., *Verr.* 2.1.146: *hoc opus bonum suo cuique facito*). Interestingly, the terms explicitly

---

[22] As noted by Martin 1989. See also Anderson 1997: 68–75 (defining the terms of *locatio conductio* contracts as a "sword of Damocles" over the neck of the contractor who had to undergo the *probatio*).

[23] Dessales 2016.

[24] Anderson 1997: 13–14 suggests that training in the legal requirements of contracting was part of the ideal theoretical education of Roman architects.

allowed for the use of recycled components (Cic., *Verr.* 2.1.147: *rediuiua sibi habeto*).

Given the visibility that public construction projects brought to their sponsors, linking the terms of payment with the *probatio* provided an effective mechanism to safeguard against the risks associated with the mismanagement of public finances. In fact, monumental building inscriptions make abundantly clear that the correct expenditure of public funds was advertised as a civic virtue.[25] Since initiating, financing, and coordinating the completion of public monuments was such an important component for the career of Roman aristocrats, technological innovation in the field of public architecture implied greater social and political dangers.[26] This is likely the reason why individual patrons of public architecture in Republican Rome tended to form lengthy connections with trusted specialists, often taking advantage of preexisting political ties among elite families. The best documented and intriguing case is by far that of L. Cornelius, *praefectus fabrum* and *architectus* of a Q. Catulus, probably to be identified with the younger Q. Lutatius Catulus, a close associate of L. Cornelius Sulla, who was responsible for the building of the Tabularium (as consul in 78 BCE) and for the reconstruction of the Temple of Jupiter Optimus Maximus (as censor in 62 BCE).[27]

Similar factors must have been at play in the logistics of urban construction projects across Roman Italy, regardless of the juridical status of the towns.[28] A passage in Polybius (6.17.2–5) is often used to demonstrate that there was an increasingly intensive use of *publicani* who accepted government contracts for public building works on behalf of Roman magistrates throughout the peninsula.[29] Polybius, however, says he is describing the industry as it existed at the start of the Second Punic War, a period for which there is no evidence of censorial contracting outside of Rome.[30] Another fragmentary testimony in Livy (41.27–28) suggests that one of the Roman censors of 174 BCE, Q. Fulvius Flaccus, used allotted funds to carry out replanning projects at the Roman colonies of Sinuessa, Pisaurum, and Potentia, but it also indicates that the move was strongly opposed by his colleague. Thus, it is hard to extrapolate from this notice how widespread the direct intervention of Roman officials was in the early period. More reliable is an inscription referring to the refoundation of Aquileia in 169 BCE (*AE* 1996.685), which demonstrates how the commissioners (*tresuiri*) sent from Rome were also responsible for configuring the

---

[25] Pobjoy 2000.

[26] On the perception of the dangers associated with large-scale construction projects in Republican Rome, see Bernard 2018b.

[27] *AE* 1971.61. For the identification and career, see Anderson 1997: 26–32.

[28] For a synthesis on the organization of public building outside of Rome, see Horster 2014.

[29] See the discussion in Sewell 2010: 110–11.

[30] The exaggeration is rightly noted by Anderson 1997: 99–100.

physical topography and urban fabric of colonies of Latin right.[31] Once colonies had been established, however, local magistrates and town councils
remained in charge of the administration of public projects. This was the case
for the Latin colony of Luceria (originally founded in 315/314 BCE), whose
fortifications were rebuilt in the late 3rd or early 2nd centuries BCE by local
*praefecti*.[32] The *Lex Puteolana* demonstrates that the same degree of autonomy
applied to Roman colonies, despite the fact that these were located on *ager
Romanus*. The corpus of Oscan building inscriptions from Pre-Roman
Pompeii and other Samnite centers in the region reveals that the organization
of public construction in allied cities followed the same principles as the
Roman *locatio conductio operis*. As we will see, the technical language normally
employed in those texts corresponds precisely with the Latin terminology.

## BASIC TERMS AND DEFINITIONS: WHAT IS ROMAN CONCRETE?

The book is organized so as to systematically document the earliest examples of
concrete construction in relation to sources of building materials through
excavation reports and, where possible, on-site examination. For each site
and region included in this study (Figure 1.1), the main goal is to establish
a reliable developmental chronology for specific building techniques and types,
and to then chart their geographical spread against the local geology. To that
end, a preliminary discussion of general terms and distinctions that I apply to
the dataset is in order, starting with the building medium.

In the specialist literature, the term Roman concrete indicates a mixture
consisting of stone fragments (aggregate) normally ranging from fist- to head-
size (0.10 to 0.30 m), hand-laid in a lime-based binder (mortar) with high-
quality hydraulic properties, and packed into place.[33] Archaeologists and
architectural historians normally distinguish the material from other forms of
mortared rubble in which the binder did not feature volcanic ash as an additive,
consisting of a simple lime-and-sand compound.[34] There is scientific evidence
for the development of volcanic ash mortars going back to the Late Minoan
period in the Eastern Mediterranean, but in the absence of a continued tradition its significance for the Roman phenomenon is negligible.[35] Builders outside of central Italy, however, had other ways to create hydraulic mortars than
simply by adding volcanic ash, so the conventional distinction appears problematic if applied more widely across the Roman Mediterranean.

---

[31] Gargola 1995.

[32] Gregori and Nonnis 2013: 495, no. 30 (= *CIL* 9.800 = $1^2$.1710 cf. p. 1028).

[33] For a comprehensive overview of the differences between modern and ancient concrete
    construction, see Wright 2005, 1: 182–85; Lancaster 2008.

[34] E.g., Ward-Perkins 1981: 98.

[35] Maravelaki-Kalaitzaki *et al.* 2003 (Late Minoan structure at Chania in Crete); Koui and Ftikos
    1998 (6th century BCE cistern from Cameiros on Rhodes).

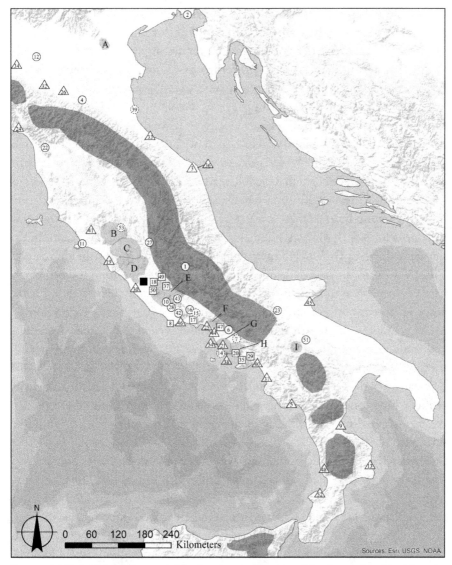

Figure 1.1  Map of the Italian peninsula showing the location of the sites analyzed in this study
with relation to volcanic geology and sources of timber (dark grey). Drawing: M. Harder. Key:
solid square = Rome; empty squares = allied cities; triangles = Roman colonies; circles = Latin
colonies; dashed circles = other (e.g., *praefectura*) or uncertain status. Sites: 1=Alba Fucens;
2=Aquileia; 3=Auximum; 4=Bononia; 5=Buxentum; 6=Cales; 7=Capua; 8= Circeii; 9=Copia;
10=Cora; 11=Cosa; 12=Cremona; 13=Croton; 14=Cumae; 15=Fabrateria Nova; 16=Fregellae;
17=Fundi; 18=Gabii; 19=Graviscae; 20=Herculaneum; 21=Liternum; 22=Luca; 23=Luceria;
24=Luna; 25=Minturnae; 26=Mutina; 27=Narnia; 28=Norba; 29=Nuceria; 30=Ostia;
31=Paestum; 32=Parma; 33=Pisaurum; 34=Placentia; 35=Pompeii; 36=Potentia;
37=Praeneste; 38=Puteoli; 39=Ravenna; 40=Salernum; 41=Saturnia; 42=Setia; 43=Signia;
44=Sinuessa; 45=Sipontum; 46=Tarracina; 47=Teanum; 48=Tempsa; 49=Tibur;
50=Tusculum; 51=Venusia; 52=Vibo Valentia; 53=Volsinii Novi; 54=Volturnum. Volcanic
districts: A=Colli Euganei; B=Monti Vulsini; C=Monti Cimini; D=Monti Sabatini; E=Colli
Albani; F=Roccamonfina; G=Campi Flegrei; H=Vesuvius; I=Vulture.

Deposits of unconsolidated volcanic materials (i.e., ash and lapilli of pumice and scoria) were readily available in the environs of Rome. These pyroclasts occur in different varieties, which are sometimes improperly identified with the catchall term "pozzolana." This term was originally associated with the volcanic ash found around Pozzuoli (ancient Puteoli), but was later applied to any volcanic material with similar properties. Geologists working in Rome use the term as a proper name to refer to specific strata of the Colli Albani volcanic district. The correct scientific word to describe materials with pozzolanic properties is "pozzolan" (a category which includes fired clay and certain organic ashes in addition to volcanic ash).[36] Volcanic ash contains enough soluble silica to react with lime when water is added to the mix (hence the term "hydraulic mortar"). As a result of the chemical reaction, cementitious gels characterized by a crystalline matrix are produced (calcium aluminum silicate hydrate, or C-A-S-H, intermingled with Al-tobermorite in lime clasts). Thus, a denser mortar is developed with stronger bonds within it, and which hardens faster than mortars made of lime and nonsoluble silica such as quartz sands of nonvolcanic origins. The reaction does not require evaporation to occur, making volcanic ash mortars well-suited for use as a binder in airtight environments (e.g., foundations and wall-cores), as well as vaulting. By contrast, simple lime mortar mixtures never achieve the same degree of strength, especially when used in thick applications, since they revert back into a type of artificial limestone by absorbing carbon dioxide from the atmosphere (hence the term "aerial mortars"), in an exchange that can occur only on the outer surface.[37]

The ancient terminology that scholars associate with Roman concrete was originally coined to denote structures built with either hydraulic or non-hydraulic mortars. *Opus caementicium* (or *caementitium*), a term derived from the Latin word for rubble (*caementa*), is often employed interchangeably with Roman concrete.[38] Architectural historians generally use the title to describe any sort of rubble mixed with hydraulic mortar featuring volcanic additives. With relation to masonry styles, the term applies to layered concrete fabric with differentiated facing of any pattern, but the usage is often vague and inconsistent from author to author. In ancient primary sources it occurs only once, as *opus cement(icium?)*, in a rather late inscription from the sanctuary of Silvanus at Philippi (*CIL* 3.633; 2nd century CE).[39] Considering the location, however,

---

[36] See discussion in Lancaster 2015: 21–23.

[37] On the chemistry of pozzolans, see Lancaster 2015: 24–25, with further bibliography. For simple lime mortars, see the discussion in Lancaster 2015: 20. The distinction between "aerial" and "hydraulic" mortars is in Rapp 2009: 265–66.

[38] Ginouvès and Martin 1985: 51–52.

[39] See Kloppenborg and Ascough 2011: 315–18, no. 68a. Oleson 2014: 11 assigns incorrectly the inscriptions to the later 1st century BCE. This is repeated in Lancaster 2015: 21. The reference is to a wall built in front of the main temple, but the actual structure has not been identified.

volcanic ash mortar is unlikely to have been employed in this case.[40] For Republican central Italy, an inscription from the Pagus Lavernae, near Sulmo and Corfinium, in the region of Paeligni, refers to the construction of a *murus caementicius* (*CIL* 9.3138; second half of the 1st century BCE), while another document from a *pagus* near Interpromium, in the region of the Vestini, has *parietes caementicii* (*CIL* 1².1801; 1st century BCE). Whether these features employed volcanic ash in their mortar is also unknown. As the etymology suggests, however, the defining characteristic of these structures was the use of rubble (as opposed to ashlars), not the composition of the mortar. A perhaps slightly earlier inscription from Carthago Nova in Spain (*CIL* 2.3434; early 1st century BCE?), which records the building of *pilae* and *fundament(a) ex caement(is?)* ("piers and foundations made of rubble"), demonstrates the wide diffusion of the basic technical lexicon.[41]

The limited epigraphic evidence corresponds well with the information we get from contemporary literary texts. Writing in the mid 2nd century BCE, Cato mentions *parietes calce et caementis* ("walls made of lime and rubble") as one of the structural features of the ideal rural residence (*Agr.* 14.1–3).[42] Vitruvius, our main source on practical Roman knowledge in architecture and construction, speaks generally of *structura caementorum*, or *caementiciae structurae* (i.e., "rubble walls"). He considers all type of mortars as potential binders (*De arch.* 2.4–6), not just mortars containing volcanic ash, although he assumes that the

---

The relative size of the wall can be guesstimated, however, by extrapolating from the overall sum paid by the patron.

[40] Lancaster 2015: 23, fig. 9A and WebCat 2-A plots only one site in Macedonia where volcanic ash might have been used (i.e., Olynthus). The early date (450 BCE) and the unidentified nature of the material (described simply as "reactive soil") does not make the data relevant to our discussion.

[41] Abascal Palazón and Ramallo Asensio 1997: 69–77, no. 1 has *ex caement(o)*. The authors present the state of the debate as to the identification of the monument, discussing the possible association with harbor installations. According to Oleson 2014: 23, the use of the term *caementa* to signify rubble poured into the sea in order to build concrete *moles* is attested in Horace (*Carm.* 3.1.33, mocking attempts by a rich villa owner to find satisfaction in extravagant architecture). If so, the inscription of Carthago Nova would be the earliest reference of the technology. The term *pila* alone, however, does not support the interpretation, because it is also used in Vitruvius with reference to other structural contexts (multistory housing: *De arch.* 2.8.17; porticoes: *De arch.* 5.1.9; *suspensurae*: *De arch.* 5.10.2), to mean "pier." See also *CIL* 1.673² from Capua (112–111 BCE: [*muru*]*m et pilas IIII*. It seems unlikely a public infrastructure as strategic as the port of Carthago Nova would have been commissioned by representatives of a presumably private association (the *magistri* of the unnamed *collegium* are all either *liberti* or enslaved people). On the dating: Barreda Pascual 2009 (Sullan or post-Sullan period). On the use of the singular to mean concrete, see Plin., *Ep.* 10.39.4 (*quia sint caemento medii farti nec testaceo opera praecincti*), with reference to a failing wall in the gymnasium at Nicaea (Oleson 2014: 31, but the interpretation is dubious).

[42] The date of Cato's work is unknown, but other sources (e.g., Nep., *Cato* 3.2–3) imply that he engaged in literary pursuits only late in life. See Horsfall 1989: 54. Von Gerkan 1958a: 188 argues that *calx* in this passage should be taken as a direct transliteration of the Greek *chalix* meaning "rubble" or "gravel," and that the correct expression for lime would have been either *calx uiua* (literally, "burnt rubble," i.e., quicklime) or *calx extincta* ("slaked lime").

mortar is always lime-based. He describes the properties of river, gravel, and marine sands, *harena fossicia* ("pit sand," i.e., quarried sand, of which he lists four types),[43] *puluis* or *cinis* from the Bay of Naples (the *puluis Puteolanus* of Plin., *HN* 16.202),[44] and crushed terracotta (mortars of this type are conventionally referred to as *opus Signinum* or Italian *cocciopesto*).[45] By Vitruvius' time, Roman builders had a fairly sophisticated understanding of these materials and of their different textural and physical properties.[46] This knowledge is demonstrated by the specific recipes that Vitruvius prescribes for mixtures using different ingredients (*De arch.* 2.5.1): The proportion of sand to lime is 2:1 when river or marine deposits are used, but 3:1 when *harena fossicia* or *puluis* is available (so hydraulic mortars required less lime). One part of crushed terracotta (*testa tunsa et succreta*) could be added for extra strength: Finely ground bricks, amphorae, and coarse ware would have been good choices (but mortars made of ground terracotta and lime alone are never considered by Vitruvius).[47] Different types of mortars called for different applications: *Puluis*, in combination with *pumex Pompeianus* aggregate, is recommended for marine-based architecture (*De arch.* 2.6.2); river sands are to be preferred for plaster instead of quarried sands (*De arch.* 2.4.3).

That Vitruvius was drawing from previously codified practice is demonstrated by the *Lex Puteolana*, whose provisions included a standard for the quality of the construction materials that the builders were required to employ. Dimensional criteria are given for the coarse aggregate (ll. 38–40: *caementa* should not weigh more than 15 *librae* when dry).[48] The structural mortar (ll. 37–38 *opus structile*) was to be lime-based, consisting of three parts of inert

---

[43] Jackson *et al.* 2007.

[44] Gazda 2001: 146–47 makes the point that the term derives from the name of the port from which this material was shipped, not from the location of the main quarries (so, "ash from Puteoli," not "ash of Puteoli"). Cf. Strabo (5.4.6) describes the same substance from the Bay of Naples in Greek as sand (*ammos*), associating it with the fiery nature of the surrounding volcanic area, and states that it was mixed with lime (*ammokonia*) and rubble (*chalix*) to make hydraulic structures. Oleson 2014: 24 (followed by Lancaster 2015: 22) translates *ammokonia* as sand-ash (i.e., the equivalent of *puluis*) and *chalix* as lime.

[45] On the diffusion of *cocciopesto* from Hellenistic Sicily into the Italian peninsula, see Vassal 2006; Tang 2006 reviews the debate concerning the terminology of decorated floors, for which a Punic origin is commonly accepted. Giuliani (1992) considers *opus Signinum* as a specific construction method for cisterns, distinguishing it from *cocciopesto* floors.

[46] Discussion in Jackson and Kosso 2013.

[47] The degree of reactivity of fired clay increases as the temperature rises above 600°C and decreases above 930°C, making fine ware not suitable (e.g., terra sigillata is fired at temperatures at or above 1,050°C). See Lancaster 2015: 25. Crushed terracotta mortar hardens more slowly than mortar made with *puluis*.

[48] Dessales 2011: 45–46 estimates that the maximum dimensions of *caementa* would have been 25 × 20 × 10 cm, assuming a specific weight of 1,500 kg/m³ for a generic volcanic tuff and a maximum weight per rubble element of 7.5 kg. The amount indicated in the inscription, however, is lower (4.85 kg). Using the same parameter for the type of stone the maximum dimensions would be approximately 20 × 15 × 10 cm.

sediment (*terra*) to one part of slaked lime (*calx restincta*), according to the same proportion that Vitruvius specifies for mortars containing *harena fossicia* or *puluis*.[49] Based on the proximity of the building site to sources of volcanic ash, the use of reactive material is in this case probable, but the possibility that reworked sediments were exploited cannot be excluded.[50]

Because of the lack of a precise parallel in the ancient lexicon, I avoid employing the term *opus caementicium* altogether. I refer to the nonhydraulic building medium as "mortared rubble" and will distinguish between clay-based and lime-based mortar subtypes when necessary. Whenever possible, I incorporate the available scientific evidence on the provenance of rocks and volcanic ash used to impart strength to the binder, with reference to the proper geologic names. In these cases, I employ the term "cemented rubble." It should be noted, however, that the presence of reactive ingredients in lime-based mortars has often been identified only through visual inspection. Not always can lime-based mortars including natural or artificial pozzolans be assumed to have achieved the same hydraulic properties (e.g., particle size and surface area significantly affect the performance). In fact, the reactive phase can only be verified using scientific methods. Most notably, the presence of C–A–S–H and Al-tobermorite can be detected through scanning electron microscopy (SEM) and X-ray diffraction analysis (XRD). Other chemical, mechanical, and mineralogical tests have been developed to measure "pozzolanicity" (i.e., how effective the pozzolan is), but they have been rarely applied to characterize mortar samples from monuments dating to the period under discussion. The broad distinction between "mortared" and "cemented," therefore, is primarily meant to help the reader know exactly which mortar composition is in play every time a building medium is named.

## THE *STRUCTURA CAEMENTORUM* IN REPUBLICAN ARCHITECTURE: TECHNIQUES AND PROCESSES

The existing glossary for the forms of concrete masonry documented in the numerous archaeological sites analyzed in this study also requires systematization. Some authors use specific terms idiosyncratically to refer to different wall

---

[49] Blake 1947: 325 translates the *quod opus structile fiat in terra* of l. 37 to mean "to make the foundations." *CIL* 10. 5837–38 from the acropolis at Ferentinum has *in terra(m)* to mean "sunken into the ground" (D'Alessio 2007a: 400). *Contra* Giuliani (2006: 196) takes *opus structile* to be synonymous with *opus incertum*. Columella (*Rust.*, 11.3.798) uses the adjective *structilis* to distinguish a built-up hedge from one made with shrubs or trees. For the meaning of "used in building," see Martial (9.75.1: *structili caemento*, i.e., rubble, which the poet cites alongside *silex durus*, hard limestone, and *lateres cocti*, fired bricks, in a basic catalogue of building materials).

[50] *Terra* in Vitruvius is a generic term that can refer to anything from fine soil to clay to mud: Rowland and Howe 1999: 179. For a survey of the evidence from Puteoli, see *infra*, ch. 6.

facings, while in other cases not enough information is provided to specify exactly which kind of technique is in play in a given usage. Given the general scope of my survey, therefore, it is necessary to create a basic classification in which every key variable of the building method is elucidated, and in which each type of masonry is identified by a unique name. The list is not meant to cover all aspects of concrete construction, but to provide a terminology that can be consistently applied to the sample presented here. Exceptions will be highlighted whenever they are encountered, explaining what limitations or ambiguity the lack of specificity creates in that specific context.

Significant parameters of concrete construction depend on the function of the structures, so a preliminary distinction must be drawn between foundations, substructures, free-standing walls, and vaults. These broad structural categories may be further subdivided according to type of binder, as defined above (i.e., nonhydraulic "mortar" or hydraulic "cement"), and to the specific construction technique.[51]

Rubble foundations built with nonhydraulic mortar typically fill shallow trenches characterized by an irregular profile, and support precinct walls, interior party walls, or walls delimiting buildings whose structural load was modest. The binder is generally clay-based, but it occasionally includes lime lumps. I will refer to this category of structures as "mortared-rubble foundations." Hydraulic cement, on the other hand, is normally employed to build deep rubble foundations laid within simple trenches, whose sides were retained and protected by formworks when the loose nature of the terrain required it. When this was the case, the impressions of the wooden planks of the shuttering are preserved on the exterior surface of the foundations. In these applications the mortar is usually prepared with abundant water so as to fill uniformly the gaps and voids between the rubble. I will refer to this category of structures as "cemented-rubble foundations," specifying each time if laid in formworks. In some cases, foundations were partly or even entirely built above ground, within shuttering or as freestanding structures using stiff mortar, before construction fills were dumped to raise the floor levels and the actual building superstructure was erected.

I employ the term "substructure" (from Latin *substructio*) to refer specifically to terracing walls (often buttressed), rows of vaulted rooms, or vaulted corridors built from the ground up on sloping terrain in order to support a horizontal embankment. The most complex forms, consisting of tiers of hollow vaulted substructures, cleverly reduced or eliminated the problem of quarrying and transporting huge quantities of soil needed to create an artificial terrace.

---

[51] For Republican concrete vaulting, see Lancaster 2005: 3–10; 2015: 29–36. Mortared rubble could be used as construction fill on top of vaults made of stone voussoirs.

I include under this heading *bases villae* and other underground structures improperly described as *cryptoporticus*.[52]

Superstructures built with mortared or cemented stone rubble in which there is little or no difference between the aggregate from the core and the exterior will be referred to simply as "mortared-rubble masonry" or "cemented-rubble masonry" (depending on the medium type). This basic definition mirrors Vitruvius' description of the *genus incertum* ("unsorted mortared rubble," *De arch.* 2.8.1), but it is not to be confused with the modern name *opus incertum*, which I apply to a different type. These walls are essentially unsorted mortared or cemented stones in their natural state or in any case unfinished. The rubble elements are mostly of irregular shape and size, lying chaotically course above course, with overlapping vertical joints in order to avoid cracks, often incorporating larger pieces that span the entire thickness of the structure. The stones could be sourced from surface material deriving from the natural fragmentation of the local bedrock, as typically found at the foot or along the slopes of reliefs. Alternatively, they could be processed from quarried blocks or recycled ashlars directly at the building site. The fact that large amounts of waste materials are usually found still in situ at or near ancient quarries suggests that quarry debris was not exploited extensively due to transportation costs (except perhaps when the quarry site was located in close proximity to the building site).[53] The shape of the rubble elements depended on the layering and texture of the stone deposits or quarried blocks from which they were extracted. They ranged from prisms with sharp edges (derived from sedimentary rocks that seamed without any distinct stratification or that were deposited in with very thick layers) to parallelepipedal blocks with parallel faces (which correspond to the stratification planes in rocks that are layered in thinner sheets), to slabs (created by hammering foliated metamorphic rocks that would break along the flat depositional planes). The structures could be raised so that outermost stones turned to present the flattest available exterior surface (this variation is loosely known as *petit appareil*). The outer surface of these walls was rough, thus requiring a thick coating of plaster if meant to be decorated or finished.

Structurally, mortared-rubble masonry has weak resistance to compression and lateral thrust. Regardless of the facing style, the height of a wall above ground would be fairly limited even with simple lime mortar unless the structure was really thick, because the material at the center would harden very slowly and would not develop the same strength. For this reason, mortared-rubble masonry normally appears combined with load-bearing ashlar elements. In the more elaborate versions, the blocks form a skeleton of piers whose function was also to counter the lateral thrust created by the non–load-

[52] The term *cryptoporticus* should only be applied to aboveground covered passageways enclosed by side walls provided with windows on one or both sides. See Zarmakoupi 2011: 54–55.
[53] Giuliani 2006: 193–94.

bearing mortared-rubble panels that they retained. Comprised in this category are some examples of the so-called limestone-framework technique (from the Italian *opera a telaio*), which was especially frequent in Pompeii and Campania (the technique is commonly but improperly known in the literature as *opus Africanum*). Cemented-rubble masonry, on the other hand, has far greater resistance to compression (the smaller the aggregate, the more uniformly distributed the mortar through the materials). It normally incorporates ashlars only for quoins and jambs, thus eliminating the need for complex lifting technology. Large ashlars could, of course, be used as facing elements of cemented-rubble fills (as seen in temple podia), but I take this mixed technique to represent a variant of *opus quadratum*.

With relation to cemented-rubble masonry, I use the conventional title *opus* to describe walls in which thin bonding layers of core concrete are laid at the same time as different facing material that bonds in with the core. These structures rose as a single unit much like in brick-faced concrete masonry, normally with two masons working on opposite sides, without using form-works (as represented in the famous painting from the Tomb of Trebius Justus in Rome: Figure 1.2). As they progressed up the wall, masons would erect wooden scaffoldings supported by poles. Bucketloads of mortar and rubble could be lifted by means of simple pulleys, or builders could carry the baskets on

Figure 1.2 Construction process of brick-faced concrete masonry as represented in a wall painting from the Tomb of Trebius Justus on the Via Latina in Rome (Photo: Wilpert, J. 1913. *Die Malereien der Grabkammer des Trebius Justus aus dem Ende der konstantinischen Zeit.* Rome: Armani and Stein; open source; image courtesy of D. Favro).

their shoulders while climbing on ladders that rested on the scaffolding. To save up on wood, socketed and cantilevered scaffolding were developed. Their use is generally indicated by the presence of horizontal rows of putlog holes covered by a small lintel. In the cantilevered version the holes go straight through the wall, and the projecting putlogs supporting the floor are reinforced by diagonal braces on the facing.[54]

*Opus incertum* refers to walls in which facing pieces consisting of prisms with polygonal or oval outer surfaces of relatively uniform size create a smooth exterior that can be clearly distinguished from the cemented-rubble core. In this construction method there was no separation between the fashioning of the stone and the laying of the wall. Both phases of the work involved skilled masons who would know how to select, cut, and fit individual rubble elements within the overall mosaic, finishing or dressing the facing blocks in situ at the time of construction. Precisely because of the different shape and size of the rubble, walls of this kind also required horizontal levels to be created at regular intervals ("leveling courses"), so as to ensure the uniform distribution of the loads across the entire section of the structure.

*Opus reticulatum* refers to walls whose facings feature pyramidal blocks cut in standardized shape and set in a diagonal grid pattern. The distinction is derived from Vitruvius' description of the *genus* current in his time (*De arch.* 2.8.1), which he criticized for its tendency to develop cracks along the diagonal joints, but the idea that masons raised wall facings separately up to a certain level before laying the rubble in the core is inaccurate: due to their shape, the quantity of mortar in which the reticulate blocks are laid increases as these penetrate the core, causing the interior section of the wall to be subject to greater compression. Whereas structural improvement was unlikely to have been an impetus, the availability of easily carved stone was probably a significant factor in the initial development of the technique. It seems that the move was primarily aimed toward a more efficient division of labor, completely separating the manufacturing of the building materials from the construction phase. Unskilled or semiskilled workers could build *opus reticulatum* walls under the supervision of a foreman, since the facing pieces could be stacked in a faster and easier process that did not require the retouching of individual elements during construction (though the speed of laying depended largely on the neatness, accuracy, and the size and treatment of the joints).[55]

A common assumption is that the reticulate facing blocks were prefabricated in bulk directly at the quarry sites, or in any case away from the building site.[56]

---

[54] Adam 1994: 151–53.
[55] Torelli 1980a, 156–57; Rakob 1983: 363–66; Pfanner 1989: 173, fig. 8 (but erroneously considering that the mortar was poured in once the facings were built up).
[56] Thus, Coarelli 1977: 18. The best depiction of this has been seen in a funerary marble relief from Ostia (Museo Ostiense, Inv. no. 132) featuring two seated workmen with a basket full of squared elements lying at their feet; in front of them are two men carrying sacks containing the finished products or the waste from the process, under the watchful presence of a supervisor holding a tally:

Contemporary *opus reticulatum* monuments from Rome and Ostia, however, show a wide variation in the average size of facing blocks per wall surface unit.[57] This strongly suggests that any standards must have applied at the level of individual projects alone, thus challenging the idea that there was mass production for the market. Evidence from a building dump excavated in the Insula dei Dipinti at Ostia (I.4.2–4) indicates that reticulate facing pieces were cut from much bigger squared blocks of roughly the required depth, which were then sawn to form a smooth face. The flat surface was marked out to a shallow depth to give a precise form to the face of the piece, while the separation and shaping of the rest of each piece was done more roughly.[58] Since smaller fragments of the same material out of which the facing blocks are made are normally also present as aggregate in the wall core, the pieces were probably finished directly at the building site.[59] Like for *opus incertum*, the first choice would have been to cut reticulate blocks out of reusable ashlars from earlier buildings in the area, as this option would bring savings in both labor and transport, unless the quarry was located near the building site.[60] The excavation of the construction levels of a mid 2nd century CE *horreum* at the Nuovo Mercato di Testaccio site has revealed the remains of what might have been one of several stations for the fabrication of the facing pieces: A repurposed travertine threshold slab placed at a short distance from the wall to be built, and used as a bench by stonecutters who would manufacture the pyramidal blocks, choosing from a pile of large tuff chunks deposited on one side and accumulating the finished facing pieces on the other (Plate I. A–B).[61]

DeLaine 2001: 265 n. 20, following Adam 1994: 44, fig. 49. Both the date and the identification, however, are problematic. Zimmer 1982: 158, no. 81 assigns the relief to the 4th century CE, when *opus reticulatum* was no longer in use. Wootton 2016: 64 dates it to the Hadrianic or Antonine period, but interprets the scene as representing the cutting of mosaic floor *tesserae*.

[57] As is indicated by both the number of facing pieces per 1 m² of wall and the standard deviation of the length of their sides from the average value. See Medri 2001: 16–24, tables 4–5; D'Alessio 2009: 240, fig. 15.

[58] See DeLaine 2001: 241 (with table 11.3 for the labor rates for crafting facing pieces from marked-out blocks). As Wright (2005: 192–93) points out, the dressing of small units of stone requires skill to keep the unit stable under the impact of the tooling.

[59] E.g., Rakob 1983: 365 (Hadrian's Villa).

[60] See DeLaine 2001: 241–44, suggesting that the progressive decrease in the availability of recyclable ashlars may have been one of the factors determining the eventual replacement of *opus reticulatum* masonry with brick-faced concrete in Rome and Ostia. The transportation of the finished pyramidal facing elements from distant quarries to the building sites would have indeed been much costlier than that of larger quarry blocks (with weight being equal, *opus reticulatum* blocks would take up more volume). The secondhand value of ashlars would have added to the overall costs, For a quantification of the labor required for the demolition of Roman ashlar walling and the economic viability of careful demolition and reuse, see Barker 2010, whose analysis reveals that the cost of secondhand ashlar blocks could be roughly 80 percent lower than the cost of newly produced blocks.

[61] Serlorenzi 2010: 113–18.

The modern term *opus quasi reticulatum* has been coined to describe a rough form of *opus reticulatum* that does not result in a regular grid, and has often been taken to correspond to an intermediate phase of progressive regularization of the *opus incertum* technique and building process. The term appears very subjective, since it has also been applied to *opus incertum* walls in which facing pieces are laid in an orderly, nestled configuration. I use the title with caution (i.e., only when facing pieces are cut to square or near-square shape fairly consistently, and then laid in place as easily as they will go, with a clear but also not rigorous netlike pattern). The distinction has limited chronological value, though, since the aspect of the facing blocks (and therefore of the wall facing) is often dictated by the more intractable nature of the building materials or by labor requirements.[62]

Finally, the use of small parallelepipedal oblong facing blocks is also attested. These are radially laid along the intrados of concrete barrel vaults, or stacked on their flat face for quoins (as specified in the *Lex Puteolana*, l. 44: *angolaria* should not be thicker than 0.12 m). Occasionally, the technique was applied to walls by laying the blocks in horizontal courses with overlapping joints. Avoiding the more generic term *petit appareil* or its Italian equivalent *opera a blocchetti*, I define this class of walls as *opus uittatum* (but I distinguish it from the later version of the technique, which normally features bands of bricks).[63]

Given the artificial nature of the facing elements, brick-faced concrete (also known as *opus testaceum*) represents a distinct category. Bricks to standardized dimensions eliminated the potential supply bottleneck inherent in large-scale masonry construction with *opus incertum* or *opus reticulatum*, allowing builders to diversify suppliers and stock up from different sources instead of having to rely on the extraction rates of a single quarry. This in turn created an incentive for producers to expand their output, given that they were no longer producing just to order for specific projects.[64] Whereas mass production developed only in the 1st century CE, the use of roof tiles (often sawed or cut into wedge shape and with their flanges broken off) in combination with cemented-rubble cores

---

[62] Thus Medri 2001: 15–16, 24. Medri describes a general trend for *opus reticulatum* over time (i.e., greater precision in the cutting of facing pieces of larger and more uniform size), but highlights the degree of variability within individual monuments and between monuments belonging to the same phase well into the Augustan period. Rakob (1983: 364) characterizes the so-called *opus quasi reticulatum* found in the limestone region outside of Rome as the local adaptation of *opus reticulatum* construction using material that was harder to shape. Conversely, Giuliani (2006: 230) places *opus quasi reticulatum* within the same broad category as the canonical form of *opus incertum*.

[63] Cf. Lugli 1957, vol. 2: Pl. CLXXXV–VI (describing Republican-era examples of the so-called *muratura a tufelli* from Pompeii and Latium as a subtype of *opus uittatum*); Pfanner 1989: 174 (but in relation to concrete construction in North Italy, Gaul, and Spain); Maggi 1996: 368–71. The masonry technique is discussed by Lamboglia 1958: 158–62 under the heading of *opus certum* (which also includes *opus reticulatum*). Giuliani (2006: 235) groups *opera a blocchetti* and *opus reticulatum* as variants of the same masonry category.

[64] Wilson 2006: 227–28.

was first introduced in the 1st century BCE.[65] Therefore, the relevance of the technique for this study is limited. There are, however, earlier examples of fired-brick architecture in which whole tiles or bricks tended to be used. These are laid on top of thin layers of clay- or lime-based bedding mortar to form overlapping courses that penetrate across the thickness of the structure.

Irrespective of facing styles, concrete has been characterized as a cheap and economical alternative for ashlar construction in terms of both the cost of basic materials and the requirements for skilled labor. With regard to the building process, the main advantage of cemented-rubble masonry over *opus quadratum* was undoubtedly its speed of assembly at the job site. DeLaine (2001) has set out the work rates involved in the fabrication of *opus incertum* and *opus reticulatum* in volcanic tuff for Rome and Ostia for both skilled and unskilled labor, expressing the values for manpower costs of the different modes of construction as multiples of a laborer's daily pay (her "man-days laborer equivalents").[66] Her analysis has found that the size and volume of facing elements and core rubble to be put in place affected significantly the overall rate of construction.[67] When rubble pieces measuring within the optimal range are employed for the core,[68] even accounting for the additional time and care needed to select, fit, and shape each block, a given unit of wall could be slightly more labor-saving if made in *opus incertum* of larger facing pieces than if faced with *opus reticulatum* of smaller pieces (of the kind most commonly found in early examples of the technique). Figures derived from standing monuments at Ostia, however, show that either type would have been at least four or five times less labor-intensive to assemble compared to volcanic tuff ashlar construction.[69]

Patrons of concrete architecture paid every cost associated with the masonry, not just its construction at the building site. For both *opus quadratum* and concrete architecture, labor expended on off-site extraction, processing, and transport of building materials greatly exceeded the cost of on-site assembly. When costs of production and supply are taken into consideration (including fuel for lime), however, the overall requirements of concrete masonry can be

---

[65]  Lancaster 2008: 264; Ferrandes and Oriolo 2019.

[66]  DeLaine 2001: 232–34 for the methodology to calculate man-days laborer equivalents (hereafter "mle"). The manpower cost for a skilled craftsman is estimated at 1.69 as much as an unskilled laborer, based on figures extrapolated from Diocletian's price edict. For more recent research on wages in Diocletian's price edict (with a slight caveat about applying the edict to the 2nd century BCE), see Groen-Vallinga and Tacoma 2016.

[67]  DeLaine 2001: 234–40, fig. 11.1 and table 11.2. The model assumes that for each mason laying the rubble there was at least one laborer preparing and supplying the material.

[68]  DeLaine 2001: 239 shows that below 300 cm$^3$ the time taken to lay a unit of wall increases rapidly, while over 500 cm$^3$ there is no significant time gained because of the handling of heavy individual pieces.

[69]  DeLaine 2001: 247–59. *Opus incertum* = 5.1 or 5.86 mle/m$^3$ (doubling the extra time needed to select and shape each facing piece compared to brick-faced masonry); *opus reticulatum* = 3.59 mle/m$^3$; *opus quadratum* = 22 mle/m$^3$.

shown to have been two or three times less expensive than *opus quadratum* (if reusing materials from demolished structures, the total cost would go down by an additional 30 percent).[70] Both *opus incertum* and *opus reticulatum*, therefore, can be described as substantially cheaper than *opus quadratum*. Limestone can be two or three times harder to work than volcanic tuff, so the production costs for concrete masonry in the limestone region were greater for rubble (as they would have been for ashlars), but the transportation costs for lime were lower than in the tuff region (urban sites in inland areas also would have had easier access to sources for timber). Finally, while *opus reticulatum* may require less skilled labor during construction than *opus incertum*, overall the demands on skilled labor are higher, so the transition from one technique to the other was not dictated solely by economic concerns.[71]

DATING CONCRETE CONSTRUCTION: A NEW TYPOLOGICAL APPROACH

The typological assessment of building materials and related facing styles represents an indispensable tool to identify comparanda for each construction technique and define their chronology and spatial distribution both within individual sites and across multiple sites. In order to establish a reliable developmental sequence of concrete construction, I combine the analysis of the masonry styles and wall-facing variants described above with that of key building types and designs with which they are associated. Strictly speaking, using formal analysis for typologically induced dating corresponds to the same method as the one adopted by previous scholars that I critique in the chapters that follow. My approach, however, departs from earlier works in significant ways.

The current reference system rests heavily on problematic ideas of linear evolution and progress. The conventional dating framework, originally developed by G. Lugli, depends on the concept of *maniera* (Italian for style). Within his catchall *opus incertum* class, Lugli distinguished three successive stages in the development of wall-facing styles, regardless of form and function of the buildings with which they are associated. These would demonstrate a progression from irregular and rough (*Prima Maniera* or First Style) to regular and aesthetically

---

[70] DeLaine 2001: 247–59. *Opus incertum*: 12.6–13.3 mle/m³ or 8.7–9.5 mle/m³ (if using recycled ashlars); *opus reticulatum*: 22–23.6 mle/m³ (the lower value is based on faster but less accurate production of facing blocks) or 14.1–15.8 mle/m³ (if using recycled ashlars); *opus quadratum* = 40 mle/m³. Production figures for the building materials (tuff rubble, brick, volcanic ash, and lime) are given in DeLaine 1997: 109–18 (based on labor and transport costs). The model assumes single source of origin for the materials, and omits items such as scaffolding, lifting devices, and the supply and repair of tools (considering that such costs were the same in all cases).

[71] DeLaine 2006: 240–41 highlights cases in which ideological ends may have prevailed over labor-saving concerns in public works, suggesting that more costly techniques might have been used to provide a wage to free unskilled laborers.

pleasing (*Terza Maniera* or Third Style) – through an intermediate phase (*Seconda Maniera* or Second Style) characterized by a more careful selection of blocks as to size and shape (blocks have a worked face, either polygonal or oval) and neater joints (less mortar is needed to fit the blocks).[72] While recognizing that the local availability of materials and organization of construction could affect the exterior aspect of any structure, thereby making straight comparisons across different sites difficult, Lugli applied the principle quite rigidly to his sample from Rome and Latium. He proceeded to identify benchmarks whose relative sequence would demonstrate the gradual transition of *opus incertum* construction from one style to the next, until the technique eventually morphed into *opus quasi reticulatum*. Using the topographical approach, Lugli inferred absolute dates for buildings who would represent the earliest possible examples of each technique and corresponding subphase from building episodes associated with historical events or characters known from textual sources. Materials from Pompeii and other select sites in Roman Italy were integrated in the same scheme.

Subsequent work has refined Lugli's canon by linking it with typologies of wall-painting styles and decorated floors in which assemblages are ordered according to similar evolutionary schemes. While these classification systems remain useful for comparison between different paintings or mosaics, their validity for dating walls can be questioned because of a basic tendency toward circular reasoning in the way paintings, floor types, and facing styles are linked.[73] Insights from recent research on Roman decorative ensembles have challenged the flawed assumptions of linear progress that characterize the sequencing of the materials. New fieldwork on the distribution of Pompeian wall-painting styles, for example, has shown that the First Style tradition was maintained alongside (and on occasion to the exclusion of) the Second Style and later variants more often than commonly thought.[74] Similarly, while decorative motifs made with irregular and sparse *tesserae* are generally considered to predate those featuring geometric ornament,[75] new findings suggest that the two types appeared side by side since the tessellated floors were first introduced in the region.[76] Thus, conventional typologies need to be approached carefully, as different styles were contemporaneous in places.

Armed with this background information, my survey of concrete masonry goes beyond the inherent limitations and biases of a typology that relies on the proposition of stylistic evolution. For each case study (Rome, the *suburbium*,

---

[72] Lugli 1957, vol. 1: 449; 456–57.

[73] As noted by Ling 1991: 23.

[74] McAlpine 2015. Erhardt 2012 surveys the complex practices for the retention, removal, integration, and conservation of painted decorations at Pompeii and other Vesuvian sites.

[75] Morricone Matini 1967; Morricone Matini 1971; Morricone 1980; Papi 1995.

[76] For examples of geometric motifs in 3rd century BCE *cocciopesto* floors, see the cases of Fregellae (houses: Coarelli 1995; baths: Vincenti 2008) and Gabii (houses: Gallone and Mogetta 2013; public building: Johnston *et al.* 2018).

Pompeii, Cosa, and other colonial sites), I set out to deconstruct the arguments underlying the currently accepted sequencing, exposing the main flaws. By acknowledging that different wall-facing styles and building techniques could be in use simultaneously, I advocate for a typology that takes the first occurrence of a wall-facing style or the use of specific building materials as a *terminus post quem* (or *ante quem non*), but then works on the expectation that, as soon as each innovation has happened, older styles or technologies would not necessarily be immediately replaced by the new ones. To identify key reference points, I assign greater weight to buildings or building phases for which I can adduce convincing stratigraphic dates using the contextual method.[77] Conversely, I strike out of the equation other monuments that traditionally have been linked with early concrete construction, but whose chronology is based solely on style or questionable links to the written sources (most notably the so-called Porticus Aemilia in Rome, or monuments built with Sarno Limestone architecture in Pompeii). As we see, this is the game changer that allows the protracted debate to move forward.

## THE STRUCTURE OF THE BOOK

The content of this book is organized around the central theme of the relationship between the problematic concept of Romanization and the formation of a distinctively Roman material culture. By providing a retrospective view on how concrete construction has come to be interpreted as a marker of *Romanitas* (i.e., Roman identity and self-image) in both specialist and popular discourse, Chapter 2 lays out the intellectual problem and then looks more closely to ancient literary representations of the technology in order to explore how building techniques could become caught up in political debates about elite self-presentation, bringing the agency of patrons and builders to the fore. In doing so, I concentrate on processes of identity construction in the domestic sphere and explore their relation to public architecture, thus establishing the underlying theme of the book.

The following analytical chapters trace the early development of concrete architecture at the listed settlement categories (primary urban centers, select rural sites, and colonial foundations). Each detailed study concentrates on a different site or group of sites spread across different environmental and cultural zones, and can be read as a self-standing essay exploring the social and cultural context of the innovation at the local level. The arrangement of the topics progresses geographically from core to periphery, but shuns the old

---

[77] As already stressed by Lamboglia 1958: 163–70. The end of the 3rd century BCE marks a radical break in the production and circulation of fine wares in central Italy (especially Black Gloss Pottery), while significant changes in the composition of pottery assemblages can also be detected after the middle of the 2nd century BCE: Morel 2008; Di Giuseppe 2012.

Romano-centric perspectives about the diffusion of the building technique. Chapter 3 investigates the origins of concrete construction in Rome, reassessing the significance of elite domestic architecture as the missing link for the initial phase of experimentation in light of the downdating of the earliest concrete public buildings to the mid 2nd century BCE. Chapter 4 complements the archaeological picture available for the tuff region by comparing urban and rural patterns. In it, I contrast the sample of villas from the *suburbium* of Rome with the contemporary limestone architecture in the territory of neighboring Tibur, in order to elucidate whether easier access to both key ingredients for high-quality mortars, volcanic ash and lime, could trigger technological change. Chapter 5 shifts the focus by detailing the distribution of both mortared- and cemented-rubble construction in relation to the urban development of Pompeii, another site located at the interface between volcanic and limestone geologies, whose exceptionally extensive archaeological record bolsters the correlation between social status and the ability and drive to innovate in the field of domestic architecture. The evidence from Capua and Cumae, two major urban sites that were incorporated under a Roman *prae-fectura* just after the Second Punic War, provides important parallels to contextualize Pompeii's pattern of public building within the regional phenomenon and to measure the impact (or lack thereof) of direct Roman political influence on simultaneous trends. Chapter 6 zooms out to the broader scale of analysis, taking up the topic in relation to the colonization program launched by Rome in the early 2nd century BCE, with particular reference to the cases of Cosa, Puteoli, Luna, and Aquileia, questioning the idea that the technology was imported as part of a package from Rome.

Taken together, the narrative presents the emergence of concrete construction as the result of complex interaction between Roman Republican political and economic power structures, local cultural traditions, and global waves of fashion. By highlighting the ways in which elite networks and personal agendas may have influenced the mobility of skilled craftsmen, it ultimately shows how technological transfer in Roman Italy could occur from the bottom up.

# TWO

# DECONSTRUCTING ROMAN CONCRETE

## ROMAN CONCRETE AND ROMAN CULTURE: WORDS AND THINGS

In the preface to his seventh book, Vitruvius attributes the completion of the colossal dipteral temple of Olympian Zeus at Athens to a certain Cossutius, proudly remarking how the creative work of a *ciuis Romanus* was celebrated as a success not only by the general public, but also by the local experts (*in paucis*).[1] The expression makes it almost certain that we are dealing with the same *Dekmos Kossoutios Popliou Rhomaios* to whom the Athenians erected an honorific statue in the area of the sanctuary (*IG* 3.1.561). Scholars have been baffled by the fact that Antiochus IV Epiphanes (175–164 BCE), the royal sponsor of what would have represented one of the most prestigious architectural commissions for the period, preferred a relatively obscure Roman craftsman over contemporary Greek stars of the caliber of Hermogenes.[2] One of the proposed explanations, therefore, has been that Cossutius was hired primarily for his quintessentially "Roman" ability to find practical solutions to the problems posed by the size and pluristratified nature of the site, which was built on Archaic foundations.[3] If so, his story would reflect one of the most commonly

[1] Vitr. *De arch.* 7.*praef.* 15–17 (the manuscript has Quossutius).
[2] See discussion in Anderson 1997: 20–21. On the temple, its Hellenistic building phase and the contribution of Cossutius to design and structural features: Tölle-Kastenbein 1994. On Hermogenes and his school: Gros 1978.
[3] As noted by Torelli 1980b: 313–14; Rawson 1975. At first glance, the decision to hire Cossutius resonates with other stories about Antiochus adopting and displaying Roman customs after his return to Syria (e.g., Polyb. 26.1). Ancient historians have cast doubts on

held views about the Romans. In modern conceptualizations, they are indeed praised for their major achievements in technology and engineering rather than in pure science and high culture, which the Greeks championed.[4]

The basic contrast between Greek art and Roman ingenuity has ancient roots. According to Strabo (5.3.8), the Romans distinguished themselves precisely because of their preference for utility over beauty, which enabled them to focus on the practical requirements of urban life, such as traffic, water supply, and sanitation. Given the pervasive scale and apparently uniform and recognizable pattern of urban infrastructure across the expanse of the Roman empire, the image of the Romans as exceptional builders has been often used to characterize the cultural implications of Rome's military expansion, in turn informing current perceptions of Rome's direct contribution to the history of the Western world. In both popular and academic discourse, Roman technological innovations are effectively viewed as examples of progress and modernity.[5] By far the most frequently cited example is that of concrete construction, the technology that shaped salient features of the Roman way of life, as it enabled builders to assemble modular vaulted structures like aqueducts, theaters, amphitheaters, shops, and warehouses.[6] The diffusion of these architectural forms has been traditionally attributed to Roman agency or influence, based on similarities between provincial monuments and Italian prototypes.[7]

Scholars have over the years questioned the real motivations behind Rome's imperial agenda from a variety of theoretical perspectives, rejecting especially the idea of its civilizing mission. The view that the success of the Romans was due to their ability to devise and transfer ready-made, simple designs from their home to the conquered areas, however, has remained fundamentally unchallenged; so much so that building process has come to represent a useful parallel

the nature of these reports, suggesting that these rather gossipy descriptions may have been intended to put Antiochus in a negative light in front of the Greek audience, and have pointed to his quite independent and aggressive foreign policy. See Allen 2006: 166–70.

[4] E.g., Greene 2004: 140, comparing the popular reception of the Parthenon with that of the Pantheon to illustrate current perceptions of the relationship between Greek science and Roman technology. Rostovtzeff 1953, vol. 3: 1230–38 is a classic reference for the idea of Rome's indebtedness to Greek theory in the field of building and military industry, with the Romans eclipsing Hellenistic precursors only in scale. For this view, see also Scheidel 2009. Flohr 2016 reassesses the value of Rome's "culture of innovation" and its effects beyond ideas of abstract economic progress or measurable growth that dominate the current debate on Roman technology.

[5] Hingley 2005: 39. Terrenato 2001a: 84, fig. 4.4 shows how public opinion in Italy regards building as the most important activity the Romans did other than fighting. On Strabo's characterization of Rome see Purcell 2017.

[6] E.g., Wilson 2006.

[7] Ward-Perkins 1970; Ward-Perkins 1979: 198 describes the emergence of the building technology as an "indigenous counter-motif" to the Hellenization of architectural forms in Republican Italy.

to describe the very nature of Roman rule. In his discussion of Roman colonial statutes deriving from the famous *Lex Ursonensis* (*CIL* 2.5439; 47–44 BCE),[8] MacMullen draws from the technical language of Roman concrete construction in order to illustrate his concept of Romanization in the West:

> Once its essential content had been more or less decided on, early in Augustus' time, the imposing of it on a population was as easy as putting up work-forms for a wall; pouring the population into it was as quickly done; and the hardening of their habits of at least partial conformity could be expected to yield an equally durable set of institutions [. . .].[9]

The powerful analogy refers to salient aspects of concrete fabrication so as to present Roman colonial charters as a form of social engineering, thus reinforcing the idea that developments in Roman technology and society were closely intertwined. Whereas the recipe for the building medium was first tested in the core region of Italy, the text drew from norms and requirements that the Romans shaped at home in the period of the conquest of the peninsula.[10] Thanks to its standardized nature, the constitution could be imposed on the provinces as easily as concrete structures could be assembled at the building site using modular elements (shuttering and centering). Colonists could be dispatched to settle in as quickly as mortared rubble could be laid into formworks. Mirroring the curing and setting process of concrete foundations, cores, and vaults, the sedimentation of shared practices of government established under the colonial statutes would inculcate new behaviors in the inhabitants, thus securing the stability and long-term reproduction of the Roman order. In this perspective, the civic institutions and the built environment in which they operated become almost inseparable, both reflecting in essence a Roman worldview.

Recent syntheses at the empire-wide level of analysis are finally reassessing the importance of both textual sources and material culture to cast Rome's relationship with its provinces in a different light, emphasizing the active role of the local elites in negotiating their place within the new political order, as well as the experience of the less powerful elements of the indigenous cultures.[11] Legislative texts like the *Lex Ursonensis* resulted from the imperfect adaptation of general statutes to local needs, and often copied and pasted clauses from different sources in a relatively careless fashion. The importance of the pre-Roman past in the social memory of provincial communities, in Spain as elsewhere in the West, was in any case never erased by the implementation

---

[8] Crawford 1996, vol. 1: 393–454 (no. 25).

[9] MacMullen 2000: 126.

[10] Entire sections of chs. 75–79 appear in almost exact form in the *Lex Tarentina*, a municipal charter of the 70s BCE (Crawford 1996, vol. 1: 301–12, no. 15).

[11] The literature is extensive. For recent reviews of the intellectual problem and the different approaches to its solution, see Hingley 2010; Terrenato 2008; Van Oyen 2015.

of the Roman charters, and references to the resilience of customary laws and practices are not infrequent in epigraphic and literary sources.[12] Similarly, the building technique presented greater challenges than generally assumed. There are notable differences between modern concrete and the Roman construction method in terms of materials, working process, mode of use, and static properties, making MacMullen's metaphor not entirely accurate. In the case of the Roman medium, mortar and rubble were obtained through different supply chains and were never premixed together. Instead of being poured, they were set in place separately by hand, building facing and core at the same time. Even when formworks were used, the construction progressed in a piecemeal fashion, layer by layer. In order to carry monumental roofing across unencumbered space – whether to span the large pool in a bath building or the sloping substructures of an amphitheater – great amounts of wood and skilled carpenters for the centering were required, as well as detailed planning and organization to remove it without damaging the structure or injuring the personnel. The goal of many innovations in vaulting was precisely that of reducing the quantity of wood needed for the formworks. In the provinces, they occur in buildings largely funded by the municipal elites independently of the imperial administration, and were probably created by native specialists to benefit the financing of public works.[13] Against this backdrop, however, the assumption often remains that at the time of contact Roman culture in Italy was a compact, homogenous entity, and that this formed as a result of a phenomenon of global acculturation similar to that which accompanied the traditional view of the empire.[14]

The early development and spread of Roman concrete construction in the core region of Italy have come to be regarded as key steps in the path toward the disappearance of pre-Roman traits, interpreting the technology as both a symbol and a symptom of Roman expansionism. In order to reframe the discussion, a deconstruction of the main arguments linking Roman concrete with the cultural consequence of the Roman conquest is first necessary.

## ROMAN CONCRETE AND ROMAN IMPERIALISM: MODERN PERCEPTIONS

The idea of concrete as a Roman cultural marker has a long history. Manuscripts of Vitruvius circulated long before the first printed edition of 1511,[15] and were crucial in the retaining or regaining of knowledge of the technology of mortared rubble construction. Architectural treatises following

---

[12] Johnston 2017.
[13] Lancaster 2015. On centering and formworks, see Lancaster 2005: 22–50.
[14] For a thorough critique of this paradigm, see Terrenato 2019.
[15] See Rowland and Howe 1999: 19.

the first translations and illustrated versions of the text closely paralleled the instructions of Vitruvius, recommending the Roman formula. Well into the 18th century, when hydraulic mortars reemerged as a building medium in the context of large-scale projects such as Louis XV's waterworks at Versailles, architects and engineers depended largely on Vitruvius' authority to understand the basic properties of cements, but were misled in attributing the exceptional strength and durability to a supposedly "lost secret," giving way to the popular idea that the Romans used either a special ingredient or procedure (e.g., by thorough ramming).[16] Direct access to the growing number of ancient monuments that were being brought to light in Rome since the early 19th century sparked more systematic investigations of the materials and methods. However, the romantic exaggeration of the excellence of Roman mortars persisted in the scientific scholarship,[17] culminating in the misconception that Roman concrete was capable of acquiring monolithic properties. The theory was formulated in *L'art de bâtir chez les Romains* by Choisy (1873), who, however, never described the material as endowed with the almost magical properties that archaeologists and antiquarians ended up attributing to it.[18]

It is difficult to judge the extent to which classicists were aware of the early theories of architects and engineers. Nevertheless, their fascination with the exceptional strength of Roman concrete was evident and cemented the idea of concrete construction as a manifestation of both Roman ingenuity and political power. This is especially evident in the works of scholars who espoused the nationalist movements in Germany and Italy, such as Mommsen. In his search for an edifying parallel for the young nation-states that were emerging out of regional diversity, Mommsen pitched the Roman model to his Prussian audience by drawing from the same contrast between elegance and utility seen in Strabo's characterization of Rome's town-planning norms. Shifting the discourse to an ethical dimension, the German historian strongly criticized the Greeks for seeking the ideal of life in the beautiful and the good, which in his view inevitably degenerated in the enjoyment of idleness and individualism, ultimately causing the political collapse of the Greek world. Conversely, he praised the Roman character for its devotion to the useful act, which compelled every citizen to unceasing work. According to Mommsen, this innate pragmatic ethos was the decisive factor that allowed the Romans to not only create a unified, centralized state that was both politically and technologically

---

[16] Gazda 2001: 147–49. For a survey of these theories, see Lea 1970: 3; Van Balen 2003; Prigent 2009: 25–26.

[17] See Frizot 1982: 229–30.

[18] On Choisy's impact and legacy, see Lancaster 2009. In *L'art de bâtir*, Choisy barely mentioned pozzolana and offered no explanation of its significance. Later, in his *Histoire de l'architecture* (1899), Choisy noted the possible relationship with the hardness of Roman mortar but concluded that in most cases the strength was simply the result of hundreds of years of curing.

advanced, but also to desire its extension.[19] In this idealist, teleological framework, Roman concrete could be easily presented as the true embodiment of
the Roman spirit, or *Romanitas*: What Mommsen described as the "everlasting"
mortar with which Roman monuments and urban infrastructure were built
would reflect and at the same time proclaim "the indestructible solidity and the
energetic vigor" of the culture that invented it.[20]

For their part, archaeologists and architectural historians doing research on
Roman concrete in the late 19th and early 20th centuries showed little interest
in the broader implications of the debate. Their main focus was on developing
systematic approaches to the dating of key monuments in Rome.[21] Van Deman
(1912) pioneered descriptive methods based on the increasingly accurate
observation of both materials and processes (e.g., the color and quality of the
mortar, type of rock or other materials used for aggregate, method of laying the
aggregate), but never investigated the origins and initial spread of the technique
in great detail, lumping the inconsistent evidence on mortared-rubble masonry
under the category of "pseudo concrete" and crediting the fortuitous invention
of the building medium to the availability of volcanic materials in central
Italy.[22] Informed by the earlier scientific scholarship, Van Deman concentrated
only on those monuments that in her view displayed a true "monolithic" mass,
as a result of both the use of volcanic ash and the alleged application of external
pressure during construction.

A notable exception was represented by scholars working in the German
*Bauforschung* tradition. Delbrück (1912) sought to identify formal precedents for
Roman vaulted architecture in the broader Eastern Mediterranean context,
tracing the possible mechanisms of transmission from external influence.
Departing significantly from the conventional opinion, he concluded that the
transfer of the lime-based technology would have occurred through cross-
cultural contact in the period of Rome's foreign campaigns in Asia Minor:
Roman engineers who followed the Roman army would have learned the
technique from direct observation of various forms of mortared-rubble construction he identified in the Greek East; alternatively, Greek architects who

[19] Mommsen 1854–56, vol. 1: 23–24. To demonstrate the connection between the Roman and
the contemporary unification processes, Linderski 1984 points out that Mommsen presented
Roman territorial expansion beyond the natural borders of Italy as the prime cause of Rome's
later decadence.
[20] Mommsen 1854–56, vol. 1: 474. For the state of the knowledge on Roman construction
techniques around the time Mommsen was writing, see Gazda 2001: 150, listing the main
reference works that would have been available to contemporary scholars of antiquity.
[21] Middleton 1892; Durm 1905.
[22] As reported by Blake 1947: 326–27 (with a date in the 3rd century BCE for the discovery). For
her part, Blake (1947: 312–13) argued for external influence from Greece (as mediated by the
colonies of Magna Graecia), highlighting the "fortunate accident" that most of the sand
available in central Italy contained pozzolan, so that even simple lime mortars would acquire
more strength.

followed Roman patrons to Rome after the conquest could have exported it to the capital.[23]

Delbrück's theory provided a first template to conceptualize the relationship between the evolution of building techniques and Roman military conquests, attracting the attention of historians. Using a similar approach, Frank (1924) mapped the sources of stone used in Mid-Republican architecture onto Roman territorial control as it developed in the 4th and 3rd centuries BCE, thus matching the supply of building materials with the geographical and historical context of Roman imperialism. In doing so, he too postulated a strong relationship between imperial expansion, mass enslavement, and the exploitation of natural resources.[24] Whereas the introduction of new building materials in stone masonry was seen as reflecting the centripetal movement of skilled builders to Rome, the evidence about the early development of concrete construction could be used to chart technological transfer from core to periphery. With few exceptions,[25] current models still reflect this basic framework (Table 2.1).

After Van Deman's plans to publish a monograph on the subject were postponed in 1925 to focus on the study of Roman aqueducts,[26] the task of systematizing the material was picked up by Lugli, who produced an influential comprehensive typology of wall-facing styles for Rome and Latium (the corpus was collected largely in the period before the WWII, and the main text had already been completed in 1939).[27] Rejecting some of Delbrück's ideas, Lugli expanded on the results of extensive surveys he had conducted in the 1920s in the countryside of Tarracina and Circeii (South Latium).[28] Lugli had identified

---

[23] Delbrück 1912: 85–90.

[24] E.g., Frank 1924: 20 (on Tufo Giallo della Via Tiberina).

[25] Modifying Delbrück's argument, Rakob (1976: 370–71 n. 24) pointed out how the use of formworks in *pisé de terre* (a technique common at Punic sites in Sicily and North Africa) might have been adapted to concrete construction as the result of the increased interaction between Carthage and Rome in the period of the Punic Wars. Cf. Gaggiotti (1988: 215–21), who once saw a connection between the *Poenica pauimenta* (listed by Cato among the examples of luxury in the *uillae expolitae*, and understood by Festus, *Gloss. Lat.* 282, as the Numidian marble popular in his day), *opus signinum* (Vitr., *De arch.* 8.6.14), and *cocciopesto*, which is often decorated with white stone fragments, suggesting that such pavements may have been derived from Punic Carthaginian models brought to Rome (and from there to Signia, after which *opus signinum* is named) by Carthaginian prisoners after the Second Punic War. Russell and Fentress (2016) contrast this view, suggesting an Italian origin for *pisé de terre* and, therefore, arguing that the direction of technological exchange went in the opposite direction, spreading from Rome to North Africa.

[26] Bergmann 2010 provides an account of the afterlife of Van Deman's project, which was inherited by Blake at the time of her mentor's death in 1937.

[27] Lugli 1957. On the events delaying the final publication, see Lugli 1957, vol. 1: 21. The many inconsistencies in the treatment of the early development of concrete construction are most likely due to these vicissitudes. The main principles of his typological approach were first applied to the architectural study of Late Republican villas in the Roman Campagna: Lugli 1923. For a review of this early work, see Billig 1944: 131–35.

[28] Lugli 1926; 1928.

TABLE 2.1 *Current interpretations of the origins and diffusion of concrete construction in Rome and Italy. All dates BCE.*

| Author | When? | Where? | Context of Innovation | Notes |
|---|---|---|---|---|
| Lugli (1957) | 3rd cent. | Rome/Latium | Concerns for economic resources; fast and cheap building method; farms | Properties of volcanic ash "discovered" in Campania; developed by Roman colonists; large-scale adoption in Rome (after 211 fire) |
| Brown (1951; 1980) | 4th–3rd cent. | Rome/Latium | Mid-Republican colonization program | Technique "imported" by Roman colonists at Cosa |
| Coarelli (1977) | Before 204 | Rome | Standardization of *opus incertum*; population pressure and influx of enslaved labor | Origins of mortar technology in Pompeii; gradual evolution of facing styles in Rome throughout 2nd cent. |
| Rakob (1976; 1983) | *c.* 200 | Rome/ Campania | Technological transfer during Punic Wars | Link with so-called *pisé de terre* (formworks) and so-called *opus Africanum* (ashlar quoins) |
| Carandini and Papi (1999) | 3rd cent. | Rome | Urban development (after 211 fire) | Diffusion of mortar technologies from Rome to Mid-Republican colonies |
| Giuliani (2006) | 4th–3rd cent. | Rome | Mid-Republican colonization program | Long period of trial-and-error prior to Testaccio Building |

there mortared-rubble architecture of a type he quickly compared with examples that were just then being discovered from the early levels of Ostia and Minturnae, both poorly documented, as well as in some canonical atrium houses of Pompeii.[29] Thus, he located the early implementation of the technique at Mid-Republican Roman colonies, providing a parallel for the kind of architecture that would have existed in contemporary Rome.[30] Following Lugli's lead, Brown (1951) assigned most of the standing remains of mortared-rubble masonry from his excavations at Cosa (launched in 1948) to the first building phase of the colony of 273 BCE, on the expectation that Cosa's colonists learned the technique at their place of origin. On the false assumption that Roman colonies were miniature copies of Rome not only in their

[29] Paraphrasing Vitruvius' description of the *genus incertum* (*De arch.* 2.8.1), Lugli (1957, vol. 1: 374) classified these walls as *opus antiquum*. The term seems to refer to clay-based mortared-rubble architecture, but there is a great deal of confusion with *opus incertum*. See also Lugli 1957, vol. 1: 378, 407–08, and 447.

[30] Lugli 1957, vol. 1: 374–75.

institutional framework but also in their physical aspect,[31] Brown's conclusion was that the technology would have been exported to Cosa from the metropolis through the agency of Roman colonists. The idea was that from colonial centers such as Cosa and Alba Fucens (where fieldwork by a Belgian team was revealing similar remains), Roman construction methods would have eventually trickled down to the newly conquered territories.[32]

Although he conceded that builders from other areas in the volcanic region could have discovered the properties of hydraulic mortars independently, Lugli interpreted the emergence of concrete construction in Rome as a regional phenomenon that likely originated at the lower level of society. He described the building medium as a cheap and unpretentious architectural expedient that would have been first developed in the rural context as an alternative to the expensive *opus quadratum*. According to Lugli's reconstruction, the new technology would have eventually made its way from the *suburbium* into the city, where decisive improvements would have been achieved over a period of experimentation in the 3rd century BCE, finally leading to the large-scale application of the building medium in public architecture by the end of that century. The sequence of fires that damaged the Forum, south slopes of the Capitoline, Forum Holitorium, Forum Boarium, the Circus Maximus, and perhaps the Palatine between 213 and 210 BCE (Liv., 24.47.15; 26.27.3; 27.11.16) would have prompted the need and opportunity for the shift.[33] The later phases of development of the technique would also demonstrate a direct link with Rome. Lugli described *opus incertum* as the standard masonry style (*muratura ufficiale*) that came to be adopted for public building projects in the 2nd century BCE, and connected the peak of diffusion of the technique outside of Rome's volcanic region with the activities of a narrow circle of Roman architects and skilled craftsmen who would have monopolized state-sponsored construction programs for at least one generation, in the period 100–60 BCE.[34]

---

[31] Brown's desire to find Roman prototypes in Cosan archaeological realities is discussed by Fentress 2000.

[32] For a similar view on the diffusion of *opus incertum* to areas beyond Latium and Campania, see Torelli 1983; Giuliani 2006: 217.

[33] Lugli 1957: 384 and 449–50.

[34] Lugli 1957, vol. 1: 445–46. The idea is partly based on the late date he assigned to monuments such as the Sanctuary of Fortuna Primigenia at Praeneste. For a similar perspective, see Van Deman 1922: 30–31. In Van Deman's model, there was a direct connection between political centralization and advances in construction methods (Blake 1947: 2, n. 3). Blake (1947: 228–49) surveyed the evidence from colonies of the Sullan period more broadly, concluding that there was a greater variability in the construction techniques. She interpreted the pattern as the result of the interplay between environmental conditions (the regularity of the facing depending on the workability of the local stone) and architectural traditions (whether imported from the homeland of the veterans or preexisting in the area).

Abandoning the nationalistic overtones and placing greater emphasis on ideas of societal progress already present in the idealist phase, material historical critiques in the post-WWII period focused on the economic motivations behind the Roman conquest and the decisive role they played in shaping cultural developments. Delbrück had seen the Late Republican architecture of Rome and Latium as the manifestation of Roman capitalism, linking its high degree of technical rationalization with the rise of an economy based on slavery.[35] To analyze the spread of concrete construction in Roman Italy along these lines, scholars looked more closely to the case of *opus reticulatum*, having recognized that the technique allowed for the de-skilling of the workforce in comparison to both *opus incertum* and ashlar masonry. Since it eliminated the need for expert masons to finish or dress the facing pieces in situ at the time of construction, the building process of *opus reticulatum* could be characterized as an embryonic form of "mechanization" of production. Betraying the evolution of Rome's society into a "pre-capitalist" state, it would demonstrate a step forward in the continued trajectory of technological progress.[36]

The idea that there was a causal relationship between the pattern of distribution of Roman concrete construction and the availability of enslaved labor has dominated the discussion ever since. In his seminal work on Roman architecture in the 2nd century BCE, Coarelli (1977) interpreted the transition from *opus incertum* to *opus reticulatum* in Rome as a response to the pressure for quick completion of multistory apartment blocks, whose need would have been sparked by demographic and physical expansion through the period of conquest (Liv., 21.62 mentions the existence of high-rise buildings as early as 218 BCE). In doing so, he emphasized the role of slaves for both the production of facing pieces and the assembly process, downplaying the mobility of free workers.[37] A similar transformation in the mode of production and the organization of workforces toward standardization and replication was thought to have affected other sectors of the Roman economy, most notably the pottery

---

[35] Delbrück 1912: 177–80. Weber (1904: 55–62) considered the mindset expressed by Cato's *De agri cultura* as the closest ancient parallel for the Protestant ideal and its unsentimental capitalism.

[36] On the progressive "industrialization" of Roman building in the 2nd century BCE, see Von Gerkan 1958a; Rakob 1976: 372–73. For a parallel in sculpture and architectural ornament fabrication, see Pfanner 1989.

[37] Coarelli 1977: 17–19, citing examples of large gangs of enslaved people such as Crassus' 500 builders (Plut., *Vit. Crass.* 2.5). Bernard (2018a: 168–71), however, rightly points out that enslavers would have been unwilling to maintain workers full-time for the sporadic and uneven demand that unskilled building labor required. On the other hand, the demand for repair and maintenance was more predictable and explains the nature of Crassus's activities. See also Maschek 2016, highlighting the availability of free unskilled workforce from rural farms in the periods when the demand for labor in agriculture was less intensive, as derived from Roman agricultural calendars, and suggests that only small permanent teams of enslaved workers (10 percent of the total workforce) were employed in any given long-term project.

industry (e.g., the Campana A and, later, the Italian sigillata productions).[38] Thus, Torelli (1980a) charted the diffusion of the technique outside of Rome, producing one of the few maps showing the extent of the phenomenon at the broader scale of analysis (Figure 2.1). Based on the occurrence of the technique at the more densely populated coastal sites (e.g., in the Bay of Naples) as well as at large villas along the major interregional roads and rivers in the interior regions adjacent to the urbanized core of Italy, Torelli linked *opus reticulatum* with the interests of Roman aristocrats in the real estate business (mass-housing projects or luxury architecture) and agricultural intensification exploiting enslaved labor. Expanding on Coarelli's model, Torelli ultimately ascribed the trend toward efficiency of construction to the growing entrepreneurship mentality brought about by Roman imperialism.[39] The adoption of *opus reticulatum* in the public architecture of the Italian *municipia* outside of the economically more advanced areas of the peninsula, although relatively late and more limited in scope, would confirm the connection with the Roman elites. The evidence in fact consists essentially of prestige types (e.g., theaters, amphitheaters, and public baths) built under the patronage of Roman senators, high-ranking court officials, or members of the imperial family with access to that building technology.[40]

Current research has shied away from structural concepts and homogenizing representations of Roman culture discussed above. The emphasis has been placed on the biographies of individual communities, and on how cultural identities were created as a result of the interplay between local groups and Roman political institutions within the broader Mediterranean setting.[41] Consequently, the characterization of the early spread of concrete construction in Italy as a manifestation of *Romanitas* has lost its original relevance.[42] In order to illustrate regional specifics, the focus has shifted to other dimensions of the archaeological record such as rural settlement, thus highlighting the survival of vernacular architectural forms into the Roman phase.[43] The evidence from field surveys has challenged our understanding of Roman colonization

---

[38] Morel 1981; Pucci 1973. For a critique of this perspective, see Roth 2007, emphasizing regional variation.

[39] Torelli 1980a: 157–58, noting that the phenomenon would have been accompanied by the progressive loss of status for the profession of the architect, as suggested by epigraphic evidence that shows how the sector increasingly relied on unskilled workforce of low social condition.

[40] Torelli 1980a: 153–54; Rakob 1983: 363–66.

[41] E.g., Van Dommelen and Terrenato 2007. Cf. Wallace-Hadrill 2008. For an artifact-oriented critique, see Van Oyen and Pitts 2017.

[42] The topic remains popular in the context of Roman provincial architecture in the Greek East: e.g., Waelkens 1987; Medri 2001; Malacrino 2006 (emphasizing how concrete was used in buildings built by or for individuals or groups with explicit western ties who wanted to express their Roman identity by imitating construction techniques from the capital).

[43] See the seminal study by Terrenato 1998. For the state of the debate, see Stek and Pelgrom 2014.

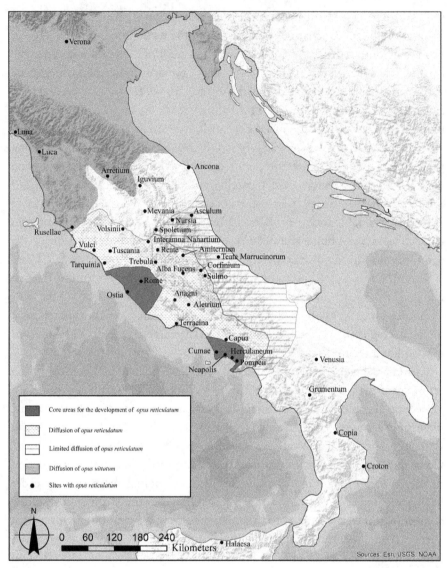

Figure 2.1 Distribution map of *opus reticulatum* in peninsular Italy. Compiled from data in Torelli 1980a. Solid circles indicate known *opus reticulatum* monuments from sites located outside the main area of diffusion of the technique. Drawing: M. Harder.

programs in Italy, cautioning against the pitfalls of the normative model of Mid-Republican colonial exploitation and our ignorance of the urban image of most colonial sites before the 2nd century BCE. As a result, Rome itself has finally begun to be regarded as one of the many communities that experienced the impact of Roman expansion rather than as a monolithic prime mover. The incorporation of established themes of Hellenized taste and tradition marked a radical departure from the local Iron Age and Archaic past, effectively reducing the cultural distance between the Romans and Italian elites in areas of the peninsula where similar styles were already widespread.[44]

Taking the lead from this discovery, I pivot from modern conceptualizations to ancient literary representations in order to investigate how the early development of concrete construction was implicated in the ensuing debates about elite self-fashioning.[45] Contemporary sources allow us to explore what social identities and interpersonal relations could have been expressed and enacted within the arena of technological practice at that crucial juncture, revealing more complex components of social agency than Roman ingenuity, mindset, or ethnicity.

## ROMAN CONCRETE AND IDENTITY CONSTRUCTION: ANCIENT REPRESENTATIONS

A famous passage in Suetonius (*Aug.* 28.3) best demonstrates how construction projects could become associated with ideology and propaganda at the highest level of society:

> He so much improved the state of the city, which he had found adorned in a way that did not conform to the greatness of the empire, and prone to flooding and fires, that he could with good reason boast about how he was going to leave made of marble a city that he had received made of mudbricks.[46]

The physical transformation of Rome was explicitly celebrated among other examples of Augustus' liberality in the *Res Gestae* (19–21), reflecting a Roman view of building as a form of public benefaction. Yet, white marble, a foreign material, had been introduced in Rome long before Augustus. Velleius Paterculus (1.11.3–5) records that the first temple made of marble was the one built by Q. Caecilius Metellus Macedonicus within his Porticus in the Campus Martius, most likely the Temple of Jupiter Stator attributed by Vitruvius to the Greek architect Hermodorus (*De arch.* 3.2.5).[47] Imported Pentelic marble features prominently in a series of temple foundations of the late 2nd century BCE,[48] while the use of Luna marble reputedly started already

---

[44] Keay and Terrenato (2001: i) refer to the process as the "Romanization" of Rome.

[45] Coarelli 1996 (especially 15–84) and Gruen 1992 describe the dynamic use of Greek cultural forms in this period as an attempt to articulate Roman values; Wallace-Hadrill 2008.

[46] *Urbem neque pro maiestate imperii ornatam et inundationibus incendiisque obnoxiam excoluit adeo, ut iure sit gloriatus marmoream se relinquere, quam latericiam accepisset.*

[47] Gros 1976: 393–96.

[48] Bernard 2010: 25–39 presents scientific evidence for the structures below S. Salvatore in Campo (Temple of Mars in Circo, built after 136–135 BCE) and some architectural elements from the Casa di Lorenzo Manlio attributed to the Temple of Neptune (built after 121 BCE?). The date and identification of the Round Temple by the Tiber, which also employs Pentelic marble, is debated. Most recently: Maschek 2014: 185–89 (100 BCE, based on stylistic analysis); Davies 2017: 96–99 (Temple of Hercules Victor, vowed in *c.* 146 BCE?).

in the time of Caesar (Plin. *HN* 36.48). In addition, only a small proportion of the buildings in Augustan Rome were converted from mudbrick to marble, and the marble buildings that were erected proved difficult to see in the cityscape. Thus, as Favro (2016) has argued, it was the sensory experience of the construction process of a few large marble structures, which in some cases took decades to be completed, that might have given the illusion of a newly clad marble city: The noises of massive marble blocks constantly being moved through the streets of Rome to reach the construction sites would have left a much deeper impression on the average Roman than the finished work.[49]

The earliest encounter with concrete construction in Latin literature betrays a similar awareness of how technological choices were capable of acquiring communicative potential and, therefore, could be used to express and manipulate salient identities. I have already referred to Cato's *De agri cultura* as providing direct evidence for the diffusion of contracts of the *locatio conductio operis* form in private building (*Agr.* 14.1–5). In his discussion of the terms and provisions to follow for villa architecture, Cato describes two basic types, both featuring the use of structural mortar. The first is the *uilla calce et caementis* (14.1–3):

> If you let the contract for a rural residence that is going to be newly built from the ground up, it will be the responsibility of the builder to make these things. All the walls of lime and rubble, as ordered, pillars of squared blocks, all the beams that are necessary, sills, posts, rafters, supports, winter and summer feeding-trough for the cattle, a horse stable, a quarter for the enslaved people, three meat-racks, a round table, two bronze boilers, ten coops, a hearth, the main entrance and another one as the owner wishes, windows, ten two-foot lattices for the larger windows, six lamps [or window-shutters?], three benches, five chairs, two looms for togas, a small mortar to crush wheat, a vat for fulling, terra-cotta revetments and two presses. The owner will provide the timber and what is necessary for this and deliver it to the site, a saw, a plumb-line (as long as the contractor fells, hews, squares and finishes the timber), stone, lime, sand, water, straw, and dirt to make daub.[50]

---

[49] Paradoxically, the Augustan period represented a decisive phase for the implementation of fired brick as a building material, using roof tiles that had their flanges cut off and were then sawed or chiseled into convenient units. See Gerding 2002: 47–48; 50. The technique was primarily employed for foundations, so it had relatively poor visibility.

[50] *Villam aedificandam si locabis novam ab solo, faber haec faciat oportet. Parietes omnes, uti iussitur, calce et caementis, pilas ex lapide angulari, tigna omnia, quae opus sunt, limina, postes, iugumenta, asseres, fulmentas, praesepis bubus hibernas aestivas faliscas, equile, cellas familiae, carnaria III, orbem, ahenea II, haras X, focum, ianuam maximam et alteram quam volet dominus, fenestras, clatros in fenestras maioris bipedalis X, luminaria VI, scamna III, sellas V, telas togalis duas, paullulam pilam ubi triticum pinsat I, fulloniam I, antepagmenta, vasa torcula II. Hae rei materiem et quae opus sunt dominus praebebit et ad opus dabit, serram I, lineam I (materiem dumtaxat succidet, dolabit, secabit facietque conductor), lapidem, calcem, harenam, aquam, paleas, terram unde lutum fiat.*

The other is the *uilla lapide calce* (14.4–5)

> When a rural residence is built with stone and lime, the foundations
> should be one foot above ground, while the rest of the free-standing
> walls should be made of mud-brick; add the rafters and the revetments
> that will be necessary. The remaining features should be just as those of
> a rural residence built with lime and rubble.[51]

At a first glance, the text seems to offer exceptionally detailed information about
the building practices current during Cato's lifetime.[52] In the case of the *uilla calce et
caementis*, mortared rubble appears prescribed in combination with an ashlar framework. The suggested proportion of sand to lime given for the foundations of the
*parietes* (2:1, expressed as volume per linear foot) might imply that the mortar was
not of the hydraulic type (*Agr.* 15.1).[53] In the *uilla lapide calce*, the reference seems to
be to a structure in which bedding lime was used to level the ashlar footing of walls
made of mud-brick.[54] The emphasis on self-subsistence points to a possible correlation between architectural types and geology: The former variant would be the
ideal choice in areas characterized by limestone geology, whereas the latter would
be common in volcanic areas, where the ready availability of soft tuff would make
ashlar masonry more convenient. The same rationale would be behind the advice
on how to establish contracts for burning lime (*Agr.* 16), whereby the burner
should be responsible for the construction of the kiln, the preparation of wood and
the transportation of lime, while the owner would provide stone and wood: The
arrangement would only make sense if limestone was available in the catchment
area of the building site (unless we imagine a separate transaction conducted by the
owner directly at the quarry), or if limekiln and farm were at a reasonable distance
between each other (which ultimately means that the farm was not far from
limestone quarries, because lime industries usually developed in close proximity
to these; *infra*, Chapter 4).

---

[51]  *Villa lapide calce. Fundamenta supra terram pede, ceteros parietes ex latere, iugumenta et antepagmenta
quae opus erunt indito. Cetera lex uti villae ex calce caementis.*

[52]  On the value of Cato as a direct source for the early development of concrete construction,
see Delbrück 1912: 89–90; Frank 1924: 35–38, n. 19; Blake 1947: 324–27; Lugli 1956: 107–08;
Lugli 1957, vol. 1: 363–74; Pesando 2011; Oleson 2014: 13–14. Archaeologists and architectural historians have often worked on the assumption that the text reflected Cato's direct
knowledge of practices that were already widespread during his early life (he was born in 234
BCE), in turn providing a convenient *terminus ante quem* for the introduction of the building
medium he describes.

[53]  On structural mortar, see also 18.7: *caementis minutis et calce harenato* for the floor preparation of
a wine press. Blake 1947: 324–27 presents Van Deman's idea that the walling techniques Cato
was speaking about should be classified as a type of masonry in which the structure is held
together by the downward pressure of the mass of *caementa*, rather than by the adhesive power
of the mortar (clay or simple lime would have been used just to keep in place the stones during
construction), but concludes that, if so, simple lime would have had a small edge over clay to
justify the expense.

[54]  The alternative translation of *lapide calce* as meaning "stone rubble" (following Von Gerkan
1958a) would leave no difference between the two villa types.

More critical readings of Cato's work as a literary whole, however, have revealed many inconsistencies, repetitions, and contradictions in the text, undermining its value as a direct source for contemporary realities, including building practices.[55] Scholars have emphasized the literary and political purposes, suggesting that Cato was first of all constructing an imagined identity for himself and for his readers. The odd advice to build the farm when the owner turns thirty-six, and only if the land has been already planted (*Agr.* 3.1) or that walls should be left unplastered until the owner turns seventy (Gell., *NA* 13.24; Plut., *Vit. Cat. Mai.* 4.4) fits well with the image of the austere freeholder striving to maximize his profits from a small landed estate, for which Cato was exploiting the classic *topos* of rustic frugality and lack of sophistication. The origins of ideas condemning the ornamentation and size of Roman houses have been traced back to his criticism of the *uillae atque aedes expolitae maximo opere*, the "villas and houses embellished to the most impressive degree" (*ORF*[4] 8.185; *c.* 152 BCE), a speech that argues against the practice of multiple consulships, lamenting that politicians who seek reelection use public office only to benefit their private interests. In other rhetorical fragments, Cato describes his own domestic architecture, like his other personal effects, as modest (*ORF*[4] 8.174; after 164 BCE?), denouncing greedy (public?) building as a form of political corruption (*ORF*[4] 8.133; *c.* 183 BCE).[56] The functional model farm that Cato presents in *De agri cultura*, unlike the highly refined palaces of his political rivals, had no place for colonnaded atria, polychrome terracottas, and painted plaster.

Cato's representation of rural architecture is clearly at odds with known rural buildings in the region of Rome (Figure 2.2). As we will see in Chapter 4, these are either older and larger, or much smaller but more nicely appointed than Cato's types. Both the *uilla calce et camentis* and the *uilla lapide calce*, therefore, should be better contextualized as abstract icons. The *De agri cultura*, therefore, was and is primarily to be understood as an exercise in Roman aristocratic self-fashioning, aimed at the larger group of would-be elites from central Italy who lacked pedigree but desired upward mobility.[57] We cannot expect male aristocrats to undertake or even supervise personally many of the rustic activities described in the book, but the fact remains that construction techniques became charged with social meaning in the contested politics of mid 2nd century BCE Rome. Building with mortared rubble was presented as one of the aspects of parsimony that could balance the dream of economic gain on a scale unseen before.

[55] See especially Terrenato 2012: 76–82, showing the shortcomings in how partial readings of Cato's *De agri cultura* have been placed side by side with some material evidence to confirm one another.

[56] On Cato's reproach of the sumptuous house, see Nichols 2017: 90–98, who points out that two out of three quotations come from defensive rather than offensive speeches, suggesting that charges of excessive expenditures did not simply pit one group of conservative Romans against another luxuriating group.

[57] Discussion in Terrenato 2012: 82–88.

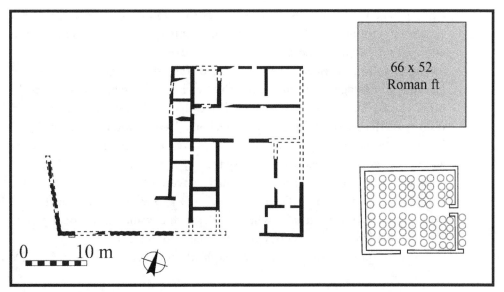

Figure 2.2 Schematic comparison between the surface of site 11 on the Via Gabina (a "Catonian" villa; left), the size of Cato's pressroom (*Agr.* 18; top right), and the approximate space that the prescribed 100 dolia associated with it (*Agr.* 10; bottom right) would take up, as characterized by Terrenato 2012. Rendered by M. Harder.

Vitruvius' discussion of the *structura caementorum* (*De arch.* 2.8) further demonstrates how concrete architecture could become enmeshed in political discourse and competition. As Nichols (2017) has demonstrated, the section of the work on masonry styles was one in which the author could more effectively respond to the social and cultural environment of his time by reinvigorating a discipline notoriously reliant on Greek sources with Roman characters, attitudes, and ideas.[58] The chapter in question begins with Vitruvius introducing the two basic types of wall-facings (2.8.1):

> The netlike work, which today everyone employs, and the one that is called irregular (i.e., consisting of elements of irregular shape), which came into use earlier. Of these the net-like work is the prettier, though it is likely to develop cracks, because in all parts the layers of aggregate (in the core) and the vertical joints (in the wall-facings) are disconnected. Rubble of irregular shape, lying course above course with overlapping joints, gives a structure which is not as pleasing to see but certainly stronger than the netlike.[59]

[58] For a salutary reaction against the conventional portrayal of Vitruvius as a conservative practitioner, see also Wallace-Hadrill 2008: 144–210, emphasizing the theoretical significance of *De architectura* and its relationship to Augustan guidelines giving importance to the Italic tradition. For a classic argument as to why Republican culture may provide the best fit for Vitruvius, see Boëthius 1939.

[59] *Structurarum genera sunt haec: reticulatum, quod nunc omnes utuntur, et antiquum quod incertum dicitur. Ex his uenustius est reticulatum, sed ad rimas faciendas ideo paratum, quod in omnes partes dissoluta habet cubilia et coagmenta. Incerta vero caementa alia super alia sedentia inter seque imbricata non speciosam sed firmiorem quam reticulata praestant structuram.*

The message that Vitruvius aims to project to his audience is that those who commission buildings should beware of contractors whose technological choices would prefer *uenustas* to *firmitas*. "Beauty" is normally used by Vitruvius to signify aspects that are immediately identifiable by members of his own knowledge community, but that are hard to explain to outsiders. In other words, the expression often signals a form of tacit knowledge that would distinguish the good architect from the bad one.[60] However, the reference here has been commonly understood in the narrower sense (i.e., in terms of aesthetics), essentially because of the symmetry of *opus reticulatum* wall-facings (although exterior surfaces were normally covered by plaster and thus not visible after completion).[61] The result of what Strabo would have characterized as a very un-Roman attitude, whereby elegance is valued more than practicality, is that structural stability would be fatally compromised.

The concept is repeated even more explicitly at the close of the chapter (*De arch.* 2.8.8):

> Therefore, whoever wishes to consider and select a type of masonry from these commentaries has the explanation of what will make it durable. Those structures made of soft (i.e., tuff) rubble finely shaped to create an attractive facing are not the ones that will not deteriorate as they get older.[62]

Vitruvius goes on to say that masonry of that sort could not last for more than eighty years, deriving this idea from an obscure law dealing with how assessors estimated the value of party walls (*parietes communes*) in a building sale.[63] He concludes that mud-brick (*lateres crudi*), not by chance the building medium used by the great kings of the past, would be the best of all (*De arch.* 2.8.9), but remarks that the need for buildings with a second floor in the crowded urban fabric of Rome unfortunately made their use in the city not feasible, since it would have required very thick walls (*De arch.* 2.8.16).

Ironically, the terms of comparison that Vitruvius singles out to criticize Roman practitioners are the long-lasting *structura Graecorum* (2.8.5) and *emplekton* (2.8.7), which in his view excelled for both the quality of the building materials (hard stone) and the incorporation of bonding blocks or rubble elements through the thickness of the wall, and despite the absence of lime

---

[60] On the strategic use of tacit knowledge in Vitruvius, see Cuomo 2016.

[61] So Torelli 1980a; Rakob 1983.

[62] *Itaque si qui voluerit ex his commentariis animadvertere et eligere genus structurae, perpetuitatis poterit rationem habere. non enim quae sunt e molli caemento subtili facie venustatis, non eae possunt esse in vetustate non ruinosae.*

[63] Jackson 2014: 23 takes the reference literally to mean that Vitruvius and his contemporaries would have considered structures built prior to about 100 BCE as made of flawed and poorly cohesive cementitious materials, and expected such walls to withstand deterioration for no more than eighty years of service life. On the concept of "depreciation" and "amortization" in Vitruvius, see Rihll 2013.

mortar. The idea we get from Vitruvius is that Greek masons build structures in which there would be no separation between core and facings, whereas Roman builders (his *nostri*) erect walls that consist of three separate parts, as if the facings were meant to be freestanding structures with the function of formwork ("lost shuttering"), just for the sake of quick construction (*celeritati studentes*). In reality, however, in both *opus incertum* and *opus reticulatum* facings and core rose together.[64] The fact is that Vitruvius, much like Cato, never intended to provide an accurate and objective representation of the built environment – on the contrary, the inaccuracy of many of his architectural rules and precepts has been a source of frustration for archaeologists.[65] His main goal was to appeal to elites and aspiring elites that were hoping to secure a position in the new Augustan order by sponsoring building projects (whether private or public in nature), crafting his authorial persona so as to emerge as a member of a community of architects who look out for the *patres familiarum*.[66]

How deeply his readers were supposed to engage with the technical and scientific content remains a controversial topic, but Vitruvius' presentation of building materials and techniques was important enough to follow right after the book on the education of the architect.[67] The concern was specifically for patrons of domestic architecture to be able to balance the Roman culture of display with the financial perils of construction, which depended first of all on the technological aspects. This was a recurring problem affecting Roman urbanism in Italy: Private sponsors who went bankrupt for indulging in conspicuous consumption had a negative impact on the overall ability of local communities to sustain the burden of urban infrastructure and maintenance (see Cic., *Cat.* 2.20 on the precarious state of Sullan colonies).[68] Hence the need arose for Vitruvius to warn his readers not to fall victim to aggressive architects and dissipate resources that could be reinvested elsewhere for their political advancement. As Nichols perceptively argues, by measuring Roman building practice against the Greek yardstick,[69] the hope of Vitruvius was to elicit the response of well-educated Romans, who could appreciate the

[64] See Wright 2005: 187–92, pointing out how the pyramidal facing blocks in the *opus reticulatum* were closely bedded only on the exterior and did not constitute a stable shuttering, so that facing and core had to be built up simultaneously (but he seems to think that a few courses of *opus incertum* facings could be built before adding the core).

[65] See Lugli 1956: 105–06 for an explicit attempt to reconcile the mismatch between the archaeological record and Vitruvius' characterization of Roman concrete as fragile.

[66] Nichols 2017: 10–15.

[67] Cf. Reitz-Joosse 2016, arguing that Vitruvius wished to present his material in the order in which a city is built from scratch.

[68] *Sed tamen ii sunt coloni, qui se in insperatis ac repentinis pecuniis sumptuosius insolentiusque iactarunt. Hi dum aedificant tamquam beati, dum praediis lectis, familiis magnis, conuiuiis apparatis delectantur, in tantum aes alienum inciderunt, ut, si salui esse uelint, Sulla sit eis ab inferis excitandus.*

[69] Tomlinson 1961 suggests that Vitruvius' discussion of the *structura Graecorum* derives entirely from written sources.

difference in emphasis between their education and that of a true architect, thus eliminating the problem of laymen preferring to manage building projects at home rather than hiring architectural impostors (*De arch.* 6.*praef.* 6–7).[70] Greek cultural standards could provide a familiar frame of reference.

Perhaps only to our surprise, then, in literary representations of the Late Republican and Early Imperial periods Roman concrete construction came to be characterized by negative connotations, particularly in the private context.[71] The specialized use of hydraulic mortars, for example, was linked with excessive expenditure in forms of domestic architecture that provoked controversy. Seaside villas provided with features built out into the sea, such as fish-pools, were an easy target: Their owners, mocked as *piscinarii*, were chastised for ignoring their political responsibilities in Late Republican Rome.[72] While the shared belief was that the grandeur of a house should correlate to the social status of its owner (e.g., Vitr., *De arch.* 1.2.9; 6.5.3), luxury in private architecture remained a stereotype connected with vice.[73] Moral injunctions about extravagant domestic construction abound in Vitruvius, who contrasts lavish spending in decoration, especially because of the high prices of pigments, with the restraint and sobriety of the *antiqui*. Based on the same principle that led him to praise the *firmitas* of the *genus antiquum* and reject the crumbling *reticulatum*, Vitruvius saw in the refinement of houses yet another dimension of the decaying state of the Roman architecture of his time.

## CONCLUSIONS

Being an exceptionally durable yet versatile building material, Roman concrete has been traditionally conceptualized as the physical manifestation of *Romanitas*. In current surveys of Roman building techniques, the impression we get is that the invention of concrete architecture in Rome was simply bound to happen. The economic implications of Rome's growth into an imperial capital and its pattern of military expansion into Italy during the Mid-Republican period seemed to provide enough context to explain the genesis,

---

[70] On the sarcasm with which Vitruvius commends *patres familiarum* who have been managing their own architectural projects, see Nichols 2017: 78–82.

[71] Pliny, too, who depends entirely on Vitruvius, criticizes *opus reticulatum* for its alleged tendency to develop cracks: *HN* 36.171.

[72] See Cic., *Att.* 1.19.6; 1.20.3.

[73] Edwards 1993: 137–72. Romano (1994) suggests that passages in Vitruvius in which he advocated for the incorporation of the magnificent forms of public buildings into private space by the *potentes* or *nobiles* (*De arch.* 6.5.2) reflect an original composition in a historical context dominated by a group of men who inhabited palatial homes that accommodated political functions, and that the moralizing elements condemning luxury were only added in a later phase to conform to Augustan policies of modesty. Nichols (2017: 83–129) prefers to see in this a demonstration of the contrasting modes of propriety of domestic display in Roman discourse dating back to the Mid-Republican period.

implementation, and subsequent dissemination of the building medium and related wall-facing styles. In this perspective, Roman colonists effectively represented the main agents in the transfer and exchange of Roman knowledge across the peninsula, building technology included.

Ancient literary sources allow us to sketch a more complicated picture of Roman attitudes toward the building industry, providing a point of entry into the socioeconomic context of concrete construction and its development. The connection is often with moralizing injunctions about domestic architecture, which were specifically meant to score broader political goals. Cato presented the use of mortared-rubble construction as an element of restraint and parsimony, contrasting the modest features of his imagined *uilla calce caementis* to the extravagant mansions owned by his political opponents. While spinning traditional rural morality to the advantage of those who, like him, were trying to break into Roman politics from a relatively underprivileged starting position, he was also speaking to the landed aristocrats in and around Rome, criticizing luxury and fragmentation of wealth.[74] Similarly, Vitruvius repeatedly cautioned the patrons of building projects against the financial dangers of construction, emphasizing the crucial relationship between technological choices and efficient resource management. In doing so, he praised the old and well-tested *genus incertum*, the technique he saw most closely aligned with the ideal norms of the *structura Graecorum*, at the expense of the Roman *opus reticulatum* current in his times.

Whereas I acknowledge the ideological biases of Cato and Vitruvius, and their interest in crafting their own authorial personae, two main points emerge from these findings. First, by the mid 2nd century BCE, self-presentation through domestic architecture played a major role for *patres familiarum*, and building with mortared-rubble technology was part of the debate about the economic concerns of individuals of higher status who had career aspirations in the increasingly crowded field of Roman politics. Although the shared understanding was that the ornamentation and size of a house should correspond to the social status of its owner, excessive spending in architecture, whether in luxurious decor or on structural repairs that could have been avoided by hiring an architect that valued *firmitas* over *uenustas*, would have squandered resources that could have been otherwise invested more profitably, for example to finance successful electoral campaigns. This suggests that cost-saving innovations in the organization of construction may have just as well occurred in the domestic sphere. It seems reasonable to assume that technological advances could have been extended to public building by the same aristocratic patrons, employing groups of builders whose new skills had been already tried elsewhere. To test this hypothesis, I turn to the archaeological record.

---

[74] Habinek 1998; Wallace-Hadrill 2008: 319–38.

# THREE

# A NEW DATE FOR CONCRETE IN ROME

## AT THE ROOTS OF ROMAN REPUBLICAN ARCHITECTURE

Rome's military expansion in the Mid-Republican period was a crucial phase for the formation of Roman urbanism and architecture. The growth of Rome into a metropolis and the launch of the colonization program in 338 BCE offered the Romans an opportunity to rethink how cities should look and function and test new ideas on the ground. Key urban elements such as fortifications, orthogonal grids, civic spaces, and religious structures were redefined between the 4th and the early 2nd centuries BCE through the creative adaptation of Greek prototypes both in Rome and in the colonies.[1] This chapter expands the analysis beyond issues of design and planning, exploring how advances in building technology became implicated in the process.

Temple building, the one category for which we have an extensive archaeological record for the period before the 2nd century BCE, provides perhaps the best example to demonstrate how the early application of imperial wealth influenced shifts in both the energetics and the aesthetics of monumental architecture. Since the early 3rd century BCE at the latest, temples were

---

[1] Sewell 2010. On the end of the 4th century BCE as a watershed in the field of Roman urbanism, see Von Hesberg 2005: 16 (arguing that "Roman architecture" from the 8th to the 4th centuries BCE must be intended simply as meaning "building Rome"). Hopkins (2017: 176), however, reevaluates Rome's architectural production of the late Archaic and early Republican periods, emphasizing its creative mixture of trends from Ionia, Etruria, and Sicily, thus downplaying the concept of Hellenization for the 3rd and 2nd centuries BCE.

being vowed in response to military concerns.[2] These monuments featured materials quarried from areas located farther away from the urban core, in the newly conquered Latin, Etruscan, and Faliscan countryside, which had physical properties better than those available locally (e.g., greater resistance to compression and tensile stresses; suitability for fine carving). Their pattern of use in public architecture, however, was the result of the complex interrelation between the organization of construction, visual culture, and aristocratic ideology, since almost all building projects in this period were overseen by magistrates who were members of the ruling elite. The abrupt change from squat to slender proportions in temple superstructures, which Davies (2012) has linked with the introduction of Greek-looking entablatures, can be understood as an innovation that was made possible by the judicious application of imported stone like the Peperino (*lapis Albanus*). Visual language could thus be exploited by patrons who knew how to take full advantage of the greater visibility that the sponsorship of public building afforded to them so as to stand out in the crowded field of Roman politics.[3]

The idea that Rome's ascendancy in central Italy created the material conditions for accessing and exploiting new building materials, and that these in turn enabled architectural innovations in response to sociopolitical needs, is quite tempting, but the model requires some modifications. First, recent work on the geochemical characterization of the tuffs used in Rome has called into question the validity of old chronological schemes and the causal connection between quarrying and conquest, highlighting the function of independent trade networks for the supply of building materials. Peperino stone was used centuries earlier than the Roman incorporation of Latium, while in other cases there was a considerable lag between the conquest of a territory to the use of that territory's material in Roman architecture.[4] Secondly, by the later Mid-Republican period building contracts had become the normal means by which public construction was arranged, progressing in parallel with the state's use of coinage. This implies a deeper institutional transformation of Rome's economy, as one increasingly relying on market-based strategies for the supply of both skilled and unskilled labor.[5] Taking these circumstances into account, in what follows I examine how the introduction of concrete fits in the developmental sequence of the monumental core of Rome, clarifying the tempo and

---

[2] Davies 2017: 42–61, 80–82; Bernard 2018a: 25–44.

[3] Davies (2017) stresses how the continued cooptation of members of allied communities into Rome's government only exacerbated the intensity of the phenomenon, since such reward systems had the effect of widening significantly the pool of eligible candidates.

[4] See Marra *et al.* 2018 and Diffendale *et al.* 2018 for an overview of the early use of Tufo Lionato from the Anio and Peperino stone at the sanctuary sites of Largo Argentina and Sant'Omobono, respectively. Bernard 2018a: 225, table 7.2.

[5] On the institutional structures that facilitated the mobility of nonagricultural labor, see Bernard 2018a: 175–85.

dynamics of its initial implementation in order to reconstruct the context of innovation and its relationship to the broader historical trajectory.

## THE LOCAL ENVIRONMENT: SOURCES OF BUILDING MATERIALS IN THE REGION OF ROME

The early history of Roman concrete construction was largely determined by the limitations of the resources that were naturally available in Rome's catchment area. Patterns in the choice of stone employed as rubble and the selection of the fine aggregates used in mortars (Vitruvius' *harenae fossiciae*) demonstrate how Roman builders expanded their empirical knowledge of the chemistry and physical properties of the materials through time. Thus, it is useful to start our discussion with a brief introduction about the environmental conditions that influenced the archaeological phenomenon.

The geology of the site of Rome and of the Roman Campagna is characterized by the products of two distinct volcanic districts, the Alban Hills and the Monti Sabatini (Figure 3.1).[6] Most notable among the Alban Hills deposits are the Tufo del Palatino (which outcrops in the valley between the Palatine and the Capitoline) and the Tufo Lionato (varieties of this stone were quarried from the foot of the Capitoline, at Monteverde, on the Via Portuensis, and on the Anio river, east of Rome, but can only be distinguished through combined petrographic and geochemical analysis). Deposits of more durable stones are located farther away. Among these are the Peperino (quarried near Marino) and the *lapis Gabinus* (quarried at Gabii) – both the result of hydromagmatic episodes – and leucititic lavas (basalt). The most common stones from the Monti Sabatini district include the so-called Cappellaccio (Grottarossa Pyroclastic Sequence, which outcrops at the top of the Palatine and is, therefore, often confused with the Tufo del Palatino), and, from the areas north of Rome, the Tufo Giallo di Prima Porta, the Tufo Giallo della Via Tiberina (also known in the archaeological literature as Grotta Oscura), and the Tufo Rosso a Scorie Nere (quarried near Fidene). All of these building stones were exploited as *caementa* in Republican concrete construction. Travertine rubble is also occasionally attested, but its presence is often secondary (i.e., obtained from recycled elements and/or waste materials). The stone, which was quarried from Tibur, 30 km east of Rome, was primarily used for architectural decorations or revetments. The earliest evidence for the use of lightweight scoria from the Vesuvian region comes from the Forum of Caesar, where it was judiciously employed for vaulting, and dates to the middle of the 1st century BCE.[7]

---

[6] DeLaine 1995; Jackson and Marra 2006: 419–21; Marra *et al.* 2016: 180–81, table 1.
[7] Lancaster *et al.* 2011.

The volcanic tuffs alternate with layers of volcanic ash deposits interspersed with paleosols, which formed when each ash deposit was exposed before it was buried by a subsequent eruption.[8] Thus, Tufo del Palatino is overlain by the Pozzolane Rosse, the younger Pozzolane Nere, the lower lithified unit of Tufo Lionato and the upper unit of Pozzolanelle. Several fall deposits created by the Monti Sabatini activities have also been identified above the Grottarossa Pyroclastic Sequence and the Pozzolane Rosse. The volcanic plateau created by the Alban Hills and the Monti Sabatini deposits was largely eroded by the Tiber River and its tributaries during periods of low sea level in the Late Pleistocene. Reworked sedimentary deposits of volcanic origins (known as Valle Giulia, Aurelia, and S. Paolo Formations) occur at the base of the Capitoline and Esquiline hills (the San Paolo Formation contains Pozzolane Rosse, whereas the Aurelia Formation contains Pozzolanelle and Tufo Lionato). Exploitation of deeper beds of volcanic ash was made feasible by tunneling the desired strata directly from the side of the natural cuts in the bedrock. The changing sea levels, together with erosion and deposition processes, influenced how minerals in these pyroclastic deposits are altered (these secondary components and their phases of mineral changes are recognizable in Roman mortars using scientific methods). In general, the Pozzolane Rosse and Pozzolane Nere are less altered (and thus more reactive) than the Pozzolanelle and the Monti Sabatini ash falls (the latter appear for the most part strongly pedogenized). Extensive quarries of both Pozzolane Rosse and Pozzolane Nere are documented in the south and east sectors of the *suburbium* (along the Marrana della Caffarella, Almone, Fosso di Tor Carbone, Fosso delle Tre Fontane, Fosso di Pozzo Pantaleo) (Figure 3.2), but tunnels functioning during the Republican period are reported in the immediate environs of Rome, on the Parioli hill, near Porta S. Lorenzo (Piazza Sisto V and at S. Bibiana), on the Viminal (Ministero delle Finanze and Stazione Termini), and near the Lateran (Via Amba Aradam).[9] The best documented case is represented by the quarries recently excavated on the Esquiline (Piazza Vittorio and Piazza Dante), perhaps extending over an area of 4 ha, whose main phase of exploitation has been dated stratigraphically to before 60–50 BCE.[10]

Van Deman's pioneering work provided the first comprehensive field observation of standing concrete architecture in Rome, characterizing both the compositional aspects of the mortar mix and the provenance of the coarse aggregate in select monuments.[11] Based on the macroscopic properties of the

[8] Jackson *et al.* 2007; Jackson *et al.* 2010; Marra *et al.* 2011; Marra *et al.* 2015.
[9] Marra *et al.* 2016: 194. For the location of possible Republican quarries, see also *Suburbium* II. D140, A120, A122, A133.
[10] Serlorenzi 2014: 93 (on the geology and the quarrying of deposits described as "pozzolana grigia"); 95, n. 15 (on the dating); 100–01 (on the extent of the quarries and the suggestion that one of them provided the material for the construction of the *Horti Lamiani*, *c.* 50 BCE).
[11] Van Deman 1912a; Van Deman 1912b.

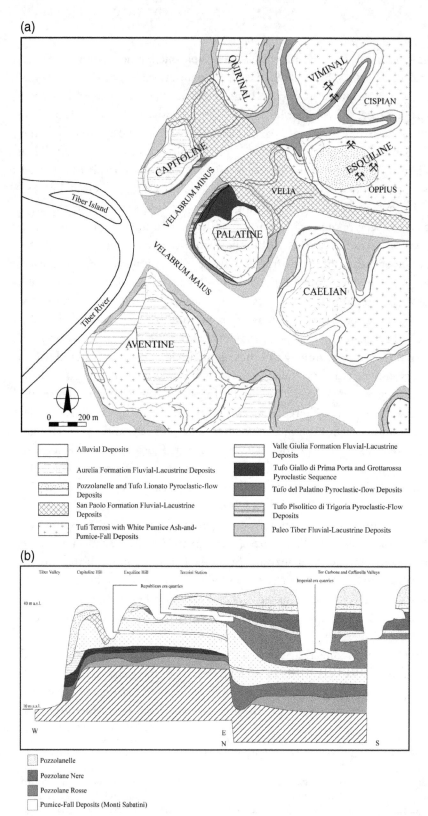

Figure 3.1 Geology of the site of Rome. A) Schematic plan (location of Pozzolana quarries based on Serlorenzi 2014); B) Schematic cross section (composite view along W-E and N-S axes; not to scale). Compiled from data in Marra *et al.* (2016: 177, fig. 1, and 191, fig. 4a). Drawing: M. Harder.

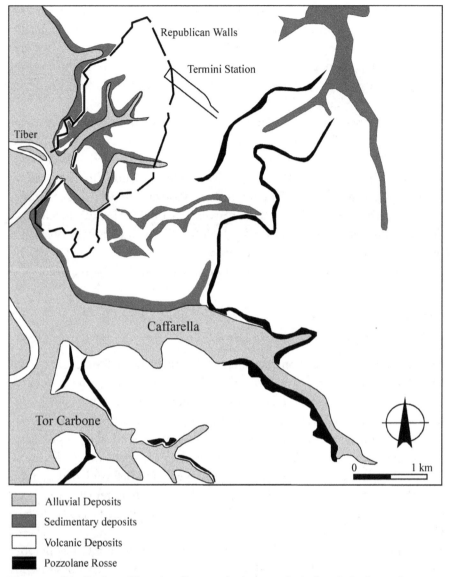

Figure 3.2  Distribution of Pozzolane Rosse and other pyroclastic deposits in the southeast *suburbium* of Rome (Tor Carbone and Caffarella Valleys). Compiled from data in Marra *et al.* (2016: 191, fig. 4b). Drawing: M. Harder.

constituent ingredients, Van Deman distinguished three main mortar types, mapping their association with specific methods of construction. Her friable "ashy gray" mortar occurs in both cemented-rubble cores and *opus incertum* walls of buildings she assigned to the late 2nd and early 1st centuries BCE. Examples from this group, which featured a darker mortar that contained less soil impurities, were pinpointed by Van Deman to the Sullan period. She then described a finer and harder "grayish red" mortar as being employed in well-dated monuments of the age of Caesar, where it appears in combination with *opus reticulatum* wall-facings and cores featuring travertine and basalt *caementa* (in addition to rubble of varied tuffs). Finally, she identified a "dusky red" mortar, whose introduction during the Augustan period would have been the result of a progressive trend toward the systematic selection of the less altered facies of the pozzolans described above.

Subsequent petrographic and mineralogical analyses of the Roman granular ash deposits and of the fine aggregate from ancient mortars have validated several of Van Deman's intuitions, establishing a shared scientific vocabulary and reference collection. While providing valuable information to define changes in the technological preferences of Roman builders through time, these studies have been relying on the conventional archaeological chronology, thus reproducing the old framework established by the traditional scholarship. In order to fully integrate these results with the newly excavated evidence presented here, a reassessment of the canonical sequence is first required.

## DATING EARLY CONCRETE CONSTRUCTION IN ROME: THE PROBLEM OF THE *PORTICUS AEMILIA*

The formative steps of Roman concrete construction in Rome have been commonly dated to the 3rd century BCE or even earlier, on account of complex arguments linking deeply rooted conceptualizations of Roman culture, evolutionary ideas about wall-facing styles, and problematic relationships between canonical monuments, ancient sources, and historical events or characters. The conventional dating system is based on the problematic identification of a large concrete vaulted building preserved on the left bank of the Tiber, near the modern Testaccio, whose scattered *opus incertum* remains had been excavated intermittently between 1886 and 1931 (hereby, Testaccio Building). Gatti (1934) realized that its design and dimensions corresponded with those of a monument represented on fragments of the Severan Forma Urbis (hereby, Marble Plan) previously associated with the Saepta Iulia in the Campus Martius (*FUR*, frs. 23 and 24 b–d).[12] Considering the location of the archaeological remains, Gatti restored the fragmentary inscription labeling the building on the Marble Plan to read [*Aemi*]*lia*. He then linked the name with one of the *porticus* claimed by Livy to have been first erected under the aedileship of M. Aemilius Lepidus and L. Aemilius Paulus in 193 BCE (35.10.12: *porticus extra portam Trigeminam*), and repaired by the censors Q. Fulvius Flaccus and A. Postumius Albinus in 174 BCE (41.27.8: marketplace *extra portam Trigeminam*, repairs of the Porticus Aemilia and a stair of approach from the Tiber). Since test-trenches

---

[12] Gatti 1934. Earlier scholarship on the fragments identified the building as the Saepta Iulia in the Campus Martius.

had not detected any traces of earlier structures below the visible remains, Gatti concluded that the original *porticus* was made with perishable material, and assigned the standing masonry to the 174 BCE rebuilding.[13]

Gatti's theory about the Testaccio Building had important repercussions for the dating of concrete architecture in Rome, because it provided a much earlier fixed point than previously available for *opus incertum*.[14] By accepting Gatti's identification, Lugli was able to push the earliest securely datable use of the technique further back in time by at least two generations. In Van Deman's canon, the *terminus ante quem* for the introduction of concrete construction was represented by the Temple of Concord (121 BCE), which in turn suggested a date around the mid 2nd century BCE for the early development of the building method.[15] The Testaccio Building, however, surpassed any other known monuments for its staggering size and complex internal organization. It was an elongated rectangle of 487 × 60 m, covering approximately 3 ha on unstable grounds. The interior was arranged into a series of 50 chambers, pierced by clerestory windows on the back wall and by arches on the long sides. Each row was spanned by record-setting barrel vaults of about 8.30 m, descending in four levels toward the river. According to Lugli, who described the archaeological remains as those of a warehouse connected with the *emporium*, such advanced features presupposed the kind of confidence which architects could only have acquired as a result of a much longer period of successful experiments with the medium.[16] Having thus established a likely context for the beginnings of concrete construction in the Mid-Republican period, Lugli used the so-called Porticus Aemilia as a term of comparison to date other monuments. On the basis of formal analysis, he produced a comprehensive typology of concrete wall-facing styles for the main public buildings known from textual sources.[17] The canonical list was further expanded and partly modified by Coarelli, who set out to identify concrete public monuments that would predate the Testaccio Building, ultimately demonstrating the progressive development and regularization of the *opus incertum* technique and its evolution into *opus reticulatum* over the course of the 2nd century

---

[13] As reported by Lugli 1957, vol. 1: 451 n. 1.

[14] See Van Deman 1912a, 245: concrete substructures incorporated in the podium of the Temple of Concord (121 BCE: App., *B Civ.* 1.26; Varro, *Ling.* 5.156).

[15] Van Deman 1912a: 235; 244–46.

[16] This line of argument had already been followed by Van Deman (1912a: 244), "the full mastery of technique in the handling of the new material, as shown in [the first dated monuments], makes it safe to assume [...] that a knowledge of its use antedated by a considerable period the time of their erection."

[17] Lugli 1957, vol. 1: 363–65. Earlier scholarship was much more cautious about the possible chronological implications of the Testaccio Building. Blake (1947: 249) accepted the identification as Porticus Aemilia, but assigned the visible remains to an unrecorded restoration dating to the Sullan period based on masonry style.

BCE.[18] This chronological framework appears crystallized in popular hand-books of Roman construction.[19]

Lugli's systematization, however, was challenged early on from a variety of perspectives. With relation to the topographical context, Von Gerkan (1958b) immediately pointed out how Gatti's original identification was based on the false idea that the Porta Trigemina opened across an hitherto undocumented stretch of the Servian walls running at a right angle from the side of the Aventine to the Tiber.[20] As a result of a more careful reading of the textual evidence, Richardson (1976) noted that the form of the Testaccio Building is hardly that of any of the *porticus* we know from Livy: These always run from one point to another, usually near, behind, or outside other buildings. The second *porticus* built by the aediles of 193 BCE led from the Porta Fontinalis to the altar of Mars in the Campus Martius and was in all likelihood a covered passageway, perhaps based on the Greek *stoa* concept (Liv., 35.10.12; *perducere*). Two other *porticus* were built *extra portam Trigeminam*: by M. Tuccius and P. Junius Brutus, the aediles of 192 BCE in the woodcutters' district (*inter lignarios*: Liv., 35.41.10); and by M. Fulvius Nobilior, one of the censors of 179 BCE (in addition to four other *porticus* elsewhere, i.e., *post naualia et ad fanum Herculis et post Spei ad Tiberim et ad aedem Apollinis Medici*: Liv., 40.51.6). Besides repairing the Porticus Aemilia, the censors of 174 BCE paved another *porticus* in stone, clearly implying that this was intended for the heavy traffic directed to Aventine (the passage is corrupt, so it is unclear whether the new building was located inside or outside the Porta Trigemina).[21] Given that none of these monuments seem to refer to a warehouse, Richardson concluded that neither the Testaccio Building nor its representation on the Marble Plan had any relationship with the Porticus Aemilia as described by Livy. He interpreted the latter as an embellishment of the new marketplace, suggesting a location closer to the Porta Trigemina toward the Forum Boarium and the Forum Holitorium, between the west slope of the Aventine and the Tiber.[22]

Other problems can be raised by looking at the internal evidence from the Marble Plan itself. The treatment of Gatti's Porticus Aemilia on the slab is

---

[18]  Coarelli 1977.

[19]  Adam 1994: 79–80; followed by Gros 2011: 22–23. See also Boëthius 1978: 128–29. Considering the complexity of the project, Giuliani (1998: 60 n. 11) suggests that the two dates recorded in Livy for the Porticus Aemilia refer to the beginning of construction (192 BCE) and its final inspection (174 BCE), rather than to different building episodes, and argues for an even longer chronological gap, placing the first trials with the building medium in the fourth century BCE. On the reliability of Livy's annalistic notices, see Bernard 2018a: 21–22.

[20]  Von Gerkan 1958b: 189. The Testaccio Building is 500 m away from the generally accepted location of the Porta Trigemina (near the *pons Sublicius*) and lies closer to both the Porta Lavernalis and the Porta Raudusculana. On the position of these gates: Säflund 1932: 198–99; Bernard 2012: 19–25; 36 fig. 16.

[21]  As noted by Tuck 2000: 176.

[22]  Richardson 1976: 57–59. Castagnoli 1980: 121; Tuck 2000: 176–77; Forni 2012.

unlike any other *porticus* appearing on it: The details are traced with a recessed outline, as done for other large structures with concrete cores, not with a single line or dot.[23] Furthermore, as Von Gerkan also objected, the inscription labeling the building as reconstructed by Gatti would have created confusion with the Basilica Aemilia, due to the lack of available space for the word *porticus*. The easiest solution for the German scholar was to assume that the building was in fact identified with a single noun rather than a family name, for which he proposed [*nau*]*alia*.[24]

Cozza and Tucci (2006) have expanded on Von Gerkan's idea, adding crucial observations about the main architectural features. By surveying representative examples of archaeologically documented shipsheds, they have provided what are to date the closest comparanda for the design and spatial arrangement of the complex.[25] Some specialists have argued against this interpretation, noting that the vaulted naves of the Testaccio Building seem too wide for triremes or quinqueremes, too far from the river bank (90 m), too high up from the projected river level, and at the wrong orientation.[26] There are plausible explanations to account for each of these objections. Blackman (2008) has identified a category of shipsheds featuring chambers with a clear width of 7–8 m, while Keay *et al.* (2012) have reconstructed Imperial-era shipsheds at Portus whose naves span up to 12 m. As reconstructed by Aldrete (2007), the Tiber levels rose and fell considerably during the seasons, and there are several known cases from the 1st century BCE when floods could have potentially reached the presumed ground level in the rear sector of the Testaccio Building (Plate II).[27] This would explain why the dockyard complex was built at some distance from the river and further upslope.[28] The intervening space could have been occupied by a sloping surface or an artificial basin, which would have

---

[23] As noted by Tuck 2000: 178.

[24] Von Gerkan 1958b: 190. Tuck (2000: 179–82, figs. 2–3) directed our attention to the traces of the last four letters of the preparatory inscription, placed just below the final one and never completely removed, as indicating something other than the "i" necessary to restore the word "*Aemilia*" (cf. Rodríguez Almeida 1981: pl. 16). His suggestion is for the family name [*Corne*]*lia*, which would refer to Horrea built by L. Sulla, otherwise unattested. The epigraphic evidence has been disputed by Arata and Felici 2011, who after an inspection concluded that only the last two letters of the preparatory inscription, [–]*ia*, are actually preserved on the slab.

[25] See also Coarelli 2007.

[26] E.g., Hurst 2010: 32–33. On the challenges of launching and shipping across stream, see Rankov 2013, followed by Yegül and Favro 2019: 23.

[27] On the magnitude of the Tiber floods in antiquity, see Aldrete 2007: 81–89 (particularly relevant is the discussion of the floods of 54 BCE and 44 BCE, possibly reaching above 13–15 m a.s.l.). It is important to note that the height of floods as recorded in the sources refers to the monumental core, where the rise would have been affected by building density. The effects might have been different in the less densely occupied areas outside the Republican walls.

[28] Cozza and Tucci (2006: 192–93 and n. 34) point out that Arsenale Mediceo on the Arno at Pisa, another example of large river shipsheds, shares the same basic features and is also located downstream from the city toward the sea. The location of the modern Papal Arsenal at Porta

facilitated the launching of the ships.[29] At a later stage, this annex would have been encroached upon by the structures represented on the Marble Plan as occupying the river bank.

Recent excavations carried out both on the exterior of the back wall and within one of the naves have demonstrated that the Testaccio Building underwent significant modifications in the late 1st century CE, as part of a broader repurposing of the complex (Plate III.A–B).[30] Some of the arches that originally opened into the transverse walls supporting the barrel vaults were blocked with brick-faced concrete masonry, further subdividing the interior space for storage. As reconstructed by the excavators, the original floor levels would have been systematically removed in order to create a new *cocciopesto* floor surface at lower elevation.[31] Portions of the solid wall that supported the arcade, which the excavators describe as foundations, would have been reexposed in the process, and subsequently coated with the same thick plaster that covers the brick-faced masonry plugs and the vaults. These foundations do not feature any offset from the upper portions of the transverse wall, and are faced with the same type of *opus incertum* as the superstructure. The walls delimiting each chamber were evidently built up as a single unit, but construction progressed in stages, adapting it to the sloping terrain. Each pier sits on a horizontal section of wall, which lies at about 0.6 m higher than the next downslope. Based on the pattern, an overall slope of 8 percent can be calculated from the base of the pier at the back to the base of the wall at the front of the building (the gradient would fit well with the parameters known for other archaeological examples of shipsheds). The excavators, however, take these drops in elevation to mark the level of the original Republican floor. Thus, they reconstruct an interior consisting of a sequence of eight platforms, which would be incompatible with Cozza and Tucci's identification. On the longitudinal axis, each step would have communicated directly with the contiguous chambers through the corresponding arch (but no sills or thresholds have been identified under

Portese, directly across from the Testaccio Building, shows that large ships could indeed be hauled on a slope at some distance from the Tiber river banks (Tucci 2012: 585).

[29] Thus Claridge 2010: 403–05. Rankov (2013) points out that launching ships in a nontidal environment requires a narrow or parallel angle of entry, ideally into a basin cut into the side of the river. Muzzioli (2009) tackles the topological issues, repositioning the *prata Quinctia* (which Liv., 3.26.7 links with the *naualia*) from the Campus Martius to the area of Trastevere across from the Testaccio Building. D'Alessio (2014: 10–12 and fig. 8) emphasizes the spatial relationship between the Testaccio Building and the findspot of an altar dedicated to Magna Mater and *Nauisaluia* dated to the Julio-Claudian period, which probably relates to harbor activities (the scene on it represents a ship that transported a statue of Magna Mater being dragged ashore).

[30] For an interim report, see Burgers *et al.* 2018.

[31] Burgers *et al.* 2018: 3, reporting that the exploration did not reveal any Republican layers. The authors do not present a stratigraphic section of the excavated deposits, so the depth to which the construction fills associated the Imperial *cocciopesto* floors were excavated. See also Contino and D'Alessandro 2014.

the brick-masonry plugs), maintaining a constant level. On the cross axis, each step would have been connected to the one immediately below by means of a short staircase or ramp. The absence of any adjoining structures for terracing or retaining the horizontal steps across the width of the aisle, however, makes the latter hypothesis quite difficult.[32]

A different solution may be proposed if one takes into consideration that the Testaccio Building lacked doorways on the side and back walls. Movement through the complex was clearly not a concern, since it was only possible to get in and out from the front. As Tucci (2012) notes, this limitation seriously undermines the traditional interpretation of the complex as warehouse for the redistribution of goods.[33] In fact, it is entirely possible that the arcades were never meant to function as communicating doorways. The *naualia* interpretation would also explain why built-up surfaces associated with the Republican remains are nowhere to be found across the entire building, as attested by the early excavation reports. Shipsheds were normally provided with elaborate wooden groundways to both support and haul the ships' keels. Similar features would have been incorporated within each aisle, ascending on a single inclined plane from front to back. In such arrangement, portions of the *opus incertum* walls below the arcades would have always remained visible.[34] The groundways would have been removed to create the *cocciopesto* floors in the Imperial phase, dumping fills to bring up the level (thus accounting for the absence of Republican-era fills below the new floors). The primary purpose of the arches, therefore, would have been to provide light (their intrados is at the same level as the larger windows on the back wall) and especially aeration, substituting for the wooden or stone post-and-lintel construction of the Greek models. Moreover, by incorporating these voids in the masonry of such colossal building, the costs of construction could be curbed significantly. These gaps eliminated the need for a considerable volume of building materials, thus saving on labor requirements for production, transport, and assembly.[35] The use of facing pieces of optimal size (7–11 cm) in the *opus incertum* masonry further

---

[32] As already remarked by Cozza and Tucci 2006: 181–83.

[33] The existing doors on the back wall seem to have been created in the Imperial period by altering preexisting windows. See Tucci 2012: 577–79, figs. 2–4; D'Alessio 2014: 14–16. Burgers *et al.* do not address the issue, stating that those features are of uncertain function (2018: 4). The doorways on the façade were originally framed by ashlar pillars (the narrower openings represented in the Marble Plan correspond to later brick-faced masonry panels), as reported in Cozza and Tucci 2006: 186. *Contra*: Arata and Felici 2011 (commercial function).

[34] Burgers *et al.* (2018, 5 fig. 4b) shows the presence of at least one groove or socket hole on the exterior face of the transverse wall, but the limited documentation does not allow to elaborate further on the nature of this evidence.

[35] Extrapolating from the measurements given in Burgers *et al.* 2018, each opening could have eliminated the need for approximately 50 m$^3$ of materials, for a total of about 17,000 m$^3$ (at 1.65–2.42 mle/m$^3$ for production and 5.10–5.86 mle/m$^3$ for assembly). For the costing of *opus incertum*, see DeLaine 2001: 247–50 and supra Chapter 1.

suggests that rate of construction might have been an important factor in determining technological choices at the site.[36]

In sum, while the old *Porticus Aemilia* identification appears seriously flawed both in terms of its topographical associations and building design, the preponderance of the evidence supports the interpretation of the Testaccio Building as *naualia* rather than *horrea*.[37] As Davies (2017) points out, the monument conforms to the requisites listed by Vitruvius (*De arch.* 5.12.7) for the former building type; its large scale makes the possibility of it being a censorial work extremely likely.[38] The existence of a ship-building industry in Rome is attested since the First Punic War (Ennius in Serv., *Aen.* 11.326). Livy refers explicitly to ships departing from Rome (36.42.1: 191 BCE), and to the storing of ships in Rome (42.27.1: 172 BCE). An *opus naualium* is attributed by Cicero (*De or.* 1.14.62) to Hermodorus, presumably the same Greek architect from Salamis who was credited with the construction of the earliest white marble temple in Rome (Temple of Jupiter Stator, after 146 BCE).[39] The context of the speech in which Hermodorus is mentioned refers to the praetor M. Antonius, who went on to celebrate naval triumph in 100 BCE, reaching the consulship in 99 BCE and the censorship in 97 BCE, although it is not at all clear from the text that the two characters were contemporaneous with each other.[40] Whether any of this refers to the Testaccio Building remains uncertain, but the unavoidable conclusion is that the monument can no longer represent a fixed point for the dating and sequencing of *opus incertum* in Rome.

## REDATING THE EARLY DEVELOPMENT OF CONCRETE CONSTRUCTION IN ROME: THE PUBLIC MONUMENTS

The demise of the *Porticus Aemilia* theory prompts a thorough reassessment of the available evidence for other buildings featured in the canonical list. Coarelli's synopsis of purported early concrete wall-facing styles in Rome (Figure 3.3) is a good place to begin such reanalysis. The diagram presents the sequence of development of *opus incertum* as inferred from those monuments which appeared

---

[36] See DeLaine 2001: 238, fig. 11.1; DeLaine 2006: 241.

[37] While rejecting the conventional identification, D'Alessio (2014: 18–23) prefers to suspend judgment on the issue, concentrating on aspects of the masonry style that would support a date in the latter part of the 2nd century BCE.

[38] Davies 2017: 175–77.

[39] Cozza and Tucci 2006: 194–98, highlighting the existence of shipsheds with similar ground plan at Salamis. The authors propose several possible dates for the project, before or after 146 BCE. On Hermodorus' career, see in particular: Gros 1973; Gros 1976 (placing his formative years ca. 175–150 BCE). His role in the Pentelic marble temple building in Rome in the second half of the 2nd century BCE is discussed in Bernard 2010. Coarelli (2007: 42–43) accepts both identification and attribution, dating the complex to the middle of the 2nd century BCE.

[40] As noted by Tucci 2012: 586, n. 37.

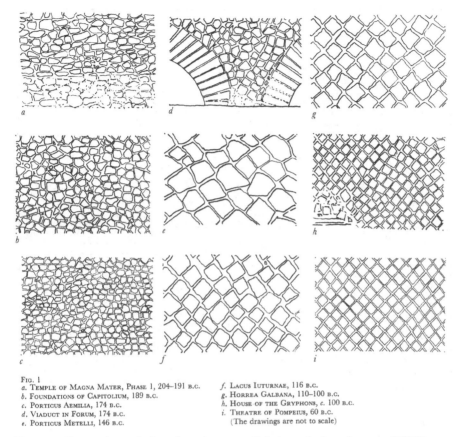

Fig. 1
a. TEMPLE OF MAGNA MATER, PHASE 1, 204–191 B.C.
b. FOUNDATIONS OF CAPITOLIUM, 189 B.C.
c. PORTICUS AEMILIA, 174 B.C.
d. VIADUCT IN FORUM, 174 B.C.
e. PORTICUS METELLI, 146 B.C.
f. LACUS IUTURNAE, 116 B.C.
g. HORREA GALBANA, 110–100 B.C.
h. HOUSE OF THE GRYPHONS, c. 100 B.C.
i. THEATRE OF POMPEIUS, 60 B.C.
    (The drawings are not to scale)

Figure 3.3  Progressive evolution of *opus incertum* wall-facing styles in 2nd century BCE Rome according to Coarelli (1977: 11 fig. 1; used by permission of the British School at Rome).

securely identified and, therefore, well-dated on the basis of textual sources. Anonymous remains were also added to the sample on account of morphological similarities with the Testaccio Building, attributing them to building episodes known from literary accounts to have occurred at or near their location around the time the Porticus Aemilia was built. The overall ordering would demonstrate the process of gradual evolution of wall-facing styles from irregular to regular, regardless of type of building material or structural context. Given that typological-induced dating was used to identify reference points, however, the argument suffers from circular reasoning. Recent excavations at some of the key sites have produced a wealth of stratigraphic data that offer the opportunity to test the traditional reconstructions (as summarized in Appendix 1; Figures 3.4–5 for position).

    The temple of Magna Mater, a multiphase building located on the southwest corner of the Palatine, is usually cited as the earliest known concrete

Figure 3.4 Schematic map of Rome showing the location of the main public monuments and domestic buildings discussed in Chapter 3. Drawing: M. Harder. Sites: 1=Sanctuary of Magna Mater; 2="Scalae Graecae"; 3=Atrium Vestae; 4=Testaccio Building; 5=Via Consolazione site; 6=Clivus Capitolinus; 7=Palatine East Slope (Fortuna Respiciens?); 8=Temple of Castor and Pollux; 9=Lacus Iuturnae; 10=Temple of Veiovis; 11=Porticus Metelli; 12=Temple of Concord; 13=Temple of Victoria; 14=Casa dei Grifi; 15=Aracoeli site; 16=Via Palermo site; 17=Northeast Slope of the Palatine; 18=North Slope of the Palatine.

monument in Rome, and therefore deserves a lengthier discussion. Coarelli's interpretation was based on evidence collected in the early 1960s.[41] A sondage excavated in the cella had revealed that the podium consisted of a grid of concrete walls raised in separate horizontal courses, clearly distinguishable on

[41] Romanelli 1963: 227–39; 260–90.

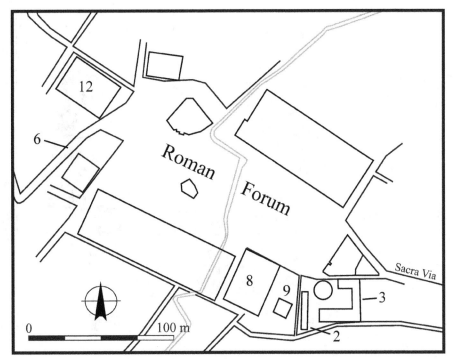

Figure 3.5 Schematic map of the Forum Romanum showing the location of the main public monuments discussed in Chapter 3 (see Figure 3.4 for site key). Drawing: M. Harder.

the basis of the prevailing types of rubble (Tufo Giallo della Via Tiberina, Peperino, and Cappellaccio; travertine and Tufo Lionato,[42] and Tufo Rosso a Scorie Nere from Fidene). Coarelli classified these walls as a rough form of *opus incertum*, assigning them to the original construction of the temple (Liv., 29.37.2, 36.36: 204–191 BCE). In Coarelli's view, the early date would correspond well with the particularly "unrefined aspect" of the masonry.[43] The large-scale excavation and mapping of the temple and sanctuary resumed between 1977 and 2006 under the direction of Pensabene. The final results reveal a completely different situation.[44]

---

[42] The excavations reports refer to both the Monteverde and Anio varieties being used, but the terminology is problematic. The recent geochemical study by Marra *et al.* (2018) has found that samples characterized by medium-grain size and a paucity of lithic inclusions, which archaeologists normally classify as Monteverde Tuff, actually come from the facies quarried along the Anio valley (i.e., Anio Tuff). For this reason, I avoid usage of these terms unless backed by scientific evidence, and describe both Monteverde Tuff and Anio Tuff as Tufo Lionato. *Supra*, n. 4.

[43] Coarelli 1977: 10–13 (followed by Adam 1994: 80).

[44] Pensabene 2017a, 126–86. For earlier reports, see Pensabene 1978; Pensabene 1980; Pensabene 1985; Pensabene *et al.* 1993; Pensabene and D'Alessio 2006; D'Alessio 2006; D'Alessio 2009. Coarelli 2012: 249–82 rejects the stratigraphic sequence as reconstructed by Pensabene for the temple, but without new arguments.

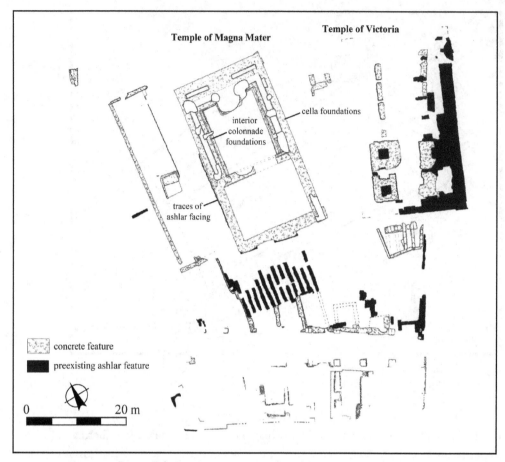

Figure 3.6 Rome, Palatine. Composite state plan of the sanctuary of Magna Mater showing the architectural remains of Phase II, *c.* 100 BCE (Mogetta 2015: 10, fig. 4; modified from D'Alessio 2006: Tav. N; used by permission).

A complex series of concrete structures has been exposed both within the temple and in the adjacent area (Figure 3.6). As Pensabene's excavations on the east side of the temple show, the perimetral walls of the podium and their foundations were built as part of a single operation.[45] The different rubble layers were placed by hand within timber formworks without a clear distinction between core and faces.[46] Thus, these structures should be described as cemented-rubble walls, not *opus incertum*. On three sides, the exterior of the podium was lined with Peperino slabs (several elements of the base have been found).[47] On the west side, however, the imprint of five courses of blocks is

[45] Pensabene 2017a: 132–38 (Trenches B and C); 133, fig. 44 (sectional drawing of temple podium).
[46] Cf. Pensabene 1980: 71; D'Alessio 2009: 237–38.
[47] Pensabene 2017a: 313, 362–64, nos. 271–82 (but these elements may refer to the Augustan redecoration of the podium).

preserved on the face of the concrete podium (the presence of a spoliation trench demonstrates that these were robbed in the medieval period).[48] At the northern end of the podium, two courses of Tufo Giallo della Via Tiberina blocks sit perfectly on axis with these traces.[49] Both structures belonged to the podium of the original temple, stretches of which were evidently reused as lost shuttering to retain the concrete mass (a practice which is also attested in the temple of Victoria).[50] The earliest concrete architecture of the Temple of Magna Mater, therefore, must be dated to its second phase. Historical sources place the reconstruction of the temple toward the end of the 2nd century BCE (post-111 BCE), connecting it with the patronage of the Caecilii Metelli.[51]

The cella and pronaos are divided by a concrete wall, which is joined to the box that delimits the podium, whereas the foundations of the sidewalls of the cella abut both the podium and the dividing wall. Parallel to the latter is another foundation, whose function was to support an inner colonnade. The direct stratigraphic relationship with the podium clearly indicates that all the sub-structures belong to the same phase. The freestanding parts of the cella are variously described as made with *opus quasi reticulatum* or *opus incertum* of Tufo Rosso a Scorie Nere (the latter title seems more appropriate).[52] The surviving mosaic floor and architectural ornaments belong to a later redecoration of the interior, which can be dated stylistically to the Augustan period.[53] The construction fill below the mosaic floor, which extended down to the bottom of the podium foundations, contained frequent building debris (e.g., fragments of an earlier *cocciopesto* floor; architectural elements in Peperino), ceramics, and votive figurines in secondary deposition.[54] The composition of the assemblage

---

[48] Pensabene 2017a: 149–57 (Trenches S and T) describes the spoliation trench. See also Pensabene *et al.* 1993: 28–34.

[49] Pensabene and D'Alessio 2006: 37–38, figs. 4–5. Their alignment differs markedly from that of other ashlar structures detected in the adjacent area and securely dated to the Middle Republican period, for which see Pensabene 1980: 67; Pensabene 1981: 104; D'Alessio 2006: 433–34; Pensabene and D'Alessio 2006: 32, fig. 2.

[50] For a reconstruction of the outline of the original ashlar podium, see D'Alessio 2009: 228, fig. 1. On the Temple, of Victoria, see Pensabene 1991: 14–15, 26–27, figs. 13–14. Fragments of Peperino column drums recycled as rubble in the concrete masonry of the podium have also been assigned to the original temple: Pensabene 2017a: 315–22.

[51] Ov., *Fast.* 4.348; Val. Max., 1.8.11; Julius Obsequens, 39 (first temple destroyed by fire in 111 BCE). See *LTUR* III.206–08 (Pensabene). For the dating of the dedication and its attribution to a member of the Metelli, see Bastien 2009: 45–47 (C. Caecilius Metellus Caprarius?); D'Alessio 2009: 234–36 (Q. Caecilius Metellus Numidicus). Based on the interpretation of related texts (Diod. Sic., 36.13.1; Plut., *Vit Mar.* 17.8), Davies 2017: 154 places the letting of the contract in 102–101 BCE, when both Metellus Caprarius and Metellus Numidicus were censors.

[52] D'Alessio 2009: 229 n. 7 (*opus quasi reticulatum*), with earlier bibliography; Pensabene 2017a: 127–28 and 133, fig. 44 (*opus incertum*).

[53] Romanelli 1963: 321–30. Pensabene 1978: 69; Pensabene 1980: 71; Pensabene 1985: 182–83. For a full description, see Pensabene 2017a: 315–22.

[54] Pensabene 2017a: 128–29 reports that several fragments of architectural terracottas were found in layers interpreted as collapse (e.g., Trench B: SU 5, 7, and 8) or associated with burnt materials (e.g., Trench E: SUs 25 and 28; Trench N, SUs 17–21; Trench B: SU 5).

suggests that temple decorations and furnishing associated with the first occupation of the sanctuary were disposed of in a systematic way, as part of the late 2nd century BCE construction activities.

A paved terrace extending to the south slope of the Palatine was built in front of the temple at this stage. This terrace is supported by a series of concrete vaulted rooms and corridors flanking a *uia tecta*, or covered passageway (the so-called *cliuus Victoriae*), built on cemented-rubble foundations. These structures feature ashlar piers connected by arches made of voussoirs of Tufo Lionato (from the Anio?) whose spandrels are faced in *opus quasi reticulatum*. Farther to the south, the platform rested on a pillared structure supported by a system of vaulted substructures, which formed the monumental front of this side of the hill, whose walls are faced with *opus quasi reticulatum* of Tufo Lionato facing pieces.[55] West of the temple podium, a lower terrace is delimited by a concrete *temenos* that includes parts in *opus incertum*. An oblong basin lined with hydraulic mortar was added here.[56] The construction fills of the lower terrace contained hundreds of pottery fragments of the same type as those found in the podium fills, providing a link between the building process of the podium and that of the platform in the reconstruction of the sanctuary post-111 BCE.[57] Thus, both *opus incertum* and *opus quasi reticulatum* were used in this phase of the sanctuary, but for different purposes within the structure (Figure 3.7). The fact that *opus quasi reticulatum* was employed selectively and only in the terrace front, and that Tufo Lionato does not appear in the podium and other ancillary structures suggests that different supply chains and perhaps also crews were used for different parts of the projects (recycled blocks probably being the norm for the cemented-rubble and *opus incertum* structures). The important implication, of which most modern building archaeologists are well aware, is that different wall-facing styles do not always represent successive building events, so any periodization based solely on building techniques must be taken with caution.

Next in Coarelli's canonical sequence are two minor monuments that have been singled out on account of morphological similarities with the wall-facing of the Testaccio Building, such as dimension and shape of the facing pieces, thickness of the mortar joints, and use of wedge-shaped oblong tuff blocks to face the intrados of concrete vaults. Based on these features, both Lugli and Coarelli interpreted the row of arches visible behind the imperial Rostra in the Forum Romanum (see Figure 3.3d) as related to the first paving of the *cliuus Capitolinus*, which was commissioned by the same censors who repaired the

---

[55] D'Alessio 2009: 231–33 (describing them as *opus reticulatum*).
[56] Pensabene *et al.* 1993: 29–30. Davies 2017: 163, fig. 4.16 reconstructs this space as a peristyle garden.
[57] For a detailed description of the finds, see Rossi 2009.

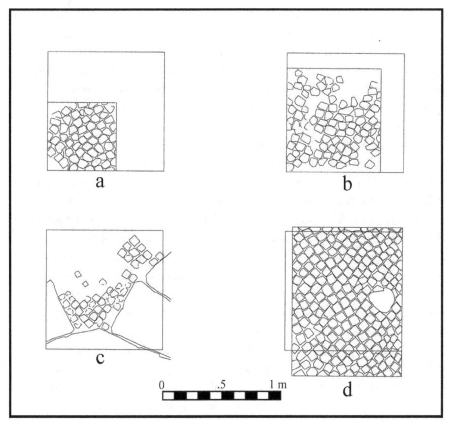

Figure 3.7 Rome, Palatine. Variants of *opus incertum* and *opus quasi reticulatum* wall-facings from Phase II of the sanctuary of Magna Mater (after D'Alessio 2009: 239, fig. 14; used by permission).

*Porticus Aemilia* (Liv. 41.27.7: 174 BCE).[58] Other identifications, however, are equally possible. Modifications to the course of the road were certainly planned for the construction of the Temple of Concord.[59] Lugli assigned another *opus incertum* structure to the same year, a terracing wall located on the east slopes of the Capitoline known as the Via della Consolazione site, on the assumption that the paving of the *cliuus Capitolinus* involved a major reorganization of the entire hill.[60] Because of the slightly less regular aspect of the wall-facing (see Figure 3.3b), Coarelli preferred an earlier date, identifying the remains with the *substructio super Aequimelium in Capitolio*, the construction of which was

[58] Lugli 1957, vol. 1: 452.

[59] For a more detailed reconstruction of the stratigraphy of the road, see Filippi 1997–98: 161–66, emphasizing the impact of the building activities sponsored by L. Opimius in the late 120s BCE. Cf. Van Deman (1922: 14–16), who described the same structure as being made of *opus reticulatum* and mortar of the "Sullan" type, and connected it with the building of new streets in the western end of the Forum in the Sullan period.

[60] Colini 1940: 227–28; Lugli 1957, vol. 1: 452 n. 2; 467.

recorded by Livy as a censorial work for 189 BCE (38.28.3).[61] The *opus incertum* stretch appears juxtaposed to ashlar structures featuring both Tufo Lionato (the identification as Monteverde Tuff is uncertain) and Tufo Giallo della Via Tiberina, but the association does not necessarily confirm the early character of the concrete facing. Even if the identification of the site were correct, the *opus incertum* walls could simply belong to a later refurbishment of the *opus quadratum* features (the original *substructio?*).[62]

With the so-called Porticus Aemilia out of the picture, then, the earliest surviving archaeological example of concrete architecture from Coarelli's canon is the Porticus Metelli. This monument was famous in antiquity because it featured several architectural innovations (Vell. Pat., 1.11.3–4; 2.1.2; Plin., *HN* 34.31; 34.64; Vitr., *De arch.* 3.2.5). Most notably, it was the first *porticus* of the peristyle type (or *quadriporticus*), built for the specific function of providing a formal columnar framework for the display of statues.[63] In the Imperial period, the monument was known as the Porticus Octaviae.[64] This is represented on the Marble Plan (*FUR*, frs. 31bb, 31cc, 31dd, 31u, and 31vaa) as a temenos featuring a single colonnade on the short sides to the north and south (the latter incorporates a hexastyle propylon), and a double colonnade on the long sides to the east and west.[65] The plan of the Republican building did not differ much from that of the Augustan version, which enclosed both the temple of Jupiter Stator, and the preexisting temple of Juno Regina into a single sacred area (105 × 92 m).[66] The original porticoes were commissioned by Q. Caecilius Metellus Macedonicus after his triumphal return in 146 BCE. According to Morgan (1971), the earliest possible date for the *locatio* of the Temple of Jupiter Stator and its enclosing porticoes is 143 BCE, when Metellus Macedonicus held the consulship (but other later dates have been suggested).[67] The exact relationship between the foundations of the temple of Jupiter Stator and the floor level of the courtyard is not known in any detail, but the erection of the temple probably started before that of the surrounding precinct, since moving heavy white marble members in and out of a raised enclosure would not have been logistically feasible. Thus, a construction date in the later 130s BCE (i.e., after completion of the temple) is the most likely for the porticoes.

[61] *LTUR* I.20–21 (Pisani Sartorio).
[62] On the relationship between the *substructio super Aequimelium* and the fortifications of the Capitoline, see Bernard 2012: 25, n. 74.
[63] Nünnerich-Asmus 1994: 39–42.
[64] Literary sources on the monument are collected in *LTUR* IV.141–45 (Viscogliosi).
[65] For a possible surviving capital from the interior order of the side colonnades, see La Rocca 2011: 9–11, figs. 8–9.
[66] Davies 2017: 129, fig. 3.59.
[67] Morgan 1971: 500 (136 BCE, i.e., the year of Metellus Macedonicus' first bid for censorship; or 131 BCE, the first year of his censorship).

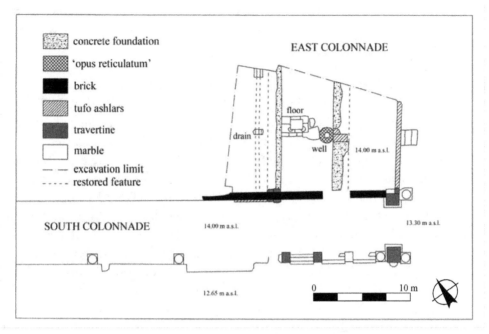

Figure 3.8 Rome, Campus Martius. Composite plan of the southeast corner of the Porticus Metelli/ Octaviae. Drawing: M. Mogetta (after Mogetta 2015: 15, fig. 7).

Parts of the south side of the Porticus Metelli were investigated first by Colini in 1950.[68] The state archaeological service carried out excavations in the 1980s and 1990s in the north side, the northwest corner, and in the monumental entrance to the south.[69] The south colonnade of the *quadriporticus* rests on a stylobate formed by two parallel concrete structures retaining a construction fill (Figure 3.8). The external retaining wall is a thick concrete foundation consisting of a Tufo Giallo della Via Tiberina rubble core faced with stretchers of Tufo Lionato ashlars (the top course of Peperino headers most likely belongs to the Augustan reconstruction). Semicircular niches are also incorporated on the front.[70] The internal retaining wall is an *opus incertum* structure made with nestled facing pieces of Tufo Lionato (see Figure 3.3e), evidently raised from the ground up.[71] The projecting propylon at the center of the south side seems to have been added only in the Imperial period since the external retaining wall and associated drain continue behind it (columns of bigger module incorporated in the current exterior colonnade probably mark

---

[68]  Cressedi 1954; Lugli 1957, vol. 1: 409, 412. A reappraisal of the old documentation is in Lauter 1980–81.

[69]  Giustini 1990; Ciancio Rossetto 1995; Ciancio Rossetto 1996; Ciancio Rossetto 2009.

[70]  Ciancio Rossetto 1995, 96–98; Lauter 1980–81: 39–40, 42 cross section C–C'.

[71]  Lugli 1957, vol. 1: 409 (describing the material as Monteverde Tuff).

the original entrance).[72] Both the southeast and the northwest corners of the *quadriporticus* feature two parallel concrete foundations built up with *opus incertum*, thus confirming the presence of a double colonnade on the long sides of the complex.[73]

The construction method employed to raise the foundations of the Porticus Metelli resembles the technique described above for the podium of the Temple of Magna Mater, whose continued development is in fact attested throughout the last third of the 2nd century BCE. The earliest known example seems to come from the second phase of the Temple of Veiovis on the Arx. Originally dedicated in 192 BCE, the temple was the object of multiple reconstructions (Liv. 31.21.12, 34.53.7, 35.41.8; Plin., *HN* 16.216; Gell., *NA* 5.12.8–10; Vitr., *De arch.* 4.8.4; Ov., *Fast.* 3.430).[74] Colini dug a series of sondages in the extant cella and podium (erected sometime after the construction of the nearby Tabularium, *c.* 78 BCE), exposing a series of concrete structures laying on a different orientation.[75] These walls feature cores made of dark-gray lime mortar and Tufo Giallo della Via Tiberina rubble, faced with reused Tufo Giallo della Via Tiberina ashlars, and sit directly on top of a lower course of blocks belonging to the original podium.[76] The construction fill excavated below the extant cella pavement included fragments of tessellated mosaics, which Colini associated with the previous phase, suggesting for it a tentative date around 150 BCE on stylistic grounds.[77] A tuff plinth with a dedicatory inscription by the consul C. Fannius (*CIL* 1².658; 122 BCE) comes from the area in front of the temple, and may relate to the building episode in question.[78] Contemporary parallels for the technique include the temple at S. Salvatore in Campo (post-136/135 BCE, whose podium features a travertine ashlar facing surmounted by Pentelic marble columns),[79] the Temple of Concord (121 BCE),[80] and the Temple of Castor and Pollux (post-117 BCE),[81] while the case of the temple along the north side of via delle Botteghe Oscure (by some identified with the Temple of the Lares Permarini of 179 BCE) remains dubious.[82]

---

[72] Ciancio Rossetto 1996: 270, fig. 4; Ciancio Rossetto 2009: 65.

[73] Giustini 1990: 71; 72, fig. 15; Mogetta 2015: 16 fig. 8.

[74] Colini 1942; Davies 2017: 92–93, fig. 3.14 with a rendering of Colini's plans.

[75] Colini 1942: 20–25.

[76] Colini 1942: 23, fig. 19.

[77] Colini 1942: 26.

[78] See Lugli 1957, vol. 1: 412 (150–120? BCE).

[79] On the identification and dating of the remains, see Tortorici 1988; Bernard 2010: 36–38; La Rocca 2011: 11–14; Kosmopoulos 2012.

[80] Hafner 1984.

[81] Nielsen 1992.

[82] See the discussion by Bernard 2018a: 10–11. Maschek (2018: 182) places the Temple of the Lares Permarini at the Largo Argentina site (Temple D).

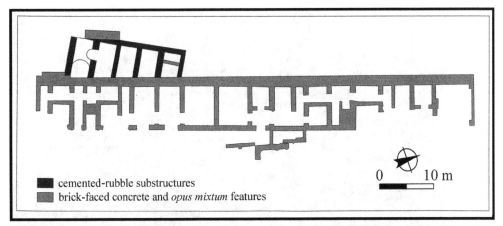

Figure 3.9 Rome, east slope of the Palatine. Simplified plan of the vaulted substructures (Temple of Fortuna Respiciens?). Drawing: M. Mogetta (after Mogetta 2015: 17, fig. 9).

The last few decades of archaeological research in the monumental core of Rome have expanded the sample of monuments originally included in the Lugli–Coarelli canon, but failed to produce conclusive evidence of concrete construction in public architecture for the early part of the 2nd century BCE.[83] The earliest datable application of the new building medium can be placed in the third quarter of the 2nd century BCE.

The first monument to discuss is represented by a series of concrete vaulted substructures located on the east slopes of the Palatine, between the sites of Vigna Barberini and the Domus Flavia (Figure 3.9). The standing remains consist of a series of five chambers, whose façade was truncated in the Hadrianic period, when the structure was incorporated into a multiphase brick-faced building. The original depth of the structure has been estimated at 50 m, whereas the front could have measured at least 27–32 m (traces on either side of the standing remains point to the existence of two additional rooms).[84] D'Alessio (2014) has noted similarities with the technique employed for the barrel vaults and archivolts of the Testaccio Building. Although much narrower in span (2.90–3.15 m), the vaults of the East Palatine substructures feature wedge-shaped oblong rectangular blocks of Tufo Giallo della Via Tiberina laid radially on the intrados (Figure 3.10). Close parallels can also be found in vaulted architecture from Campania in the 2nd century BCE (e.g., Cumae, Terme Centrali; Puteoli, "Criptoportici"; discussed in Chapters 5

[83] Tucci 2018: 15–16, fig. 4; 18, fig. 5 reports that isolated *opus incertum* walls were discovered in 1999 during excavations in the area of the Temple of Peace, and identifies the remains as pertaining to the Macellum (Liv., 40.51.5: 179 BCE). The excavation data is unpublished, so the relationship and date cannot be verified. Tortorici 1991: 40–44 places the Macellum in the area of the Forum of Nerva adjacent to the Basilica Fulvia/Aemilia. See also *LTUR* II.312–13 (Morselli and Pisani Sartorio).

[84] Anselmino 2006: 237.

Figure 3.10  Rome, east slope of the Palatine. Detail of vaulting technique (D'Alessio 2014: 19, fig. 14; used by permission). Note the use of oblong, wedge-shaped facing pieces laid radially at the intrados.

and 6, respectively).[85] The walls are made with cemented rubble of Tufo Lionato of various shapes and sizes, most frequently rectangular parallelepipedal with an exterior flat face (a form of *opus uittatum*?).[86] A narrow corridor (0.60 m) running at the back of the rooms separated the structure from the natural bedrock, serving both as insulation and to collect surface waters. Such a feature appears in monumental substructures from other contexts in Latium that can be generically dated to the second half of the 2nd century (e.g., Praeneste, Via degli Arcioni; lower terrace of the forum of Cora) or early 1st century BCE (the extra-urban sanctuary at Tusculum).[87]

The lack of contextual data makes it difficult to reconstruct the function of the structure. Given the widespread association of this type of vaulted architecture with sacred buildings,[88] scholars have interpreted the monument as the platform of a temple. The generally accepted identification is with the site of the Temple of Fortuna Respiciens, which sources locate on the east flank of the Palatine between the *Septizonium* and the *Curiae Veteres*.[89] The theory rests

---

[85] On the comparison with Puteoli, see D'Alessio 2014: 19–20.

[86] Anselmino 2006: 234, fig. 14 (*opera cementizia in paramento*); the same features are labeled as *opus incertum* in the sectional drawing on 232, fig. 19.

[87] As noted by Anselmino 2006: 233–34.

[88] D'Alessio 2007a: 425–30; 2007b; 2011.

[89] For the topographical context, see Coarelli 2012: 200–19.

primarily on the topographical relationship with the find spot of the famous terracotta sculptural group known as the "Via di S. Gregorio pediment" (recovered within the post-64 CE fill 75 m south of the vaulted structure, but considerably farther down the slopes).[90] In fact, the structure seems large enough to support a temple whose width can be estimated at about 20 m (as inferred from the overall dimensions of the pediment at 15–16 m), but there are no traces of the podium at the site. The relative position of the surviving elements, the iconography, the meaning of the scene, and the identity of the main deity in the group have been the object of considerable debate. Other associations have been proposed with temples located elsewhere on the Palatine or on the Caelian farther away from the actual place where the statues were discovered (Mars, Venus, Victoria). Differences of opinion on style and attribution have influenced to a great degree the dating of the sculptural pieces, ranging from as early as the 3rd century to as late as the first half of the 1st century BCE.[91] Combining the architectural evidence from the east slopes of the Palatine and related masonry style with a new reading of the iconography for the sculptural group, Anselmino (2006) has proposed a date within the first half of the 2nd century BCE, narrowing down the window for the construction of the temple to the 167–150 BCE period (on account of the missing notice in Livy), and suggesting a possible connection with L. Aemilius Paullus (but the supporting evidence is very tenuous). Strazzulla (1993) accepts the identification of the site but prefers a date immediately after 150 BCE based on her stylistic analysis of the pediment, hinting to a possible association of the temple with Scipio Aemilianus (*c.* 146 BCE).[92] It is important to note that the later history of the monument contrasts with the accepted interpretation as a temple structure: The terrace was eventually incorporated into a larger structure that seems to have been used as an apartment block in the 2nd century CE, a transformation that would have erased any religious connotation.[93] The possibility that the terracing was part of an elite residential complex in the previous period cannot be dismissed.[94] If so, the Temple of Fortuna Respiciens would have to be located closer to the find spot of the sculptures.

[90] Anselmino *et al.* 1990–91: 198–201; Anselmino 2006: 224–25.

[91] For a complete reference to early scholarship on this monument, see Anselmino *et al.* 1990–91: 179, table 1; Anselmino 2006: 239, n. 33. The most recent comprehensive treatment is Di Cesare 2010 alongside Strazzulla 2010; Ferrea 2002. On the dating, see especially Strazzulla 1993: 326–30.

[92] Anselmino *et al.* 1990–91: 252–62; Anselmino 2006: 238. Cf. the more cautious approach by Davies 2017: 90–92, figs. 3.12–13 (end of 2nd century BCE?).

[93] Anselmino 2006: 240–41.

[94] For possible contemporary parallels, see the *opus incertum* terracing structure under the church of S. Pudenziana on the *uicus Patricius* (Angelelli 2010: 279, n. 5); the *opus reticulatum* building on the east slopes of the Viminal (Ramieri 1980); the remains from Vigna de Merode (Morricone Matini 1971: 17; Blake 1947: 250, plates 41.3 and 52.3); the *opus incertum* substructures on the north slopes of the Viminal at Via Palermo (De Caprariis 1988: 29–39; 42–44, fig. 25).

A more circumstantiated case can be made for the selective use of cemented-rubble technology in the Temple of Castor and Pollux. Cemented rubble was employed for minor repairs of the ashlar foundations of the front part of the podium, whose original construction dates to the 5th century BCE.[95] Probably around the middle of the 2nd century BCE, but certainly before the complete overhaul of the podium and cella in 117 BCE by L. Caecilius Metellus Dalmaticus (Cic., *Scaur.* 46; *Verr.* 2.1.154), the façade of the temple was radically modified (Phase IA). The first row of columns and several courses of Cappellaccio blocks were dismantled in order to accommodate a lower step in the podium, consisting of Peperino slabs. In the area of the pronaos, the ashlar grid was reinforced by laying predominantly Cappellaccio rubble (probably recycled from the original blocks; but Tufo Lionato and Peperino pieces are also attested) in hydraulic mortar (Figure 3.11; Plate IV.A). Based on the macroscopic properties of the binder, which contains coarse "blackish-gray pozzolana" clasts of up to 1.5 cm in diameter, these concrete features can be clearly distinguished from the later structures. Furthermore, while the podium of the Metellan temple was raised using timber shuttering, the irregular surface of the concrete walls of Phase IA indicates that mortar and aggregates were placed directly into the trenches so as to fill the voids resulting from the removal of the Cappellaccio blocks.[96] By removing the original frontal steps, the lower platform was effectively transformed into a *tribunal* that could be accessed from the sides through staircases set at right angle. The excavators have linked this restoration with a broader building program affecting both the temple and the nearby Lacus Iuturnae, tentatively attributing it to the censorship of L. Aemilius Paullus (164 BCE).[97] Davies (2017), however, has argued convincingly

---

[95] Nielsen and Poulsen 1992a. Drawings and photos from the excavation archive are available online at http://da.acdan.net/.

[96] Nielsen and Poulsen 1992b: 80. These concrete fills are not uniformly attested across the pronaos, suggesting they may relate to an intermediate stage of repairs dating sometime between Phase IA and the construction of the Metellan temple. As a result of later modifications to the podium, however, there is no solid stratigraphic basis to demonstrate whether parts of the ashlar foundations were ever reexposed a second time in order to replace damaged blocks.

[97] Nielsen and Poulsen 1992b: 80. The argument has been developed in a series of contributions by Steinby (1985; 1987; 1988; 1993; 2011; 2012a: 61; Steinby 2012b: 34–70), based primarily on a passage in which Minucius Felix (*Oct.* 7.3) relates that the Dioscuri were said to have appeared by a *lacus* to announce Paullus' victory at Pydna (168 BCE). Since Minucius Felix also mentions consecrated statues of the gods, which she takes to be the ones found by Boni during excavations in the area of the Lacus Iuturnae (Boni 1901: 88–92, figs. 2–4; Davies 2017: 106, figs. 3.33a–d), Steinby speculates that these were dedicated on that occasion as part of a bigger project involving the reconstruction of both the temple and the Lacus. Florus (1.28.12) is the only source linking the episode specifically with the Lacus Iuturnae, but the text does not mention the statues. All the other sources dealing with the episode (Cic., *Nat. D.* 2.6; Val. Max., 1.8; Plin., *HN* 7.86, on the relay of sound over long distances; Plut., *Vit. Aem.*, 24.4–6) imply that the Dioscuri manifested themselves far from Rome, possibly by Lake Regillus (with which their memory was associated). Another message from the Dioscuri was received after the victory over the Cimbri in 101 BCE (Plin., *HN* 7.86), but the location of their appearance is unknown.

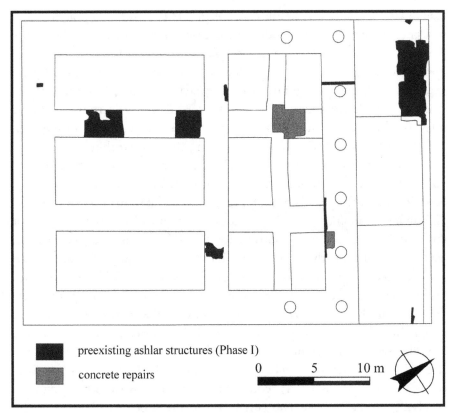

Figure 3.11  Rome, east side of the Forum Romanum. Restored plan of Phase IA of the Temple of Castor and Pollux with indication of the concrete repairs, *c.* 139–137 BCE? (Mogetta 2015: 19, fig. 10). Drawing: M. Mogetta.

that this reconfiguration could have been designed to accommodate the physical requirements of voting reforms enacted between 139 and 137 BCE, which changed the spatial dynamics of the Forum with relation to the electoral process.[98]

The dating of the Lacus Iuturnae and associated concrete structures is controversial. Three concrete phases have been identified for the monumental basin on the basis of facing styles and stratigraphic relations (Steinby's Phases II.1–3; Plate IV.B).[99] The precise dimensions of the concrete basin in the earliest stage are not known, but it originally had an oblong rectangular shape. Its retaining walls were made with *opus incertum* lined with *cocciopesto*, on top of which is a course of tuff blocks that create a projecting rim. In the second phase, the level of the rim was raised by about 1 m. To the south, a new retaining wall in *opus quasi reticulatum* was built up from the bottom of the

[98] Davies 2017: 102–04.
[99] Steinby 2012b. For schematic phase plans, see also Mogetta 2015: 20, fig. 11a–c.

basin on the south side.[100] To the east, the edge of the basin was brought to the same height by laying two additional courses of tuff ashlars on top of the previous ones,[101] while cemented rubble was used on the west side. The north side was rebuilt so as to transform the rectangular basin into a square structure. Other modifications in *opus reticulatum* belong to a third phase. A lower step abutting the inner face of the retaining walls runs on all four sides: It was probably added in order to facilitate maintenance of the pool after the edges had been raised. Built using the same technique and with the same materials is a rectangular platform located at the center of the pool, which sits on top of an earlier ashlar base. In the absence of stratified deposits, the absolute dating of the architectural remains is uncertain. Following Coarelli's chronology, Steinby sees no obstacles for a date of the *opus incertum* phase to shortly after 168 BCE (thus, the first phase is dated essentially on the basis of the building technique).[102] Rather than with the reconstruction of the Temple of Castor and Pollux by Metellus Dalmaticus, the raising of the basin rim in Phase II.2 can perhaps be linked with the generalized reorganization of the Forum pavement in 78–74 BCE.[103] This building episode likely impacted the area of the Temple, which in fact underwent another restoration by Verres shortly after (Cic., *Verr.* 1.129–54: 73 BCE). If so, the original construction of the concrete basin (Phase II.1) could be connected with other activities involving the cult of the Dioscuri in the period between the end of the 2nd and the early 1st centuries BCE.[104]

The area of the Lacus Iuturnae is delimited to the east by a row of vaulted rooms supporting a ramp that spanned the elevation drop from the Via Nova to the Via Sacra. Commonly referred to as the *Scalae Graecae* or *Scalae Anulariae*, the structure served as a public route to reach the site of the Porta Romanula on the northwest corner of the Palatine without having to pass through the Forum.[105] In aspect and function, the structure can be compared with the viaduct of the Clivus Capitolinus on the opposite side of the Forum (it had

[100] *LTUR* III.169 (Steinby); cf. Steinby 1985: 82 (cemented rubble).
[101] Mogetta 2015: 21 fig. 12.
[102] Steinby 1987: 168 and n. 122.
[103] Giuliani and Verduchi 1987: 55–66. The floor surface on the east side of the podium of the temple of Castor and Pollux is reconstructed by Nielsen (1992: 112) at 13.10 m a.s.l. The elevation of the crepidoma of the Metellan temple is 13.40 m a.s.l. The raised rim of the Lacus sits between 13.37 (Steinby 1985: 77) and 13.44 m a.s.l. *Contra* Steinby 2012b: 54–56.
[104] Bastien (2009: 45) emphasizes the links between Temple of Castor and Pollux, Lacus Iuturnae, and the triumph by the Caecilii Metelli (M. Caecilius Metellus and Metellus Caprarius) in 111 BCE, on the *dies natalis* of the temple. Coins of A. Postumius Albinus depicting statues of the Dioscuri on horses near a wellhead on the reverse, minted in 96 BCE (*RRC* 335/10b), could refer to the dedication of the sculptural group by members of his family. The Postumii were indeed connected with the original dedication of the temple of Castor and Pollux: Palmer 1990.
[105] Hurst 2006.

wedge-shaped oblong tuff blocks laid radially at the intrados),[106] although its vaulted chambers are wider (2.80–5.00 m), and one of them was also embellished with an engaged Doric façade in Peperino.[107] Steinby thought that the construction of the ramp predated that of the Lacus, placing it between the end of the 3rd and the first third of the 2nd century BCE.[108] It is important to note that the feature formed an integral part of the Atrium Vestae, since some of the chambers (Rooms 7–8) were actually open toward it. Most likely, therefore, the ramp was built in connection with one of the building phases known for the precinct. Recent stratigraphic excavations have dated the earliest occurrence of concrete architecture in the sanctuary to the early 1st century BCE (but a date in the late 2nd century BCE is also possible).[109] The concrete ramp seem to have replaced a previous structure in *opus quadratum*: The limit between the Atrium Vestae and the Lacus Iuturnae in the early 2nd century BCE was represented by a stretch of blocks of Tufo Giallo della Via Tiberina found east of the podium of the round temple.[110]

Two roughly parallel concrete foundations of considerable thickness (1.30–1.50 m) run north of the basin, truncating part of the wall that delimited the concrete ramp to the north (Figure 3.12a–b). Scattered remains of a floor at approximately the same level as the Sullan pavement of the Forum are associated with these structures.[111] A third foundation with square buttresses, not perfectly aligned and perhaps later than the other two, was found razed in test-trenches excavated along the eastern side of the temple of Castor and Pollux (Figure 3.12c). Steinby (2012b) assigns these structures to two building phases. The original complex (*c.* 164 BCE?) would have consisted of a simple portico, later transformed into a *basilica* with the addition of a second nave (1st century

---

[106] Boni (1901: 63) gives the dimensions of the facing blocks of the intrados, but the variety of tuff is not specified.

[107] Reconstruction in Steinby 2011: 9, fig. 3.

[108] Steinby 2011: 7. Carandini *et al.* (2017: 215–16) assigns it to 150/125–100/80 BCE (Phase 12; Arvanitis).

[109] Arvanitis *et al.* 2010: 54–59; Carandini *et al.* 2017: 216–217 (Phase 13: 100/80–27 BCE; Arvanitis). Only foundations survive (in one case associated with a superstructure of Tufo Lionato blocks). The mortar used in these structures has been described as purplish in color, with pumice inclusions, and yellow and green tuff (including Tufo Giallo della Via Tiberina and Tufo Lionato), with rare Cappellaccio aggregate. See Carettoni 1978–80: 330–32. It is worth noting that 2nd century BCE construction activities seem exclusively represented by structures in *opus quadratum* of Tufo Giallo della Via Tiberina: Arvanitis *et al.* 2010, 48–51. Based on sporadic finds from the foundation trench of the round podium of the Temple of Vesta, Scott (2009: 18–24, 28–29) had tentatively dated the concrete phase between the late 3rd and the middle of the 2nd century BCE, but his reconstruction must now be rejected. See also Carandini *et al.* 2017: 242–43 (N. Arvanitis).

[110] Arvanitis *et al.* 2010: 49, fig. 21s (148–100 BCE); Filippi 2010: fig. 6. See also Steinby 1985: 77 (blocks under the first level of Room 7 of the concrete ramp). But cf. Arvanitis (in Carandini *et al.* 2017: 215–16) now assigns Steinby's concrete ramp to Phase 12 (150/125–100/80 BCE).

[111] Steinby 1985: 81–82; Steinby 2012b: 60–70.

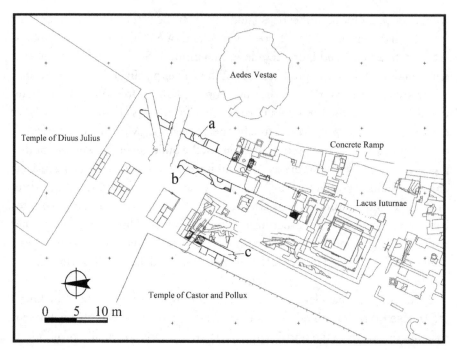

Figure 3.12 Rome, east side of the Forum Romanum. Simplified map showing the location of the three concrete foundations (a, b, and c) associated with the Lacus Iuturnae (adapted from Steinby 2012b: 62, fig. 17; © Quasar; used by permission).

BCE).[112] On account of a radically new interpretation of the relevant literary sources, Steinby identifies the monument with the Basilica Aemilia mentioned by Cicero (*Att.* 4.17) by the middle of the 1st century BCE, distinguishing it from the Basilica Fulvia.[113] Regardless of the topographical problems, the archaeological sequence indicates that the foundations postdate both Lacus and concrete ramp, making the 164 BCE date untenable.

## ARCHAEOMETRIC EVIDENCE ON THE EARLY DEVELOPMENT OF MORTARS IN PUBLIC BUILDING

The architectural and stratigraphic data discussed above can be complemented with the results of scientific analyses of the mortars carried out on select

[112] Cf. Steinby 1988: 32–33, fig. 1. Carnabuci 1991: 280–87 considers it implausible that the three foundations formed part of a single building. Cullhed *et al.* 2008 interpret the buttressed foundation as a retaining wall connected with the raising of the levels in the area of the Lacus Iuturnae, rejecting the idea that it supported a colonnade. Carnabuci 1991 sees the structures as part of yet another ramp connecting the Forum with the Palatine, possibly of the kind reconstructed by Zink (2015: 366–67, with 365, fig. 7) in the area of the Temple of Apollo on the Palatine (Phase 4: end of the 2nd century BCE?); cf. Pensabene 2017b: 67–69.

[113] Steinby 1987: 172–76. The interpretation is rejected in *LTUR* I.173–75, 183–87 (Bauer). See also Ertel and Freyberger 2007: 110–17. The issue is ignored in the final publication of the most recent architectural survey carried out at the site: Freyberger and Ertel 2016 (15–60 for the Republican phases).

monuments. The material characteristics of samples taken from the Testaccio Building, the first concrete phase of the Temple of Concord, and the podium of the Metellan Temple of Castor and Pollux (Phase II) suggest that builders exploited volcaniclastic sediments outcropping near the construction sites as fine aggregates, mixing them with the sieved fragments of the same tuff varieties that were used as rubble in the cores and wall-facings.[114] In the case of the Testaccio Building, rubble-grade and crushed fragments of Tufo Lionato were combined with the less coherent fraction of the same pyroclastic-flow deposit, a transitional facies that in the region of Rome overlays the incoherent Pozzolanelle, occurring on the Aventine. The material used as fine aggregate, therefore, could have been quarried from the same site where the Tufo Lionato was extracted. Similarly, the mortar of the Temple of Concord features fragments from the sedimentary deposit of the Aurelia Formation, which outcrops on the Capitoline above the Tufo Lionato sequence. The mortar of the Metellan Temple of Castor and Pollux is composed of crushed fragments of Tufo del Palatino and Tufo Lionato, both of which occur as rubble in the core.[115] The earliest known occurrence of Pozzolane Rosse aggregate comes from podium and cella of Temple B at the Largo Argentina site, a structure commonly identified with the Temple of Fortuna Huiusce Diei and dated to *c.* 101 BCE.[116] The material is associated with lightweight white pumice whose chemical signature suggests an origin from the Monti Sabatini products, pointing to a source in the region of Rome (where white pumice occurs below the Pozzolane Rosse deposits).[117] Pozzolanelle and Pozzolane Nere, on the other hand, were detected only in monuments dating from the 2nd century CE onwards.

The archaeometric evidence from the public monuments suggests that by the early 1st century BCE at the latest builders were purposely selecting better materials that were more difficult to access than the reworked volcanic sands normally used in 2nd century BCE concrete construction.[118] The available sample size is too small to draw generalizations, meaning that it remains to be demonstrated whether the presence or absence of Pozzolane Rosse necessarily represents a precise chronological reference. An important implication, however, is that the quarrying of the highly reactive material started earlier than previously thought, and that suitable deposits were identified at the site of

[114] Marra *et al.* 2016: 185–87. Jackson *et al.* (2010: 41, table II) include concrete features from the podium of the Temple of Saturn, which the authors assign to a building phase dated to the 4th century BCE, known only from a late source (Macrob., *Sat.* 1.8.1). If at all historical, this building episode probably represented a minor restoration of the original ashlar architecture: *LTUR* V.234 (Coarelli).

[115] Marra *et al.* 2016: 191.

[116] Davies 2017: 153.

[117] Marra *et al.* 2016: 187–89.

[118] Marra *et al.* 2016: 191–94.

Rome before the less valuable deposits in the *suburbium* began to be exploited on an extensive scale, thus undermining Van Deman's idea of gradual development.[119]

## REDATING THE EARLY DEVELOPMENT OF CONCRETE CONSTRUCTION IN ROME: THE HOUSES

The progress of stratigraphic investigations in the deeper levels of Rome is shedding more light on long-term trends in elite domestic architecture. An intensive phase of house construction has been documented for the 6th century BCE, when new types of aristocratic residences with expensive architecture surfaced both in the urban core and in the *suburbium*.[120] These buildings were carefully maintained for centuries with little structural modification other than the periodic reconstruction of floor levels in the 4th and 3rd centuries BCE.[121] Another peak of activity is attested in the 1st century BCE. A series of literary accounts vividly portray the phenomenon of elite competition for real estate on the Palatine hill.[122] At least twenty-three domestic contexts are known archaeologically from legacy data, all featuring a phase in *opus reticulatum* dating to the early or middle part of that century.[123] The record for the 2nd century BCE is much less consistent: *opus incertum* architecture has been securely identified only at a handful of sites (cf. Figure 3.4 for their location), whose dating is difficult due to the lack of contextual evidence.[124] The recently published

---

[119]   Marra *et al.* (2016: 194) argue that the sudden innovation and widespread implementation of mortars containing Pozzolane Rosse resulted from the spike in construction activities following the fire of 111 BCE, and link the later exploitation of the upper layers of volcanic ash outcropping in the southeast *suburbium* of Rome with the increasing demand for building materials during the Imperial period (see also Marra *et al.* 2015: 123–24).

[120]   Carandini and Carafa 1995; Carandini *et al.* 2007.

[121]   For incomplete plans of ashlar domestic architecture commonly assigned to the Mid-Republican period, see Andrews 2014 (atrium house below the church of Santi Sergio e Bacco in the Subura); Colini and Matthiae 1966: 11–15 (house on the Oppian beneath S. Pietro in Vincoli, with *opus incertum* subphase); Meta Sudans (Schingo 1996: 154); house abutting the Republican walls of the Quirinal at the Salita del Grillo (Specchio 2011); S. Cecilia (Parmegiani and Pronti 2004, with subphase in *opus reticulatum*). Torelli and Marcattili 2010: 44–46 show that the style of architectural decorations and moldings, too, remained anchored to Archaic conventions for most of the 3rd century BCE.

[122]   An early survey is in Patterson 1992: 200–04. Royo 1999: 72–75 lists twenty-eight house plots known to have been the object of successive transactions (including inheritance, confiscation, sale, or rental) between 200/150 and 36 BCE. See also Guilhembet and Royo 2008: 196–209.

[123]   For the quantification, see Papi 1998: 50–52; Carandini *et al.* 2010: 78–225; Coarelli 2012: 112–26; 287–346.

[124]   Synopsis in Mogetta 2015: 22, fig. 13. Capitoline: Santa Maria in Aracoeli (Tucci 2019: *opus incertum* sewer associated with a multistory *opus reticulatum* building); remains by the Temple of Veiovis (Morricone Matini 1967: 4; 1971: 8, nos. 3–4; Morricone 1980: 19). Palatine: Casa dei Grifi (Pensabene 2017b: 3–11; late 2nd century BCE); Aula Isiaca (Vlad Borrelli 1967: 23–28, 24 fig. 11; plan in Iacopi 1997: 7, fig. 1). South slopes of the Velia: Via dell'Impero site

results of large-scale excavations on the north slopes of the Palatine now provide a more detailed picture of building practices for that phase.[125]

A series of concrete features has been documented across a city block facing onto the Via Sacra (Figure 3.13). Measuring approximately 7,000 m², the insula is delimited by the so-called *cliuus Palatinus* to the east and by an east–west road leading from the *cliuus Palatinus* to the so-called *Scalae Graecae* to the south (perhaps this corresponds to the Nova Via mentioned in historical texts).[126] A north–south alley separates this private sector from the neighboring block to the west, which is occupied by public buildings (Carettoni's Domus Publica, the Atrium Vestae, and the Sanctuary of Vesta). The block is organized into terraces that adapt to the morphology sloping from south to north, and from east to west. Property boundaries have been tentatively reconstructed on the basis of design features and elevation points, but the poor preservation of structures in the east sector of the block poses serious problems for the definition of individual houses. The excavators identify four units accessible from the Via Sacra and the *cliuus Palatinus* (labelled Houses 5–8), built on top of decapitated *opus quadratum* remains dating to the Archaic, Early, and Mid-Republican periods.[127] At least two other units faced on the south street (for one of which we know only its 1st century BCE occupation),[128] whereas no contemporary structures have been preserved in the west side of the blocks (where the available space could have accommodated two additional units).

According to the excavators, the development of the block was prompted by the 210 BCE fire.[129] The relative sequence has been reconstructed as follows: Building activities would have begun in House 6, continued in House 5 and

---

(Colini 1933: 85 fig. 8); Temple of Venus and Rome site (Cassatella 1985: 102–05). Esquiline: structures under the "peristilio rettangolare" of the Domus Aurea (Sanguinetti 1958: 45; Morricone Matini 1971: 11–12; 1980: 27). Aventine: S. Sabina site (Darsy 1968: 20–21, figs. 7–8; Morricone 1980: 31). Quirinal: Via Sistina site (Fiorini 1988: 53, fig. 11). For the Viminal see *supra*, n. 94.

[125] Carandini and Papi 1999.

[126] Carandini *et al.* 2010: 98 and 102, fig. 43 (the road in question is interpreted as a *uicus*, while the toponym Nova Via is connected with a minor alley between the Atrium Vestae and the Lucus Vestae). For other identifications, see Hurst and Cirone 2003: 23, fig. 4.

[127] Gualandi and Papi 1999a. For the early remains, see Carandini and Carafa 1995 (Phase 9, Activity 23, Houses 1–4). According to the restored plans, Houses 5 and 6 would maintain the size and proportions of their Archaic precedents (Houses 1 and 2, whose plans, however, are even more fragmentary), with stretches of earlier party walls repurposed to support the new foundations; Houses 7 and 8, on the other hand, would be slightly bigger than their precedents, but much more elongated in shape. If confirmed, this evidence would suggest that, in spite of the generalized reconstruction of the city block, the previous system of land division was not altered radically, but it remains difficult to say whether there was continuity in ownership patterns.

[128] Santangeli Valenzani and Volpe 1986. See also Carandini *et al.* 2010: 110–11 and 108, fig. 46.

[129] Carandini *et al.* 2010: 98–111 (reorganization of the city block: 210 BCE; modifications: 70–20 BCE). Cf. Carandini 2005: 10, fig. 8 (175–125 BCE phase plan showing property plots).

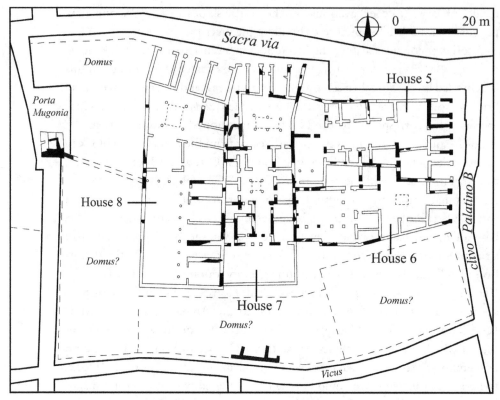

Figure 3.13 Rome, north slope of the Palatine. Map of the city block excavated by A. Carandini, showing the hypothesized property divisions. The actual remains of the houses are indicated with solid line (adapted from Carandini *et al.* 2010: 102, fig. 43). Drawing: M. Harder.

House 8, and ended with House 7, whose internal walls abut both the west boundary of House 6 and the wall delimiting House 8 to the east. Moreover, a later subphase is documented by minor modifications involving Houses 5, 6, and 7. The best case for a canonical atrium plan can be made for House 6, which preserves an *ala* and enough space for an axial *tablinum* opposite the *fauces*. For House 7, the excavators restore an internal organization centered on two atria separated by a *tablinum*, an arrangement for which they suggest a parallel with the Casa del Criptoportico at Vulci (late 2nd century BCE),[130] but the actual evidence for it is scanty. In House 8, the back part of the plot can be confidently said to have included a row of nicely appointed rooms facing onto an open space, quite possibly a formal garden (but no traces of the supposed L-shaped portico have been found).

Whereas some uncertainties surround the individual house plans, the construction process can be described more precisely. The project started with the systematic demolition of the Archaic buildings, which were razed to a uniform

[130] Gualandi and Papi 1999a: 42 n. 118.

level across the extent of the city block. Next, construction fills were dumped to regularize the undulating topography. Trenches up to a few meters deep were dug through these deposits in order to lay concrete foundations for load-bearing walls.[131] When the course of the foundations coincided with that of preexisting ashlar walls, these were dismantled down to the appropriate level, suggesting that concrete was deemed structurally superior. The depth of the foundations, seemingly built without formworks, implies the use of cemented rubble.

Based on the macroscopic properties of the mortars (color, compaction, and granulometry), the provenance of the aggregates, their relative proportion to rubble, and the method of construction of the foundations, Misiani (1999) has identified seven different variants of concrete being employed in the Late Republican occupation (Tables 3.1–2).[132] The evidence is not as detailed and systematic as that available for the public monuments, but it allows for a comparison. Types 1 and 2 contain a great proportion of Cappellaccio rubble (50 percent or more) and only a small percentage of Tufo Lionato and Tufo Giallo della Via Tiberina, placed by hand in roughly horizontal layers interspersed with a dark gray mortar containing coarse volcanic sediments (described by Misiani as "pozzolana" without any qualification other than color and grain size) and a relatively small quantity of lime (M1). Both types are evenly distributed across the four houses. Cappellaccio was the predominant material with which the Archaic structures were built (Tufo Giallo della

TABLE 3.1 *Republican houses on the north slopes of the Palatine. Composition and distribution of cemented-rubble foundations within the different property plots. Compiled from data in Misiani 1999.*

| Cemented Rubble Type | Mortar Type | Aggregate | Spatial Distribution |
|---|---|---|---|
| *Type 1* | M1 | C | House 5; House 7; House 8 |
| *Type 2* | M1 | C (>50%); TL; TGVT | House 5; House 6; House 7 |
| *Type 3* | M2 | TL (>50%); TGVT; C | House 5; House 6 |
| *Type 4* | M2 | Other tuffs (>50%); Tr (rare); B (rare); Tile (rare) | Houses 5 and 6 (second phase) |
| *Type 5* | M6 | TGVT (>50%); TL; C | House 8; Houses 5 and 6 (second phase) |
| *Type 7* | M6 | TGVT (>50%); Other tuffs | Houses 5 and 6 (second phase) |
| *Type 10* | M4; M6 | TGVT; B; Tr (rare); Other tuffs (rare) | House 7 |

[131]  Gualandi and Papi 1999a: 41.
[132]  The evidence is collected by Misiani 1999: 179–86. Lab tests included microscopic analysis of thin sections, thermal analysis, and calcimetric measurements (Misiani 1999: 180), but the raw data and results have not been published.

TABLE 3.2 *Republican houses on the north slopes of the Palatine. Mortar types associated with the earliest cemented-rubble foundations. Compiled from data in Misiani 1999.*

| Mortar Type | Color | Composition | Compaction |
|---|---|---|---|
| M1 | Dark gray | Coarse volcanic sediments (max 5 mm); smaller proportion of lime | Friable |
| M2 | Light to dark gray | Fine volcanic sediments; smaller proportion of lime | Friable |
| M4 | Gray | Volcanic sediments; tuff fragments; higher lime content | Hard |
| M6 | Gray | Gray to reddish volcanic sediments; higher lime content | Hard |

Via Tiberina occurs only in minor restorations dating to the 4th century BCE). Thus, it is possible that most of the rubble was recycled directly from the demolition of the walls that stood in the area. It is also probable that Tufo del Palatino and Tufo Lionato were quarried on purpose from the deposits out-cropping near the building site. Type 3, which is characterized by the pre-dominant use of Tufo Lionato rubble, is attested only in Houses 5 and 6. The mortar associated with it, a light gray mixture containing finer volcanic sedi-ments, also occurs in association with *opus reticulatum* construction. Finally, the variants with prevailing use of Tufo Giallo della Via Tiberina rubble (types 5, 7, and 10) are mostly employed for later modifications. In House 8, the boundary walls have foundations built with the Cappellaccio-based cemented rubble, but the series of small rooms in the back part of the house feature a reddish mortar (M6; containing Pozzolane Rosse?). Type 10 appears associated exclusively with House 7, the last one to be built in the lot. On the assumption that different recipes were used by different groups of builders, the pattern has been interpreted as evidence of multiple crews moving from house to house as work progressed in the block.[133]

*Opus quadratum* was employed in combination with the cemented-rubble foundations, both for exterior façades and internal walls. In House 8, the walls of the rooms facing onto the Via Sacra, the west boundary wall, and at least one of the internal subdivisions have freestanding parts in Tufo Lionato ashlars. Both Tufo Lionato and Cappellaccio blocks were used for load-bearing walls in House 6 (on the west and southwest sides), while earlier Cappellaccio walls' were maintained for internal subdivision in the front and back of the house. The party wall separating House 5 from House 6 is made of Tufo Giallo della Via Tiberina ashlars. In House 7, ashlars were used for internal subdivision on

---

[133] Gualandi and Papi 1999a: 20.

the northwestern side of the larger court, and negative impressions of blocks have been detected on the top surface of the foundation that separates the central part of the house from the shops on the front. The evidence, therefore, demonstrates that concrete construction was used selectively. The new building medium was to be developed as a rapid and economical way of building solid foundations for the new houses, making extensive use of recycled building materials. Its use for freestanding walls is poorly documented, due to the levelling of the city block in the subsequent phase, but some of the foundations may have supported concrete walls (as documented in one case for House 8).

The dating of the earliest concrete phase of these houses is difficult. Unfortunately, the construction of semisubterranean quarters in the middle of the 1st century BCE caused the almost complete destruction of the original stratification.[134] The foundation trenches of Houses 7 and 8 cut beaten earth-floors, which were in use from the 5th through the 3rd centuries BCE.[135] This sequence provides only a generic *terminus post quem*, since the demolition of the archaic houses down to the level of the foundations most likely caused the razing of successive surfaces. The original floor levels are preserved only in House 8, which seems to come later in the sequence of occupation of the block. This building features decorated *cocciopesto* floors with comparanda dated stylistically from the middle of the 2nd century BCE onwards.[136] One of these floor surfaces is associated with a wall painting in the First Style, the remains of which seem to fit with that date.[137] A small assemblage of (early?) 2nd century BCE pottery has been recovered from a construction fill in House 7,[138] but deposits of this kind normally contain frequent residues, and at best provide a *terminus post quem*. The excavators have derived a *terminus ad quem* from the possible identification of one of the houses located in this block with the *domus* of Cn. Octavius, which Cicero (*Off.* 1.138) specifically connects with Octavius' election to the consulship in 165 BCE.[139] The link between the

---

[134] Medri 1999: 70 (Phase 12, Activity 300); Gualandi and Papi 1999b: 112–17.

[135] Papi 1995: 338–39.

[136] Papi 1995: 343–46.

[137] Gualandi and Papi 1999a: 46–51. The introduction of the First Style in Latium has been dated to the second quarter of the 2nd century BCE, though its diffusion peaked in the last quarter of that century: Caputo 1990–91; Torelli and Marcattili 2010. The surviving decoration from House 8 shows a red band, above which is a white ground possibly divided in stretchers by vertical red lines (only one is actually preserved). The absence of elements in relief would suggest an advanced stage in the development of the First Style, but the evidence is too meager to provide a secure chronology.

[138] Gualandi and Papi 1999a: 39 (citing Black Gloss pottery and tile fragments of unspecified types). Based on the single fragment of basalt collected in the same layer, the excavators suggest that the construction of the houses "unequivocally" progressed in connection with the building of the new course of the Via Sacra (174 BCE?). See Gualandi and Papi 1999a: 17.

[139] Carandini 1986: 263–68 connects the reference in Cicero with the *Octavi domus* mentioned by Sallust (*Hist.* fr. 2.45). The latter belonged to L. Octavius (consul in 75 BCE and grandson of Cn. Octavius), and was located near the Via Sacra, adjacent to the house of M. Aemilius

excavated remains and literary accounts, however, should be taken with caution. Overall, the archaeological evidence from the site seems to be consistent with a date between the second and the last quarters of the 2nd century BCE.

A more reliable date can be assigned to another group of aristocratic residences located on the northeast slopes of the Palatine, just 200 m away from the previous site, in the area now identified as the Curiae Veteres.[140] Immediately adjacent to the Curiae Veteres precinct are the fragmentary remains of a 1st century BCE house, which is delimited by a Tufo Lionato ashlar sitting on top of deep cemented-rubble foundations.[141] To the same property can be associated a mosaic-paved room located behind a series of shops that open onto the main road coming from the Forum. A small rectangular open court bounded by party walls faced with *opus incertum* and paved with a cement floor probably belongs to an earlier stratum (Figure 3.14).[142] The associated foundations consist of Cappellaccio rubble laid in lime-based mortar containing "pozzolana" of unspecified type (but the mortar is certainly of the hydraulic type). The rubble may have been obtained from the debris. As revealed by deeper excavations, the structures that occupied the area in the previous period were predominantly built with Cappellaccio ashlars. The pottery assemblage recovered from the construction levels dates the *opus incertum* house to *c.* 150 BCE.[143] The remaking of the neighborhood probably followed the overall reconfiguration of the urban infrastructure in this sector of the city, an undoubtedly lengthy project started by the censors of 174 BCE (Liv. 41.27.5). This likely involved the laying out and paving of both the Via Sacra and the east–west road leading from it to the valley of the Colosseum.

Scaurus (into which it would be eventually incorporated). On the basis of the topology, Carandini identifies the monument with his House 5. The identification is accepted by Coarelli 2012: 290–92. *Contra* Tamm 1963: 32, placing the domus of Scaurus on the north side of the Domus Tiberiana.

[140] A general interpretation of the remains and of their broader topographical context is attempted by Zeggio 2006: 74–75, fig. 8, nos. 11–13. Carbonara (2006) presents a phasing of the architecture. For contemporaneous structures on the southwest slope of the Velia, see Panella 1990: 46–47.

[141] Carbonara 2006: 19–27; Panella 2006: 278–281 identifies the property as the house where Augustus was born. On the Republican phases of the Curiae Veteres building, see Panella *et al.* 2014:167–72, with figs. 9 and 29; Panella *et al.* 2019.

[142] Carbonara 2006: 16–19, figs. 2–3.

[143] Panella 1990: 46–47. A *terminus post quem* around the late 3rd or early 2nd century BCE has been derived from the stylistic analysis of a tuff *impluvium* cut by the foundations of the *opus incertum* walls (Carbonara 2006: 19 fig. 5). To reconcile the discrepancy with the date suggested by Carandini and his team for the concrete houses on the north slopes of the Palatine, Panella (2006: 283–84) argues that the refashioning of the old aristocratic houses began in the neighborhoods closer to the Forum around 200–175 BCE, spreading to more peripheral areas only in a subsequent period.

Figure 3.14 Rome, house on northeast slope of the Palatine (Area I). Detail of *opus incertum* party wall on top of a cemented-rubble foundation (Carbonara 2006: 18, fig. 3; Photo: S. Zeggio; used by permission).

## THE SOCIAL AND CULTURAL CONTEXT OF THE TECHNOLOGICAL INNOVATION

The survey of excavated urban sites for which stratigraphic data are available allows us to lay some firmer groundwork to interpret the genesis of concrete architecture in Rome. Thanks to the new material, elite house construction can be brought into the picture, complementing previous reconstructions based mainly on the role of public architecture. The private building industry emerges as a context, in which important steps toward the development of concrete may have been achieved. Starting around the middle of the 2nd century BCE, long-lived aristocratic compounds that had stood unaltered for centuries were torn down and rebuilt, particularly in the areas closer to the monumental and political core. As already discussed with reference to Cato and Vitruvius in Chapter 2, the theme of private expenditure in the domestic sphere featured prominently in contemporary literary accounts, establishing a link between the consumption of luxury building materials and self-aggrandizement. The idea we get from these sources is that architectural developments were linked with the semipublic function of the Roman house.[144] The spread of First Style stucco decorations in elite houses of this period, for

[144] See especially Coarelli 1989; Drerup 1957. For a reappraisal of the problem, see Sewell 2010: 137–65.

example, may have primarily had the function of visually recreating the ashlar masonry exteriors of political buildings such as the *basilicae* and *quadriporticus* within the domestic space, and perhaps even of alluding to the white marble environment of Classical Greece.[145] Innovations in both design and decoration could be exploited as powerful tools in the competition for public office, as clearly demonstrated by the case of Cn. Octavius mentioned above. Crucially, the development of concrete construction in domestic architecture can be contextualized as part of an overarching process in which the display of new styles (including more elaborate house plans) suddenly became more important than emphasizing the continuity of occupation of centuries-old homes, as had been the norm throughout the Mid-Republican period.[146]

The earliest public monument for which a construction phase in *opus incertum* can be pinpointed with a certain precision is the Porticus Metelli, whose date is within a couple of decades of that of the earliest datable houses. The judicious use of cemented rubble for the repair of podium foundations is attested in the temple of Castor and Pollux (Phase IA), which may be contemporary with the Porticus Metelli, if not slightly earlier. The chronology of the concrete vaulted architecture of the substructures on the east slope of the Palatine and of the Testaccio Building remains uncertain due to the problems of identification and the lack of external evidence, but a date within the second half of the 2nd century BCE seems likely. Temple architecture demonstrates that by the last quarter of the 2nd century BCE at the latest, the use of the technology was widespread, particularly in connection with the rebuilding of temple podia on existing sites (e.g., Veiovis, Concord, Castor and Pollux, Magna Mater, and Victoria), that is, in a structural context that mirrored the construction process and needs described for the houses. The Temples of Magna Mater and Victoria are associated with the earliest datable examples of freestanding concrete vaults (i.e., the *uia tecta* and the monumental front of the southwest corner of the Palatine, *c.* 102/101 BCE). The state of the evidence may have suffered from the radical transformation of the monumental core in the Imperial period, but the available archaeological information on those public buildings that can be securely identified and dated to within the first half of the second century BCE, such as the Basilica Fulvia (179 BCE; Liv. 40.51.5) and the Basilica Sempronia (169 BCE; Liv., 44.16.8–11), demonstrates the exclusive use of ashlar technology (both had Tufo Giallo della Via Tiberina subterranean foundations paved with more durable travertine).[147]

[145] Torelli and Marcattili 2010: 50–53; Russell 2015; Veyne 1979.

[146] See the discussion in Gros 2006: 38–60. Welch (2006) connects the diffusion of peristyles in the elite domestic contexts with the increasing need for spaces to formally display war booty. Cf. Jolivet (2011) stresses continuity with Archaic atrium houses.

[147] On the original remains of the Basilica Fulvia, see Freyberger and Ertel 2016: 37–43, 56–58 (but the travertine pavement belongs to a later subphase). On the remains of the Basilica

Precisely because we have so little archaeological data about Rome's public architecture, to conclude that the use of the technique was initially limited to the private context would risk being an argument ex silentio. The group of public buildings adjoining the aristocratic houses on the north slopes of the Palatine received concrete additions only in the course of the 1st century BCE, but the time lag may have more to do with the need for preserving the ancestral character of those particular monuments.[148] It may be that concrete construction was first introduced in domestic architecture, but, in any case, the transmission of the technology to public building would not have taken very long, since public architecture was sponsored and controlled by the same aristocratic patrons who commissioned the refashioning of the old elite residences in the urban core.[149] The organization of public construction in Republican Rome provides a plausible context to explain why the widespread adoption of concrete in public construction went in parallel with experiments in the private sphere: Magistrates could assign contracts to builders whose skills would have already been tested in private projects, thus minimizing the social and political risks associated with innovating in public architecture.[150] An example may be Cn. Octavius, the possible owner of one of the concrete houses on the north slope of the Palatine, who also built a *porticus*, perhaps of the same general kind as that built by Metellus Macedonicus (which we know incorporated cemented-rubble foundations).[151] In theory, he could have used the same professional builders for both projects.

The growth of Rome's public construction industry can be inferred from the nature of the building works let by the aediles in the early 2nd century BCE, which included structures related to the delivery, storage, and distribution of building timbers (e.g., *emporium extra Porta Trigeminam*; *porticus inter lignarios*: Liv., 35.41.9–10). The demands of censorial building programs, which were characterized by increasing complexity in terms of both building types and scale of the interventions, must have contributed to the development of higher levels

Sempronia: Carettoni and Fabbrini 1961. Neither of these buildings features concrete architecture.

[148] *Supra*, n. 109 for the Atrium Vestae. For the so-called Domus Regis Sacrorum, see Carandini *et al.* 2017: 397–99 with plates 71–72 (Phase 6; Filippi). For the so-called Domus Publica, see Carandini *et al.* 2017: 443–44, with plates 84–85 (Phase 5; Filippi).

[149] See Morgan 1973 on the Caecilii Metelli; Wiseman 1993 and D'Alessio 2014 on the Aemilii.

[150] Biscardi (1960: 433–34) suggests that the practice of assigning the task of inspection to the same individuals who originally contracted the work even though they were no longer in (the same) office, known epigraphically, was an attempt to transfer at least part of the risks (*uitium operis*) from the *conductor* (i.e., the contractor) to the *locator* (i.e., the individual or group who let the contract).

[151] Sources collected in *LTUR* IV.139–41 (Viscogliosi). Pliny (*HN* 34.13) describes it as a *porticus duplex*, but it is unclear whether his terminology refers to a quadriporticus. The construction of the monument is dated between 167 and 163 BCE, making it contemporary with the *domus Octaui* on the Palatine.

of organization and specialization among craftsmen.[152] Problems such as those experienced by the censors of 169 BCE, whose contracted projects were so extensive that it was not possible to perform the required inspections within the statutory period of 18 months (Liv., 45.15.9), would have represented an incentive for the magistrates in charge of public building to foster technological innovations in the economics of construction (the pair applied for prolongation in order to have the projects completed and approved but were unsuccessful, therefore losing much social and political capital).[153] Throughout the middle and late 2nd century BCE, the implementation of a building method that could streamline and expedite the construction process, and thus make sure that deadlines would be met, responded to the ambitions of magistrates that conceived of monumental architectural sponsorship as a powerful weapon for career advancement.[154]

## CONCLUSIONS

I have focused here on reconstructing the pattern of distribution of early concrete architecture in Rome as revealed by the systematic survey of legacy data and newly excavated evidence. Challenging the orthodox view about the phase of experimentation during the period when Rome's colonization program unfolded, I have argued that the technology surfaced rather suddenly in the middle of the 2nd century BCE. Consequently, the developmental sequence of *opus incertum* should be compressed within a shorter period of time through the last three or four decades of the 2nd century BCE, allowing for significant overlaps between different variants that depended primarily on structural function and related economic concerns. In terms of building process, I have highlighted the role of the private building industry at the root of the phenomenon, acknowledging the influence of the socioeconomic structures that informed the organization of construction. I have attributed the impetus for the technological innovation to the political ambitions of members of the ruling class, which are manifested especially in the radical change affecting domestic architecture close to the monumental core. The fact that the actual sponsors of public projects happened to be the same elite patrons that commissioned the refashioning of the outdated houses to reflect current architectural styles provides a crucial link to model the transmission of the technology through the agency of contractors.

---

[152] Anderson 1997: 98–99 (on the *societates* of builders mentioned by Livy for the period). Cf. DeLaine (2006: 249–50) regards the pace of construction activities in the Republican period as slow and gradual, arguing that the construction industry received greater impetus only in the Imperial period.

[153] As noted by Anderson 1997: 99.

[154] Davies 2017: 104–05.

The earliest datable contexts suggest that cemented rubble was implemented as a building medium capable of transforming demolition or quarry waste into a versatile, durable, and fast material, offering some insights into how the technology came about. Other important factors that must have been at play in this context include the taste for stucco and plaster decorations,[155] and the use of *cocciopesto* for floor revetment and waterproofing.[156] The continued spread of these lime-based technologies in both private and public building probably triggered an expansion of production in the limestone region around Rome. The hydraulic properties of *cocciopesto* made it well-suited for use as a binder in airtight structural environments such as foundation trenches and podium or wall cores, where the hardening of simple lime mortars would not be possible. Roman builders were familiar with its higher resistance to shrinkage and cracking during the hardening process, and would have easily realized that these properties could minimize problems of separation between facing and cores in freestanding mortared-rubble walls. Yet, they never used *cocciopesto* for structural purposes on a large scale.[157] The main reason for this was that the mass production of ground terracotta as an additive would have had much higher costs than the quarrying of volcanic ash, making it unsustainable for concrete construction.[158] Conversely, there is scientific evidence that volcanic sediments were often added to the *cocciopesto* mix,[159] though it never really replaced ground terracotta (perhaps so that the building medium preserved the red hue that made it popular in the first place). The conclusion seems to be that Roman builders had an empirical knowledge of ground terracotta and volcanic ash possessing very similar properties. Vitruvius (*De arch.* 2.6.3–4) connected the superior quality of *puluis Puteolanus* with the effects of intense fire on certain natural deposits, and the same may have been true for the *harenae fossiciae* of the Roman Campagna. The dry state (*ieiunitas umoris*, or "want of moisture") and latent heat with which the material was left in the process would explain its reactivity (especially if it came in contact with water).[160] Terracotta was similarly obtained by firing natural deposits and thus could be conceptualized

[155] As noted by Giuliani 2006: 185–86, mortar used as a primer for plaster moldings typically contained volcanic ash.

[156] Morricone Matini 1971: 7. On the specialized use of the mix in Republican Italy, see Trümper 2010; Fumadó Ortega and Bouffier 2019.

[157] Giuliani (2006: 223) lists examples in which *cocciopesto* was used selectively as a conglomerate. Vitruvius (*De arch.* 2.5.1) recommends adding ground terracotta to the mortar mix when riverine or marine sands are used instead of volcanic ash.

[158] Based on the figures in DeLaine 1997: 111–13, tables 6–7, and 116–18, tables 8–9, the labor requirements per m³ of finished product can be calculated as 0.468 mle equivalents for volcanic ash, versus 2.95 for bricks (*bessales* with average thickness of 0.04 m), not including fuel costs to fire the bricks and the work required for the subsequent grinding.

[159] Bugini *et al.* 1993: 271; Giuliani 2006: 222 (but the evidence dates mostly to the Imperial period). For early examples from Pompeii, see Piovesan *et al.* 2009.

[160] Jackson and Kosso (2013: 273) read in this passage the influence of the Empedoclean theory of the four classical elements on Vitruvius.

as an artificial variety of *puluis*; it simply involved more processing. The switch from ground terracotta to volcanic ash must have been easier to implement than one would assume knowing that the Romans did not understand the actual chemistry behind it. It happened, however, only when the societal and economic needs presented themselves.

# FOUR

# A VIEW FROM THE *SUBURBIUM*

According to the scientific evidence presented earlier, the initial phase of concrete construction in Rome was based on the exploitation of volcanic sediments that outcropped near the construction sites. Deposits of volcanic ash were readily available in the *suburbium* of Rome too, but their systematic use for public monuments in the metropolis seems to have developed only in the Imperial period. Presumably, the expansion was a response to the increasing demand for both imperially sponsored monuments and private construction. This important discovery prompts new questions regarding the relationship between the availability of raw resources, the intensification in the production and supply of building materials, and processes of technological innovation.

In this chapter, I explore the issue further by shifting the focus on building sites located at the interface between the limestone and volcanic landscapes of Latium. Builders in this buffer zone had easier access than in Rome to *both* ingredients for high-quality mortars, volcanic ash and lime. If masons had rocks or breakable stone and quarriable pozzolanic material in the vicinity of the job site, the expectation would be that cemented rubble was going to be the cheapest option, but also the one that needed the most lime for plaster if the wall was to be decorated. Logically, builders at sites in close proximity to sources of lime production may have had an incentive to develop the building medium independently. To test this hypothesis, I turn my attention to the relatively large datasets of villa architecture from Rome's countryside (Roman Campagna). Moving eastward along the Anio valley and toward the foothills of the Monti Tiburtini limestone formation, I detail the spatial distribution of building techniques with relation to the underlying geology across different environmental regions.

In offering this assessment, I compare the evidence from the Roman Campagna with the building practices attested for the main urbanization phases of the towns within whose territories the villa sites fell. Included in this sample area is Gabii, which sits midway between Rome and Tibur. The emphasis on rural settlement offers the opportunity to revisit old ideas about the origins of concrete construction as a form of vernacular architecture that was first implemented to build modest farms of the type archaeologists correlated with Cato's *uilla calce et caementis*. Moreover, the discussion of villa sites allows us to investigate the links between the early diffusion of concrete technology and elite domestic architecture from another angle, thus complementing the interpretation of the urban phenomenon. The results of this analysis should be read in parallel with the main insights drawn from Chapter 2.

## ROMAN REPUBLICAN VILLAS AND TECHNOLOGICAL INNOVATION: PREVIOUS APPROACHES

The evolutionary framework of earlier typological studies rested on the paradox that initial experiments with structural lime-based mortar would have been characterized by an inherently inferior quality of the medium. Both Lugli and Blake described Mid-Republican villas and farms as the most likely context for the development of a method designed on the basis of local needs, traditions, and availability of building materials, and far simpler than what the technology of the time was capable of sustaining. They approached the problem from different perspectives, thus reaching alternative conclusions as to which factors influenced the diffusion of concrete construction.

Stressing the practical advantages of using field stones instead of ashlar, and pointing to the apparent disregard for the unrefined and hasty aspect that would have characterized the early variants of the masonry style by their patrons, Lugli was among the first to suggest that the origins of concrete construction ought to be found in private architecture of modest means or function.[1] Starting in the early 1920s, Lugli had been cataloguing sites in the *suburbium* of Rome according to the same classification system he later applied to urban monuments.[2] Given that most visible remains in the Roman Campagna belonged to the Imperial period, he looked particularly to the region of South Latium, still largely unexplored, in order to provide the missing link. Thus, Lugli identified extensive ashlar terracing structures in the environs of the Mid-Republican

---

[1] Lugli 1957, vol. 1: 374. *Contra* Billig 1944: 139–40 and table I (showing that adoption of the technique in urban housing predated its introduction for villa architecture).

[2] Lugli 1923: 22–25.

Roman colonies of Tarracina and Circeii, in which lime-based mortared-rubble construction often appeared, employed for interior features.[3] Although Lugli assigned the majority of these walls to the mid 2nd century BCE, describing them as *opus incertum*, the underlying assumption was that the masonry style would have been adopted for elite rural residences only after the structural viability of the building medium had passed the test of time in those smaller-scale projects. Having acquired a "rustic" feel because of its association with unpretentious rural buildings,[4] *opus incertum* would have been first introduced selectively to build the less visible, secondary components of villas (e.g., interior party walls or cisterns). Eventually, the technique would have replaced *opus quadratum* or polygonal masonry in the more structurally important parts of villa sites, becoming a marker of local identity.[5] While recognizing that the pattern could have been influenced by local geology, particularly where more intractable stones like limestone or basalt were predominant, Lugli explained the fact that *opus incertum* continued to be used extensively in the region even after the supposedly more refined *opus reticulatum* became predominant elsewhere in terms of cultural choice.

In contrast, Blake downplayed aspects of technological style to give greater importance to economic concerns. Her approach was based on the assumption that villa patrons always sought to reduce construction costs by systematically exploiting the material resources available on their property.[6] In this scenario, concrete construction would still originate in the rural context, but at the higher level of society. Overlooking the ideal of self-subsistence and parsimony that underpins the text, Blake pointed to the example of building contract in Cato's *De agricultura* (14.1–5), in which the honest owner (*dominus bonus*) is described as responsible for providing all building materials, including lime and sand, and in which the overall cost was calculated using a pricing formula that included such contribution (14.3). Because of the larger scale, elite buildings necessitated more resources in terms of both raw materials and labor, but landowners of medium or large estates had privileged access to unskilled or semiskilled manpower needed for extraction and processing. These conditions could have sparked innovation. Since *opus incertum* represented a method of construction requiring less specialization in comparison with *opus reticulatum* or brick-faced concrete, Blake suggested that the technique could have remained in use for a longer period of time not only in the limestone region, but also in the tuff areas closer to Rome. The implication was that not all of the *opus incertum* villas found in the *suburbium* should necessarily belong to an early phase

[3] Lugli 1926; 1928.
[4] Lugli 1957, vol I: 384 (with reference to the supposed 3rd century BCE precedents).
[5] Lugli 1957, vol I: 461–62.
[6] Blake 1947: 241.

of development, thus undermining dating systems based solely on masonry styles.[7]

Paying more attention to the integration of urban and rural economies, recent research has highlighted the role that rich landowners played in the building industry serving Imperial Rome, especially for the procurement of bricks for *opus testaceum*.[8] The mass production of bricks is associated with estates scattered along the Tiber valley and its main navigable tributaries (Nera, Farfa, and Anio rivers), which incorporated extensive clay beds. Studies have demonstrated that the brick industry developed during the 1st century CE from preexisting infrastructure, taking advantage of kiln sites which in previous periods produced tiles, dolia, and other terracotta artifacts.[9] In this case, then, elite landowners were quick to reorganize the production units in order to meet the increased demand for bricks in Rome. The growth of the lime industry, on the other hand, is less understood. DeLaine (2001) has quantified the labor requirements of lime production, characterizing the material as the most expensive ingredient for concrete construction in Rome. In comparison to quarried sand (*harena fossicia*), it required as much unskilled labor but over four times as much skilled labor per volume unit of *opus incertum* masonry (when manufactured on a large scale, and not including fuel costs).[10] Since the supply of lime limited the builder's ability to save on costs, its sourcing affected significantly the building process and must have played an especially important part in the early development of concrete construction. Thus, investigating the lime production cycle may reveal clues as to how and when the relationship between local geology, topology, and land tenure patterns brought about favorable conditions for the switch.

## AGRICULTURAL INTENSIFICATION AND THE SUPPLY OF LIME

Vitruvius (*De arch.* 2.5.1) notes two qualities of "white stone" as suitable to be burnt for obtaining lime, the *saxum* and the *silex*. The former term has been taken to mean the soft, porous calcareous tufa deposited at the mouths of thermal springs rich in calcium carbonate, which are common in the *suburbium*; its spongy texture corresponds well with the characterization by Vitruvius (*fistulosum*). The latter has been interpreted as referring to the marine limestone from the Apennine bedrock, which can in fact be described as compact and

---

[7] Blake 1947: 251.

[8] Steinby 1993.

[9] E.g., Graham 2006; Uroz Sáez 2008.

[10] The proportion is based on the recommended 3:1 ratio of volcanic ash to slaked lime for hydraulic mortars, assuming a 250 percent increase in volume of quicklime after slaking. For the figures in man-days laborer equivalents (mle), see DeLaine 2001: 260, table 11.B1 for volcanic ash (0.380 unskilled mle/m³ and 0.045 skilled mle/m³); 261, Table 11.B2 for lime (2.25 unskilled PD/m³ and 1.45 skilled PD/m³ and 2.75 tons of fuel, based on the output of a large kiln with overall volume of 100 m³).

harder (*spissus et durior*). Vitruvius recommends that lime made from *saxum* be used for nonstructural purposes (i.e., plaster), prescribing lime burnt from denser stones for masonry work.[11] Deposits of *silex* outcrop as an uplift of the Apennine Mountains within the claystone bedrock of Rome (Figure 4.1), at the Monti Cornicolani 25 km northeast of Rome, and at the Monte Soratte, an isolated relief in the *ager Capenas*, 40 km northeast of Rome (Vitr., *De arch*. 2.7.1 mentions it as a source for dimension stone, but characterizes the material as of medium strength). Both formations are close to the Tiber, which provided convenient transportation.[12] The foothills of the Apennines at the Monti Tiburtini above Tibur, 35 km east of Rome along the Anio valley, represent another close source of the material served by a major waterway.[13] Just below Tibur, at the interface with the volcanic geology, was the Acque Albule basin, where a variety of calcareous tufa known as travertine formed. The quarrying of this sedimentary rock for architecture in Rome started in the 2nd century BCE.[14] It is uncertain if travertine was burnt to produce lime, on account of its superior strength and durability (Vitr., *De arch*. 2.7.1. includes it in the same class as the Soratte stone).[15] Although Cato does not explicitly address the different properties of lime for building purposes, his advice to use only "good stone" (*lapis bonus*), "as white and as uniform as possible" (*Agr*. 38.2: *quam candidissimum, quam minime uarium*), would seem to reflect a similar preference for quarried stone.

For the period under discussion, Cato is the only author who treats the process of lime-burning in some detail.[16] He sets out the terms for the model contract between the villa owner and the *calcarius* in a passage that follows the section on the *uilla calce caementis*, so the reference has been assumed to be to the provisioning of lime for building purposes (*Agr*. 16). According to the stipulations, the owner was tasked with providing the stone and wood for the kiln (it is unlikely that charcoal was used for burning lime: Calcination of pure limestone requires temperatures around 900°C, so natural woodland or farmed coppice could do). The contractor was responsible for the construction of the kiln at the building site, the cutting of the wood (probably meaning the centering on top of which the stone charge was laid), the burning of the lime, and the collection of the burnt lime (quicklime) from the kiln.[17] The *calcarius* was to be hired then

[11]  Jackson *et al.* 2007: 42–43.
[12]  Quilici (1986: 211) includes the Sabinum, further upstream, as another region that could have played an important part in the lime trade.
[13]  On the role of the Anio for the transportation of other building stones (e.g., Tufo Lionato and travertine), see DeLaine 1995: 559, with Strabo 5.3.7–11.
[14]  Bernard 2018a: 32.
[15]  On the properties of travertine, see Jackson and Marra 2006: 425–26 with fig. 10.
[16]  See, in general, Adam 1994: 65–72; Coutelas 2009; Dix 1982; Traini 2013.
[17]  *Calcem partiario coquendam qui dant, ita datur. Perficit et coquit et ex fornace calcem eximit calcarius et ligna conficit ad fornacem. Dominus lapidem, ligna ad fornacem, quod opus siet, praebet.*

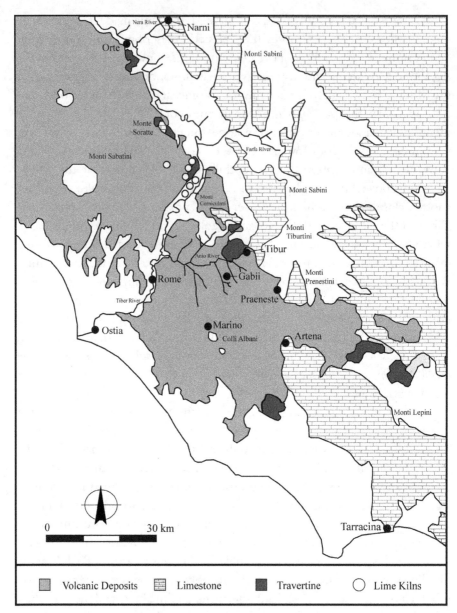

Figure 4.1 Distribution of travertine and other limestone resources in the region of Rome, showing the location of known limekilns. Compiled from data in DeLaine 1995 and Jackson and Marra 2006. Drawing: M. Harder.

as a skilled craftsman (in Diocletian's Edict, the *calcis coctor* was entitled to receive a daily wage twice the amount of an ordinary laborer; 7.1.4).[18] This sort of arrangement would make more sense for villas located close enough to suitable limestone deposits, or at least along waterways at the interface with the

[18] DeLaine 2001: 247, Appendix A.

limestone region, which would have defrayed the high costs of transporting raw resources (including fir: see Figure 1.1) over longer distances (Vitr., *De arch.* 1.2.8 on how the architect is to avoid the use of materials that are not easily procured and prepared on the spot).

After taking into account the fact that after calcination the stone loses as much as 44 percent of its original weight and 20 percent of its volume,[19] the transportation of quicklime produced near the quarry would have been much more advantageous, provided that appropriate containers were used. In addition, the grading requirements of the stone elements, which had to be carefully adjusted to the overall volume and height of the limekiln chamber in order to ensure the uniform burning of the charge, make it unlikely that the owner would have acquired the stone without some form of guidance or specifications for the task. In fact, employing builders who could supply sound and reliable material directly, or resorting to specialist suppliers if the contractor did not have direct access to the required materials, would have represented a much more cost-effective method.[20] A 2nd century CE funerary inscription from Capua mentions a *negotia(n)s calcararius* (*CIL* 10.3947), thus demonstrating that a private lime trade business operated in central Italy in the Imperial period. Seaborne or riverborne transport of lime for large-scale public contracts in Rome is attested epigraphically for the Neronian period.[21] The existence and eventual extent of such networks during the formative period of concrete architecture, however, is unknown.

Cato returns to the topic in a different section of his work (*Agr.* 38.1–4), where he describes two types of kilns. The main difference between them consists in the number of stokeholes they possess, whether a single one or two separate ones. Both types, however, are of relatively modest dimensions, approximately 3 m in diameter and 6 m tall (10 × 20 Roman feet). The resulting overall volume (approximately 17.5 m³, giving a capacity of less than 12 m³) appears considerably smaller than the largest archaeologically

---

[19] These figures refer to limestones with pure compositions, like those of the Monte Soratte and Monti Cornicolani (containing 95 percent calcium oxide and less than 0.5 percent combined oxides). The discrepancy with the weight loss given in Vitr., *De arch.* 2.5.3 (one third of the original weight) has been noted by Van Balen (2003: 2044), who suggests either that limestone with clay content was also used, or that normally the charge was not burned enough to convert completely into quicklime.

[20] The practice is particularly well documented in Roman Gaul. The analysis of the residues collected from sets of basins for the slaking and aging at five villa sites in the Haut-Limousin has demonstrated that quicklime came from sources located 80 km away. In each case, the basins were incorporated in the original plans of the villa, which suggests that they were meant for long-term use. See Loustaud 1983.

[21] See Panciera 2000 on a bronze tablet of the middle or late 1st century CE that refers to tax immunity for a ship that transported lime for contracts let out by a L. Arruntius Stella as public official. The same magistrate is mentioned in another bronze tablet (*CIL* 15.7150) originally set up on a *nauis harenaria* operating on the Tiber by the *Horrea Aemiliana*, which evidently transported sand for building purposes relating to an unspecified *cura*.

known examples from the *suburbium* of Rome (none of which, however, predates the Augustan period).[22] Nowhere in the text does one find indications that any of the lime produced in such kilns was intended for building purposes. In fact, we would expect Cato to provide at least some advice on the correct procedure to obtain slaked lime through hydration – a notoriously hazardous process.[23] While we may assume that he took for granted that the slaking of quicklime fell under the responsibilities of the *calcarius*, a separate set of structures would have been needed at the site for this process (these consisted of pits or tanks full of water, often dug in the bedrock), but are not described in the contract.

Cato's description of limekilns and their operation is part of a broader discussion of fertilizers for crops and of crops with fertilizing properties (*Agr.* 36–37), so the evidence can be read in relation to the use of lime for agricultural purposes. If applied to the land, quicklime encourages the decomposition of waste matter and corrects for soil acidity, thus preventing the spread of harmful weeds and improving the texture of clay soils, making them suitable to sensitive crops like legumes.[24] The results of regional surveys in central and southern Italy have consistently shown that there was an explosion of rural sites in the Mid-Republican period.[25] Despite the known interpretive problems (visibility and recovery rates; demography; identification of socioeconomic regimes), the survey data presents a general picture of more intensive landscape activity by the 3rd century BCE at the latest,[26] and of growing exploitation of marginal lands. This trend toward agricultural intensification, therefore, may have represented a significant impetus for the early development of the lime industry, whose output would then be extended over time to cover lime for construction, as a result, and not a cause, of the diffusion of concrete.[27]

That the supply of lime as building material eventually came to represent an economically important activity for wealthy landowners of estates located in the limestone region is demonstrated by the evidence from Lucus Feroniae, a 1st century BCE veteran colony in the *ager Capenas*, not far from Monte

---

[22] For a catalog of kiln sites in the *suburbium*, see Traini 2013: 57. Most of them are not datable, but are probably late, based on type of the excavated load (e.g., Proconnesian marble at the Via Poppea Sabina site), or their repurposed nature (e.g., the Via delle Vigne Nuove site was originally a pottery kiln).

[23] On slaking, see Dix 1982: 338–39; Malacrino 2010: 62–64. Quicklime reacts exothermically with water at temperatures of 90°C–100°C to form calcium hydroxide. Violent steam escapes were controlled by adding more water as the mix thickened into a putty.

[24] Dix 1982: 341–42.

[25] For recent syntheses at the supra-regional level: Coarelli and Patterson 2008; Attema *et al.* 2010. For the *suburbium* of Rome: Quilici 1974; Volpe 2012. For Latium: Attema and Van Leusen 2004.

[26] See discussion in Goodchild and Witcher 2010.

[27] DeLaine 1995: 560 presents a similar case for the origins of lime production at Tarracina, which late texts (*Cod. Theod.* 14.6.3; Symm., *Relat.* 40.3) describe as supplying Portus (and perhaps Rome) with both lime and firewood.

Soratte, and with easy access to the Tiber. The urban site developed around an old cult place that had become an important regional market (Liv. 1.30.5), which was still functioning in the early Imperial period (Strabo, 5.2.9).[28] The area was characterized by dense rural settlement from early on.[29] Three clusters of limekilns have been excavated in the environs of town. The largest fully excavated feature for which there is sufficient stratigraphic information is associated with a villa site located on the road to Capena (Figure 4.2).[30] Its volume would have approximated the 100 m³ hypothesized by DeLaine as a standard production unit of moderately large size (66 m³ capacity).[31] Ancillary structures are attached to the kiln and include two rooms, possibly dormitories, flanking a central space with an annexed cooking area, which has been interpreted as a watching post on account of its open front: Limekilns operated continuously overnight, and a careful eye was to be kept on them at all times to ensure correct burning. A pair of smaller kilns, more similar in size and shape to those described by Cato were located at some distance, closer to the villa. The reduplication would ensure a continuous cycle: Workers could unload one of the kilns while the other one would be lit. These smaller structures were abandoned in the early Imperial period, as a result of the expansion of the

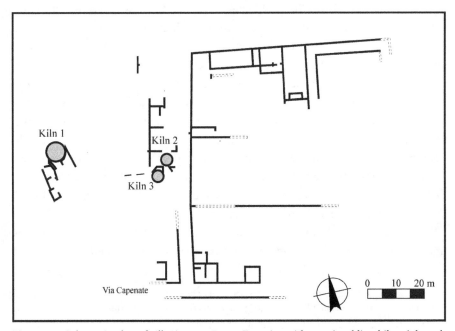

Figure 4.2 Schematic plan of villa site near Lucus Feroniae with associated limekilns. Adapted from data in Fontana 1995: 564–65, figs. 2–3. Rendered by M. Harder.

[28] Russo Tagliente *et al.* 2017.
[29] Jones 1962; Jones 1963.
[30] Fontana 1995.
[31] DeLaine 2001: 260. For the estimate of the kiln capacity, see DeLaine 1995: 560.

residential complex. The obliteration of the larger kiln cannot be dated precisely, but it is probable that at least for some time the three units functioned together, since the precinct wall surrounding the larger unit extended all the way toward the two smaller ones. In the absence of scientific analysis on the lime residues, it is unclear if the production exploited the travertine bedrock in which the kilns are cut or the limestone outcrops from the surrounding area (Monte Soratte).

The excavators have proposed to link the production site with the activities of the Volusii Saturnini, an elite family who owned large estates in the area, and whose members had been made *patroni coloniae* by the late 1st century BCE. Inscriptions confirm that they were involved in the monumental development of Lucus Feroniae, which spiked in the Augustan and Julio-Claudian periods.[32] It is likely that projects sponsored by the Volusii (e.g., the Temple of Divus Augustus, 14–20 CE; *AE* 1983.399) would have employed building materials produced at their villa sites, but their limekiln operation could have served Rome too. The largest excavated kiln had a total volume well above 100 m³, whose output would have exceeded 60 m³ of quicklime per firing.[33] To provide an order of magnitude, that amount of quicklime would have sufficed for mortar to build about 1 linear km of *opus incertum* masonry 3 m tall and 0.59 m thick. Two other limekiln sites were functioning at around the same time. At the south outskirts of the monumental area, recent excavations exposed a pair of kilns (one of which is of large size).[34] The third group of limekilns, consisting of smaller, canonical features set in pairs, is located north of the town and was probably connected with a villa site along the Via Tiberina.[35] None of the excavated sites have revealed slaking pits, thus suggesting that lime was not used locally for structural purposes (i.e., the slaking would have happened directly at other building sites). Assuming that the whole operation could be managed as part of estate production, the difference in size between structures may betray smaller manpower availability. In any case, the cumulative output under constant production of the sites around Lucus Feroniae would not have been negligible.[36]

Given our limited knowledge of the lime industry, pinpointing when it was first expanded to include building and how early was the development of the

---

[32] Cf. Torelli 1973–74, with reference to a funerary inscription of an enslaved member or freedman of the Volusii who worked as overseer/controller of construction work (*CIL* 6.37422: ll. 1–2: *Epigono Volusiano / operi(s) exactori ab Luco Feroniae*).

[33] See DeLaine 2001: 260–61.

[34] Savi Scarponi 2013: 8–10 (nos. 6–7); a bronze *as* dating to 21–22 CE was recovered from one of the levels of debris deposited while the kiln was in operation.

[35] Savi Scarponi 2013: 10–13 (nos. 8–11).

[36] DeLaine 1995: 560 calculates that seven kilns of 60 m³ capacity operating continually (i.e., firing ten times each year) for 20 years would have sufficed to supply the lime for the entire Hadrianic rebuilding of Ostia.

type of lime industry documented for the Augustan period is difficult (although the spread of the First Style in wall decorations probably determined a first spike by the early 2nd century BCE). One notable pattern, however, is that all known limekiln sites are located in the north or northeast quadrant of the *suburbium* (i.e., in the area closest to sources of limestone but farthest away from the most accessible deposits of volcanic ash, which are found in the southwest sector of the Roman campagna).

## BUILDING TECHNIQUES IN THE VOLCANIC REGION: VILLA ARCHITECTURE IN THE ENVIRONS OF ROME

Rescue excavations carried out in the last few decades in the suburban sprawl of Rome have revolutionized our knowledge of rural settlement patterns through the Republican period.[37] Two recently published gazetteers provide a critical mass of data on sites for which architectural plan and building techniques are reported (Figure 4.3).[38] This robust sample can be complemented with legacy data collected in a series of general works focusing on the emergence of classic villa architecture and economy in central Italy.[39] On this basis, it is possible to study the distribution of building techniques in the *suburbium* of Rome with relation to both settlement type and location, with the caveat that precise dating evidence is available only for the smaller subset of sites that have been the object of targeted stratigraphic excavations. By plotting the combined use of *opus quadratum*, *opus incertum*, and *opus reticulatum* by site, the spread of concrete construction can be observed and characterized with greater resolution than before.

At least ninety-four Republican rural sites with mapped architectural remains have been identified in the region (Table 4.1). At least forty-five of these sites feature ashlar masonry; in about half of the cases, the structures have been securely dated to before the 2nd century BCE. The few Early Republican sites (5th–4th centuries BCE) can be grouped in two subtypes: large complexes (surface area up to 1,500 m$^2$) with articulated plans and often rich decorations (of the kind most notably exemplified by the Auditorium site),[40] or much smaller farms lacking any kind of refinement (e.g., Torrino; the Casale Nuovo di Grottarossa site, among the largest in this group, covers a surface of 240 m$^2$).[41] As for the former sites,

---

[37] For a first synthesis, see Volpe 2012.

[38] *Suburbium* I–II.

[39] Romizzi 2001; *VAR*; Marzano 2007.

[40] Terrenato 2001b; Carandini *et al.* 2007. See also the Monte delle Grotte site (Terrenato and Becker 2009); Quadrato di Torre Spaccata site (*Suburbium* II.D39); Gregna (*Suburbium* II.D44); possibly Grotte Celoni (*VAR*.57) and the Via Barbarano Romano site (*Suburbium* II.B99).

[41] *Suburbium* I.B93; limited remains found under the villa of Via Togliatti (*VAR*.63); Viale Tiziano, Phase 1 (Piranomonte and Ricci 2009); Dragoncello, Site G (*VAR*.89); Torrino, site 8 (Bedini 1984); Via Aldini (*Suburbium* II.D43); Via Lucrezia Romana (*Suburbium* II.D41).

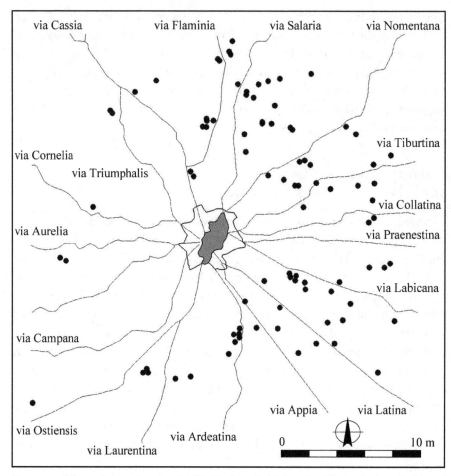

Figure 4.3 Schematic map showing the distribution of ashlar rural residences in the *suburbium* of Rome, 5th–2nd centuries BCE. Compiled from data in Volpe 2012. Drawing: M. Mogetta.

occupation often continued through the Imperial period, with only minor modifications attested in the intervening phase (in *opus incertum* at Gregna; in late 1st century BCE *opus reticulatum* at the Via Barbarano Romano site). Most smaller sites were abandoned by the Late Republican period, if not earlier (Via Aldini, Via Lucrezia Romana, Dragoncello), with no evidence of concrete construction used in combination with *opus quadratum*. At the Casale Nuovo di Grottarossa site, Torrino and most likely at the Via Togliatti sites, the Late Republican villas were built on top of thick post-abandonment levels. At the Viale Tiziano site, the Early Republican structure appears exceptionally replaced by a larger complex already in the 3rd century BCE. The latter can be taken as the local manifestation of the new settlement type emerging in central and southern Italy in the Mid-Republican period: the medium-sized farmstead (up to *c.* 700 m²). This class of rural sites is referred to in the literature as the precursor of classic villa architecture, albeit often

TABLE 4.1 *Distribution of building techniques in Late Republican villa architecture from the* suburbium *of Rome. Compiled from data in* Suburbium *I–II;* VAR*; Romizzi 2001; Marzano 2007.*

| Building Technique | Number of Sites (Percentage) |
|---|---|
| *Opus quadratum* only (5th–3rd century BCE) | 8 (8.5%) |
| *Opus quadratum* only (2nd century BCE or later) | 4 (4.25%) |
| *Opus quadratum* and *opus incertum* in the same building phase | 3 (3.25%) |
| *Opus incertum* with previous phase in *opus quadratum* | 6 (6.4%) |
| *Opus incertum* only | 17 (18.05%) |
| *Opus reticulatum* with previous phase in *opus quadratum* | 24 (25.5%) |
| *Opus reticulatum* only | 29 (30.8%) |
| *Cemented-rubble foundations* only | 3 (3.25%) |
| **TOTAL** | **94 (100%)** |

imprecisely.[42] Nine other examples have been identified in the area, all of which can be dated to within the 3rd century BCE.[43]

The original phase of construction of the medium-sized farms employs exclusively *opus quadratum*; tuff ashlar masonry continues to be used for their maintenance throughout the latter part of the 3rd and early 2nd centuries BCE (e.g., site 11 on the Via Gabina, Phase 1 C; *c.* 200 BCE; see Figure 2.2). In contrast with the larger sites created in the previous period, these buildings typically show substantial renovation phases in the middle to late 1st century BCE, with extensive additions in *opus reticulatum* that transform their plans quite radically. Subsequent reconstructions in *opus incertum* are attested both at the villa at Giardini di Corcolle and the villa of Centocelle *ad duas lauros*. At Corcolle, the *opus incertum* phase has been dated to the late 2nd century BCE,

---

[42] Viale Tiziano, Phase 3 (Piranomonte and Ricci 2009). For a critique of the terminology, see Terrenato 2001b: 17–28; Torelli 2012.

[43] Site 11 on the Via Gabina (Widrig 1987); Centocelle, Villa della Piscina, Period II (Gioia and Volpe 2004: 393–402) and most likely the villa *ad duas lauros*, Period 2 (Gioia and Volpe 2004: 363–68); Giardini di Corcolle (*VAR*.50); S. Palomba-Palazzo (*VAR*.94); Via Ardeatina (*VAR*.80); Mazzalupo-Via di Boccea (*Suburbium* II.B114); Parco di Roma, Site 86 (*Suburbium* II.B95); Vigne Nuove-Val Melaina (*VAR*.25).

but the evidence is limited. The Centocelle case is exceptional because the new structures present a completely different orientation; these have been dated on the basis of stratified ceramic contexts to the 1st century BCE.[44] A mixed technique employing tuff ashlars in combination with large tuff rubble and abundant mortar (of an unspecified kind) has been reported as being used sporadically in an earlier subphase to create internal subdivisions (other 2nd century BCE restorations of load-bearing walls were made in *opus quadratum*).[45] Concrete construction seems to be more securely attested in the open area southwest of the Villa della Piscina, where a large cistern preserves in its western corner a cemented-rubble wall tentatively dated to the late 2nd and 1st centuries BCE on the basis of the type of aggregate (Tufo Giallo of the same kind as that employed for the ashlar and rubble masonry of the villa in this phase).[46] Isolated cemented-rubble foundations predating an *opus reticulatum* phase have been detected at the Val Melaina site, but their relationship to the *opus quadratum* structures is unknown.

*Opus quadratum* remains have been detected in at least twenty-three other sites generically assigned to the Late Republican period (2nd–1st centuries BCE) based on the occurrence of the building technique, the presence of cisterns of the tunnel type (*cuniculi*), and the association between masonry and decorated *cocciopesto* floors (or more rarely First Style decorations). Four sites predating the middle of the 1st century BCE display a single phase in *opus quadratum*.[47] Only three contexts suggest that *opus incertum* and *opus quadratum* were used in combination in the same building period, although only at Veii-Campetti was concrete construction ever used in substantial amounts.[48] Remarkably, none of these sites follow the pattern attested in the urban context, where ashlar superstructures were frequently built on top of concrete foundations. The other sixteen sites include *opus reticulatum* modifications, the extent of which varies considerably from case to case.[49] In buildings character-ized by complex plans featuring canonical atria and ten or more rooms, the

---

[44] Gioia and Volpe 2004: 368–71, fig. 13 (Period 3).

[45] Gioia and Volpe 2004: 366, fig. 7.

[46] Gioia and Volpe 2004: 435–38, figs. 53–55 (Period 3).

[47] Tor Carbone (*VAR.*78); Capannelle (*Suburbium* I.D49); Romanina, Via Alimena (*Suburbium* II.D42); Via del Quadraro (*Suburbium* II.D37).

[48] *VAR.*2 (but the interpretation of the complex as a villa has been seriously challenged: Fusco 2013–14). In the other examples of Cecchignola (*VAR.*84) and the Via Tiberina km 0.550 site (*Suburbium* II.B87) the use of *opus incertum* is limited to only a few rooms, suggesting that concrete structures belong to later restorations.

[49] This group includes the villa of Castel Giubileo, Site 15 (*VAR.*13); Casal de' Pazzi (*Suburbium* II.D175); Casale Monfalcone (*VAR.*29); Casalone dell'Osa (Marzano 2007: Site L204); Fosso di Montegiardino (*VAR.*48); Grotte di Cervara (*VAR.*46); Ospedaletto Annunziata (*VAR.*10); Prima Porta, villa *ad gallinas albas* (*VAR.*7); Torre Maura (*VAR.*64); Via Ripa Mammea (*VAR.*45); S. Alessandro, Site C (*VAR.*30); Torre Spaccata (*VAR.*65); Fosso Lombardo (*VAR.*76); La Cecchina-Podere Rosa (*Suburbium* II.D180; *VAR.*34); S. Basilio (*VAR.*35).

technique is used for minor additions, most often consisting of a bathing room and/or water-related infrastructure (e.g., Casale Bianco; Casale Monfalcone; Grotte di Cervara; Ospedaletto Annunziata, Prima Porta, S. Alessandro Site C; Casalone dell'Osa). In other cases, the preexisting *opus quadratum* building was either completely obliterated or altered substantially in plans (Castel Giubileo; Fosso di Montegiardino, *ad gallinas albas*, Torre Maura, Torre Spaccata, Fosso Lombardo; La Cecchina; the site of Via Ripa Mammea is too poorly preserved to judge), as has also been observed for the smaller 3rd century BCE farms. The mixed use of ashlar masonry foundations and concrete superstructures has also been reported (Casale dei Pazzi; S. Basilio; at La Cecchina, ashlars, *opus incertum*, and *opus reticulatum* were apparently used simultaneously).

The overall impression we get from the evidence for the *suburbium* of Rome is that throughout the 2nd century BCE, and therefore well beyond the supposed period of experimentation with concrete construction in the rural context, the predominant building tradition remained based on cut-stone masonry. Mortared-rubble architecture (including clay-based variants) is practically absent during the Mid-Republican period, even in small farms. When continuity of occupation is attested through the Late Republican period, it is only with the 1st century BCE that concrete structures make a substantial appearance. However, the number of *opus incertum* villas that were built ex novo is surprisingly small, tallying up to seventeen sites in the most optimistic estimates.[50] If we include preexisting sites that received *opus incertum* modifications, the total will give a maximum of twenty-six contexts. By contrast, *opus reticulatum* is associated with at least twenty-nine newly built sites, in addition to twenty-four sites with an earlier *opus quadratum* phase, bringing the total to fifty-three contexts.[51] (At three other sites the structures are preserved only at

---

[50] Only isolated walls have been identified at the Via di Santa Bibiana (*Suburbium* II.A121) and Via Regina Margherita (*Suburbium* II.D123) sites; an *opus incertum* cistern is connected to a 1st century BCE possible villa site at the Tenuta Torre Serpentara-Borgata Fidene (*Suburbium* II. B9). More extensive remains have been found at the Via Tiberina km 18 (*Suburbium* II.B88); Castel di Guido (*VAR*.54); Torricola (*Suburbium* II.D4 and D5); Vigna Casali (*Suburbium* II. D18; Quilici 1987); Centroni (*Suburbium* II.D51); Via Latina, 3rd mile (*Suburbium* II.D62); Acqua Traversa (*VAR*.19); Tor de' Schiavi, Gordiani (*VAR*.53); Via Carciano (*VAR*.42); Quarto Cappello del Prete (*VAR*.55; Caspio *et al.* 2009); Tor Vergata, Carcaricola (*VAR*.73); Via della Magliana (*VAR*.86); Dragoncello, Site A (*VAR*.90); Viale Serenissima, Site AAI (Caspio *et al.* 2009).

[51] Borgata Ottavia (*VAR*.18); Via della Marcigliana (*VAR*.9); Via della Serpentara (*VAR*.22); Prima Porta, Via Tiberina km 0.850 (*VAR*.6); Prima Porta, Valle Lunga (*VAR*.3); Via Tiberina, km 3.500 (*Suburbium* I.B90); Prima Porta, Cimitero Flaminio (*VAR*.5); Borgata Massimina (*Suburbium* I.C3); Casale Tor Carbone (*Suburbium* I.C82); Casal Bianco, Settecamini (*VAR*.36); Casal Bruciato (*VAR*.51); Casale Ghella (*VAR*.16); Castel Giubileo, Site 1 (*VAR*.12) Cinecittà, Subaugusta (*VAR*.67); Cinquina (*VAR*.11); Fosso dell'Osa (*VAR*.49); Fortezza Tiburtina (*VAR*.44); Macchia Piana di S. Vittorino (Marzano 2007: Site L224); Villa of Maxentius (*VAR*. 69); S. Anastasio (*VAR*.27); Tomba di Nerone (*VAR*.20); Via Capobianco (*VAR*.26); Via Pollenza (*VAR*.33); Via Vigne Nuove (*VAR*.32); Borgata Ottavia (*VAR*.18); Casale di Aguzzano (*VAR*.41); Via Lucrezia

the level of the foundations.)[52] These numbers demonstrate that in areas of the *suburbium* closer to Rome the diffusion of concrete for villa architecture was quite a late phenomenon, which took off only in the middle to late 1st century BCE. In many cases a generic 2nd century BCE date has been assigned on the basis of the wall-facing style alone, due to the absence of external evidence. At least four of these sites (Via della Magliana; Acqua Traversa, Via Tiberina, and Castel di Guido) are located in areas where pozzolana was not available, and thus it is unlikely that they should have been among the earliest examples of use of this technique.

Where most complete, the architectural and stratigraphic evidence from *opus incertum* sites located in the southern and eastern quadrants of the *suburbium* show that these villas are normally of the classic type, extending over wide surfaces (e.g., 2,500 m² at Dragoncello, Site A) and possessing very articulated plans, including *bases uillae* with vaulted substructures on four sides (e.g., Tor de' Schiavi), two atria (e.g., Carcaricola), and monumental water-features (e.g., Quarto di Cappello del Prete, an exceptional site extending over 1 ha). The exploitation of local volcanic ash deposits located within the villa estates has been demonstrated in a number of cases (Centroni; Quarto di Cappello del Prete, Fosso di S. Maura) and easy access to this material can be reasonably assumed for the other contexts (especially at Torricola and Vigna Casali, not far from the quarries of Tor Marancia, and the Via Carciano site, close to the Tenuta di Capannacce). Ceramic assemblages from well-documented sites suggest construction dates in the second half or end of the 2nd century BCE (Carcaricola, Serenissima, Campetti, Centroni; at Quarto di Cappello del Prete the material is not associated with the structures, but has been recovered from the pozzolana quarry fills, and may not be readily indicative of building activities at the site). In any case, *opus incertum* was still used in the early 1st century BCE (as seen for the Villa della Piscina, as well as Serpentara, Acqua Traversa, Tor de' Schiavi).

In neighboring areas of the Colli Albani volcanic district, regional surveys have detected a very similar pattern. In the territory of Tusculum, for instance, concrete architecture emerges only in the late 2nd or early 1st century BCE.[53] The relatively higher attestations of new *opus incertum* buildings (at least eighteen, as opposed to seventeen *opus reticulatum* villas) may be in part explained by the intensive use of local basalt deposits, a material that is much harder to shape into small square blocks in comparison with the soft volcanic stones. For the late 3rd and early 2nd centuries BCE, buildings in *opus quadratum* or polygonal

Romana (*VAR*.82); both L'Annunziatella (*Suburbium* II.C70) and Casale di Vigna Murata (*Suburbium* II.C77) are near 3rd century BCE pottery scatters.

[52] Via Ipogeo degli Ottavi (*Suburbium* II.B102); Borgata Massimina (*Suburbium* II.C3); Via P. A. Micheli (*Suburbium* I.D141).

[53] Valenti 2003; Marzano 2007: 591–627.

masonry are also attested, in most cases receiving significant modifications or additions in *opus reticulatum* only in the middle to late 1st century BCE.

Social and economic issues must surely have influenced the architectural development we see in the countryside of Rome. Whether the first appearance of large *opus incertum* villas in the *suburbium* correlates with changes in land tenure patterns and agricultural productivity is a much bigger question that goes beyond the scope of the present discussion.[54] The spread of concrete villas from the Gracchan period onwards may have been driven by processes of a socioeconomic nature (e.g., concentration of land, intensification of wine production). It is worth noting in this regard that about two thirds of the *opus incertum* buildings do not have architectural predecessors on site, a trend that could indeed be read as the result of major shifts in settlement forms. From the point of view of architecture, the most interesting implication of this pattern is that a much greater amount of newly quarried material was required for the construction of classic villas in comparison with elite housing in the urban context, where both aggregate and facing blocks could be easily obtained from the demolition of preexisting structures.

## CONCRETE CONSTRUCTION AND URBAN DEVELOPMENT IN THE VOLCANIC REGION: GABII

Some of the villa sites described above are located along the border between the east sector of Rome's *suburbium* and the notional territory of the Latin town of Gabii. a top-tier center with close political and cultural ties with Rome. Ten years of extensive excavations in the urban area of Gabii have produced a wealth of data, providing a comparative sample to study architectural developments in the volcanic region.[55] The archaeological sequence documented for the 3rd and 2nd centuries BCE is particularly relevant.

Two main types of building stones were used at Gabii, both extracted from local deposits: the *lapis Gabinus* (geologically, the Valle Castiglione ground surge deposit, which forms the bedrock beneath the city itself, and whose main quarries lie just beyond the city walls to the northeast) and the Tufo Lionato (from the Villa Senni eruption unit, outcropping along the Fosso del Osa, just west of Gabii). The *lapis Gabinus* appears frequently throughout Rome, where it has been identified in numerous monuments dating from the mid 2nd century BCE onwards, attesting to the existence of a trading network.[56] Volcanic ash deposits were accessible directly east and south of

---

[54] See Panella 2010.

[55] On the broader relevance of Gabine archaeology for early Roman urbanism, see Becker *et al.* 2009; Mogetta and Becker 2014; Johnston and Mogetta 2020.

[56] Jackson and Marra 2006: 420–21; Farr 2014; Farr *et al.* 2015 for the geochemical identification.

the site, whereas the sources of limestone were closer to Gabii than to Rome. Despite the ready availability of the main ingredients required for concrete, however, most of the Republican-era architecture at Gabii is based on fine *opus quadratum* techniques.

The predominance of ashlar construction undoubtedly reflects the early date of both public and domestic architecture within the orthogonal layout, whose surge can be placed with precision between the early decades and the middle of the 3rd century. The so-called Tincu House, a middle-range courtyard building created around 280–260 BCE, utilized courses of ashlar blocks of *lapis Gabinus* (probably associated with superstructures in perishable materials), while Tufo Lionato slabs were selectively employed for water-related features.[57] Rubble of both types was used in combination with clay mortar for subsequent modifications of the house dating to the middle or second half of the 2nd century BCE.[58] A more complex system can be observed in the Area F Building, a monumental structure of over 2,000 m² facing onto the main thoroughfare intersection and arranged on multiple terraces, dating to the mid 3rd century BCE (Plate V.A).[59] Tufo Lionato ashlars appear in the middle and lower terraces (waste from the dressing of the blocks is recycled for the preparation layer of the decorated *cocciopesto* floors in the main rooms), where *lapis Gabinus* slabs pave the open spaces. *Lapis Gabinus* blocks line the cut for the top terrace, whose sides and back wall are in a form of polygonal masonry of small module bonded with clay-based mortar (Plate V.B). A reorganization of the building is documented by minor *opus incertum* structures in the secondary atrium and in the back corridor of the middle terrace, a subphase that can be tentatively assigned to the late 2nd or early 1st century BCE.

The agency of Roman patrons is attested epigraphically at two temple sites. Sometime in the second half of the 3rd century BCE, a Roman consul (perhaps a Fabius) set up an altar within the area of the extra-urban Santuario Orientale, just north of the fortifications.[60] This dedication does not seem to be connected with any major building episode in the temple and ancillary structures (with the possible exception of repairs to the drainage system). The first phase in which concrete architecture was introduced at the site is represented by a portico structure that has been dated to the first half of the 2nd century BCE on the basis of its wall-facing style (*opus incertum*) and wall-painting decoration (First Style).[61] The construction of this feature, whose internal configuration has been interpreted as evidence for the identification of the cult of Demeter-

[57] Opitz *et al.* 2016.

[58] Farr 2016. A similar pattern has been found to characterize the Area C house, where elements from the canonical atrium design were inserted into a preexisting structure. For a preliminary presentation, see Mogetta and Becker 2014: 179–80 fig. 9.

[59] Johnston *et al.* 2018.

[60] Fabbri *et al.* 2012: 236–40.

[61] Fabbri 2012: 28–29, fig. 8.

Ceres, determined a radical overhaul of the sanctuary, but the absolute chronology remains an open problem in the absence of associated finds.[62] At the urban sanctuary of Juno, the refashioning of the temple as a *peripteros sine postico* with Italo-Corinthian columns, the dedication of an inscribed Doric altar, and the creation of the *triporticus* around it, for which only ashlars of *lapis Gabinus* were employed, have been linked with the activities of a member of the Cornelii Cethegi, a Roman family possibly originating from Gabii.[63] An axial semicircular *cauea* is also assigned to this phase, so the monument is commonly identified as the earliest example of temple-theater complex, a class of sanctuaries that spread to Rome and Latium in the late 2nd and especially 1st centuries BCE.[64] A grid of massive cemented-rubble foundations dated stratigraphically to the early 1st century CE has recently been exposed in the southeast corner of the ashlar precinct, which was backfilled to raise an artificial terrace.[65] Finds from earlier excavations at the site indicate that there was a phase of redecoration occurring within the first quarter of the 1st century BCE, but this is not associated with any concrete architecture.[66] Directly downslope and just across from the north–south street that borders the east side of the sanctuary, *opus incertum* walls delimit a lower terrace paved with slabs of *lapis Gabinus* and lined by a colonnade. The structure, which has been interpreted as representing the original phase of a public square created anew in the 1st century BCE,[67] presently provides the earliest term of comparison for monumental concrete construction at the site.

Several factors must have been involved in the choice of building materials and techniques seen in Gabine architecture, including cost, availability, and the physical properties of the stones. The existence of a local industry specializing in the quarrying and carving of *lapis Gabinus*, a material which was heavier and harder to cut than the varieties of tuff in Rome, but, for these reasons, more durable and endowed with greater load-bearing capacity, probably explains why *opus quadratum* remained the method of choice for monumental building. Roman sponsors of architecture at Gabii could simply rely on the existing infrastructure, whose continued development is demonstrated by the increasing adoption of *lapis Gabinus* in the metropolis. Furthermore, the absence of any substantial phase of urban redevelopment after the mid 3rd century BCE

---

[62] Fabbri 2012: 35 (noting how the architectural ensemble would seem to predate the regional phenomenon by at least a half century).

[63] Coarelli 1982 with a date in the second quarter of the 2nd century BCE. The typological study by Maschek 2012: 52, 125–29 suggests a slightly later date (150–125 BCE). On the origins of the Cornelii Cethegi, see Palombi 2015.

[64] Coarelli 1987; Rous 2010. On the broader diffusion of this class of monuments, see D'Alessio 2016.

[65] Glisoni *et al.* 2017.

[66] For a synthesis of the phasing, see Almagro Gorbea 1982: 581–624. On the 1st century BCE architectural ornaments, see Almagro Gorbea 1982:184–93 (Dupré).

[67] Angelelli *et al.* 2012: 187–88; Angelelli and Musco 2013: 731–32, 737 fig. 9.

meant that the kinds of economic needs we can associate with innovations in the private sphere at Rome also were missing. The introduction of *opus incertum* at the site in the 1st century BCE may, therefore, reflects a quite late adaptation to the new realities of the economics of construction in the region of Rome, thus mirroring the pattern seen in the rural sphere.[68]

## CONCRETE CONSTRUCTION AND URBAN DEVELOPMENT IN THE LIMESTONE REGION: TIBUR

By the time concrete architecture was implemented on a large scale in Rome and Gabii, the territory of Tibur, located farther upstream along the Anio valley, played a significant role for the production and supply of building materials. Sitting at the foot of the sub-Apenninic limestone formations, the town also controlled a portion of the volcanic landscape at the edge of the Roman campagna. The Anio river traversed the area of the travertine quarries and provided easy access to the interior, where denser marine limestone deposits suitable for burning lime also outcropped. The river bottom was a source of gravel and sand, which outcropped particularly on the right bank, to the north. On the left bank, several tributaries of the Anio eroded the superficial scoria and ash-fall layers, thus exposing deeper pyroclastic deposits, within a radius of 5–10 km from the city.[69] This made the material readily available for construction both at the urban and rural levels. The logical question to ask then is whether there would be a greater chance of detecting early experiments with cemented-rubble architecture in the catchment area of Tibur than in the *suburbium* of Rome, where the widespread presence of tuff varieties that were relatively soft and easy to work influenced the continued preference for *opus quadratum*.

Analyzing the spread of *opus reticulatum* from Rome to Latium Vetus and Adiectum, Torelli (1980a) singled out the case of Tibur and the *ager Tiburtinus* to demonstrate a basic contrast in the distribution of building techniques. Whereas public monuments within the urban area employed almost exclusively *opus incertum*, villa architecture in the immediate environs of Tibur featured predominantly *opus reticulatum*.[70] The trend would demonstrate how the landscape of Tibur essentially became the focus of luxury residential architecture from the middle of the 1st century BCE onwards. The extensive nature of the urban building program in *opus incertum*, commonly assigned to

---

[68] Historical sources characterize the 1st century BCE as a period of rapid decline for Gabii: Almagro Basch 1958.

[69] Jackson *et al.* 2010: 38, fig. 2.

[70] Drawing from the data collected by Giuliani (1970), Torelli 1980a: 143–44 lists five villas in *opus incertum* as opposed to ten in *opus reticulatum*, in addition to two sites showing the two techniques juxtaposed.

the decades immediately before and after the Social War, seemed to provide a plausible explanation for the lack of any substantial phase in *opus reticulatum*: The gigantic effort would have left little room for later additions. More recent topographic fieldwork in the broader territory of Tibur, however, has revealed a much richer dataset for the diffusion of *opus incertum* in rural contexts.[71] The evidence from these surveys can be used for a more detailed reassessment of the early stage of concrete construction in the limestone region.

Two major phases of urban development at Tibur have been dated to the 4th and the early 1st centuries BCE, respectively.[72] The fortification circuit and the main terracing structures that regularized the sloping topography of the site belong to the first phase, but the internal organization of the city blocks is not known in any detail because of the later architecture masking the deeper levels. The early features are built with ashlar masonry, whose blocks were quarried from the top layers of the sequence (the so-called *testina*) at the Acque Albule basin.[73] The bedrock at the site of Tibur consists of the old riverbed deposits, which possess different physical properties. This material (known as *tartaro*) appears stratified in thin layers, from which slabs or small blocks could be obtained. Builders, therefore, had to look elsewhere for stone deposits suitable for monumental ashlar construction. The lack of compact limestone levels near the site can in part also explain the absence of polygonal masonry in this period, which is in contrast with the frequent occurrence of the technique in the countryside. The introduction of volcanic tuff for ashlar architecture may date to as early as the 3rd century BCE. The stone, a type of Tufo Lionato quarried at the site of Acquoria, just 1 km west of the city walls,[74] was utilized for repairs of the fortifications. Selective use of the building material continued in the 2nd century BCE (e.g., for the revetment of temple podia, as in the so-called Tempio Rettangolare on the Acropolis, dated to *c.* 150 BCE).[75]

In the second phase, the use of concrete construction was frequent both on the Acropolis and in the lower town, rivalling in scale and complexity of technical solutions the more famous examples from neighboring Praeneste. New retaining structures making extensive use of concrete vaulting were built in order to expand the main public areas in the northeast quadrant. A platform abutting the fortification walls (the so-called Mercato Coperto) was erected across an extra-urban side street branching off of the Via Tiburtina, thus transforming a stretch of that road into a *uia tecta*. Alternating semicircular and rectangular vaulted rooms lining one of the long sides supported an extension of the old forum, whose original space had shrunk as a result of the

[71]  Mari 1991; Mari 2003; Tombrägel 2012.
[72]  Giuliani 1970.
[73]  Mari 1983: 361–70, no. 380.
[74]  Mari 1992.
[75]  Mari 2013: 25–26.

construction of a new civic building (basilica) and temples.[76] An even wider open terrace (known as the Piazza Tani site) was created not far from the old forum square. It is supported by substructures consisting of two parallel barrel-vaulted corridors on the same alignment as the Mid-Republican city walls, which it evidently replaced. The exterior façade is decorated with a series of engaged tuff voussoir arches resting on piers of *testina* blocks, whose spandrels are faced with *opus incertum* made with rubble of both limestone and travertine, using facing pieces with round edges and finished exterior surface. The same technique was adopted for the interior walls.[77] An inscription mentioning the erection of *fornices* by the *quaestores* M. Turpilius and M'. Popilius (*CIL* 1.1498 = 14.3686) may refer to any of these terracing projects. Since it contains the formula *de s(enatus) s(ententia)*, the text certainly dates to the period predating the Social Wars.[78]

The remodeling of the urban core progressed in sequence with the monumentalization of the extra-urban sanctuary of Hercules Victor.[79] The most impressive component of the temple-theater complex is represented by its system of tiered vaulted substructures, which span a stretch of the Via Tiburtina to create the main sanctuary platform. The latest research at the site suggests that these features were built in a piecemeal fashion, but the dating remains controversial. A variant of the *opus incertum* technique using oblong *tartaro* elements has been documented in the southwest front of the sanctuary (the so-called Via del Colle site), the vaulted substructures underneath the stage building continuing along the west and northwest sides, and in other terracing walls at the back of the temple.[80] These fragmentary structures seem to define a sequence of parallel covered passageways that retained the slope crossed by the Via Tiburtina, later repurposed to fit the redevelopment of the area for the monumental theater complex.

Other clues would seem to indicate that the final aspect of the sanctuary does not reflect the original design.[81] The temple itself is not centered on the main axis of the open court. The vaulted rooms lining the south side of the Via

---

[76] Boëthius and Carlgren 1932; Giuliani 1970: 218–22, no. 114; Mari 2013: 30; Mari 2017 (first half of the 1st century BCE).

[77] Giuliani 1970: 95; Giuliani 1973: 86–87 (with a date in the middle of the 1st century BCE); Vecchi 2013.

[78] [*M(arcus) Tu]rpilius L(uci) f(ilius) M(anius) Popilius M(anii) f(ilius) Q(uaestores)* | [*f]ornices de s(enatus) s(ententia) c(urauerunt)*. Mari (2013: 29) refers the inscription to the Piazza Tani site, which he considers earlier than the sanctuary of Hercules Victor on the basis of the masonry style. On the changes in the administrative and legal framework of allied communities following municipalization, see Bispham 2007.

[79] For a general contextualization of the monument, see Giuliani 1998–99; Giuliani 2009; Tombrägel 2012: 55–66; Mari 2012a; Giuliani and Ten 2016.

[80] Ten 2010: 17–22, figs. 14–17; Tombrägel 2012: 57, figs. 30–31; Mari 2013: 27–28, fig. 5; Giuliani and Ten 2016: 37–41; 38, fig. 91. Deposits of the material outcropped in situ, so the rubble elements were probably obtained from the regularization of the slope in that part of the building site. See Giuliani and Ten 2016: 35–36.

[81] As noted by Tombrägel 2012: 60–61.

Tiburtina, which are built with a type of *opus incertum* featuring smaller lime-stone rubble, are at a right angle with the roadway, unlike those to the north, which conform to the orientation of the portico of the sanctuary. The technique of the archivolts is also quite different: Those on the south side feature segmental arches with bosses at the keystone and haunches; the piers are comprised of travertine blocks, whereas those to the north combine what has been described as "irregular" *opus reticulatum* and ashlar. This has been taken to mean that the *uia tecta* was completed only at a later stage, and that in its hypothetical earlier version the sanctuary above would have had a different plan (an L-shaped colonnade?), subsequently extended to the north to form a triporticus. It is plausible that the isolated concrete structures incorporated in the first monumentalization date to the 2nd century BCE, though in the absence of external evidence it is impossible to say precisely how early they are. All the building inscriptions found at the sanctuary site postdate the Social War (e.g., *CIL* 14.3667, 3668, 3664, mentioning the *quattuoruiri*; the latter refers specifically to a *porticus pone scaenam*), so the idea that work on the monumental phase had already begun by the late 2nd century BCE, was interrupted in 90 BCE, and resumed only in 87–83 BCE, is unwarranted.[82]

## BUILDING TECHNIQUES AND REPUBLICAN VILLAS IN THE *AGER TIBURTINUS*

The archaeological record for the period between the two major phases of urban renewal at Tibur is rather poor, especially in terms of domestic architecture. Most of the evidence comes from extraurban sites whose distribution has been linked with the formation of luxury villas in the region.[83] A distinctive feature of rural architecture in the *ager Tiburtinus* is the presence of terracing structures built with polygonal masonry, whose main function is to retain earthen embankments. Most of the examples correspond to either the Second or the Third Style of Lugli's conventional typology (though a great deal of subjectivity is involved in many identifications).[84] In the former type of walling, the blocks are worked to fit more closely and the faces are dressed, but the joints between blocks are irregular, with resulting gaps that are filled in with rubble. The Third Style corresponds to a more refined variant, which features dressed blocks whose tight

---

[82] Cf. Tombrägel 2012: 64–65 (pushing the earliest concrete features on site to the middle of the 2nd century BCE); see also Giuliani and Ten 2016: 44. On the epigraphic evidence, see the discussion in Coarelli 1987: 94–103; Giuliani 1998–99: 105–08; Giuliani 2009: 87–90.

[83] Mari 2005.

[84] Lugli 1957: 51–165. For the limited application of Lugli's typology in current research, see the *Seminario internazionale di studi sulle mura poligonali* series: Attenni and Baldassarre 2012 (referring to it for descriptive purposes only). For a recent synthesis, see Helas 2016 (focusing on fortifications).

joints create a geometric pattern. Comparanda for the building type are widely attested from the Sabinum (Cures Sabini; Palombara), the Sacco valley, the Pontine region, South Latium (between Tarracina and Minturnae), and northern Campania (Monte Massico).[85] Both types are commonly dated from the late 4th to the 1st centuries BCE, though most monuments concentrate in the 3rd and 2nd centuries BCE, as has been demonstrated by extensive surveys and targeted excavations at various sites.[86] Unlike elsewhere in the limestone region, however, at Tibur the technique was never employed for public building.[87] Because of the massive size of the blocks and their polygonal shape, the masonry style is not only expensive in terms of transportation and lifting requirements, but also extremely labor-intensive for the care and skill with which elements had to be selected one by one, uniquely crafted, and laid out as construction progressed. Thus, the extensive use of polygonal masonry has been generally interpreted as a form of conspicuous consumption through architectural display.[88]

In his comprehensive study of villa architecture from the *ager Tiburtinus*, Tombrägel (2012) has identified a group of forty-five platform sites whose main construction phases have been dated to the 2nd century BCE based on masonry style and building design (Figure 4.4; Table 4.2).[89] Twenty-one of these feature ashlar masonry, which is almost exclusively of the polygonal types discussed above.[90] These platforms are located predominantly on the slopes or at the foot of the Monti Tiburtini, both north and south of the Anio, in close proximity to sources of limestone. The lack of data on mortar composition makes it difficult to distinguish between mortared-rubble and cemented-rubble architecture, although the scale of the structures suggests that hydraulic mortars were used. Early variants of cemented-rubble masonry are recorded at thirty-five sites, but the exclusive use of it has been verified in fifteen of these contexts.[91] In the majority of the cases, concrete construction appears juxtaposed with ashlar masonry, which is most frequently of the polygonal type (thirteen examples). At these sites, cemented rubble and *opus incertum* were employed for

[85] For a general survey, see Lafon 2001: 27–30.
[86] For Norba: Carfora *et al.* 2010; Quilici Gigli 2003. For Signia: Cifarelli 2013. Cf. the bath-sanctuary at the Colle Noce site, with tuff polygonal masonry: Alvino *et al.* 2003; Cifarelli 2014. The polygonal masonry terrace at the coastal site of Villa Prato near Sperlonga has been dated to 150–110 BCE by Broise and Lafon 2001: 162–64.
[87] The contrast is noted by Mari 2013: 26–27.
[88] Becker 2007; 2012.
[89] Tombrägel 2012: 116–66; 104; 118, fig. 49. The site catalog is published online at https://arachne.uni-koeln.de/drupal/?q=de_DE/node/300.
[90] Polygonal masonry: Tombrägel 2012: nos. 1, 2, 4, 6, 7, 9–12, 14, 16, 18, 26, 28, 33, 36, 37, 43, 55, 58, 60. See also Mari 2012b. Tombrägel 2012: nos. 9 (lower terrace), 10, 28, 37, 60 feature polygonal masonry with rusticated blocks whose courses approximate *opus quadratum*. The technique has been dated elsewhere to the 2nd century BCE: Cifarelli 2012. *Opus quadratum* appears at Tombrägel 2012: no. 39 (but its early date is speculative).
[91] Tombrägel 2012: nos. 8, 20–24, 27, 32, 38, 40, 49, 50, 52, 54, 59.

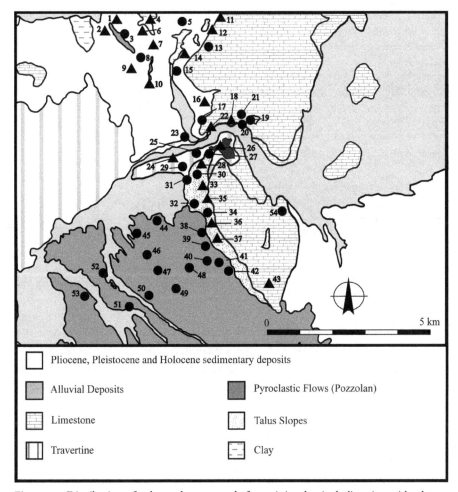

Figure 4.4 Distribution of polygonal masonry platforms (triangles, including sites with a later concrete subphase) and other monumental villas (circles) in the countryside of Tibur. Compiled from data in Tombrägel 2012. The sites are plotted against the local geology; the urban area of Tibur is indicated in dark gray (near no. 26). Drawing: M. Harder.

restorations of or extensive modifications to earlier platforms.[92] Their occurrence at sites featuring *opus reticulatum* construction is less frequent (nine cases).[93] Despite the possible overlap in their pattern of use,[94] Tombrägel's reconstruction works from the assumption that polygonal masonry, cemented rubble, *opus incertum*, and *opus reticulatum* represented mutually exclusive techniques. The transition from polygonal masonry to *opus incertum* would have

---

[92] Tombrägel 2012: nos. 9–12, 14, 16, 18, 26, 27, 33, 36, 37, 43.

[93] Tombrägel 2012: nos. 15, 17, 29, 25, 31, 34, 35, 42, 57.

[94] Tombrägel 2012: no. 6 (featuring a cemented-rubble fill poured in after the removal of the original earthwork retained by a polygonal masonry substructure); cf. also Tombrägel 2012: no. 2 (rock-cut cistern lined with cemented rubble).

TABLE 4.2 *Distribution of building techniques in Late Republican villa architecture from the ager Tiburtinus. Compiled from data in Tombrägel 2012.*

| Building Technique | Number of Sites (Percentage) |
|---|---|
| *Polygonal masonry* only | 9 (15%) |
| *Cemented rubble* or *opus incertum* with previous or contemporary phase in *polygonal masonry* | 13 (21.7%) |
| *Cemented rubble* or *opus incertum* only | 15 (25%) |
| *Cemented rubble* or *opus incertum* with later phase in *opus reticulatum* | 9 (15%) |
| *Opus reticulatum* only | 14 (23.3%) |
| **TOTAL** | **60 (100%)** |

occurred sometime in the first quarter of the 2nd century BCE.[95] Given the absence of fixed points for both polygonal masonry and cemented-rubble architecture from the urban context for most of the 2nd century BCE, the chronological scheme rests on the problematic idea that villa patrons at Tibur would have imported the technique from the capital.[96]

Based on the analysis of the standing remains, Tombrägel has distinguished five masonry types of *opus incertum* (Figure 4.5), whose patterning would demonstrate the progressive evolution of the technique from coarse to refined, mirroring the conventional typology of concrete architecture in Rome.[97] Thus, Types 1 and 2 are characterized by irregularly shaped and unfinished rubble elements (Fig. 4.5A–B). In the former class, the size of the exterior pieces varies greatly, between 0.10 and 0.35 m, with larger elements being more frequent. In the latter, the grading of the material is more accurate, and facing pieces range between 0.10 and 0.15 m in size (cf. the Testaccio Building at 0.07–0.11 m). Neither wall type, however, presents a finished exterior surface that can be clearly distinguished from the core, so the "cemented rubble" title seems more appropriate. Types 3a and 3b feature oblong, narrow facing pieces with the flatter face on the exterior (Fig. 4.5 C–D). In the latter variant, the facing pieces appear smaller and more regularly coursed, but they are not cut to standardized parallelepipedal shape, so the technique should not

---

[95] Tombrägel 2012: 32–38; 104.

[96] For a thorough critique of the argument, see Maschek 2013: 1130–34.

[97] Tombrägel 2012: 73–103, taking the Testaccio Building (for which he accepts the traditional Porticus Aemilia interpretation) as a reference point for the absolute chronology; Tombrägel 2013.

Figure 4.5 Classification of concrete wall-facing styles documented in the Tiburtine villas (Tombrägel 2012: 94, fig. 78; used by permission).

be classified as a form of *opus uittatum*. Finally, Types 4 and 5 feature small facing pieces with rounded edges and finished exterior face, which are laid with thin mortar joints, occasionally in nestled configuration (Fig. 4.5E–F); the title *opus incertum* should be applied only to these. In terms of relative chronology, Tombrägel has suggested that Type 1 evolved first into Type 2, and eventually into Type 4. Since Type 3 does not fit clearly in the supposed linear sequence of development, Tombrägel has interpreted it as a short-lived, distinct tradition coexisting with Type 2, and emerging as a result of the same trend toward regularization (in this case, using brick-shaped blocks). The number of sites with walls of this type is indeed very small, but the chronological value of this evidence is dubious.[98]

The distribution of the main classes of cemented-rubble masonry is quite even within the overall sample of villas (Type 1: eleven sites; Type 2: twelve sites; Type 4: ten sites; Type 5: twelve sites, associated in three cases with Type 2). Types 1 and 2, however, are predominantly used in buildings located on the talus slope at the foot of the Monti Tiburtini, where piles of debris and fieldstones naturally occurred. Ten or eleven out of the twelve villas there feature either Type 1 or Type 2 walls (see Figure 4.4 for the location).[99] These figures account for 50 percent of known examples of each type, thus suggesting a strong correlation between masonry style and underlying geology.

Type 4 is the only category that finds convincing comparanda from urban monuments at Tibur (e.g., the first phase of monumentalization of the Sanctuary of Hercules at Tibur). Defined as the "Praeneste type" on account of formal similarities to the kind of *opus incertum* documented at the Sanctuary of Fortuna Primigenia, whose construction can be assigned to the last quarter of the 2nd century BCE,[100] Type 4 would thus represent both the *terminus ad quem* for the dating of the Sanctuary of Hercules, and the *terminus ante quem* for structures characterized by the less regular types of wall facings. Consequently, Tombrägel has proposed a date around the middle of the 2nd century BCE for the emergence of Type 2, assigning Type 1 to the early 2nd century BCE on the assumption that there was a gradual evolution from one to the other. As already discussed, the inscriptions from the Sanctuary of Hercules are consistent with a 1st century BCE date, which undermines the framework for absolute chronology. Furthermore, examples such as the so-called Villa di Cassio, a monumental complex on two terraces with a previous phase in polygonal masonry, demonstrate that different techniques could be used judiciously together depending on structural purpose (Figure 4.6).[101] Much larger facing pieces were selected to build the thicker retaining wall of the lower platform, whereas masonry made of smaller rubble was employed in the upper terrace,

[98] Mari 2013: 28, n. 19 compares the few examples from suburban villas with the southwest substructures of the sanctuary of Hercules Victor at Tibur. See also Mari 2013: 32 and n. 41, assigning a generic 2nd–1st century BCE date. At Signia, the diffusion of other forms of *opus uittatum* has been dated tentatively to the end of the 2nd or early 1st centuries BCE: Cifarelli 2008; 2013: 44–45.
[99] For Type 1 see Tombrägel 2012: nos. 27, 29–32. For Type 2, see Tombrägel 2012: nos. 26, 33–35, 37. Types 1 and 2 are combined at Tombrägel 2012: no. 36. The *incertum* type at Tombrägel 2012: no. 28 has not been determined.
[100] Gatti 2013. The dating is based primarily on epigraphic evidence: Degrassi 1969.
[101] Tombrägel 2012: 136, fig. 108 (no. 36).

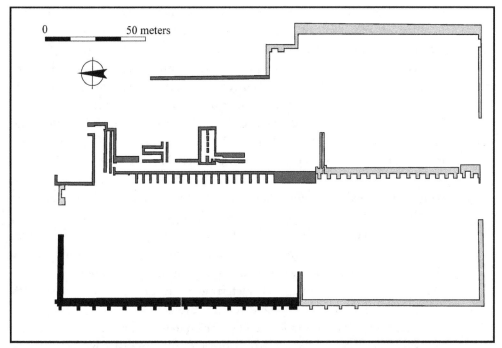

Figure 4.6 Schematic composite plan of the so-called Villa di Cassio near Tibur. Black = Tombrägel's *opus incertum* Type 1 (cemented rubble); Dark Gray = Tombrägel's *opus incertum* Type 2 (cemented rubble); Light Gray = *opus reticulatum* (adapted from Tombrägel 2012: 136, fig. 108). Rendered by M. Harder.

which might just as well belong to the same phase. The relatively thinner walls of the vaulted substructures of the residential quarter and the back wall of the terrace, which lined a cut in the bedrock and thus had no load-bearing function, both feature Type 2 only. In the absence of targeted stratigraphic excavations, however, the precise sequencing of the masonry types remains an open problem.

The number of ex novo foundations indicates that the introduction of concrete construction in the *ager Tiburtinus* was connected with a substantial expansion of rural residential architecture. Most polygonal masonry platform sites ranged from 600 to 900 m², but several examples included two terraces, which normally communicated by means of a staircase or ramp flanking one of the sides.[102] The largest ones could reach a total surface of up to 4,000 m².[103] Hardly any of these sites, however, present evidence of permanent occupation. Stretching into the lower slopes of the limestone formations, the early concrete villas occupy much larger surface areas: fifteen are 5,000 m² or above (six of which are over 10,000 m²)[104] and often feature multiple foci of habitation.

---

[102] Only in one case were the two terraces connected by axial ashlar vaulted ramps. See Tombrägel 2012: no. 39.

[103] Tombrägel 2012: 117.

[104] Tombrägel 2012: 130.

Thus, the introduction of the new building technique correlates with a change in function of the platform sites. The newly built villas located closer to Tibur are the most impressive in this category. Their main terracing walls have undecorated exterior surfaces, simply lined with plaster, though they are often buttressed.[105] The more advanced examples feature grids of cemented-rubble substructures or saw-toothed foundations that sink into and brace the fill they retain (the *diagoniae structurae* of Vitr., *De arch.* 6.8.7), and architectural ornaments on the façade.[106] The residential part, on the other hand, often incorporates elements of classic villa design, including elaborate *bases uillae* with double naves (whose long side can reach 150 m in length, while keeping spans within 4 m), as well as water-related features (basins; nymphaea), such as in the so-called Villa di Quintilio Varo.[107] Based on the present state of the evidence, it is not possible to confirm independently whether any of the sites featuring Type 1 and 2 masonry were created within the first half of the 2nd century BCE, as Tombrägel's developmental sequencing of the technique suggests.[108] On the other hand, the overall characteristics of the group would fit well with a date in the second half of the 2nd century BCE.[109]

Given the sheer volume and extent of the built-up components at the luxury villa sites, the shift from polygonal masonry to cemented-rubble architecture was probably dictated by broader concerns about the rate of construction. The monumental villa sites controlled large estates with a hierarchy of settlement types, from which the patrons could draw material resources, so even building sites located further upslope on the limestone spur of Tibur likely could have had access to volcanic ash deposits. The Anio Vetus and Aqua Marcia, both running along the ridge just south of Tibur, could be tapped into to supply the water that such "wet technology" needed. Different species of forest trees were available on the slopes of the Monti Tiburtini for use in architecture (especially oak at lower elevations; beech and fir at higher altitudes, above about 1,000 m a.s.l.), and could be exploited for carpentry, centering, and scaffolding (but the demands of urban consumption in Rome by the early 2nd century BCE may have accelerated deforestation).[110] Rubble could be obtained in situ. Several early sites fall or are in close proximity to the talus slope, where suitable material occurred in its natural state. Moreover, builders could also recycle the waste from the regularization of the terraces where bedrock was exposed. Finally, unskilled or semiskilled labor working in the agricultural fields could also

---

[105] Tombrägel 2012: nos. 16, 17, 29, 31, 33.
[106] E.g., Tombrägel 2012: no. 35; 72, fig. 52 (engaged Doric order).
[107] Tombrägel 2012: no. 17; 132, fig. 99; 150–56.
[108] Tombrägel 2012: 104 remarks that his chronological scheme is only meant to represent an approximation of the phenomenon, and that the date of the earliest phase of concrete villa architecture may in fact fluctuate widely between 200 and 150 BCE.
[109] Mari 2013: 26–27; Zarmakoupi 2014: 4–5.
[110] Bernard 2018a: 37–38.

become available in the off-season, together with animals and carts for trans-portation needs. Thus, the local environmental and socioeconomic conditions may easily explain why the *ager Tiburtinus* is characterized by a greater con-centration of concrete villa architecture than that detected in the volcanic areas of the Roman Campagna, where the availability of suitable tuffs may have caused a lack of incentive. Most villas located in the catchment area of Tibur where volcanic geology outcropped feature cemented rubble or *opus incertum* (six out of ten sites), demonstrating local preference (in two cases tuff *opus incertum* is actually found in combination with limestone *opus incertum*).

Several causes may account for the range of concrete construction techni-ques documented in the monumental complexes. Multiple crews who had been trained in different craftsmanship traditions may have been at work simultaneously at these larger sites. Far from demonstrating the slow-paced linear development of the technique over generations, the diversity of solutions attested across different sites may also reflect a rapidly evolving phenomenon. The density of villa sites suggests that a large number of architects and private contractors may have operated in the environs of Tibur at around the same time.[111] Interaction and competition among peers probably represented a mechanism for the spread of designs and construction systems in domestic architecture. The eventual adoption of limestone *opus reticulatum*, for which local conditions were rather unfavorable, may on the other hand have been influenced by contemporary developments in the volcanic region. By the 1st century BCE, most *opus quadratum* rural residences in the *suburbium* of Rome were being replaced by *opus reticulatum* structures. Roman aristocrats owned famous mansions in the *ager Tiburtinus* (e.g., the Caecilii Metelli), so their agency may have been in part responsible for later developments in the catch-ment area (perhaps also influencing innovations at the urban level).[112]

## THE VILLA ARCHITECTURE OF THE *AGER TIBURTINUS* IN ITS REGIONAL SETTING

Other areas of the limestone region of Latium located farther away from sources of volcanic ash offer a much more varied picture for the transition from polygonal masonry to cemented rubble architecture: Polygonal masonry appears associated with mortared-rubble cores, whereas cemented-rubble and *opus incertum* walls normally belong to extensions of earlier platform sites dating

---

[111] For later literary evidence on the phenomenon, see Rawson 1976 (on the brothers Cicero contracting for their villas).

[112] Cicero (*De or.* 2.263 and 2.276) makes a joking reference to the villa of Metellus Numidicus, the consul of 109 BCE, which would have been so big as to be visible from the Porta Esquilina (the fictional dialogue is set in 91 BCE). On the activities of the Caecilii Metelli at Tibur and their possible association with the Sanctuary of Hercules: Hölscher 2008. Roman senatorial presence at Tibur is mapped by Granino Cecere 2014: 241–45.

from the later 2nd century BCE onwards.[113] These sites have been linked with elite presence, although their common identification with specific villa categories (e.g., "Catonian" or "Varronian") remains extremely problematic.

The best-researched context in relation to broader settlement patterns is that of the Lepine Mountains bordering the Pontine plain. The district between the Latin towns of Cora and Setia has been the object of intensive pedestrian surveys and subsequent pottery analysis.[114] A total of 181 sites have been identified, making this the largest sample to study the development of rural occupation and related building types. Polygonal masonry is widely employed in both public and private architecture, with similar applications in city walls, urban terraces, road infrastructure, and rural platforms (nineteen sites, mostly dating to the 3rd century BCE). These building activities have been interpreted as a direct manifestation of the prosperity of local colonial elites. The Late Republican period was characterized by an increase in the complexity of the rural settlement hierarchy. Besides simple farms and polygonal masonry platforms, platform sites built with durable mortared rubble ("stone-and-cement"; using simple lime?)[115] make their first appearance (but the three examples are a small fraction of the sample), along with sites with evidence for high-status residential architecture. In the majority of the cases (twenty), the built-up features are not preserved, but the site identification is supported by the type of associated surface material (mosaic floors; painted plaster; columns and other architectural ornaments). Some of the polygonal masonry sites were also upgraded with luxury features at this time (nine cases). Finally, a few platforms built with cemented rubble or *opus incertum*, much larger than the polygonal masonry sites, seem to appear only during the 1st century BCE (four cases).[116] Given the investment in monumental architecture, they have been interpreted as the primary estates of the local elite.[117]

The monumental platforms of the Pontine region were part of a structured landscape and primarily geared toward agricultural production, whose roots went back in the Mid-Republican period. Top-tier villa sites developed in the Late Republican period as part of a broader phenomenon of urban and rural growth.[118] In light of this general trend, some of the concrete platforms located

[113] For Latium Adiectum: Andreussi 1981; De Spagnolis 1982; Venditti 2011; Cassieri 2013: 55–58 (on building techniques). For the Sabinum: Quilici 1995; Mari 2005; Franconi et al. 2019: 113–17 (Roman villa at Vacone, dated archaeologically to the late 2nd century BCE).
[114] De Haas et al. 2011–12; Attema et al. 2013–14.
[115] For another well-dated example of mortared-rubble construction using simple lime in the limestone region, see now the large cistern from the Prato Felici site at Signia (with a *terminus post quem* of 160–140 BCE): Cifarelli et al. 2017.
[116] Zaccheo and Pasquali 1972, noting the absence of this building type in the territory of Norba.
[117] De Haas 2011–12: 201–03, figs. 3–4.
[118] For a discussion of contemporary triggers for economic growth in the region, see Attema 2018, emphasizing the interests and activities of Roman elites, such as the Aemilii Lepidi and the Sulpicii Galbae.

in areas that are poorly suited for arable farming have been interpreted as possible cult places: Site 11632, on the slopes south of Cora, belongs to a class of platforms sitting on bare limestone bedrock at the edge of the Lepine Mountains. Its main terrace, which is retained by a polygonal wall of the Third Style, is occupied by what are described as "stone-and-cement" features, associated with an assemblage that includes tiles, *tesserae*, and fine wares, whose diagnostic elements date to 200–125 BCE.[119] This example serves as a useful reminder of the need to reevaluate the interpretation of the Tibur platform sites as buildings focused exclusively on *otium* using comparable data on layout, topography, and land use.

## CONCLUSIONS

While the intensification of farming during the Middle Republican period probably influenced the expansion of the lime industry for agricultural purposes, and the increased demand for plaster and stucco decoration for both private and public buildings from the early 2nd century BCE onwards likely provided another impetus for rich landowners to become involved in the lime production cycle, the implementation of structural lime-based mortar for monumental construction in the *suburbium* of Rome seems to have lagged behind the early development of the technique in the metropolis. Whereas *opus incertum* appears at only a handful of sites, and mostly for minor additions to preexisting structures, the diffusion of *opus reticulatum* villas is a much wider phenomenon, typically associated with radical modifications of earlier *opus quadratum* buildings. By the middle of the 1st century BCE, then, cemented rubble had practically become the medium of choice for rural luxury residences, reflecting a generalized conversion of the building industry to the new construction standards. The spike in building activities in the southeast sector of the Roman Campagna most likely expanded the knowledge of sources of suitable volcanic ash in the region, setting the conditions for their intensive exploitation in the Imperial period.

In areas of the *suburbium* located farther away from Rome and closer to the interface between the volcanic and limestone geologies, the pattern is more complicated. The case of Tibur demonstrates that *opus quadratum* dominated the technological shelf at the urban level well into the 2nd century BCE. The builders of rural platform sites of the *ager Tiburtinus* made extensive use of polygonal masonry, thus adopting a distinctive style that was common in the broader limestone region in the 3rd and 2nd centuries BCE. Although commonly interpreted as *bases uillae*, the early platform sites actually lack any evidence of superstructure, suggesting that their residential character was fairly

---

[119] De Haas 2011–12: 213–14. On this class of sites, see also De Haas 2011–12: 205.

limited. Based on their spatial distribution in the environs of Tibur, we can exclude the possibility that early experimentation with structural mortar was simply dictated by preferential access to the raw materials. The switch from polygonal masonry to concrete construction was sparked by the introduction of new architectural forms around the middle of the 2nd century BCE. The extra-large terracing structures on the sloping terrain just outside the urban center are commonly cited as the earliest examples of luxury villas, given the presence of elements of classic architecture such as gardens and large *piscinae* and of increasingly elaborate vaulted structures providing multiple ways to access those spaces. Thus, scale and extent of the new designs created the economic need for the technological change: Curbing building costs without compromising the desired monumentality. In this case, building types first documented in the countryside were extended to redesign the main public spaces of Tibur in the early 1st century BCE, projects for which villas could also have provided the necessary manpower.[120]

---

[120] Cf. Maschek 2016, who explores the possible interaction between construction and the agricultural cycle in their demand for labor resources with relation to the Late Republican sanctuary at Tusculum.

# FIVE

# BUILDING SAMNITE POMPEII

## PRE-ROMAN POMPEII AND ROMAN REPUBLICAN ARCHITECTURE

Because of its exceptional state of preservation, Pompeian architecture has often been used as a proxy to characterize the building periods that, in Rome, are less visible archaeologically. The analysis of the urban development of Pompeii between the late 4th and the late 2nd centuries BCE has focused on those classes of monuments, both public and private, whose introduction would demonstrate the adoption of Roman town-planning and architectural ideas prior to the foundation of the Roman colony in 80 BCE. In the context of monumental construction, the most emblematic cases are represented by the Roman-style baths, the theater, the *basilica*, and the *quadriporticus*. These building types happen to be examples of the earliest application of concrete construction for vaulting, terracing walls, and foundations in Pompeian public building. Traditionally, their appearance at Pompeii has been placed in the course of the 2nd century BCE and described as strongly influenced by Roman models.[1] In this perspective, which goes back to the scholarly conventions established by Mau in the late 19th century, the Samnites (the then inhabitants of the city) are regarded as the active agents in bringing Roman architecture and urbanism to Pompeii. Ongoing fieldwork in the urban core has reignited the argument, with some pushing the chronology of key monuments back into the Roman phase (post-89 BCE), therefore suggesting that Rome had a major,

---

[1] On the image of 2nd century BCE Pompeii as a "Romanized" town, see especially Pesando 2006. Cf. Ward-Perkins 1979 for the idea of an independent local origin for these designs.

direct impact on Pompeian archaeology.[2] For most of the period under discussion, there is an apparent lack of any coherent public building program besides fortifications and temples. This has significant implications for our understanding of the emergence of concrete technology at the site, because it once again brings the role of domestic architecture to the fore.[3]

Unlike in Rome, the built environment of Pompeii makes it easier to study domestic architecture as part of the broader process of urbanization. In the recent debate, however, the interpretation of the archaeological phenomenon has been informed by the same Romanocentric ideas affecting the interpretation of public architecture. Although the occupation of some areas took centuries to realize, extensive evidence collected from recent excavations suggests that the citywide street network was designed and executed around 300 BCE or shortly thereafter, during the height of the Samnite occupation phase (which conventionally starts from *c.* 450–425 BCE).[4] It has been argued that the impetus for this innovation came from Pompeii's incorporation into Rome's political sphere of influence, perhaps under the hegemony of nearby Nuceria.[5] Several other cities in Campania were given new fortifications and effectively replanned on orthogonal grids between the late 4th and early 3rd centuries BCE, most notably Cumae and Capua, possibly as a result of Roman annexation and the granting of *civitas sine suffragio*.[6] The spread of specific architectural designs such as the Tuscan atrium in the Vesuvian area has been described as mediated by Rome, following the territorial gains at the end of the Samnite wars.[7] Similarly, the kind of lower-class domestic architecture attested in the east neighborhoods of Pompeii (i.e., the so-called row houses of Regions I and II) has been taken as a sign that the Samnite town was being reorganized to mimic the layout of contemporary Roman colonies, featuring orthogonal city blocks subdivided into standardized property plots.[8]

Based on the rich sample of mortared-rubble architecture from habitation contexts throughout the city, the origins of Pompeian concrete construction have been linked with these overarching regional trends and dated to as early as the middle of the 3rd century BCE, suggesting a cause-and-effect relationship

---

[2] For a detailed account of the controversy, see Dobbins 2007; Ball and Dobbins 2013; Cooper and Dobbins 2015; Ball and Dobbins 2017.

[3] Cf. Zanker 1998: 32–53 contrasts the richness of domestic architecture with the scarcity of public construction for most part of the 2nd century BCE, attributing the pattern to the private interests of local elites prevailing over communal goals.

[4] Poehler 2017: 31–39, and 41 (noting some anomalies in the creation of streets and the discontinuous occupation through the 3rd century BCE).

[5] Coarelli 2002: 18–19. Polybius (3.91.4) lists Nuceria as one of the cities on the south coast of Campania, despite it being 9 miles inland, but never mentions Pompeii and Herculaneum.

[6] Rescigno and Senatore 2009.

[7] Pesando 2008: 159; Coarelli and Pesando 2011. For a review of the problem, see Anderson and Robinson 2018a.

[8] Wallace-Hadrill 2007: 122; Wallace-Hadrill 2008: 127–36; Sewell 2010: 120, 130.

with demographic growth.[9] At the local level, settlement nucleation would have provided the actual economic need for the introduction of a cheaper and more efficient building medium to support a phase of intensive urban development for the middle and lower classes: an explanation that mirrors the conventional model previously proposed by Coarelli for Rome.[10] The building materials needed to manufacture lime mortar were easily available in the catchment area of Mt. Vesuvius, so the notion of an early stage of experimentation predating the monumental examples of the early 2nd century BCE, whether originating independently or not, seemed highly plausible.[11] More or less explicitly, the further refinement of the technology, its large-scale implementation (especially for vaulting), and the rationalization of the building process have also been interpreted as advances brought about by Roman presence in the region. The influx of Roman colonists at the sites of Liternum, Volturnum, and Puteoli (founded in 194 BCE), and the spread of Roman traders (*negotiatores*) and rich villa owners in the countryside (e.g., in the area of Cumae),[12] have been singled out as particularly relevant factors. Hence the common opinion that the Romans themselves further developed their technology while testing the highly reactive materials available in the bay of Naples.[13]

The new date for concrete in Rome calls for a recasting of these theories. In what follows I concentrate on the broader trends seen in private architecture, reassess their relationship to public building, and locate the place of Pompeii within the regional setting. In doing so, I question the extent to which the diffusion of the technology in Pompeii and Campania compares with contemporary Roman developments, and, more broadly, with the historical narrative of Roman expansion in the region.

## BUILDING MATERIALS AND THE ARCHITECTURAL HISTORY OF PRE-ROMAN POMPEII

The study of Pompeian architecture is complicated by the poor historical record for the early period, and, consequently, by the lack of reliable construction dates.

---

[9] Lugli 1957, vol. 1: 379–83 (300–250 BCE). Adam 1994: 127; 2007: 106 (3rd century BCE).

[10] For this reconstruction, see especially Johannowsky 1976: 270–72.

[11] Lugli (1957, vol. 1: 382–83) suggested that local builders discovered the properties of pozzolana from observation of natural phenomena caused by volcanic activities, such as the natural calcination of limestone outcrops hit by pyroclastic flow.

[12] D'Arms 1970.

[13] The importance of the area of Roman Puteoli for the origins of the formula of hydraulic mortar is stressed in Oleson *et al.* 2004: 199–200. Zevi 2003: 80–87 links developments in vaulted concrete architecture at Rome and Puteoli, based on the synchronism between the foundation date of Puteoli and the construction of port infrastructures along the Tiber (i.e., the Emporium and the Porticus Aemilia of 193 BCE, which he identifies with the Testaccio Building).

Strabo (5.4.8) speaks of different waves of political domination that succeeded one another in the region: Oscan, Etruscan, Samnite, and Roman. The participation of Pompeii in the rebellion against the Romans during the Social War (App., *B Civ.* 1.50; Vell. Pat., 1.16.2), which led to the siege of the city by Sulla in 89 BCE and eventually resulted in the planting of a Roman colony in 80 BCE, provides the only fixed point for the period in question. While there is evidence that elite groups of the Samnite period retained some of their influence in the long term, the political life in the early years of the colony was dominated by the Roman settlers, who controlled the key magistracies under the new constitution (i.e., the *duouiri*; *quattuoruiri* are also occasionally attested). Cicero (*Sull.* 60–62; 61 BCE) represents the colonists and Pompeians as having separate identities and legal status.[14] Latin became the official language in public affairs, quickly replacing Oscan also as the main spoken language. Thus, when Oscan inscriptions are found in association with standing buildings, a generic date in the period 150–80 BCE is inferred for their construction (although some argue that the official use of Latin may have already been introduced by the Samnite elites by the end of the Social War, in the expectation of receiving Roman citizenship).[15]

Thus, the conventional periodization of Pompeii's building phases is mostly based on the combined analysis of historical dates, construction techniques, and associated building materials (Table 5.1).[16] The origins of this archaeological system can be traced back to the work of Fiorelli, who directed the excavations at the site in 1860–75. Fiorelli was the first to link the variety of construction methods documented at the site with Strabo's historical account. Even though most of the neighborhoods east of Via Stabiana had yet to be uncovered, Fiorelli looked to the distribution of domestic architecture featuring an atrium of the Tuscan type and interpreted its initial diffusion as evidence of the alleged Etruscan domination.[17] These houses were built primarily with ashlars of the so-called Sarno Limestone, a variety of calcareous tufa (travertine) outcropping in the river plain southeast of Pompeii (Figure 5.1).[18] Hence his conclusion that exploitation of the material started with the arrival of the Etruscans, but was abandoned when the Samnites took over. Mau subsequently argued that this "Limestone period" continued well into the Samnite phase, until the Nocera Tuff (a volcanic stone imported from farther away) was introduced, thus marking the start of a "Tuff

[14] An overview of the problem is in Santangelo 2012: 421–23.
[15] Lauter 2009: 163–70. On the Romanization of Oscan-speaking elites (in the linguistic sense) in the 2nd century BCE, see Adams 2003: 113–14 (with particular reference to Cumae and Delos). On Oscan epigraphic habits in Pompeii, see Vetter 1953; the most recent update by Crawford 2011 collects a total of 147 texts. For the conventional dating, see Mau 1908: 38; Castrén 1975.
[16] For a seminal review of the problem, see Fulford and Wallace-Hadrill 1999: 37–39.
[17] Fiorelli 1873: vii–xiii.
[18] Kastenmaier *et al.* 2010: 50–51. For the reconstruction of the pre-79 CE topography of the countryside of Pompeii, see Vogel *et al.* 2016 (with bibliography).

TABLE 5.1  *Stones used as building materials in Pre-Roman Pompeii. Compiled from data in Kastenmeier et al. 2010.*

| Archaeological Term (Richardson 1988) | Geological Term (Kastenmeier *et al.* 2010) | Lithology |
|---|---|---|
| *Pappamonte* | Tuff | Welded tuff with scoriae and calcite inclusions |
| *Sarno Limestone* | Calcareous Tufa | Porous carbonate of karstic origin |
| *Sarno Limestone* | Travertine | Harder carbonate with some crystallization |
| *Cruma (Spongia or Pumex Pompeianus)* | Basaltic Trachyandesite | Scoriaceous lava (dusky red) |
| *Lava (Lapis Pompeianus)* | Basaltic Trachyandesite | Compact lava (dark grey) |
| *Lava* | Latite/Tephriponolite | Compact lava (for road pavements) |
| *Nocera Tuff/Sorrento Tuff* | Campanian Ignimbrite | Welded tuff |

period."[19] Because of the greater transportation costs, the new building material was used rather selectively (i.e., for façades and architectural moldings). Nevertheless, Mau was convinced that the introduction of the expensive stone happened at a time of prosperity, which in his opinion could only mean the period after the Second Punic War.[20] Subsequent excavations below the floors of some of the Sarno Limestone atrium houses by Maiuri, however, revealed that they were much later in date than previously posited.[21] Furthermore, evidence of preexisting structures on the same orientation came to light. These structures were made of another kind of volcanic stone, the so-called Pappamonte, which can be found at shallow depths in the southwest area of the lava spur where Pompeii lies.[22] Maiuri adapted the chronological framework accordingly, assigning the use of Pappamonte to the Archaic period (6th–5th centuries BCE) and pushing the widespread diffusion of Sarno Limestone into the Samnite phase.

Early Pompeianists specifically linked the genesis of mortared-rubble construction at Pompeii with the architectural developments of the so-called Limestone period. The typological study by Carrington (1933) identified two mixed techniques featuring Sarno Limestone: "drystone masonry" and the "limestone framework" (from the Italian *opera a telaio*). The former title refers to walls in which flat pieces of limestone are laid horizontally in clay mortar, in combination with bigger corner blocks.[23] The latter refers to walls in which

[19]  Richardson 1988: 370. The deposits of Nocera Tuff are part of the Campanian Ignimbrite formation: Kastenmeier *et al.* 2010, 41; 49–50.

[20]  Mau 1908: 36–38.

[21]  E.g., Maiuri (1973: 1–14) dated the Casa del Chirurgo not earlier than the 3rd century BCE, undermining the idea of an Etruscan "Limestone" phase. For a comprehensive review of Maiuri's findings from select houses of Pre-Roman Pompeii, see Chiaramonte Treré 1990: 7–13.

[22]  For the geologic characterization of this material, see Kastenmaier *et al.* 2010: 50.

[23]  Carrington 1933: 129.

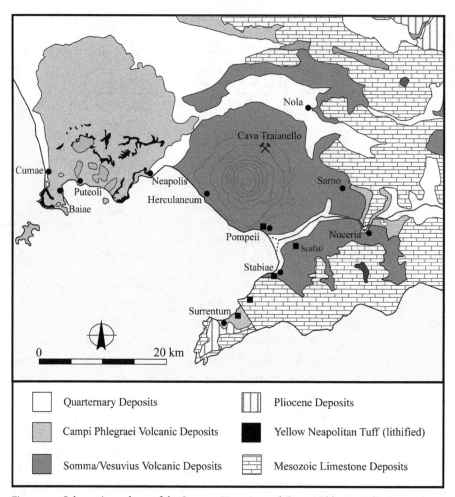

Figure 5.1 Schematic geology of the Somma-Vesuvius and Campi Phlegraeai districts with location of pre-79 CE outcrops (squares; the quarry sign marks the location of lightweight rubble sourced from lava flows accessible on the north side of Vesuvius). Compiled from data in Kastenmeier *et al.* 2011; Vogel *et al.* 2016; Lancaster *et al.* 2011. The so-called Sarno Limestone outcropped along the river plain. Drawing: M. Harder.

ashlar blocks are laid horizontally (stretchers) and vertically (uprights) in alternation to build rows of load-bearing piers separated. The gaps, which may vary in width, are filled in with either flat blocks (in what can be described as an approximation of isodomic masonry) or mortared rubble. The technique has come to be commonly referred to as *opus Africanum*. The term is not attested in ancient sources, but is a modern definition based on the idea that the technique originated in Punic North Africa, spreading subsequently to the Punic sites of Western Sicily, and from there to the peninsula.[24] The variants attested at

[24] Lugli 1957, vol. 1: 379–82 (describing the rubble panels as coarse "*opus caementicium*"); Adam 1994: 120–21. Based on examples of the technique from Archaic Etruria, Stopponi 2006 notes similarities with the *mur à piliers* ("pier-and-panel technique") of Levantine origins.

Pompeii and in Campania, however, find closest parallels with a technique documented primarily at Greek sites in East Sicily from the 5th through the 3rd centuries BCE, thus questioning the direct Punic connection.[25]

Following the accepted conventions, Carrington assigned these masonry types to the 4th and 3rd centuries BCE, noting different combinations: houses with *opus quadratum* façades featuring sidewalls and interior partitions in limestone framework; houses built either with limestone-framework or with drystone masonry in all their parts; houses with limestone-framework façades and drystone masonry party walls. According to Carrington, the pattern did not imply a chronological variation as much as it depended on wealth, with houses of the first class at the top and houses where drystone was employed at the bottom.[26] Construction with lime-based mortar and Sarno Limestone rubble would have emerged in parallel with a temporary but generalized decline in the supply of ashlars during the latter half of the 3rd century BCE.[27] The Casa di Sallustio (VI.2.4) and Maiuri's excavations in the Villa dei Misteri seemed to provide supporting evidence for this transition phase. Dated to the late 3rd century BCE on account of the prevailing use of Sarno Limestone for the rubble elements and the absence of Nocera Tuff, these domestic structures were taken to demonstrate the first selective use of durable lime mortar for *opus incertum* wall-facings. Quoins and doorposts associated with these walls featured ashlars laid horizontally and vertically so as to grip the rubble fills, thus providing a link with earlier practice.

In sum, previous scholarship has anchored the chronology of Pompeian construction methods in domestic architecture, identifying the limestone-framework technique as the precursor of concrete masonry, and placing the formative stage in the Early Samnite period. More recently, systematic architectural survey and subsurface excavations have shifted the focus from individual houses to broader topographical units. The available data allows for the contextualization of building techniques within the major phases of Pompeii's structural development.

## REFRAMING THE LIMESTONE PERIOD

In the most comprehensive study of limestone-framework architecture in Pompeii, Peterse (1999) has plotted the distribution of variants of the technique

Camporeale (2016: 62–65) has found that the technique appeared at Carthage in the 7th century BCE, but that the more complex versions are found only from the 2nd century BCE onwards (e.g., at Bulla Regia and Carthage).

[25] Camporeale 2013 (Type 3A). Di Luca and Cristilli 2011 plot the diffusion of the technique in Campania in the 4th through 2nd centuries BCE. On the complex network of interactions between Greek and Punic elites in Sicily, along with their influence on the cultures of central Italy, see especially Fentress 2013.

[26] Carrington 1933: 128–29.

[27] Carrington 1933: 130.

across the site (Figure 5.2), reconstructing a model of gradual evolution of the masonry style.[28] Three types of structures can be singled out on the basis of variation in the spacing of the pillar-like features, the shape of the rubble elements, and the composition of the mortar (Figure 5.3). Type A can be described as an approximation of isodomic masonry, while Type B resembles Carrington's "drystone masonry." In both types, the walls feature closely spaced pillars and panels of predominantly flat blocks, using little or no clay-based mortar. By contrast, the distance between pillars in Type C walls appears wider, and the gaps are filled in with rubble laid in a clay-based mortar containing greater proportions of lime and reactive materials.[29] According to Peterse's evolutionary scheme, the continued improvement of the recipe caused the pillars to lose much of their original structural function, since the increased strength of the binder would have made the mortared-rubble panels capable of bearing heavier loads. Becoming an unnecessary expense, the limestone framework would be eventually

0                    100 m

☐  *Opus Africanum* Type B      ■ *Opus Africanum* Type C      ▨ *Opus Africanum* Types B and C

☐  *Insulae* featuring elite domestic architecture

Figure 5.2 Pompeii. Spatial distribution of variants B and C of the limestone-framework technique ("*Opus Africanum*") in relation to city blocks featuring "rich" 2nd century BCE houses. Compiled from data in Peterse 1999; Lauter 1975. Drawing: M. Harder.

---

[28]  Peterse 1999: 36–55; cf. Adam 2007: 105.

[29]  Peterse 1999: 19–48. Only a handful of contexts demonstrate a significant increase in the average spacing of pillars in load-bearing walls: see Peterse 1999: 20–31; 70–75, tables I.1–4.

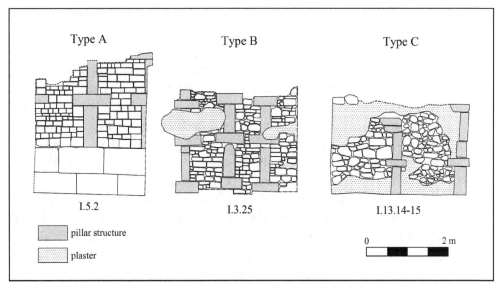

Figure 5.3  Examples of limestone-framework masonry types according to Peterse's classification (Mogetta 2016: 49, fig.1). Drawing: M. Mogetta.

eliminated altogether, thus bringing about true *opus incertum*.[30] The results of mineralogical and chemical analyses carried out on mortar samples collected from both cores and wall facings, however, show a substantial overlap between walls of Types B and C, whereas hydraulic mortar was detected only in two cases (IX.1.22 and II.3), in which the lime content appears suspiciously high.[31] In what is perhaps the best documented of the cases for load-bearing Type C walls (VI.11.12), the wider spacing of the pillars does not correlate with higher lime content in the clay mortar.[32] Because of the heterogeneous composition of the local volcanic sediments, the tests could not determine whether separately sourced volcanic material was added to the mix. Furthermore, because calcite inclusions are known to occur naturally in both clay and volcanic ash deposits at the site, it remains unclear whether burnt lime was used at all.[33] On the other hand, a stark compositional difference has been verified between Type C and *opus incertum*.[34]

Peterse has assigned each type to a bounded phase on the basis of horizontal stratigraphy and data from old excavations: Type A would have been short-

---

[30] See especially Peterse 1999: 56–63; Peterse 2007: 378.

[31] Peterse 1999: 87 considers these walls as later repairs, excluding the samples from the cluster analysis.

[32] Peterse 1999: 106, table II.6.

[33] The absence of artificial lime in clay-based mortars used for limestone-framework architecture has been confirmed by the analysis of samples from the Insula of the Centenario (IX.8). See Bonazzi *et al.* 2007: 127 (mortar type D). Santoro and Scagliarini Corlàita (2005) date the first phase of occupation of the block to the first half of the 2nd century BCE.

[34] Peterse 2007: 376, fig. 1.

lived (450–420 BCE), with Type B replacing it completely thereafter, until the advent of Type C in the first quarter of the 3rd century BCE.[35] The overall picture, however, is not convincing. Although Type A is concentrated in and around the so-called *Altstadt* (i.e., the central sector of Archaic Pompeii into which the settlement retreated for most of the 5th–4th centuries BCE), the numbers are too small to be statistically significant. Façades of Type B are attested mainly in the west side of town, while those of Type C appear to concentrate in the easternmost parts of Regions I, V, and IX, as well as in Region II, in association with the so-called row houses. Type B walls, however, have also been found in blocks I.9; IX.10 and 14, as well as in the irregular strip of blocks east of the Via Stabiana (IX.8; I.7 and 8). Conversely, Type C walls are also documented in the northwest sector (in blocks VI.2 and VI.5, this is the only type of limestone-framework ever attested).[36] The early chronology proposed by Peterse is also problematic. One of the oldest documents of limestone-framework construction comes from the Casa del Centauro (VI.9.3–5), whose original occupation has been dated stratigraphically to the middle of the 3rd century BCE.[37] This medium-sized house had a testudinate plan and featured a façade in limestone *opus quadratum* and interior walls in packed clay and mud-brick.[38] Although the rooms were finely decorated with painted plaster, *cocciopesto* floors and mosaics, lime mortar was not employed for structural purposes. Two broad phases have been identified in the urban development of the neighboring city blocks. Sustained activities started in the 3rd century BCE, picking up especially in the second half of the century.[39] In the second phase of development, beginning in the early 2nd century, several houses received substantial modifications, but the same old building techniques were used, at least initially. This has been observed in detail for both the Casa del Centauro and the Casa del Chirurgo (VI.1.10), whose main

[35] Peterse 1999: 56–60.
[36] See Mogetta 2016: 51 for a full discussion.
[37] Pesando 2005: 82–88; Pesando 2006: 229–33; Pesando 2008. Limestone-framework masonry is also attested at the Casa del Naviglio (VI.10.11), whose construction levels contain materials of the first half of the 3rd century BCE: Pesando 2005; Cassetta and Costantino 2006, 322–36 for the pottery evidence. Sewell 2010: 130 rightly takes this date as a *terminus post quem*.
[38] Similar house plans are reported by Giglio (2014; 2017a: 243–53) for Region IX, where the type remained in use through the 2nd century BCE. Pesando 2013: 123 describes the packed-clay and mud-brick technique as *opus formaceum*.
[39] According to Coarelli and Pesando 2006b, the urbanization in this sector of Pompeii progressed from north to south (i.e., starting from the periphery and slowly occupying the plots closer to the core of the so-called *Altstadt*). See also Coarelli and Pesando 2011: 51. Pesando 2013: 121–23 lists other houses datable within the 3rd century BCE, including VI.14.40 and VI.5.5 (Casa del Granduca Michele, *c.* 200 BCE, whose façade's technique can be described as Peterse's Type C). A late 4th century BCE date has been proposed for the Casa degli Scienziati (VI.14.43), but this is based on material collected from levels for which no direct stratigraphic relationship with the standing masonry structures can be established: De Haan *et al.* 2005; Peterse 2007: 377–78.

structural phase can be placed anytime between 200 and 130 BCE.[40] The pattern of occupation finds a parallel in other sectors of town. In the Casa di Amarantus (I.9.11–12), flimsier limestone architecture employing clay-based mortar can be as late as 200–150 BCE.[41] Similarly, controlled excavation in the "row houses" of Region II has demonstrated that most of the plots were first occupied only by the end of the 3rd century BCE, and that their progressive infill during the 2nd century BCE occurred without noticeable changes in building methods.[42] In the city's forum, poorly preserved structures below the Eumachia Building and the east portico of the Sanctuary of Apollo (discussed below) represent a possible parallel in public architecture.

Thus, the archaeological sequence shows that the diffusion of limestone-framework construction is a much later phenomenon than previously posited, spanning the latter part of the supposed Limestone period (from *c.* 250 BCE) and continuing well into the so-called Tuff period.[43] Excavations in the deeper layers have revealed that Sarno Limestone was normally mixed with other materials, including Pappamonte and Lava rubble, as seen below the atrium of the Casa delle Nozze di Ercole (VII.9.47; 4th–3rd century BCE).[44] The excavated evidence, therefore, undermines any sharp distinction between periods based solely on the use of different building materials.[45] As has been noted by Richardson (1988), in houses dating to the first half of the 2nd century BCE, limestone-framework masonry and Nocera Tuff architecture (i.e., ashlar façades, columns, impluvia, and moldings) consistently appear juxtaposed.[46]

Another important implication of this reanalysis is that the archaeological phenomenon appears significantly influenced by socioeconomic factors. If plotted against the spread of elaborate Pompeian houses of the pre-80 BCE period (including those having Sarno Limestone ashlar façades), the spatial distribution of Peterse's types highlights the impact of wealth and social status on the development of the limestone-framework technique.[47] Types A and B are more frequent in those city blocks in which the richest and more elaborate houses are located.[48] Type B occurs particularly in large buildings of the canonical atrium type. While the quasi-isodomic masonry may have

---

[40] Anderson and Robinson 2018b: 74–83 (Phase 3).

[41] Fulford and Wallace-Hadrill 1999: 112–15. A reassessment of the excavation data is in Pesando 2013: 118–21 and 124–25.

[42] See especially Nappo 1997; Gallo 2001: 69–77 (Casa di Epidio Rufo, IX.1.20). See also Pesando 2010a; Pesando 2010b; Pesando 2013.

[43] Cf. Richardson 1988: xv–xvii suggested a late date after the First Punic War for the urban growth of Pompeii, linking it with the involvement of the main centers of the Sarno valley district in the shipbuilding industry.

[44] D'Alessio 2008.

[45] Ball and Dobbins 2013: 463–64 with reference to the Tuff period.

[46] Richardson 1988: 376–78.

[47] Mogetta 2016: 52, table 2; 70, Appendix.

[48] As mapped by Lauter 1975: 149–51 and fig. 136.

represented a slightly cheaper solution as opposed to the canonical ashlar masonry (individual blocks could be fitted by hand without requiring complex lifting devices, and the lack of refined dressing may also be interpreted as a labor-saving choice), the close relationship between these techniques is signaled by the fact that interior walls of houses featuring ashlar façades are often executed in the former construction method. In contrast, Type C is associated either with smaller atrium houses or with the so-called row houses of Regions I and II, whose diffusion at Pompeii has been taken as evidence of lower-class housing.[49] Thus, its diffusion seems to correlate with quicker and more economical methods of house construction for the underprivileged, for which builders used a greater proportion of rubble than of dressed blocks.[50] The available scientific evidence suggests that lime mortar in these structures was used primarily for the rendering of the exterior surface of the clay-based mortared-rubble panels (in early walls the rendering has in most cases disappeared, but traces of the lime mortar revetment may remain in the exterior joints, thus giving the impression that the structures consisted of lime-based facings and clay-based cores).[51] The obvious conclusion is that the switch from mortared-rubble to cemented-rubble construction in Pompeii did not come about as the result of the gradual evolution of the so-called *opus Africanum*, but as the outcome of a different innovation process.[52]

## THE ORIGINS OF CEMENTED-RUBBLE CONSTRUCTION IN POMPEIAN HOUSES: MATERIALS AND PROCESSES

Having been devised in parallel with the study of ashlar masonry, the current periodization of Pompeian concrete construction reflects a similar methodology. The developmental sequence of wall facings has been linked with changing patterns in the exploitation of different sources of rubble as identified through visual inspection. With relation to the formative phase of the technique, Mau first hypothesized that the building materials would have been quarried primarily from the upper part of the lava flow on which the city was built.[53] This idea was expanded by Nicotera (1950) in his study of the geology at Pompeii. He proposed that the dark scoria (*cruma*) visible in most standing architecture was the refuse from construction trenches that the builders dug down into the natural deposits in order to lay their foundations on more

---

[49] Sewell 2010: 116–21.
[50] Richardson 1988: 370 casts doubts on the idea that packing Sarno Limestone rubble in clay necessarily predated the standardized use of lime mortar.
[51] Adam 1983 discusses the use of the technique in the post-62 CE phase.
[52] Cf. Camporeale 2016: 68–69 describes lime-based *opus Africanum* in North Africa as a Roman-period innovation dating to the Augustan period.
[53] Mau and Kelsey 1907: 39; followed by Adam 2007: 105–06.

compact terrain.[54] Carrington recorded the use of scoriaceous lava in combination with Sarno Limestone in walls built with the clay-based framework technique. He also detected the material in structures featuring lime-based mortared rubble throughout, as seen in houses he assigned to the late 3rd century BCE (e.g., the Casa di Sallustio), though noting that it appeared in smaller proportions (he erroneously posited that the structures consisted of a mortared rubble fill poured in the core only after the wall facings had been raised separately). During the 2nd century BCE there would be a progressive decline in the use of Sarno Limestone in favor of the more compact type of lava that was available locally.[55] The Casa del Fauno (VI.12) and the Casa di Pansa (VI.6.1), where both materials appeared employed in equal proportions, were identified as key examples of this transition. Carrington pointed out that the rubble in these walls was laid in harder mortar made of "black volcanic sand" and a higher lime content. He argued that the final switch to compact lava would have been completed before the end of the 2nd century BCE, based on the pattern documented in the Basilica, whose walls were made entirely of lava rubble.[56] Blake attributed the general trend outlined by Carrington to the diffusion of Nocera Tuff architecture. Greater amounts of Sarno Limestone rubble would have become available as older ashlar structures were being dismantled to make room for the new façades. The depletion of sources of recyclable blocks would have eventually provided the impetus for the introduction of compact lava (on the assumption that this option would have been more economical than quarrying Sarno Limestone rubble).[57] Lugli, on the other hand, highlighted the process of progressive regularization of the mortar joints that would have resulted from the switch, although he used the term *opus incertum* inconsistently for both types of masonry, including examples for which no clear distinction between facing and cores could be made.[58] Richardson pointed to the technological aspects linking choice of broken lava as a building material, advances in the composition of mortar, and the method of laying the rubble. Being a harder and heavier stone, lava produced smoother fracture surfaces that were not ideal for the packed-rubble panels seen in the limestone-framework technique, since it required laying the elements in heavier beds of mortar.[59]

In light of our reanalysis of limestone-framework architecture, the above reconstruction requires important modifications. First, the continued use of the

---

[54] Nicotera 1950: 415.

[55] Richardson 1988: 371–72 identifies this material with the *lapis Pompeianus* that Cato (*Agr.* 22.3–4; 135.2) mentions as the best material available in central Italy to craft mills. Kawamoto and Tatsumi (1992) map the distribution of compact lava in Pompeian masonry.

[56] Carrington 1933: 131–32.

[57] Blake 1947: 228–29.

[58] Lugli 1957, vol. 1: 411–12, 447–48, 475–76. On the misuse of *opus incertum* as a catchall term to describe concrete architecture in Pompeii, see Wallace-Hadrill 2007: 280.

[59] Richardson 1988: 376–78.

technique through the 2nd century BCE suggests that Sarno Limestone quarries would have been still active by the time compact lava rubble started to be exploited in greater quantity. This implies that the shift from one material to the other might not have been dictated by scarcity. Moreover, the context for the local supply of *cruma* rubble can be presented as more problematic than originally thought. The long-distance trade of this lightweight material, which can be probably identified with the *spongia* or *pumex Pompeianus* described by Vitruvius (*De arch.* 2.6.2–3), existed by the mid 1st century BCE. Geochemical testing for provenance attribution of samples from monuments in Rome (the earliest of which is the Forum of Caesar) and Pompeii shows that the rubble was sourced from lava flows that outcropped on the north side of Vesuvius, perhaps also accessible in the Campanian plain east of the volcano.[60] The new data implies that land and river transport of building stones around Mount Vesuvius, for which Pompeii probably represented one of the main hubs, was much more developed than commonly assumed. Thus, the introduction of *cruma* rubble for concrete construction may not have originated from the exploitation of in situ superficial deposits, but rather have derived at a later stage from Pompeii's participation in the exchange network. The presence of that material in any given structure, therefore, should not necessarily be taken as evidence for an earlier date, especially if based only on standard identifications. With the progress of stratigraphic excavations, more dates based on ceramic finds are being published from both domestic and public contexts across different regions of Pompeii, including from sites that had been singled out as benchmarks in the supposed evolution of the technique during the so-called Limestone period (Figure 5.4). These ceramic assemblages are normally retrieved from small trenches, whose placement is often constrained by preservation concerns, and which result in low recovery rates that produce few diagnostic elements. Most excavated deposits are secondary in nature, consisting of construction fills and leveling layers, and thus contain a high proportion of residual pottery.[61] At best, they provide a *terminus post quem* for the buildings with which they are associated, even when analyzed in a cumulative fashion.[62] Despite these difficulties, however, it is possible to sketch a trajectory.

Cemented-rubble architecture first surfaced in the rich *domus* of the Late Samnite period, especially those occupying the west and southwest neighborhoods of Pompeii (as summarized in Appendix 2).[63] The earliest manifestation of the phenomenon is likely represented by the Casa del Fauno (VI.12), the grandest mansion within the upscale neighborhood located just north of the

---

[60] Lancaster *et al.* 2011: 720–21 and fig. 8. On the geology of the lava outcrops in Pompeii (I.2.2–4; *Insula Meridionalis*; Villa dei Misteri), see also Kastenmaier *et al.* 2010: 44, table 2 (but the term "soft lava" appearing in this work should be avoided).

[61] Dicus 2014.

[62] For Region VI, see Coarelli and Pesando 2006a. Unfortunately, the sum total of limited data points collected from a larger number of small trenches does not eliminate the problem.

[63] For a more detailed survey of the evidence, see Mogetta 2016: 57–66.

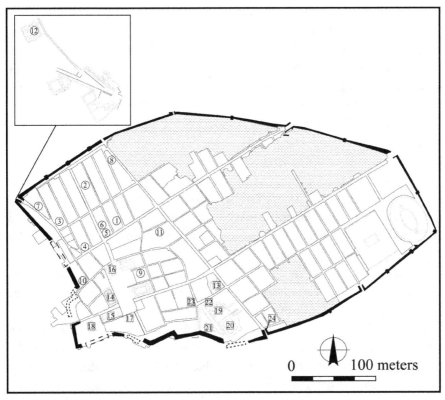

Figure 5.4 Pompeii. Schematic map showing the location of the main public monuments and domestic buildings discussed in Chapter 5. Drawing: M. Harder. Sites: 1=Casa del Fauno; 2=Casa del Centauro; 3=Casa di Sallustio; 4=Casa di Pansa; 5=Casa del Naviglio; 6=Casa dell'Ancora; 7=Casa del Chirurgo; 8=Houses near Porta Vesuvio; 9=Casa delle Nozze di Ercole; 10=Insula Occidentalis (Casa di Maio Castricio); 11=Southwest Quarter (House VIII.2.18); 12=Villa dei Misteri; 13=Stabian Baths; 14=Temple of Apollo; 15=Basilica; 16=Temple of Jupiter; 17=South Buildings; 18=Temple of Venus; 19=Theater (Teatro Grande); 20=Quadriporticus; 21=Foro Triangolare; 22= Samnite Palaestra; 23= Republican Baths; 24=Fortifications (Porta Stabia).

Forum area. German excavations carried out in the 1960s, whose finds have only been recently published, show that the construction of the compound was part of an extensive redevelopment of the city block. This followed the complete obliteration of contiguous property plots which were originally occupied by smaller buildings dating to the second half of the 3rd century BCE. The structures from this lower stratum, presumably also domestic in function, conform to the same alignment as the Casa del Fauno, but are made of clay-based mortared rubble of Sarno Limestone, chunks of compact lava, and tile fragments.[64] Coins and diagnostic Black Gloss pottery from the construction fills place the building episode in the middle of the 2nd century BCE

---

[64]  Faber and Hoffmann 2009: 33–34; 47–50.

(175–150 BCE), downdating the conventional sequence by a few decades.[65] At this stage, the Casa del Fauno featured a dressed Nocera Tuff façade, two atria, a *hortus*, and a peristyle, thus spreading over two thirds of the *insula* (Figure 5.5).[66] In the core part of the house, sidewalls and interior partitions have lower portions consisting of layers of heavier, compact lava rubble laid in lime mortar (Figure 5.6). These stretches retained construction fills that raised the ground level in order to cover the earlier remains. The superstructure, on the other hand, was made of lighter Sarno Limestone rubble with sporadic scoria and tile fragments and quoins. The grading of the materials, therefore, seems dictated by function (in addition, compact lava ensured better insulation).[67] The load-bearing walls appear built on top of mortared-rubble foundations laid in shallow trenches that cut through the early deposits. The "black volcanic sand" reported by Carrington as being used for the mortar of the freestanding walls was presumably quarried from the layer of dark-gray to black sediments reported elsewhere in nearby areas, directly below the archaeological deposits (e.g., at VI.1; VI.13; V.1).[68] The mixture probably had hydraulic properties, but these have not been confirmed scientifically.

The spatial distribution of the building technique can be mapped in detail across other city blocks of Region VI. Once seen as a reference point for the earliest type of lime-based mortared rubble, the Casa di Sallustio has been redated to 150–140 BCE on the basis of stratified ceramics,[69] thus undermining the conventional sequencing of the gradual transition from Sarno Limestone to compact lava architecture.[70] Now, contemporary examples of *opus incertum* walls combining compact lava and Sarno Limestone rubble are documented in the Casa del Centauro (VI.9.3–5; after 175–150 BCE),[71] demonstrating that the

---

[65] Faber and Hoffmann 2009: 82–84 give a date range of 175–150 BCE, but this should be taken as a *terminus post quem*. Most of the Campanian A types collected from the early level of the house date to the first half of the 2nd century BCE, but some specimens are more closely datable to the second quarter of the century. Early 2nd century BCE materials were retrieved from occupation layers sealed by the floors of the Casa del Fauno: Faber and Hoffmann 2009: 80–81. Previous studies dated the original occupation of the house to 185–175 BCE, based solely on stylistic evidence: Richardson 1988: 115–17; Zevi 1991.

[66] See Flohr 2010: 1168–69 for a critical review of the phasing methodology.

[67] As noted by Dessales 2011: 50–51, who provides density values for both Sarno Limestone (2,100 kg/m³) and compact lava (2,800 kg/m³).

[68] On the nature of the subsoil in the area, see Anderson and Robinson 2018b: 64–66.

[69] Laidlaw and Stella 2014: 127–41.

[70] For other examples of Sarno Limestone–based architecture dating to the second half of the 2nd century BCE, see Zampetti 2006: 109–11 (VI.10.3–4). Cassetta and Costantino 2008: 316–18 (Casa del Naviglio, VI.10.11; late 2nd century BCE). In contrast, Verzár-Bass *et al.* 2008 and Verzár-Bass and Oriolo 2009 (especially 496, n. 14) date walls featuring predominantly Sarno Limestone rubble in city block VI.13 to the first half of the 2nd century BCE, based solely on the building technique.

[71] Pesando 2005: 84–87 (Greco-Italic amphorae embedded in a *cocciopesto* floor). Pesando 2006: 229–33 reports the presence of pottery dating to the second half of the 2nd century BCE from the construction fills that obliterate the original floor.

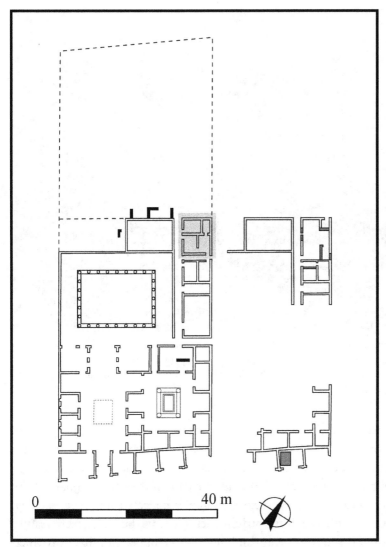

Figure 5.5  Pompeii. Schematic plan of the Casa del Fauno, Phase 1 (left: *c.* 175–150 BCE or shortly after) and later modifications (right: *c.* 100–75 BCE). Compiled from data in Faber and Hoffmann 2009. The light-gray shaded box indicates the location of the features seen in Figure 5.6. In black are shown the preexisting structures. Drawing: M. Harder.

building technique rapidly spread to medium-sized properties.[72] Houses in the Porta Vesuvio area (e.g., VI.16.26–27; 140/130–110 BCE) are characterized by the predominant use of compact lava rubble but feature Sarno Limestone blocks for quoins (Sarno Limestone rubble and *cruma* are employed for walls

[72] For an example from outside the so-called *Altstadt*, see Pesando and Giglio 2017: 18–19 (front of a testudinate atrium house below the Casa degli Archi at IX.7; first half of the 2nd century BCE).

Figure 5.6 Pompeii, Casa del Fauno. Archival photo showing the cemented-rubble foundations under the later floor of Room 42, northeast of the south peristyle, viewed from the northwest. For the position of the features, see the box in Figure 5.5 (Photo: Koppermann, Neg. D-DAI-ROM-62.2193; used by permission).

in the back part of the house, which may date to a later phase).[73] The Casa di Pansa, an atrium-peristyle house whose size and complexity are on a par with those of the Casa del Fauno, offers important information as to the development of the building medium. Although the date of the original phase of the complex to *c.* 140 BCE is less secure,[74] samples collected from *opus incertum* walls associated with the main atrium sector of the house, which feature compact lava in the lower portion and *cruma* in the upper part, have provided reliable scientific evidence for the geochemical characterization of the early mortars.[75] These were found to contain poorly sorted Vesuvian ash (whose elemental composition is comparable to products of the 79 CE eruption), which combined with lime to form cementitious gel.[76]

The Casa dell'Ancora (VI.10.7; *c.* 140 or 150–100 BCE) provides one of the earliest examples for the application of concrete vaulting. A sunken garden was created as part of a generalized redevelopment of the house when the older

---

[73] Seiler *et al.* 2005: 228–29. Construction fills contain pottery dating to 140–120 BCE.

[74] Richardson 1988: 124 (140–120 BCE, based on style of decoration).

[75] For the position of the samples, see Miriello *et al.* 2010: 2221, fig. 12 (Phase 1).

[76] Miriello *et al.* 2010: 2216–18 (Group I); 2220, fig. 7 for evidence of reaction rims between natural pozzolan and lime.

property expanded to the adjacent plot (VI.10.8).[77] This new open space was bordered on one of the short sides by a set of three rooms whose walls consist of Sarno Limestone rubble laid on top of compact lava foundations. These chambers are spanned by cemented-rubble barrel vaults (the largest one at the center measures 5.10 m in width), which support the area occupied by the *tablinum* at ground level (where walls are built entirely in *opus incertum* of compact lava).[78] The same construction method was employed on a larger scale for the expansion of habitation to the lower slopes adjacent to the fortifications. In the so-called Southwest Quarter, aristocratic houses had been encroaching upon the unoccupied space in the course of the 2nd century BCE, including the area of respect.[79] Early features abutting the fortification are documented in the area of both the Casa di Championnet (VIII.2.1) and the Casa dei Mosaici Geometrici (VIII.2.16).[80] Recently analyzed mortar samples from the perimetral wall of House VIII.2.18 (later incorporated into the Sarno Baths) demonstrate how the use of fine fragments of the locally quarried *cruma* as additive imparted a high degree of pozzolanic reactivity to the binder.[81] Examples of more extensive vaulted substructures dating to the late 2nd century BCE or early 1st century BCE are documented in the so-called *Insula Occidentalis*, between the Casa del Bracciale d'Oro to the north (VI.17.42–44) and the Casa di Maio Castricio (VII.16.17) to the south, as well as in the area located between Porta Ercolano and the Vico dei Soprastanti.[82] These features employ predominantly compact lava rubble and are associated with similar *opus incertum* restorations of the fortification circuit, which still remained accessible (as implied by an *eítuns* inscription, which provides spatial coordinates with reference to houses existing around the time of the Sullan siege in this district).[83]

Taking the evidence together, cemented-rubble architecture can be seen to have first surfaced in the rich *domus* of the Late Samnite period, especially those

---

[77] Pesando *et al.* 2006: 227–28 (*c.* 140 BCE); 235 (150–100 BCE).

[78] Pesando *et al.* 2006: 204–07.

[79] See Noack and Lehmann-Hartleben 1936. The first building phase is represented by houses in Sarno Limestone (*opus quadratum* and limestone-framework technique), whose flat-roofed basements were supported by ashlar retaining walls (e.g., at VIII.2.30 and 34). The Casa di Giuseppe II demonstrates that structures of this kind were still being built in the second half of the 2nd century BCE: Carafa and D'Alessio 1995–96: 139.

[80] On recent fieldwork in the Casa di Championnet and the Casa dei Mosaici Geometrici, see Giglio 2017b.

[81] Secco *et al.* 2019: 268–72 (Group 3: tephritic foam lava).

[82] See Cassetta and Costantino 2008: 197–202; Grimaldi 2011: 142–45. Dates are based primarily on stylistic grounds. First Style paintings are preserved in the atrium of VII.16.12–14, a house whose *tablinum* features Italo-Corinthian capitals variously assigned to 130–120 BCE (Cassetta and Costantino 2008: 204–05, n. 27) or 110–80 BCE (Lauter-Bufe 1987: 43–44, nos. 122–23; 79).

[83] Vetter 1953: 25. On the problem of the *eítuns* inscriptions, see Castrén 1975: 44–45; Henderson 2014.

occupying the west and southwest neighborhoods of Pompeii – earlier and resulting from different impetuses than previously assumed. The evidence from the *suburbium* of Pompeii fits well with the picture outlined above. The most notable site is the Villa dei Misteri, which has often been included in the canonical list for the early development of *opus incertum* due to the presence of Sarno Limestone architecture in its nucleus.[84] Laid out on steeply sloping terrain, the complex extends atop a large square platform (2,500 m²), which is retained by a U-shaped *basis uillae* featuring cemented-rubble barrel vaults (span: 2.65 m). The façade of the substructure is decorated with blind arches made of Sarno Limestone voussoirs, engaged to cemented-rubble wall with mixed Sarno Limestone and scoriaceous lava pieces. The inner walls of the *basis uillae* are entirely composed of compact lava *opus incertum*. The residential part above is comprised of an atrium-peristyle building. The peristyle has Doric columns made of Sarno Limestone drums, founded on a stylobate of Nocera Tuff slabs. The walls are built with mixed rubble (Sarno limestone, scoriaceous lava, and an unspecified variety of tuff rubble), framed by Sarno Limestone quoins. Above the door lintels are relieving arches made of small wedge-shaped blocks of Sarno Limestone, a technique that finds a parallel in houses of Region VI (e.g., the Casa del Naviglio, VI.10.11; late 2nd century BCE).[85] Maiuri pointed to the presence of different varieties of tuff being used in smaller flat-faced pieces for the rooms around the peristyle, describing the technique as a form of *opus reticulatum* with unusually thick mortar joints. On this basis, he dated the atrium core to the first half of the 2nd century BCE, assigning the tuff *opus reticulatum* extension to the early Roman period (90–70 BCE).[86] Recent fieldwork has demonstrated that the idea of a progressive development of the plan is entirely conjectural, given that the complex featured a peristyle since its establishment.[87] Variation in building techniques has been interpreted as evidence that different groups of builders were working at the same time in different parts of the house.[88] Wall paintings and decorated floors in the core of the house, all in the Second Style,[89] suggest a construction date in the early 1st century BCE.[90]

---

[84] The building techniques are described by Maiuri 1947: 42–43, 61–71, 89–93. An updated architectural study is in Kirsch 1993. Esposito 2007 incorporates the results of recent fieldwork.

[85] *Supra*, n. 70.

[86] Maiuri 1947: 17, 42–45. Subsequent scholarship has accepted Maiuri's relative sequence, revising the date of the original core to the second half of the 2nd century BCE. E.g., Dickmann 1999: 170–76 and 245–46; Mielsch 1987: 41; Pesando and Guidobaldi 2004: 164–69.

[87] Esposito 2007; Kirsch 1993; Richardson 1988: 171–76.

[88] Esposito 2007: 446.

[89] Esposito 2007: 448–53. No traces of preexisting layers of plaster were found under the Second Style decoration in the atrium.

[90] See Esposito 2007: 454–59; Kirsch 1993; Richardson 1988: 174 (all proposing a post-80 BCE date). *Contra* Zevi 1996, 135 (accepting Maiuri's sequence and interpreting the Second Style decoration as evidence that the villa was eventually confiscated by a Roman colonist).

The results of our survey of Pompeian domestic architecture reveal that a much greater overlap existed between building traditions at the site than previously acknowledged. The emergence of cemented-rubble masonry construction can be pinpointed within a specific building phase in the urban development of the Pompeii. Beginning around the middle of the 2nd century BCE, a number of elite properties were remodeled on a larger scale. Mansions like the Casa del Fauno and the Casa di Pansa adapted standardized atrium designs in order to incorporate new and fashionable architectural elements such as formal peristyles.[91] Builders at these top-tier sites expanded on the preexisting mortared-rubble tradition by developing lime-based mortars for which they exploited local volcanic sediments.[92] While the supply of Sarno Limestone rubble was still ongoing, partly to satisfy the demand for cheaper limestone-framework architecture for lower-class housing projects (the "row houses") in the eastern half of the site, compact lava was also introduced. At first, the material was used judiciously to build the lower portions of load-bearing walls, which functioned as retain structures for the dumps that raised the terrain across the building site (often by more than 1 m). Most varieties of Sarno Limestone feature cavities and porous concretions derived from the dissolution of plants, so the rubble tends to be larger in size and irregular in shape. Superstructures made with this type of rubble normally do not feature a finished surface nor a clear distinction between faces and core, and still required thick coats of plaster. Throughout the second half of the 2nd century BCE, compact lava started to be exploited in greater proportions for the upper parts of walls, which can be described as an embryonic form of *opus incertum*. The rubble pieces are generally smaller and more uniform in size and are placed with their flatter face on the exterior. Occasionally, compact lava is found in combination with lighter *cruma* for the upper portions. The new method, however, did not immediately replace the Sarno Limestone technique: The use of mixed materials is still attested by the end of the 2nd century BCE (e.g., in the Casa delle Nozze di Ercole at VII.9.47).[93]

---

[91] Wallace-Hadrill 2013: 41 downdates the Hellenization of Pompeii to *c.* 150 BCE, describing the previous phase as dominated by Punic influence in light of the diffusion of the so-called *opus Africanum* and *cocciopesto* floors.

[92] De Luca *et al.* 2015 report that pozzolanic mortars were used for joints in the first phase of I.8.12 (Garum Shops), which the authors date conventionally to the 3rd or early 2nd century BCE. Based on the published plan (De Luca *et al.* 2015: 348, fig. 13), the samples are associated to walls that appear to belong to subsequent modifications of an original "row house" of Nappo's "Tipo 3," whose basic spatial organization is still legible (e.g., the position of an axial threshold on the main façade; the siting and overall dimensions of Room 3; Rooms 4, 7, 8, and 11 probably formed the original open court or *prostas*; Rooms 12 and 6 seem to reflect the presence of an axial *tablinum*). A later date in the 2nd century BCE is, therefore, possible.

[93] D'Alessio 2008: 280, table 1. As seen in the façades of block V.1 (Casa di Cecilio Giocondo, V.1.23; Casa degli Epigrammi Greci, V.1.18), Sarno Limestone and compact lava stretches can also be found juxtaposed within the same building phase. See Leander Touati 2008:

## THE DIFFUSION OF CONCRETE TECHNOLOGY IN PUBLIC BUILDING

A group of Oscan inscriptions predating the establishment of the Roman colony informs us on the system that regulated the public building industry at Late Samnite Pompeii. The legal framework for the sponsorship of monumental public construction corresponded closely to the Roman *locatio conductio operis*, as demonstrated by the similarities between the Oscan terminology and the technical language found in building inscriptions from Rome, such as the *probatio* (Oscan *prúfatted*, Latin *probauit/probauerunt*) or the use of fine money to finance construction projects (Oscan *eítiuvad múltasikad*, Latin *pecunia multaticia*).[94] The texts record elected officials – occasionally the chief magistrate (*meddix tuticus*), but more commonly the *kvaísstur* (Latin *quaestor*) – letting out building contracts or acting as final approvers upon successful inspection (and sometimes both).[95] These magistrates were drawn from the same elite groups that hired builders in order to redevelop their houses. Comparing the developmental sequence of public architecture with the trajectory observed in the private sphere, therefore, might provide clues as to the direction of the technological exchange.

Very few public monuments in Pompeii can be said to predate the late 2nd century BCE. With the notable exception of the fortifications and the street system, monumental public construction seems virtually nonexistent for most of the 3rd and early 2nd centuries BCE. The earliest projects exploiting concrete technology focused on communal monuments of old tradition, such as the Temple of Apollo and the Doric Temple in the Foro Triangolare, which not by chance represented the main foci for collective rituals organized by gender and age groups throughout the Samnite period.[96] The Theater and annexed Quadriporticus provided a stage for public assemblies and must have played an important political function prior to the development of the South Buildings and the subsequent monumentalization of the forum square, which was marked by the reconstruction of the Temple of Jupiter. In what follows, I set out to reassess the dating of the concrete features associated with these spaces, concentrating on those monuments for which recent fieldwork has produced reliable stratigraphic evidence (summarized in Appendix 3).

The remains of the Stabian Baths, a large complex occupying the south part of an irregular block located at the junction of Via Stabiana and Via

---

121–22 (and figs. 5–9), interpreting the pattern as evidence that different crews worked at the same time on different sides of these buildings.

[94] E.g., Vetter 1953.12 (Stabian Baths).

[95] Vetter 1953.13–15 (*meddix tuticus*); 11–12 and 16–19 (*kvaísstur*). The *aediles* were mainly responsible for road construction projects: see Vetter 1953.8 (*Via Púmpaiiana*); Crawford 2011.Pompei 14 (ramp leading to the extraurban temple of S. Abbondio). On Pompeian road building in general, see Poehler and Crowther 2018. For an example of the same magistrate letting the contract and inspecting the building, see Vetter 1953.14.

[96] Osanna 2015.

dell'Abbondanza (VII.1), have played a major role for the sequencing of both wall-facing styles and building materials. The traditional reconstruction is based on the combined results of limited excavations below the 79 CE levels carried out by Maiuri (in 1928 and in 1931–32) and Eschebach (1971–73).[97] Both scholars focused their attention on the north wing of the complex, consisting of a row of five small vaulted cubicles built with lime-based, mortared Sarno Limestone rubble that open onto a vaulted corridor, and whose entrance from Vico del Lupanare to the west (at VIII.1.50) was framed by dressed Nocera Tuff blocks. An adjacent larger vaulted space was located directly to the north of this set of rooms. It was accessible from a door on the short east side, which could be reached from a vaulted passageway, narrower than the one to the south, but framed by an identical portal facing onto Vico del Lupanare (at VIII.1.48). West of these features is a deep well flanked by two smaller tanks, which were fed by means of a water-lifting device. In turn, the tanks discharged into a rooftop reservoir supported by the vault spanning the northern room.[98] Maiuri identified this part as the original core of the monument, which he dated to the late 3rd or early 2nd century BCE, distinguishing it from the suite of bathing rooms that occupied the east wing. Since they featured predominantly compact lava *opus incertum*, Maiuri assigned those structures to the second half of the 2nd century BCE. The phasing would be consistent with the style of the Nocera Tuff portico that decorated the exercise courtyard, whose existence in the Pre-Roman period was inferred from an Oscan inscription recording the installation of a sundial.[99] The west sector of the city block, which appeared originally occupied by a private house, would have been eventually incorporated only in the Roman phase.

Maiuri's reconstruction was subsequently modified by Eschebach, who hypothesized three successive phases of development for the early complex.[100] He discovered a lower layer of (tuff?) rubble structures directly underneath the Sarno Limestone walls in some of the cells and an isolated Pappamonte wall in the well room. He interpreted these spaces as part of a Greek-style bathing complex provided with hip bathtubs, which he dated to the 5th century BCE, associating it with an early version of the *palaestra*. Both sectors would have been progressively modified during the 4th and 3rd centuries BCE, rebuilding the cells in Sarno Limestone and transforming the hip baths into individual immersion baths; a Roman-style sequence of progressively heated rooms would have been added in the second half of the 3rd century BCE, prior to the construction of the east wing and incorporation of the west lot in the 2nd century BCE.

[97] Maiuri 1973: 44–48; Eschebach 1975; 1979.
[98] Maiuri 1973: 32–34.
[99] Maiuri 1973: 44–48. *Supra*, n. 525 for the inscription.
[100] As summarized in Eschebach 1979: 51–53. An early critical review of Eschebach's recon-struction is in Richardson 1988: 100–05; DeLaine 1989: 117–20; Fagan 2001: 408–14.

In order to reexamine Eschebach's argument and evidence systematically, Trümper *et al.* (2019) resumed excavation and architectural survey at the site, thus providing controlled archaeological data to reconstruct the original layout and clarify the construction date of the baths.[101] The results show that the project began around or after 125 BCE and progressed according to a highly coordinated master plan that transformed a previously unoccupied block (Figure 5.7).[102] The original complex included separate men's and women's sections, both fitted with an apodyterium, caldarium, and tepidarium, some of

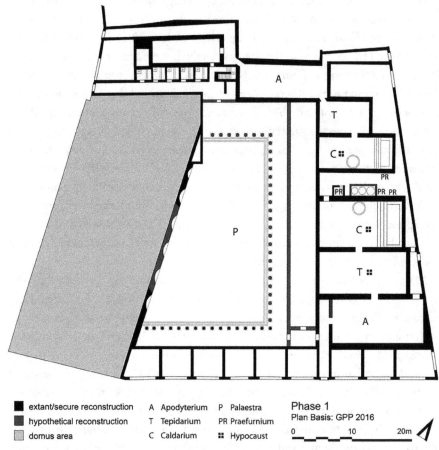

| | | | Phase 1 |
|---|---|---|---|
| ■ extant/secure reconstruction | A Apodyterium | P Palaestra | Plan Basis: GPP 2016 |
| ■ hypothetical reconstruction | T Tepidarium | PR Praefurnium | |
| ▨ domus area | C Caldarium | ▮▮ Hypocaust | 0    10    20m |

Figure 5.7 Pompeii, Stabian Baths. Schematic plan of the original phase of the complex, *c.* 125 BCE (Trümper *et al.* 2019: 148, fig. 32; used by permission).

---

[101]  Trümper *et al.* 2019: 127–43 (stratigraphy); 149–53 (finds).

[102]  Thick fills (about 2 m in depth) are also documented in the Casa di N. Popidius Priscus, at VII.2.20 (Pedroni 2011: 166). The area of the Casa dei Postumi, which occupies a city block south of the Stabian Baths, seems to have been first built up between the late 3rd and the first half of the 2nd centuries BCE, but the earliest *opus incertum* stuctures there have been assigned to the late 2nd or early 1st centuries BCE (Dickmann and Pirson 2005: 164).

which were provided with hypocaust systems. These were supplied by *prae-furnia* located in a communal service section (but type of hypocaust – whether pillars or channels – and number of furnaces remain undetermined). The north wing included the well annex, five cells, and two corridors supporting the *castellum aquae*, whose function was to provide pressurized water to the rest of the complex. The cells featured high vaulted ceilings, nonwaterproof floors, narrow doors, and simple benches, and were probably frequented only by men for some form of relaxation. Sumps placed on one corner were used to discard water, oil or other cosmetic liquids, and urine or feces.[103] A row of shops opened onto Via Stabiana.

The new reconstruction implies that compact lava *opus incertum* construction and Sarno Limestone masonry were used simultaneously, depending on function. In the north wing, intentional grading of materials can be seen in the masonry of the rooftop reservoir system: The 3.80 m wide barrel vault supporting the tank was made with Sarno Limestone wedges set radially in abundant mortar, whereas the basin itself was built using lighter scoriaceous lava rubble. In the east wing, compact lava was employed probably in order to obtain better insulation for the heated rooms. Those in the men's sector feature concrete vaults spanning up to 7 m, the largest known from Pompeii. Given the advanced design and technology of the bathing suite in comparison with other mid 2nd century BCE examples,[104] it is conceivable that that part of the complex was contracted to a specialized firm that sourced its materials separately, or that the same contractor hired a different group of masons whose skills matched the complexity of the project. As verified both in the north wing and in the women's apodyterium, however, construction of the foundations progressed using the same method throughout the building: All walls were built on top of very hard, dark grey-brown pozzolanic mortar fills poured into shallow trenches (depth: about 0.60 m) (Plate VI.A). The mixture ("earth mortar") consisted of local silica-rich sediments and finer volcanic ash combined with slaked lime, and also included frequent white plaster and lime inclusions.[105]

Another group of monuments whose dating is crucial for the sequencing of early concrete public architecture in Pompeii includes the Temple and Sanctuary of Apollo, the Temple of Jupiter (also known as the Capitolium), and the Basilica. These buildings have been traditionally assigned to the second half of the 2nd century BCE and linked with the monumental development of the forum area (Figure 5.8). The available archaeological evidence, however, points to later construction dates for most of these projects, with important repercussions on the tempo and dynamics of the spread of the technology at the site.

[103]  Trümper *et al.* 2019: 146–49.
[104]  Trümper *et al.* 2019: 123, fig. 11.
[105]  Trümper *et al.* 2019: 143–45.

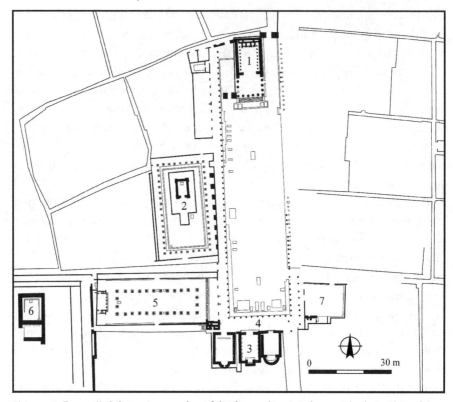

Figure 5.8 Pompeii. Schematic state plan of the forum showing the spatial relationship of the
main public monuments discussed in Chapter 5 to the forum portico and square. Key:
1=Capitolium; 2=Sanctuary of Apollo; 3=South Buildings; 4=Porticus of Popidius; 5=Basilica;
6=Sanctuary of Venus; 7=Comitium. Drawing: M. Harder.

The Sanctuary of Apollo, located on the west side of the forum north of Via
Marina, has been by far the most extensively researched of these sites (Figure 5.9).
Early excavations by Maiuri within the precinct and limited soundings by P. Arthur
along its east side toward the forum demonstrated that a sacred complex had existed
in that location since the Archaic period.[106] The architecture and stratigraphy
documented within the sanctuary testify to a complicated sequence of building
activities extending through the early Roman period. A mosaic inscription in
Oscan mentioning the *kvaísstur* Oppius Campanus places the construction of the
current cella pavement, and probably of the standing cella, squarely in the Late
Samnite period.[107] Cooper and Dobbins (2015) have noticed several irregularities
in the spatial relationship between the cella, the extant peristasis, and the precinct
colonnade. To reconcile these anomalies, they propose to reconstruct an original

---

[106] Maiuri's findings are published in De Caro 1986; Arthur 1986. For an early assessment of the
results, see Richardson 1988: 89–95.

[107] Vetter 1953.18 = Crawford 2011.Pompei 23. On the type of mosaic and its distribution at
Pompeii, see Westgate 2000: 259–60, 263. Pesando 2006 identifies it as a *scutulatum* and

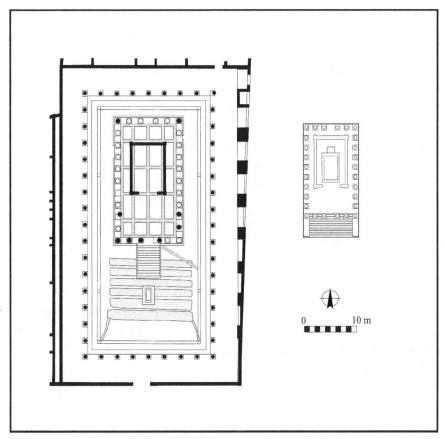

Figure 5.9 Pompeii. Schematic plan of the Sanctuary of Apollo, post-130–120 BCE. Compiled from data in De Caro 1986. Note the location of the grid of foundations below the cella and the position of the cisterns in the forecourt. Compare the hypothetical extent of the first temple associated with the precinct colonnade as reconstructed by Cooper and Dobbins (2015), at the same scale (right). Drawing: M. Harder.

shrine of smaller dimensions (to which they refer the Oscan mosaic), whose podium would have been incorporated within an expanded cella. The corner capitals of the cella respond precisely to the placement of the extant precinct colonnade, suggesting that the two projects were contemporaneous. In a third phase, the current temple peristasis, which features Corinthian columns of larger module and with wider intercolumniations, would have been installed in place of the previous one, requiring the further extension of the podium.[108] This modification would have been part of the same program of redecoration of the precinct colonnade (whose original Ionic capitals were covered with stucco to transform

suggests a date in the 140s BCE based on the earliest mention of the floor type in Pliny (Capitolium? 149–146 BCE; *HN* 36.185). Tang 2006: 95–96 dates the earliest archaeologically attested examples from Rome to the late 2nd century BCE.

[108] Cooper and Dobbins 2015: 5, fig. 5. For the surviving elements, see Lauter-Bufe 1987: 38–39, nos. 99–103.

them into Corinthian capitals).[109] Based on the state of the architectural remains exposed by Maiuri within the podium, however, the idea of an earlier and much smaller structure encased in a later one does not seem to stand, since the extant cella foundations (blocks of Sarno Limestone) appear joined to the grid of cemented-rubble substructures that extend across the entire platform, thus not leaving room for the frontal staircase as hypothesized in the alternative reconstruction.[110]

The podium revetment rests on top of a foundation course made of blocks of Nocera Tuff and Sarno Limestone, which are placed in parallel rows on the bottom of a shallow foundation trench, with gaps filled with packed rubble and pottery fragments (a technique employed also for the foundations of the colonnade).[111] The freestanding section, on the other hand, consists of two adjoining parts, which Maiuri assigned to different phases. The inner one is composed of two horizontal courses of Sarno Limestone blocks topped by an upper course of Nocera Tuff ashlars. The concrete grid was erected in parallel with the construction of the ashlar frame, in horizontal layers of coarse rubblework of both Sarno Limestone and Nocera Tuff laid in mortar containing volcanic ash. Sarno Limestone and Nocera Tuff chips deriving from the dressing of the blocks are interspersed with the soil deposits dumped within the grid. These concentrations possibly identify the surfaces at which the work was stopped to let the cemented rubble set. The exterior facing is composed of four courses of Nocera Tuff blocks on top of an Attic base, partly carved and partly built in masonry and stuccoed,[112] whereas nothing survives of the crown molding. The cross-sectional drawing by Maiuri indicates that the Nocera ashlars are associated with a different type of cemented-rubble masonry, which may support the phasing.[113]

A frontal staircase in travertine abuts the extant podium. It was probably added by the mid 1st century BCE *terminus*, when a new limestone altar was positioned with its short side on axis with the podium.[114] The Latin inscription repeated on both long sides (*CIL* 10.800 = *CIL* 1².1631) records that it was dedicated by *quattuoruiri* (probably meaning the *duouiri* and the two *aediles* acting collectively). One of the dedicants was the same M. Porcius, former commissioner for the

---

[109] On the redecoration of the portico (affecting also the original Doric frieze) see Richardson 1988: 94; Carroll and Godden 2000: 746–48, with 752–53 for the dating. On the first phase of the colonnade: Richardson 1988: 90–91. Moorman 2011: 84–85 provides a comparison with the north peristyle of the Casa del Fauno.

[110] For a description of the remains, see De Caro 1986: 10–13.

[111] This specific technique for foundations is well documented in domestic architecture from the 2nd century BCE onwards (e.g., Casa di Sallustio; Casa di Pansa): see Pesando 2012.

[112] Lauter 1979: 422 dates it stylistically to 110–100 BCE. The date is considered too late by De Caro 1986: 28 n. 72. La Rocca 1993: 30 compares the base molding profile with that of the Temple B from Largo Argentina, thus dating it to after 100 BCE.

[113] Osanna 2015: 88, figs. 10 and 12 show a row of large Sarno Limestone blocks laid below the stylobate of the west portico, possibly representing spolia from the earlier temple.

[114] The idea that the original temple had a wooden staircase, or that it did not have one at all, is discussed in Rescigno 2017: 48.

foundation of the colony in 80 BCE, who was also involved in the construction of the *theatrum tectum* (as *duouir*) and of the amphitheater (as *duouir quinquennalis* acting *sua pecunia*).[115] Altar and staircase are built on top of a series of narrow underground cisterns made of cemented Sarno Limestone rubble (width 1.35 m), all connected by conduits and covered with barrel vaults of oblong wedge-shaped Sarno Limestone blocks. These structures collected rainwater from settling basins located at the four corners of the precinct portico, so they were planned as part of a single project predating the erection of the altar.[116]

Another text in Oscan is carved on a tuff statue base that sits directly atop the lower course of ashlars abutting the stylobate of the peristyle delimiting the precinct.[117] The inscription has been assigned to the class of the *tituli Mummiani* and dated to 144–142 BCE,[118] even though it presents problems of interpretation.[119] Some scholars have used it to provide a *terminus ad quem* for the monumentalization of the entire complex.[120] The base, however, appears to be in secondary position, so its value to pinpoint the construction date can be questioned.[121] It may just as well refer to a gift dedicated somewhere else within the precinct by a person with links to the Roman general (a friend, colleague, or ally to whom Mummius had distributed a share of his booty), and whose base was later reused to support another statue (the inscription itself was concealed under a thick layer of plaster).[122] Recent fieldwork at the site has

---

[115] See Gregori and Nonnis 2017: 244–45. His tomb, erected by the city council, is in the Porta Ercolano necropolis (*CIL* 10.997 = *CIL* 1².1631, *c.* 70 BCE).

[116] De Caro 1986: 13; Rescigno 2017: 43–44 and 45, fig. 13. Earlier stratigraphic investigations in the courtyard have shown that the compact layer covering the crest of the third, fourth, and fifth cistern contains pottery of the late 1st century BCE: Carroll and Godden 2000: 746–47. The same material was found in the fill of the fifth cistern. Because this level was razed in the course of the first excavations of the temple in the 1800s, the risk of intrusions is extremely high. For evidence of WWII bomb damage, see also Ball and Dobbins 2017: 468–70.

[117] Vetter 1953.61; Martelli 2002; Martelli 2005; Crawford 2011.Pompei 1: *l(úvkis) mummis l (úvkieís) kúsúl*. On the base type, see Martelli 1996: 128; Lippolis 2004: 35–36.

[118] See Gregori and Nonnis 2017: 244. The *tituli Mummiani* are commonly associated with the year of L. Mummius's censorship: Lippolis 2004.

[119] Known *tituli Mummiani* from allied Italian towns are normally in Latin and include the official name of the community to which the gift was made. A close parallel for the Pompeian inscription comes from Fabrateria Nova, where another statue base inscribed in Latin only with the name of Mummius in the nominative has been found: *L. Mumi(us) L(uci) f(ilius) co(n) s(ul)*. One interpretation is that it was brought from Fregellae after the destruction of the colony in 125 BCE and the subsequent relocation of the inhabitants on the new site: Bizzarri 1973; Pietilä-Castrén 1978: 121. Bloy 1998: 59–60 interprets the abbreviated formula as specifically indicating that the statue was taken when Mummius was consul to signify the lengthy retention of booty, questioning the idea that the gift was dedicated at Fregellae (cf. Plin., *NH* 34.93 on the case of L. Lucullus's minor son, who dedicated booty taken by his father between 74–67 BCE only after his death in 57 BCE).

[120] E.g., Pesando 2006: 233–34 speculates that Mummius himself would have paid for the actual construction of the colonnade using spoils from Corinth, and that the Porticus Metelli in Rome would have provided the architectural model for the overall project.

[121] Ball and Dobbins 2013: 487–90.

[122] On the sculptural assemblage and related supports from the site, see Rescigno 2017: 53–60.

revealed that between the 3rd century and the third quarter of the 2nd century
BCE the east side of the sacred area was delimited by a row of limestone-
framework *tabernae*. These opened onto the forum square, responding to the
ones documented under the Eumachia Building,[123] and were eventually razed
to build the forum portico and the pier structure that separated it from the
sanctuary, which carried the roofs of both the precinct colonnade and the
forum portico. Excavation data indicate that the project started sometime in the
last quarter of the second century BCE (after 130–120 BCE).[124] It is unclear
whether the back wall of the shops could have supported the roof of the
precinct portico prior to the construction of the pier structure.

Unlike the pier structure and the stylobate of the precinct colonnade, whose
foundations are built using recycled blocks, the back walls of the colonnade on
the west, north, and south sides of the colonnade have deep continuous
concrete foundations made of mixed Sarno Limestone, Nocera Tuff, and lava
rubble.[125] The irregularities these walls create in the street pattern have been
interpreted as evidence for alterations intended to make room for the colonnade, namely by abolishing the supposed continuation of the north–south
Vicolo del Gallo.[126] Ball and Dobbins link these building activities with
a text (*CIL* 10.787) that records the purchase by *duouiri iure dicundo* of the

[123] Rescigno 2017: 40–41, fig. 5; 48; 61–62. Cf. Arthur 1986: 34–35 identified the original limit
between the sanctuary and the forum with a ditch whose alignment was at an odd angle with the
main axis of the square. For the structures below the Eumachia building, see Maiuri 1973: 53–63.

[124] Osanna and Rescigno 2018. According to Cooper and Dobbins (2015: 4), only the two
southernmost ashlar piers of the ensemble, and possibly part of the third, seem to have been in
place before the Augustan period. The late date of the pier structure plays a major role in the
reconstruction proposed by the Pompeii Forum Project, given the precise correspondence
between the position and width of its doors and the intercolumniations of the precinct
colonnade: Dobbins *et al.* 1998; Carroll and Godden 2000; Dobbins 2007; Ball and Dobbins
2013; Cooper and Dobbins 2015; Ball and Dobbins 2017. For the ceramic evidence, see Ball
and Dobbins 2017: 478 ("not earlier than 40 BCE").

[125] De Caro 1986: 15–18. A linear cut in the natural deposits documented by Dobbins on the
exterior of the precinct and below the Augustan levels may represent the original foundation
trench of the back wall of the colonnade: Dobbins *et al.* 1998: 744–46. Maiuri recorded the
continuation of the cut about 10 m south of Dobbin's Trench 1: De Caro 1986: 131, Trench
V. The edge of the cut is at about the same level as the lower offset visible in the mortared-
rubble structure and was backfilled by a layer containing nondiagnostic black-gloss pottery of
the 2nd–1st centuries BCE.

[126] A test-trench excavated by the Pompeii Forum Project at the putative intersection of the
restored street grid predating the construction of the northwest corner of the sanctuary failed
to confirm the actual presence of a road. The stratigraphy documented by Maiuri across the
alley shows that the east boundary wall of the Casa di Trittolemo sits on top of an ashlar wall
of Pappamonte, which De Caro (1986: 5–6) interprets as the precinct wall of the Archaic
sanctuary. Alternatively, this feature may have represented the original façade of the house on
the supposed continuation of Vicolo del Gallo in the Samnite period (Ball and Dobbins 2013:
475, n. 74; 476). In this scenario, a structure built with mixed rubble (including Pappamonte)
and clay mortar, found at the corner between the west and south colonnade running roughly
parallel to the ashlar wall, could perhaps belong to the west limit of the road. See De Caro
1986: 9 and plate Ib, Trench IIe; Osanna and Rescigno 2018.

right to block windows (*ius luminum opstruendorum*) of an unnamed building, possibly the nearby Casa di Trittolemo (VII.7.2), which is separated from the sanctuary by a blind alley.[127] It is also possible that the inscription simply refers to the blocking of this passage, challenging its relevance for the dating of the main building events.[128]

Sitting at the center of one of the short sides, the Temple of Jupiter represented the main focal point of the square in the Roman phase, generating with its orientation the main axis of the forum portico.[129] The broad consensus is that the cult building predated the establishment of the Roman colony, and that it was transformed into a Roman-style Capitolium upon or after the incorporation of Pompeii into the Roman state, thus marking the new status and identity of the settlement.[130] Excavations by Maiuri below the main altar in front of the temple revealed traces of a small-scale shrine frequented from the second half of the 4th century BCE and obliterated sometime in the 2nd century BCE by the construction of the larger rectangular platform, which consisted of cemented rubble with ashlar facing (imprints of the blocks were preserved in the masonry).[131] The aspect of the first monumental temple can be reconstructed on the basis of the layout of the vaulted substructures (Figure 5.10).[132] These comprise three chambers, each covered by a segmental concrete vault laid directly on wooden centering (span: about 4 m), and resting on top of a continuous foundation platform made of

[127] Dobbins *et al.* 1998: 744–52. On the date of the inscription (before 3/2 BCE), see Gregori and Nonnis 2017: 245–46. Rescigno 2017: 61 casts doubt about the original position of the inscription, suggesting that the block on which it is carved may have been recycled to rebuild the cult statue base in the cella. He cites modifications to the small portico abutting the north precinct wall or the east pier structure itself as other possible contexts for the building activities mentioned in the text, if one accepts its reference to the Sanctuary of Apollo.

[128] Note that the north section of the southeast corner of VII.15.7 is perfectly aligned with the east wall of the Casa di Trittolemo, which was built on top of a preexisting structure. This suggests that the alley between the sanctuary and the Casa di Trittolemo may have originally continued up to that point. The reconstruction documented by Dobbin's Trench 1997–2 may have been planned to connect the east–west road separating blocks VII.7 and VII.15 with the north branch of Vicolo del Gallo, allowing pedestrians to reach the houses facing on this street from Via Marina.

[129] Ball and Dobbins 2013: 478.

[130] E.g., Zevi 1996: 128; Zanker 1998: 53–60; Crawley Quinn and Wilson 2013: 139–40. For other possible dates, see Lauter 1979: 416–23, 430–34 (100 BCE); Lauter 2009: 163–70 (89–80 BCE). *Contra* Richardson 1988: 138 (proposing a single phase based on classicizing features of the design and similarities in the masonry style with other known monuments traditionally attributed to the Sullan period). Richardson's view is followed (with caution) by Ball and Dobbins 2013: 479. The authors believe that the example from Pompeii would not fit with Samnite urban, temple, and precinct designs, citing the examples of Saepinum and Pietrabbondante. The case of the forum temple at Cumae (3rd century BCE: Gasparri *et al.* 1996, 46 fig. 3; converted into a Capitolium in the Flavian period) indicates that top-tier sites of the coastal area and minor inland settlements followed different trajectories.

[131] Maiuri 1973: 116–19. For a reassessment of the evidence, see Lippolis 2017: 132–34. Lepone and Marchetti 2018 discuss the possibility that the structure represented an early version of the temple.

[132] Maiuri 1973: 103; D'Alessio 2009: 50–51; Lippolis 2017: 122–23.

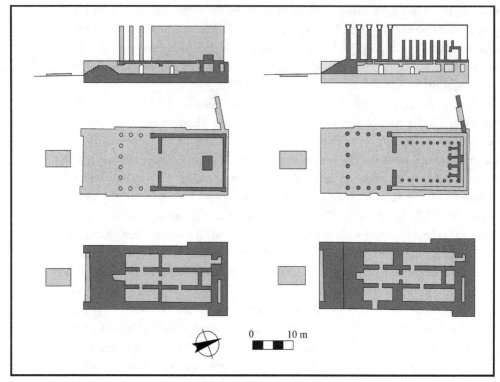

0    10 m

Figure 5.10 Pompeii. Temple of Jupiter (Capitolium). Sectional plans of the first monumental temple and its post-80 BCE reconstruction, showing the layout of the podium vaulted sub-structures. Adapted from data in Lippolis 2017. Drawing: M. Harder.

cemented compact lava rubble. Access to the basement was originally through steps built into the frontal staircase, betraying an important role of this semisubterranean space for the liturgy. An east–west wall divides the substructures into two long-itudinal sectors, a shorter one on the front and a longer one on the back, whose proportions correspond to those of the original pronaos and cella. Directly on top of this east–west foundation Maiuri found the remains of an earlier wall in Sarno Limestone and compact lava rubble, razed under the floor of the extant cella.[133] This suggests that in a second phase the cella was completely rebuilt on a slightly larger plan, accommodating an interior Ionic order whose columns are placed on the crown of the basement vaults, and a new base for the cult statues.[134] Furthermore, the podium was expanded on the front (and perhaps also on the back) in order to make room for a much deeper hexastyle Corinthian pronaos, thus incorporating part of the earlier frontal staircase and suppressing the access to the

[133] Maiuri 1973: 107–08.
[134] Maiuri 1973, 108–09; D'Alessio 2009: 51–53; Lippolis 2017: 123–25. Richardson 1988: 141–42 finds a parallel for such placement of the columns in the Basilica at Cosa.

basement. These features are all made with *opus incertum* of compact lava. In a third phase, the staircase was further modified by inserting on it a new altar, which replaced the older platform (this was abolished as a result of the construction of the travertine pavement of the forum).[135] Based on design and vaulting technique, the original temple can be assigned to the late 2nd century BCE at the earliest.[136]

On the exterior, the podium substructures featured a stepped profile, with a base formed by four receding courses of Nocera Tuff ashlars. As seen by Maiuri on the west side, the bottom course was covered by a preparation level of packed building debris that sealed the foundation trench. In turn, this level was framed by a Nocera Tuff structure, parts of which were found by Maiuri under the later travertine pavement along the east side of the square, in the northwest corner and in front of the pier wall delimiting the Sanctuary of Apollo, forming a ring of three abutting rows of slabs.[137] The top surface of the inner slabs presents a shallow depression, which most likely functioned as a drain, channeling surface water in the system of underground concrete channels.[138] Maiuri saw these features as connected with a continuous Nocera Tuff portico running on all sides of the square, whose original ashlar foundations would have been dismantled to make room for the current travertine colonnade and its continuous concrete foundations, but his reconstruction has not been unanimously accepted.[139]

At the opposite end of the square, the fronts of two of the so-called South Buildings were carved out to insert the tuff colonnade.[140] An Oscan inscription found in a house on the south side of Via dell'Abbondanza near the entrance to the forum (VIII.3.4) records the construction of a colonnaded structure by the *meddix tuticus* Vibius Popidius, son of Vibius, but its connection with the forum portico is dubious.[141] A Latin inscription (*CIL* 10.794) recovered near the

---

[135] Lippolis 2017: 125–27; 133.

[136] See the architectural analysis in Lippolis 2017: 138–41.

[137] Maiuri 1973: 108; 63–70.

[138] Maiuri 1973: 66–67. On the overall design of the Forum drainage system, see Poehler 2012: 107–08.

[139] Maiuri 1973: 70–73, fig. 34; Rescigno 2017: 47, fig. 15 (stretch by the Mensa Ponderaria). Ball and Dobbins 2013: 477 and 480–87 assign such a master plan to 89–80 BCE (though they do not discuss the drainage system described by Maiuri). Both Lauter (1979: 430–34) and Zanker (1998: 56–57) believe that in its original phase the forum portico was present only on the south side.

[140] Maiuri 1973: 99–101, figs. 54–55; Kockel 2008: 282–84; Ball and Dobbins 2013: 483–85, figs. 5–7. An *opus incertum* wall parallel to these structures was found also in the west building, but farther south. Maiuri interpreted this structure as the inner party wall of a vestibule. The difference in alignment is otherwise taken as evidence that the three South Buildings were not planned organically, and that the south portico formed a freestanding structure. Cf. Osanna and Rescigno 2018, who offer a new reading of the evidence in light of recent fieldwork, reconstructing a row of limestone-framework *tabernae* obliterated for the construction of *both* the South Buildings and the portico. See Giglio 2017b.

[141] Vetter 1953.13. The house in question is also known as the Casa dei Popidii because of a cluster of electoral slogans mentioning members of the *gens Popidia*. Della Corte (1922: 110–12) suggests that the inscription in question was kept as a family heirloom, taken from the forum and placed in

entrance of the Basilica names the magistrate responsible for the construction of a *porticus*, the *quaestor* Vibius Popidius, son of Epidius.[142] Onorato (1951) dated the document to 89–80 BCE, interpreting the choice of Latin as a sign of self-Romanization. The *quaestura*, however, is attested in early *programmata* for candidates with a Roman name, suggesting that the office was initially maintained in the constitution of the colony, but progressively lost its importance.[143] Thus, the portico inscription, which in all likelihood recorded the conclusion of the works, may even date to the early years of the colony. In any case, it provides a *terminus ante quem* for the sequence of urban development of the forum area. As demonstrated by Dobbins, the tuff portico is connected to the surrounding buildings by means of wedge-shaped structures that regularize the different alignments.[144] In the southwest corner, the ashlar foundations of the portico structure abut the Basilica's façade (or Chalcidicum), whose construction date would therefore provide a *terminus post quem* for the project.

The Chalcidicum, a Nocera Tuff *opus quadratum* structure, was built in a single operation with the space behind it, since their walls are joined at the level of both foundations and superstructure.[145] Tiles with Oscan stamps (*Ni[umsis] Pupie[diis?]*) were found in the fill of the well located on the south side of the Chalcidicum.[146] The Basilica itself features an advanced form of *opus incertum* of compact lava, with fist-sized facing pieces laid in pozzolanic mortar, which contains volcanic sand purportedly quarried from coastal deposits.[147] Quoins are made with small parallelepipedal blocks of Nocera Tuff, but larger Sarno Limestone ashlars are occasionally used (e.g., on the south side).[148] On the back wall opposite the Chalcidicum is a tribunal, which is supported by a cemented-rubble substructure spanned by a barrel vault (approximately 5 m). Based on such features, Maiuri suggested a date shortly after that of the Temple of Jupiter (130–120 BCE).[149] Richardson argued for a slightly later chronology, with a construction date toward the end of the century.[150] On stylistic grounds,

---

the house after the damages of the earthquake of 62 CE. The term *passtata* in the Oscan text has been interpreted as the equivalent of Greek *pastadas*, which in known building inscriptions usually refers to colonnades around temples (e.g., *IG* $2^2$ 1126.22, from Delphi).

[142] On the findspot, see Ball and Dobbins 2013: 485–86.

[143] Degrassi 1967: 46–49; Castrén 1975: 88.

[144] Dobbins 2007: 169–72.

[145] Maiuri 1973: 191–223 (especially 207–09); Ohr 1991: 26–30.

[146] Vetter 1953.43; Maiuri 1973: 196–99; Castrén 1975: 207–09; Dobbins 2007: 172 accepts the connection with the *gens Popidia*, since the family maintained a high status also in the early colonial period. Nonnis (1999: 80–81) considers also a possible *Pupie(ns)* = *Pupienus*. See also Nonnis 2015: 372.

[147] Ohr 1991: 35–36.

[148] Ohr 1991: 27.

[149] Maiuri 1973, 223.

[150] Richardson 1988: 99 (though he assigns the Chalcidicum to a later phase contemporary with the portico of Popidius). Cf. Lugli 1957, vol. 1: 475–76.

Ohr proposes a much broader range (150–100 BCE).[151] A more precise *terminus post quem* of 112 BCE can be derived from the closing date of a ceramic assemblage that Maiuri retrieved from a sealed construction fill below the *cocciopesto* floor of the Basilica.[152] A graffito left on the First Style plaster decoration of the north interior wall by a visitor on October 3 of 78 BCE (*CIL* 4.1842) provides a *terminus ante quem*.

The forum ensemble testifies to a dramatic increase in the scale of concrete construction. Both the Temple of Jupiter and the Basilica show signs of departure from the previous building tradition: the tendency toward a clear separation between facing and core in *opus incertum* walls; the preference for compact lava as opposed to Sarno Limestone (which, however, was still used for quoins) for superstructures; the introduction of cemented-rubble foundations, as well as of concrete vaulting for substructures. The Stabian Baths (*c.* 125 BCE) provides in this sense a well-dated example for the transition. Given the impressive number of monuments under construction in this relatively short period of time, builders with different backgrounds and training must have been at work, thus explaining the overlaps between old and new.

The sequence excavated at the Sanctuary of Venus demonstrates that works in the core sector of the so-called *Altstadt* continued well beyond the early colonial period. The construction fills on top of which the temple, forecourt, and porticoes are built date to the post-Sullan phase.[153] Both the cemented-rubble foundations of the podium and associated triporticus and the *opus incertum* and *opus quasi reticulatum* superstructures documented at the site consist mostly of Sarno Limestone and *cruma*, but also incorporate larger fragments of architectural elements (e.g., plastered Sarno Limestone blocks and Nocera Tuff capitals). This building program encroached upon a lower stratum dating to the second half of the 2nd century BCE. The area was previously characterized by a radically different spatial organization, whose function is still undetermined: A north–south alley branching off of Via Marina divided the neighborhood into two city blocks (Figure 5.11). The east sector (possibly domestic?) was razed to the ground in order to make room for the construction site of the adjacent Basilica, while the one to the west seems to have remained in use for a longer period. The structures are predominantly made with cemented Sarno Limestone rubble (Plates VII.A–B), but features made of compact

---

[151] Ohr 1991: 78.

[152] The construction fill covered the crest of preexisting structures that had been demolished to make room for the Basilica, and was sealed by a thin layer of mortar, which probably represented the surface where the binder was mixed during construction. The finds included a cache of Rhodian amphorae whose latest stamps can be assigned to 115 BCE (eponym: *Arkhibios*; Maiuri 1973: 220 no. 4) and 112 BCE (eponym: *Aristanax* II; Maiuri 1973: 220, no. 1). For the dating of the Rhodian eponyms, see Finkielsztejn 2001: 195, table 21f.

[153] Compare the mid 1st century BCE date proposed by Carroll 2010. Curti 2008: 53–56; Coletti and Sterpa 2008; Coletti *et al.* 2010 argued for a 130–120 BCE date but the results of subsequent fieldwork at the site undermine their initial reconstruction: Battiloro *et al.* 2018; Battiloro and Mogetta forthcoming.

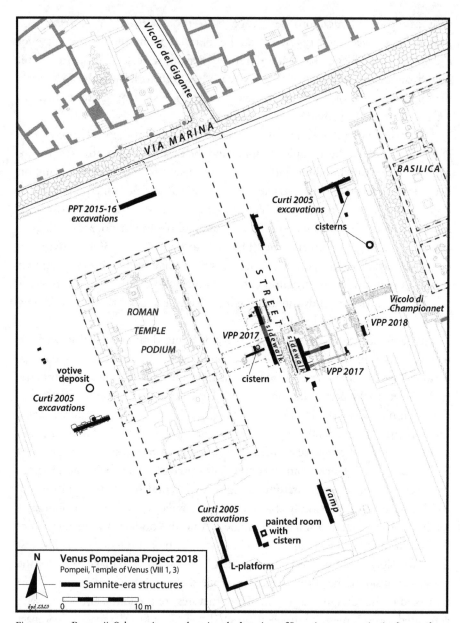

Figure 5.11 Pompeii. Schematic map showing the location of Samnite-era remains in the area later occupied by the Sanctuary of Venus (© Venus Pompeiana Project). Drawing: D. Diffendale.

lava rubble and decorated in the First Style are also present on the south terrace, most notably in an L-shaped platform abutting a stretch of the Nocera Tuff fortifications.[154]

---

[154] Varriale 2010 (with a different interpretation of the stratigraphic sequence, now fully revised).

The earliest application of concrete construction to the city walls can also be placed between the late 2nd and the early 1st centuries BCE. The Sullan siege of 89 BCE has obviously represented an important fixed point to date the extensive compact lava *opus incertum* stretches seen in the curtain walls – whose longest sections are preserved south of the amphitheater, at Porta Nola, east of Porta Ercolano, and on both sides of Porta Stabia, and the terracing wall supporting the Sanctuary of Venus – as well as in the associated towers and gates. The early debate saw most of these features either as hasty restorations and updates executed at the outbreak of the Social War or as later repairs of the damages caused by the siege.[155] Recent archaeological research has found that, whereas most concrete sections of the curtain represent post-siege construction activities,[156] the insertion of towers into the preexisting circuit and the refurbishment of the gates may have reflected a careful program rather than a panicked response to military threat. The strategic location of the towers at the end of streets would have provided the inhabitants of Pompeii with a sense of security, since the structures would have been prominently visible not just from the outside to those coming to Pompeii, but also from within. Stratigraphic evidence places the construction of the concrete vault of Porta Stabia (and thus of the adjacent tower) to around 100 BCE.[157] The addition of a vaulted gate against the field side at Porta Vesuvio is roughly contemporary.[158] The date of the thick stepped *opus incertum* foundations of Porta Nocera, the single example of its kind, is uncertain.[159] The historical context provides a variety of possible reasons for why Italian allies might have had concerns about their own defenses,[160] but the investment in the upgrading of one of the main civic symbols of Pompeii may have been part of a broader program of urban beautification, as also seen in Latium Vetus and Adiectum.[161] In fact, the towers were ornamented with First Style decoration, and stone architectural elements were incorporated in some of the *opus incertum* stretches.[162] The arched structures of the gates and the interior barrel vaults of the

[155] Van der Graaff 2019: 11–13 offers a thorough discussion of earlier scholarship and the relationship of the main theories to ideas about the urban development of Pompeii.

[156] E.g., Tower IX and its adjacent stretch dates to the early years of the colony. See Etani 2010: 208. Cf. *CIL* 10.937 = I².1629, recording the letting of the contract for, and final inspection of, a portion of the walls by the *duouiri*.

[157] Devore and Ellis 2008: 13–15.

[158] Seiler *et al.* 2005: 224 (late 2nd century BCE).

[159] Van der Graaf (2019: 60–62) assigns it to his third Samnite phase, making it contemporaneous with the 2nd century BCE refurbishing of the adjacent fortification stretch.

[160] Van der Graaff (2019: 66) suggests the Cimbri and Teutones threat.

[161] Cf. Gabba 1972; Gabba 1976; Jouffroy 1986: 16–26. Gregori and Nonnis (2013) collect the epigraphic evidence on fortification building in peninsular Italy, identifying 10 or 11 inscriptions dating to the latter part of the 2nd century BCE or the first decades of the 1st century BCE (the Oscan inscription from Porta di Nola at Pompeii is the only known example from South Italy, with the possible exception of Herdoniae: Vetter 1953.8).

[162] See Cassetta and Costantino 2008: 200 for the engaged Doric colonnade incorporated in the *opus incertum* stretch along Vicolo dei Soprastanti (dated stylistically to the late 2nd century BCE).

towers may have been among the earliest adaptations of vaulting to Pompeian public architecture.[163]

Another important cluster of concrete monuments is located on the southern edge of town, in what was formerly a sparsely built area dominated by the Archaic Doric temple of the so-called Foro Triangolare. The Theater (VII.2, usually referred to as Teatro Grande, or Large Theater, to distinguish it from the Odeum or Theatrum Tectum) probably represents the earliest building in the urban development of the neighborhood.[164] Most of its standing remains belong to the Augustan reconstruction (*CIL* 10.833–34), but some can be attributed to the early colonial period (e.g., the compact lava *opus incertum* features of the west *aditus* and rectilinear *cauea* terracing wall).[165] In its original phase, the seating area adapted to the natural topography, wrapping the sloping terrain west of Via Stabiana, and faced a detached stage (none of which remains). Elements of the original freestanding structure, in dressed Nocera Tuff ashlars, were possibly reused in later walls (e.g., the keystone with sculpted female head placed over the west *aditus*). Excavations by Maiuri exposed parts of the oblique retaining wall (*analemma*) of the early *cauea*, which consisted of Sarno Limestone rubble of quite large dimensions mixed with compact lava in lime mortar, with buttresses capped by Sarno Limestone blocks.[166]

The Foro Triangolare was refurbished sometime after the construction of the Theater. The Samnite Palaestra (VIII.7.29) and the Quadriporticus (VIII.7.16) were also built in short succession. Some scholars have assumed for these structures a functional coherence focusing on the athletic and military activities of the Pompeian youth association (*uereiia*), thus including the Republican Baths (VIII.5.36) as part of the complex.[167] Recent fieldwork has clarified the sequence of construction of the individual buildings, which appear separated by streets and located at different levels, suggesting that urban development progressed in a piecemeal fashion and was not the result of a coordinated plan.[168] Comparable building techniques are attested across the various monuments. The shallow *opus incertum* boundary wall delimiting the open area of the Foro Triangolare on the east side (a *xystus*?) has been dated to around 130 BCE on the basis of stratified materials,[169] thus providing a close *terminus post quem* for both the Quadriporticus and the Samnite Palaestra. The

---

[163] On the typology of the towers, whose variants seem based on location and military function rather than chronology, see Van der Graaff 2019: 73–78.

[164] Richardson 1988: 85–90 (first half of the 2nd century BCE); Sear 2006: 49–50 (2nd century BCE). For the regional phenomenon, see Lauter 1976.

[165] Fincker *et al.* 2018.

[166] Maiuri 1973: 183–89, figs. 104, 106–07.

[167] Avagliano 2013 (with earlier bibliography).

[168] Trümper 2018.

[169] Carafa 2011: 95–98; Osanna 2017: 82–83. The date of the Doric portico remains problematic.

chronology corresponds well with the content of the *uereiia* inscription associated with the Palestra, which contains a formula that reflects Roman legislation passed in 123 BCE.[170]

The first phase of the Quadriporticus, a large peristyle courtyard with associated terracing structures that connected the area of the Theater with the Foro Triangolare above, featured mixed techniques.[171] A series of voussoir arches, one of which survives embedded in the exterior façade of the north side, supported the monumental staircase that provided access to the sanctuary from below. At an intermediate level is a retaining wall made of Sarno Limestone rubble that lies farther down the slope along the west side. Parallel to it, at ground level, is a thick concrete wall built with Sarno Limestone rubble and Nocera Tuff corner blocks (perhaps recycled from earlier structures). This structure continues to the southwest, where it consists entirely of *opus incertum* of locally quarried compact lava rubble;[172] the masonry featured Sarno Limestone ashlar quoins. Remains of the original back walls have been identified on all sides, and the position of the stylobate seems to have been maintained throughout the subsequent changes. Other traces suggest that the complex had rooms on at least three sides from the very beginning, whereas the organization of the entrance cannot be determined due to the modifications caused by the construction of the Odeum after 80 BCE. Because of its plan, the possible lack of controlled access, and the absence of bathing facilities, use of the original complex as a *palaestra* or gymnasium seems highly unlikely, while its function as *porticus post scaenam* at this stage would be much earlier than any other known case. The presence of small rooms in the porticoes points toward a variety of purposes (e.g. storage, production, retail, dining, or lodging), which would make sense given the proximity of the building to both sanctuaries and entertainment facilities.[173]

First excavated by Maiuri, who correctly identified them as a Roman-style complex with separate sections for men and women that later had been incorporated into a private property (Casa della Calce, VIII.5.28), the so-called Republican Baths may represent the earliest building from this group. Initially described as public and linked with the Samnite Palaestra,[174] the baths have been reinterpreted as a for-profit private installation as a result of new excavations.[175] The first phase can be dated within the second half of the 2nd century BCE. The complex was developed in a lot that was previously

[170]  Vetter 1953.11. On the dating of the inscription, see McDonald 2012: 12. On the connection between the inscription and the building phases, see Trümper 2018: 91–93.

[171]  Poehler and Ellis 2011: 4–5; 2012: 5–6; 2013; 2014.

[172]  On the quarrying of lava deposits in the south of Pompeii, before and after the construction of the Quadriporticus, see Poehler 2017: 42–43.

[173]  As noted by Trümper 2018: 94–95.

[174]  Pesando 2002–03 (late 2nd century BCE).

[175]  For a first synthesis of the findings, see Trümper 2018: 97–103.

occupied by sparse industrial installations, arranged around a Sarno Limestone ashlar well. This was repurposed to serve the baths, rebuilding it in lava *opus incertum* to feed a reservoir placed on top of an adjoining vaulted room. Both the water management system and the heating technology, which consisted of six arched firing chambers (Plate VI.B), appear less developed than those attested in the Stabian Baths, pointing to the earlier date of the Republican Baths. Significant examples of the same "earth mortar" technique, however, have been detected.[176] A series of structural modifications and updates can be assigned to the first half of the 1st century BCE. In addition to the redecoration of several rooms and features, the baths were modernized by reconfiguring both the reservoir and the *praefurnium*, and a *laconicum* was also added, for which mixed rubble materials were employed.

## TECHNOLOGY AND SOCIOECONOMIC STATUS: THE INNOVATION OF CONCRETE CONSTRUCTION IN POMPEII

Whereas its large-scale implementation in public building can be verified only in contexts dating from around 130–120 BCE onwards, concrete construction is well documented in the private sphere by the middle of the 2nd century BCE. Self-aggrandizement and self-presentation through investment in lavish domestic architecture, therefore, can be identified as the pulling forces behind the introduction of the new building medium and technique. Stark variation in house size represents a clear index of social stratification for this period, while the diffusion of Hellenized stylistic features in their ornamentation demonstrates intense competition and status display within the upper strata.[177] Oscan stamps naming families of probable Pompeian origins on *dolia* and Greco-Italic amphorae testify to the economic interests of landed elites in both regional and international trade during the 2nd century BCE.[178] In fact, the simultaneous spread of *tabernae* within the built environment of Pompeii reflects the increasing viability of agriculture as a form of investment for the aristocracy.[179] Closely intertwined with the expansion of the urban population, which is demonstrated by the development of neighborhoods that had remained unoccupied for over a century, as well as with the increasing demand for food and goods that this brought about, the retail revolution generated part of the profits that were spent on private building projects.

   The Nocera Tuff façades of the earliest concrete houses, whose planning and construction show in other respects little care for internal arrangement of the

---

[176] M. Trümper (personal communication, June 2020).
[177] Dickmann 1997.
[178] Nonnis 1999: 81–83; Nonnis 2015: 558–60 with table II.6; Panella 2010: 49. For a list of traders of possible Pompeian origins at Delos, see also Castrén 1975: 39, n. 6.
[179] Ellis 2018: 129–49.

city blocks in the previous periods, may be interpreted as one of the few communal acts of urban renewal that were achieved within the third quarter of the 2nd century BCE. The spatial distribution of these ashlar structures suggests that they also had the effect of embellishing the main urban axes leading to and from the forum (i.e., Via dell'Abbondanza, Via Stabiana, and Via della Fortuna), and thus the city as a whole.[180] The main public monuments that can be safely assigned to this first phase are concentrated in the Theater's neighborhood but were not part of a single functional ensemble. Although the podium of the Temple of Apollo and the site of the Temple of Jupiter had received prior attention, the monumentalization of the forum area as a whole probably took off only with the turn into the 1st century BCE. Previous reconstructions assumed a much more gradual development of the urban core throughout the second half of the 2nd century BCE, but nevertheless interpreted the evidence as yet another indication that private interests prevailed over public ones until relatively late in the Samnite period.[181] It would be tempting to see in the appearance of building types such as the baths, the theater, and the *quadriporticus* the same powerful process of acculturation that brought about the new forms of domestic architecture. Reference to the local version of the *probatio* in the Oscan epigraphic dossier implies that private builders were hired as contractors, thus providing the link between public building and private entrepreneurship, and, more importantly, identifying the mechanism for the technological transmission from domestic architecture to the public building industry.

The scale of private construction in Pompeii can be appreciated in greater detail than in Rome. The many projects progressing in parallel in the early phase of urban development determined the economic need for versatile building methods that would make extensive use of rubble for the less visible parts (foundations and interior walls), thus offsetting the costs of the imported Nocera Tuff exploited for the decorative elements. The area of *Stabiae*, in the Lattari mountain ridge (at a distance of 5 km from Pompeii by sea, or 15 km by land), was the closest source of limestone for producing lime and provided access to deposits of Campanian Ignimbrite for ashlar construction (Sorrento Tuff), in addition to woods that grew on the low-mid slopes (e.g., evergreen oak). Other limestone deposits were located farther away (15–25 km), to the east of Sarno and Nocera, at the interface with the region from which other varieties of tuff were sourced, and closer to the higher elevations of the central Apennine Mountains where alpine fir (for timber) and beech (mostly for fuel) grew (see Figure 5.1). The spike in lime production can be interpreted as closely intertwined with shifts in the trade of both dimension stones and timber

[180] As noted by Wallace-Hadrill 2013: 41.
[181] E.g., Zanker 1998.

for building purposes and wood fuel supply. Charcoal assemblages recovered from the construction fills for 2nd century BCE houses suggest that the peak in building activities put strong pressure on natural wood resources, bringing about the need for woodland management.[182]

Volcanic sands and clays derived from the weathering of the volcanic deposits of Vesuvius near the site included large amounts of nonreactive materials, so they required extensive processing to become suitable for hydraulic mortars.[183] Well-sorted pozzolana was available from the ashfalls distributed among the carbonate formations,[184] but there is no evidence of its quarrying in the late Samnite period. Scientific evidence on the use of hydraulic mortars in the early period comes from domestic architecture only, although the use of volcanic ash is also reported from macroscopic observation for public monuments. In any case, previous experience with other types of hydraulic binders would have been instrumental in implementing the new technique: Crushed volcanic material was already used as a substitute for terracotta in floor surfaces of the so-called *lavapesta* type.[185] Observation of the physical properties of *lavapesta*, which can be compared to those of *cocciopesto*, could easily have provided local builders with the empirical knowledge to switch from clay-based to pozzolanic mortars, allowing them to make extensive use of rubble (including recycled and waste material) also in load-bearing elements.

In terms of building technique, some interesting common features indicate the sharing of common building practices in both public and private contexts. The builders selected different building materials for different structural purposes, demonstrating an empirical knowledge of the local geology. Lighter Sarno Limestone rubble could be obtained in part by recycling blocks (as implied by the extensive dismantling of earlier features that stood in the redeveloped plots), but also as a by-product of ashlar quarrying, which continued well into the 2nd century BCE to provide elements for late *opus quadratum* façades and limestone-framework construction. The extraction of compact lava, on the other hand, had to be newly organized, since the material was never used intensively in the previous period. Covered by a thick sequence of Pappamonte and scoriaceous lava elsewhere at the site,[186] compact lava layers were directly accessible on the slopes of both the Western plateau and

---

[182] See especially Veal 2018, pointing out that wood that grew on the low-mid slopes, such as oak, would also have grown on Mount Vesuvius and the Sarno plain, but in competition with other cash crops (grapevines and cultivated trees for fruits and nuts).

[183] Piovesan *et al.* 2009: 76–77.

[184] Kastenmeier *et al.* 2010 identifies four deposits of ashfalls predating the 79 CE eruption on top of the older Campanian Ignimbrite: Codola, Pomici di Base-Sarno, Mercato-Ottaviano, Avellino (these are mainly from the explosive activity of the Somma-Vesuvius).

[185] Dunbabin 1999: 33; Piovesan *et al.* 2009.

[186] See Nicotera 1950: 406–16.

the eastern Stabian Ridge across the Via Stabiana valley.[187] Quarry faces and fractures on parallel ridges have been identified through a combination of excavation and geophysical survey in the south of Regions VIII and I.[188] The construction of the Quadriporticus provides a date for the end of the active exploitation of the western sector of the exposed bedrock by 130 BCE (if not earlier), and probably for the subsequent shift of the extraction activities farther to the east, where occupation lagged until late in the 1st century BCE. This evidence suggests that the introduction of compact lava rubble for building purposes preceded the large-scale adoption of the same material for road paving, which is commonly placed in the late 2nd or very early 1st century BCE.[189] The pattern, therefore, confirms that the transition to the new construction method would have not been possible without a considerable investment of resources, bolstering the view that the innovation happened at the high level of society.

## POMPEIAN CONCRETE CONSTRUCTION IN ITS REGIONAL CONTEXT

The discovery of such simultaneous and convergent developments at Rome and Pompeii brings us back to our starting point, raising the question of whether direct Roman influence lies behind the introduction of concrete to Campania. The issue can now be tackled in a more pragmatic fashion, challenging past ideas that saw the refinement of the technology, its large-scale application, and the rationalization of the building process as advances brought about by Roman presence in the region. Roman builders were hardly ever involved in the construction of the aristocratic concrete houses of Pre-Roman Pompeii. The design of the Casa di Pansa, one of the key sites for the dating of the early development of the technique, was based on the Oscan foot,[190] thereby suggesting that local specialists were in charge. Although it is possible that Pompeian masons learned of the new technique as this was being introduced at Rome, it is unlikely that they were adopting it so as to imitate the way of doing things seen in Rome's aristocratic residences. The fact that important features of the earliest concrete houses at Rome (e.g., the use of *opus quadratum*

---

[187] On the underlying geology and morphology of this sector of town, see Holappa and Viitanen 2011.

[188] Poehler 2017: 42–44.

[189] Poehler and Crowther 2018: 588–91 (Phase 1: 100–20 BCE). For the Oscan inscriptions referring to road making in the *suburbium* of Pompeii, see Vetter 1953.8 (mentioning the *Vía Stafiiana*/Via Stabiana, the *Vía Púmpaiiana*/Via Pompeiana, the *Vía Iuviia*/Via Iovia, and the *dekkviarim* [acc.]/Decuvia[?]); nos. 9–10 (*terminatio* of the *Vía Saŕínu*). Mogetta 2016: 69 links the generalized raising of floor levels inside the houses with the first phase of road paving within the urban area, suggesting an earlier date in the 2nd century BCE for the project, which would make compact lava rubble as a by-product of the quarrying of slabs.

[190] Peterse 1985.

on top of the mortared rubble foundations, even for interior partitions) do not appear in the Pompeian examples undermines ideas of diffusion centered on the metropolis. On the contrary, it has often been remarked how the local architects and builders working for the wealthy Samnite patrons who commissioned the new houses produced quite an original class of monuments. The reason for this has been sought in the greater degree of political and ideological "freedom" that the Pompeian elites enjoyed in the reception and display of Hellenistic luxury than their Roman counterparts had.[191] According to this perspective, it was away from the metropolis, in their villas on the Bay of Naples, that Roman senators could embrace those models on a grander scale.[192] It is indeed plausible that Romans themselves developed their technology by experimenting with the highly reactive materials available in the area in this context, but the possibility that they could have relied on local knowledge should not be excluded a priori.

To reach firmer conclusions on the tempo, dynamics, and direction of the technological transfer of concrete technology, a broader survey of contemporary architecture from primary urban centers of Campania is required. Moving from nearby contexts in the Vesuvian area and the Campi Phlegraei to important centers farther to the north and closer to the Roccamonfina volcano, I focus especially on those sites for which a pattern of early interaction with the expanding Roman Republic is attested (see Appendix 4 with Figure 1.1 for location; for Puteoli and other Roman colonial sites in the region, see Chapter 6).

Herculaneum is the only major site in the region whose sample of domestic architecture is on a par with that of Pompeii, at least in quantitative terms. Qualitatively, however, the limited extent of excavation below the 79 CE levels means that house construction of the Samnite period cannot be studied with the same high level of resolution, even if the structures are generally better preserved than in Pompeii. Furthermore, none of the known public buildings predates the Augustan period,[193] thus precluding a comparative analysis. The local geology presents some notable differences with that of Pompeii, influencing the development of building techniques.[194] The site is located on the southwest slopes of Vesuvius, but far away from any sources of limestone other than pebbles from coastal sands and gravels, which probably accounts for the complete absence of the limestone-framework technique (though a system of alternating tuff uprights and stretchers is used for quoins). In addition to scoriaceous and compact lavas, the sequence of volcanic deposits features a welded reddish-brown tuff (the so-called Tufo Rossiccio), which was better

[191] Zanker 1998: 32–43.
[192] Zarmakoupi 2014.
[193] Monteix 2010: 245–49.
[194] Ganschow 1989: 23–27.

suited for ashlar construction than the Pompeian Pappamonte. It was also utilized in the form of rubble.

Based on the building materials, the aspect of the exterior surface (i.e., shape and size of facing blocks; thickness and regularity of joints; general composition of the mortar), and the vertical stratigraphy of standing structures, four main variants of concrete construction have been identified for the pre-Roman period at Herculaneum.[195] Type A is composed of large fragments of lava (up to 0.30 m). The surface of the facing blocks is unfinished, so that a thick plaster rendering was applied to regularize the exterior of the wall. Frequent pebbles are included in the lime mortar mix, indicating a low degree of selection of the sands used for the mortar. By contrast, Type B is made with slightly smaller fragments (0.10–0.25 m) featuring at least a flat face (but the joints are irregular; the mortar is often coarse and includes lumps of lime). Type C features large facing pieces of Tufo Rossiccio and Yellow Neapolitan Tuff, a material that outcropped in the Campi Phlegraei (see Figure 5.1). These techniques should be described as forms of cemented rubble. Types A and B can be found in association with ashlar masonry (e.g., Casa del Rilievo di Telefo; Casa della Gemma, I.2–3, 1; Casa di M. Pilus Primigenius Graianus, I.2–3, 1a), but not with *opus reticulatum*. Type A walls are significantly less frequent than structures built with Type B, but it is not known whether the distribution is determined by structural function. Finally, *opus incertum* of Tufo Rossiccio rubble is normally used for façades, but also for foundations and lower portions of interior walls whose upper part features predominantly scoria rubble (e.g., in the Casa del Mobilio Carbonizzato, V.5).[196] The system is clearly based on the grading of building materials, and finds a parallel in the construction method attested in the earliest concrete houses of Pompeii, where Tufo Rossiccio is substituted for with compact lava, and Sarno Limestone is used instead of scoria.

Despite the close Pompeian parallels, there are no fixed points for the dating of the techniques documented in the domestic architecture at Herculaneum. In the core areas of some atrium houses, *opus incertum* is associated with First Style paintings (e.g., Casa della Fullonica, IV. 5–7; Casa del Sacello di Legno, V.31; Casa del Mobilio Carbonizzato, V.5), but the chronology is uncertain, and, as in most cases, only a terminus *ante quem* of 80 BCE can be tentatively provided.[197] The group of houses in the so-called *Insula Orientalis* I, in which a combination of *opus quadratum* and types A and B is recorded, are among the

---

[195] Ganschow 1989: 37–41; Monteix 2010: 226–29. These studies do not provide specific information on the composition and development of lime-based mortars. Ganschow 1989: 30 points out that extensive restorations and mortar repointing would make mortar analysis misleading.

[196] Frequency table in Ganschow 1989: 110–19.

[197] Ganschow 1989: 103; 108–09, table 6; Monteix 2010: 250, fig. 119.

earliest to encroach upon the fortification walls. Ganschow suggests a date in
the early 1st century BCE, because some of the ashlar blocks used for the *opus
quadratum* walls and for the quoins of the *opus incertum* structures were spolia
from the fortifications.[198] The transition to Tufo Rossiccio and Yellow
Neapolitan Tuff rubble, which would have replaced the more intractable
lava for faster processing, has been interpreted as a sign of Roman influence,
following the settlement of Romans from the Bay of Naples after the Social
Wars.[199] If so, however, the pattern would be different from that observed in
Pompeii, where the monuments of the colonial period (e.g., Amphitheater;
Odeum; Forum Baths) feature only local materials.

The Terme Centrali at Cumae are often cited among the earliest concrete
monuments known from the Campi Phlegraei.[200] The layout of the building can
be reconstructed with some difficulties due to modern truncation of the façade and
the limited extent of the excavations (Figures 5.12–13).[201] Its core consists of six
rooms arranged around an oblong rectangular chamber whose walls feature a series
of niches lined with *cocciopesto* (Room A, probably an *apodyterium/tepidarium*). Built
with tuff *opus quadratum* (Yellow Neapolitan Tuff) on top of cemented-rubble
foundations, this central space is covered by a barrel vault whose intrados is made
with smaller oblong blocks laid radially with little lime-based mortar.[202] The span
is on a par with the largest Pompeian examples (*c.* 7 m). On the back wall, the area
between the impost and the intrados is filled by an *opus incertum* panel; the recess
below it, framed with *opus quasi reticulatum* masonry, belongs to a later phase, when
a basin was inserted into the ashlar masonry. Communicating with Room A and
built with the same technique are two smaller rooms (Rooms B, of uncertain
function, and D, occupied by a pool), separated by a vestibule (Room C). On the
east short side is a large vaulted cistern (Room E). Adjacent to this is a service room
of uncertain function, perhaps also related to water supply. Another vaulted room
(possibly a *tepidarium* or *caldarium*) extended south of Room A. It is delimited to the
east by a narrow corridor in *opus incertum*, whose initial stretch is covered with flat
slabs (Room G). The complex continued to the north, east, and south, but those
spaces have not been explored. The location and type of the heating technology is
unknown, and so is the specific arrangement of the heated rooms. Thus, it remains
difficult to specify the place of the monument in the developmental sequence of
Hellenistic to Roman-style baths.

The construction fills of the first phase of the baths are not preserved, because
the floor levels inside the complex were subsequently lowered. In Room A, the

---

[198] Ganschow 1989: 98.

[199] Ganschow 1989: 120–22.

[200] Johannowsky 1976: 270. The building is also known in the literature as the "Sepolcro della
Sibilla."

[201] Volpicella 2006–07.

[202] For other local examples of barrel vaults made with tuff voussoirs, see Munzi 2019 (north
necropolis at Cumae; 2nd–1st century BCE).

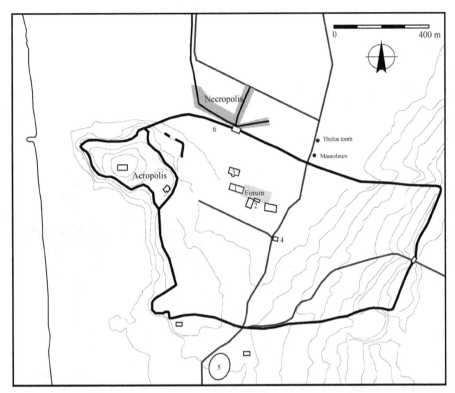

Figure 5.12 Schematic map of Cumae showing the location of relevant sites. Compiled from data in Brun and Munzi 2010. Key: 1=Capitolium; 2=Temple-portico complex; 3=Forum Baths; 4=Terme Centrali; 5=Amphitheater; 6=Stadium. Drawing: M. Harder.

original pavements were removed, and a new surface was created about 0.75 m lower, perhaps by dismantling a system of *suspensurae*, or by digging down into the bedrock, thus exposing part of the concrete foundations.[203] As a result of this process, the niches came to stand at a height of 2 m from the new pavement; having lost their original function, they were closed off with cemented rubble. In the absence of stratigraphic data, and because of the incompleteness of the plan and design, the evidence to date the remains is scanty. A fragmentary Oscan inscription on a marble *labrum*, which records its purchase by the *meddix* of the local *uereiia*, Mamercus Heius, was found in the fill of Room A.[204] The basin stood originally on a base placed outside the main building, on top of a marble pavement that was in turn supported by subterranean structures in *opus reticulatum*, thus making its relevance to the first phase of the baths dubious. Nevertheless, the inscription has been taken to provide a *terminus ante quem* of 180 BCE for the construction of the monument.

---

[203] Volpicella 2006–07: 218, n. 18.
[204] Sgobbo 1977: 256–57 pl. X–XI; Volpicella 2006–07: 213–14, fig. 15.

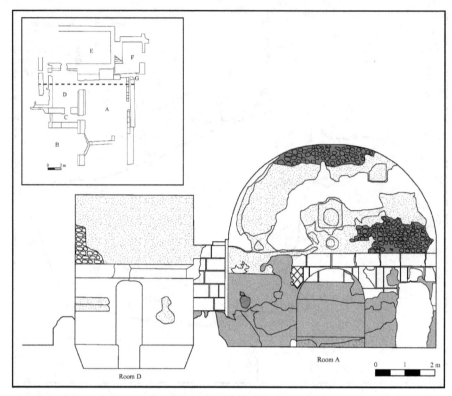

Figure 5.13 Cumae. Terme Centrali, *c.* 150 BCE (?). Cross section and elevation drawing of the back wall of Room A (*apodyterium*?) and Room D. Note the *opus incertum* features associated with the original phase as reconstructed by Volpicella 2006–07 (in dark grey on top of the *opus quadratum* remains; later restorations in light gray). Drawing: M. Harder.

The date is based on the testimony of Livy (40.43.1), who records for that year a Cumaean petition asking the Senate to grant the use of Latin instead of Oscan for the conduction of official business (Livy's text refers specifically to *praecones*, i.e., heralds, so it applies mainly to public speaking).[205] In this period Cumae was already integrated into the Roman political system: The Cumaeans were granted *ciuitas sine suffragio* in 334 BCE (Livy 8.14.11), and since 210 BCE had been placed under the jurisdiction of elected Roman magistrates (the *praefecti Capuam Cumas*).[206] The rationale for the request, therefore, might have been

---

[205]   Another idea is that Greek had lingered alongside Oscan, and Latin was formally introduced to replace it. See Adams 2003: 113–14 (on Italians presenting themselves as Latin- rather than Greek-speakers at Delos).

[206]   On the *praefectura Capuam Cumas*, see especially Bispham 2007: 95–100 (with Festus, *Gloss. Lat.* 262). The Campanian praefecture included cities that had lost autonomy (Capua, Casilinum, Atella, Calatia, and perhaps Suessula) as a consequence of their defection during the Hannibalic war (Liv., 26.16.7–8) but also towns with municipal status (Cumae, Acerra), so it could either substitute or coexist with municipal structures. The *praefecti* acted as channels of communication with Rome and served the interests of Roman citizens.

offered by the increased activities of Romans in the area.[207] Oscan, however, continued to be used into the later 2nd and 1st centuries BCE, as attested by epitaphs, religious dedications, and curse tablets (though none of these are state documents).[208] The rich funerary evidence dating to that period demonstrates the strong presence of both Oscan names and burial customs.[209]

Recent extensive excavations in the monumental core of the lower town revealed that the spread of concrete construction was a relatively late phenomenon. Most of the known features in the area of the Forum have wall facings in *opus quasi reticulatum* or *reticulatum*. These structures, which modified radically a preexisting phase in *opus quadratum*, have been dated to the middle of the 1st century BCE.[210] The earliest concrete monuments in the north necropolis belong to the same period.[211] A late 2nd or early 1st century BCE date has been proposed for the amphitheater (*opus quasi reticulatum*).[212] By contrast, *opus incertum* is rarely attested. In the Stadium, a massive ashlar stepped structure built on top of an earthen embankment abutting the north stretch of the fortifications, the technique is used to erect a platform that modified the original layout of the *cauea*.[213] The structure consisted of two superimposed concrete boxes, which probably served as a formal stage to host the panel of judges and award ceremonies. A block with an Oscan inscription recording the dedication of a statue by another *meddix* of the *uereiia* was found in secondary deposition on the lower podium.[214] Ceramic materials from the fills suggest a date between the second half of the 2nd century BCE and the early 1st century BCE, while the style of the podium moldings would fit with a date in the final decades of the 2nd century BCE.[215] In light of the general pattern at the site, it seems reasonable to assign the Terme Centrali to the middle/second half of the 2nd century BCE, based on the mixed technique and the connection with the youth corporation, whose role and visibility continued throughout the period.[216]

---

[207] D'Arms 1970: 17. Velleius Paterculus (2.4.44) reports on the presence of 20,000 Roman viritane settlers in Campania in the post-Hannibalic period.

[208] See Lomas 1993: 172–73. For other 2nd century BCE Oscan inscriptions referring to public building, see Sgobbo 1977: 249, pl. IX; Poccetti 1981: 96–97, no. 133 (construction of the floor of the Forum temple by a Minius Heius, son of Pacius, *meddix* of the *uereiia*; Petacco and Rescigno [2007: 80–81; 99] date the podium to the first half of the 2nd century BCE); Poccetti 1981: 95–96, no. 132 (gift to Jupiter Flagius; 2nd century BCE).

[209] Munzi 2019.

[210] Gasparri 2009; Gasparri 2010: 585–95. For an overview of the building techniques in the post-Sullan phase, see Covolan 2017.

[211] Brun and Munzi 2011: 155–62.

[212] Caputo 1993.

[213] Giglio 2010: 621–26.

[214] Camodeca 2012 (second half of 2nd century BCE).

[215] Giglio 2015: 82–83.

[216] Avagliano and Montalbano 2018: 78–79.

Textual evidence from Capua confirms the generalized burst in construction activities in the region during the late 2nd century BCE. An important corpus of twenty-eight inscriptions, known as the records of the Campanian *magistri*, details the activities of annual boards of local officers who were related to various local sanctuaries. These documents provide a vivid picture of the social context of construction in a major town of Campania in the late 2nd and early 1st century BCE. Although their date does not make them immediately relevant to our discussion of early concrete construction, the texts give us an idea of how the administration of public building may have functioned in Pompeii in the last decades of the Samnite period.[217] Almost all of the Capuan inscriptions can be dated in the 112–71 BCE period, with the exception of a few whose chronology cannot be specified. In the majority of the cases, the texts explicitly record the construction of buildings of various function; these inscriptions were clearly intended to be placed on the monuments to which they referred (as indicated by the use of expressions such as *hoc opus*), or in any case to stand in their proximity. For this reason, it is probable that those inscriptions in which the actual nature of the work undertaken is not preserved also relate to some sort of building activities. Several examples describe the construction activities in generic terms: unspecified walls (*muri*), parapets (*plutei*), foundations (*pilae*), although in some cases measurements are also provided.

A subset of five inscriptions provide more specific details about the erection of the *t(h)eatrum*. These texts inform us on the sequence of the works, and indirectly on their duration.[218] This building project was started in 108 BCE, when the *magistri* of Jupiter let the contract for the earthen embankment supporting the *cauea*. Activities continued in 105 BCE under the supervision of the *magistri* of Castor and Pollux and of Mercurius, with the construction of vaulted substructures (*fornices*), presumably for an expansion of the seating area (*gradus*). Other blocks of seats (*cunei*) were added in three separate installments before 94 BCE, when the theater is mentioned in another inscription as already functioning. Other works in the urban core followed at an undiminished pace in the early decades of the 1st century BCE: pavements and weights in 98 BCE; gardens and a portico of uncertain date; a second portico in 94 BCE; a monumental fountain in 84 BCE.

Outside the urban area, considerable extensions were made to the sanctuary of Diana Tifatina. In 108 BCE the temple was completely rebuilt, adding a new decorated floor (which features a mosaic inscription recording the event) and columns.[219] Recent excavations in the cella revealed that the ashlar podium of the original temple had at some stage been extended on its eastern (back) side,

---

[217] Frederiksen 1959: 126–30.
[218] Frederiksen 1959: nos. 6, 10, 14–16.
[219] Pobjoy 1997: 85–88. Cf. Frederiksen 1959: no. 19 (74 BCE)

by means of retaining walls described as faced with *opus incertum*.[220] Although no direct stratigraphic relationship has been as yet documented between the floor and the concrete walls, it is likely that both features belong to the same construction phase. In 99 BCE other *magistri* were involved in the reconstruction of the western terracing wall, where the monumental access was probably located (the inscription mentions the building of a *murum ab gradu ad chalcidicum*, of the *chalcidicum* itself, and of a *porticus*). The remains on this side have been variously described as *opus incertum* or *opus reticulatum*, probably reflecting multiple construction phases. Embedded in this wall is an inscription recording the benefaction of Ser. Fulvius Flaccus (cos. 135 BCE), who let the contract to build a *murus* using spoils (*de manubeis*: *CIL* 12.635).[221] On the east side, the boundary wall is in *opus reticulatum* with bands of brickwork, but it sits on top of an ashlar foundation.[222]

In addition to the monuments known from epigraphy, other structures demonstrate the spike in public works at Capua in this phase. The area of the forum was thoroughly reorganized, creating a new terrace supported by vaulted substructures.[223] The radial concrete foundations of a preexisting amphitheater have been discovered not far from the Flavian Amphitheater (Anfiteatro Campano).[224] The west stretch of the fortifications received substantial repairs too, perhaps in the period between 91 and 83 BCE.[225] To pay for these construction projects, the *magistri* exploited heavily the treasuries of the sanctuaries they oversaw. Some inscriptions, however, make clear that they could dispose also of secular money (for instance, the fountain erected in 84 BCE was partly paid from the treasury of Jupiter, partly from funds of the *magistri* themselves). What Frederiksen has rightly pointed out in his analysis of the dossier is that, despite a certain measure of direct control by Rome and the absence of a formal municipal constitution,[226] the elaborate monumentalization schemes undertaken by the *magistri* demonstrate that local affairs were characterized by a striking level of emancipation.

The sites of north Campania seem to provide the earliest available evidence from the wider region. The best researched case is that of Teanum, an allied town located on the southeast slopes of the Roccamonfina volcano, at a short distance from the Latin colony of Cales. A series of concrete features has been identified in a pluristratified sanctuary complex on a hilltop near the north gate,

---

[220] Melillo Faenza 2012: 201–04, fig. 3.

[221] Johannowsky 1989: 67.

[222] De Franciscis 1956: 338, n. 8. For a general reconstruction of the sanctuary in the late 2nd century BCE, see Quilici Gigli 2009.

[223] Quilici Gigli 2008.

[224] Sampaolo 2010: 78–81.

[225] Sampaolo 2010: 73–78. Large fragments of architectural spolia were used as aggregate in the concrete.

[226] For the discussion of the *praefecti Capuam Cumas*, see *supra*, n. 206.

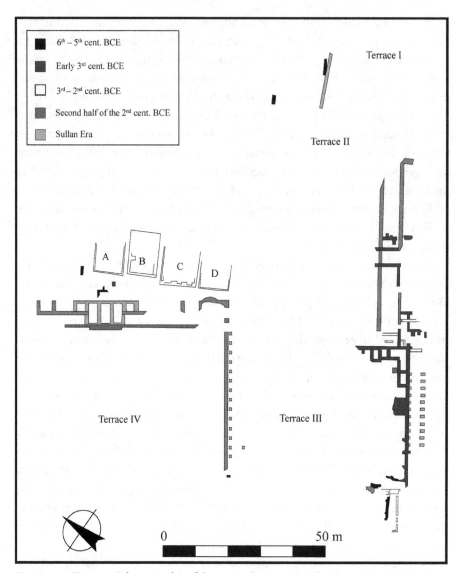

Figure 5.14  Teanum. Schematic plan of the terraced sanctuary at the Masseria Loreto site (Juno Pupluna?) as reconstructed by Johannowsky (1963). Drawing: M. Harder.

within the lower urban area (Masseria Loreto; Figure 5.14).[227] The sanctuary was first established in the Archaic period and further developed in the Hellenistic period on a series of terraces (I–III) delimited by tuff ashlar walls, and included a series of precincts, altars, and small temples (Temple C: second half of the 3rd century BCE?; others are known from geophysical survey).[228] Three small podium temples were subsequently built next to Temple C in

[227] Johannowsky 1963: 131–42; Sirano 2007; Sirano 2013: 103–07.
[228] Sirano 2017: 85–89.

relatively short succession: Temples D (in *opus quadratum*); A (with podium foundation and cornice in *opus quadratum*, and clay-based mortared-rubble core); and B (in *opus incertum* of large tuff pieces laid in reddish mortar, lined with tuff ashlars).[229] Their fronts measure 9.15 m in width (Temple B, the only one for which full dimensions are known, is 13.10 m long, including the frontal staircase). At this stage, terrace II was expanded with an annex built with cemented tuff rubble resembling *opus uittatum*.[230] A fourth terrace (IV) was also created, changing the main orientation of the complex. The perimetral walls of terrace IV feature the same technique as the terrace II extension, but the front includes vaulted substructures made with a type of *opus incertum* characterized by nestled facing pieces of small dimensions. The latter masonry style is used for the ramp connecting terraces III and IV.[231]

A new temple building was erected in this intermediate phase at the south edge of terrace III, covering a preexisting ashlar altar with annexed platform, perhaps dedicated to the local goddess Pupluna (Figure 5.15). The podium consists of a cemented rubble box (about 18.50 × 12.50 m, oriented north–south), whose thick walls (1.48 m) adapt to the slope: They are raised from the ground up on the north and west sides, and built into a cut in the bedrock on the south and east sides. The exterior was originally faced with tuff ashlars.[232] This massive foundation ring possibly supported a peristasis, enclosing a deep pronaos and a recessed cella (about 8.50 × 6.50 m) built with cemented rubble of mixed limestone and tuff rubble (0.74 m thick). The overall proportions recall especially the layout of the Temple of Apollo at Pompeii.[233] The occupation levels are not preserved due to postdepositional damage, making it difficult to establish its chronology. The assemblage collected from the construction cut and floor preparations of the cella consists of spoils and votive objects from the previous phase (mostly dating to the 4th–3rd centuries BCE), and therefore provides only a *terminus post quem*.[234] The surviving architectural ornament associated with the podia of Temples A and D may provide a parallel within the first half of the 2nd century BCE, but only on stylistic grounds; comparanda for Temple B point to the middle of the 2nd century BCE.[235] This broad periodization is consistent with coin finds from the construction fills excavated in and around the temple (the latest of which were minted after 211

[229] Johannowsky 1963: 138.
[230] Johannowsky 1963: 140.
[231] Johannowsky 1963: 141–42 ("Sullan"); Sirano 2013: 107 (second half of the 2nd century BCE). Johannowsky 1963: 164, n. 104 compares the vaulting technique to that employed for the Terme Centrali at Cumae.
[232] Sirano 2007: 77, fig. 9. The author suggests that the basic module was based on the Roman foot, but the listed significant measurements give odd proportions.
[233] Sirano 2013: 105, figs. 5–6; Sirano 2015: 211–14.
[234] Sirano 2007: 71–73. For other terracotta decorations associated with temples A–D, see Sirano 2017: 87–88, figs. 7–8.
[235] Sirano 2007: 78 (Temple D on the Arx at Cosa).

Figure 5.15 Teanum, Masseria Loreto site. South edge of Terrace III. View of the concrete foundations of the podium and cella of the Temple of Juno Pupluna (Sirano 2013: 105, fig. 5; used by permission).

BCE).[236] The debris recovered from spoliation trenches around the temple suggests that the superstructure was in *opus incertum* with tuff entablatures and possibly Corinthian or Italo-Corinthian columns, which could push the dating down to the second half of the century.[237]

The continued tradition with concrete construction at Teanum accounts for other important architectural innovations achieved in the Temple-Theater complex, which dates to the end of the 2nd century or early 1st century BCE.[238] This monument provides perhaps the earliest example of a freestanding masonry theater in central Italy. The *cauea* is entirely supported by radial *opus incertum* corridors, spanned by concrete vaults. The stage building, however, is still detached from the *cavea*, and the *parodoi* are oblique, betraying that this was still an adaptation of Greek prototypes (as seen in Pompeii). The axial temple *in summa cauea* sits on an upper terrace, which features similar concrete vaulted substructures. These corridors consist of sections in *opus incertum* and sections in *opus reticulatum* that appear perfectly juxtaposed, so both techniques were utilized simultaneously at this

---

[236] Sirano 2007: 74–75, 91–92 n. 29–35; Johannowsky 1963: 138; 140, fig. 8 for profiles of podium moldings.

[237] Sirano (2007: 79) leaves open the possibility that these fragments belonged to a later reconstruction.

[238] Sirano 2011. For the subsequent penetration of the building type farther inland from Teanum, see the case of the Monte San Nicola sanctuary at Pietravairano: Panariti 2018.

site.[239] Another peculiarity concerns the two L-shaped ramps that connected the *cauea* with the temple terrace. The sections of these corridors are spanned by barrel vaults, so they create a cross vault where they meet.[240] This technical solution does not have any parallels at contemporary Late Republican sanctuaries of Latium, where temple-theater complexes are otherwise common.[241] While the architectural type demonstrates close links with Roman context, such advanced features of the construction method suggest that architectural innovations could develop independently.

## CONCLUSIONS

The analysis of the socioeconomic factors that influenced the early development of concrete architecture in Late Samnite Pompeii helps us make better sense of an archaeological phenomenon that has previously been conceived of as just happening. While early scholars like Lugli and Blake once too simplistically described it as an accident of the local geology, Pompeian concrete technology was the manifestation of deeper cultural developments. The emergence of the new building medium occurred in the middle of the 2nd century BCE, therefore later than previously thought, and with little relation to pre-existing forms of vernacular architecture. The roots can be found in the new social and cultural milieu within the expanded horizons brought about by Rome's imperialism, when participating Samnite elites started to look to other sources of monumental display to express status and cultural identity. Famous houses such as the Casa del Fauno signal the scale of the phenomenon in the private sphere. The adaptation of building types of Greek derivation, such as leisure baths, theaters, and spaces for athletic activities, provides a parallel in the public sphere. Just as in Rome, the system governing public construction accounts for the rapid adoption of the technique from one sphere to the other.[242] The case of the Republican Baths, one of the earliest monuments in the series, demonstrates the blurred boundaries between private initiatives and public architecture.

The trajectory I have sketched for Pompeii fits well with the trends attested at peer sites in Campania, where the spike in public building can be similarly detected in the latter part of the 2nd century BCE, with a few possible earlier

[239] Balasco 2011: 75 attributes this to structural needs.
[240] Balasco 2011: 75 fig. 4.
[241] Coarelli 1987; Rous 2010.
[242] Along similar lines, Leach 2004: 262–64 analyzes the spread of decorative schemes executed by the same workshops in public buildings and houses in Roman Pompeii, asking whether public contracts influenced the taste of private clients or whether the workshop began operating in the private domestic sector first to then make the leap to the public context, and pointing out that the same individuals involved in *publica magnificentia* were also calculating self-promotion through visual culture within the private sphere.

exceptions. Extensive building programs at top-tier sites like Cumae were funded by the local communities and managed by Oscan-speaking ruling classes who had strong connections with the regional trade network. The epigraphic dossier from Capua, albeit in Latin, shows that these projects were often the result of a cumulative process involving magistrates from different leading families. It is conceivable that innovations in Pompeii happened through contacts with both patrons and private entrepreneurs from the major centers, whose craftsmanship has been identified behind architectural developments in previous periods (most notably in the case of decorated roofs), and, therefore, that they were unrelated to Roman presence in the area.

# SIX

# COLONIAL NETWORKS

## ROMAN URBANISM AND ROMAN EXPANSION: REORIENTING THE PERSPECTIVE

The aftermath of the WWII was a groundbreaking phase for the study of early Roman urbanism in Italy. With the reopening of the borders, foreign archaeological missions were allowed to launch new expeditions, which targeted specifically Mid-Republican colonial sites. American and Belgian excavations started almost simultaneously at Cosa (1948) and Alba Fucens (1949). Extensive but less systematic fieldwork by the Italian state archaeological service was resumed at Paestum (1950; 1952).[1] These projects produced discoveries that influenced significantly the next generation of scholars. One of the main expectations by the excavators was that large-scale research at these supposedly pristine Roman towns would finally reveal material evidence of Republican monumental architecture, thus bridging the knowledge gap that had hampered the study of contemporary developments in Rome.[2] For the most part, Republican era monuments in the urban core were known only indirectly through textual sources, their actual remains appearing to be hopelessly masked

---

[1] For early reports, see Brown 1951 (on Cosa); De Visscher and De Ruyt 1951 (on Alba Fucens). Neutsch 1956: 374, and fig. 119 (on the exploration of the forum area at Paestum); Lugli (1957: 457) briefly reports on the results of the 1950 campaigns funded by the Cassa del Mezzogiorno.
[2] For this approach, see especially Brown 1980. Fentress 2000 thoroughly critiques Brown's desire to find Roman prototypes for Cosan archaeological realities. On Alba Fucens: Mertens 1969. MacKendrick 1954 is an important early document for the enthusiastic reception of the new finds.

by the Imperial and later layers of the city. The recovery of entire city plans featuring unusually well-preserved standing remains, which were quickly assigned to the original phase of the colonies, reinforced the notion that Roman imperialism and urbanism were closely linked. In turn, this provided more fuel to the idea that Roman colonies functioned as epicenters for the propagation of newly imported technology and styles from Rome to Italy, especially thanks to the agency of Roman colonists.[3] Scholars pointed to the famous passage in which Aulus Gellius (NA 16.13.9) described colonial settlements as small-scale reproductions (*quasi effigies paruae simulacraque*) of the greatness and majesty of the Roman people. Even though the author's emphasis was on the people and institutions (the context discussed the difference in legal standing and purpose with the *municipia* as it was understood in the Hadrianic period), archaeologists conveniently stretched the meaning so as to apply the replica concept to the physical aspect of the urban layout and public architecture of colonial sites.[4]

Whereas the cultural implications of the Roman conquest of Italy undoubtedly affected architectural production in Rome, the view that Roman models and underlying ideas spread from core to periphery as a result of Roman expansionism has been put to stricter scrutiny, exposing both ancient and modern biases. The deconstructive trends that have characterized the scholarship on Roman colonization in the last two decades have challenged many of the traditional assumptions about the Romanizing outlook of the colonies. The lack of uniformity of material cultural assemblages from colonial contexts has been highlighted for the Mid-Republican phase, most notably in the case of the Capitoline cult, thus undermining the old "statist" model of a formally codified Roman package radiating from the center.[5] A different reading of the epigraphic evidence suggests that the creation of colonial sacred landscapes was primarily the result of local initiatives in response to colonial anxiety or other identity concerns and preoccupations emerging from migration or frontier situations, rather than the direct outcome of Roman imperial strategy.[6] Meanwhile, new systematic fieldwork at the urban level has demonstrated that Mid-Republican colonies literally resembled empty boxes. In their first phase they consisted of massive fortification circuits surrounding largely underdeveloped city blocks, with virtually no evidence of monumental architecture

---

[3] Torelli 1999a. Cf. the discussion in Stek 2018a: 275–78.

[4] On the use and misuse of this passage to describe architectural developments, see Sewell 2014.

[5] See especially Bispham 2006: 78–85; Crawley Quinn and Wilson 2013, also questioning the link between *Capitolia* and colonial status; Bolder-Boos 2019: 110–19.

[6] The famous example of the Latin colony of Ariminum (268 BCE), where Roman place names are associated to the local topography (e.g., Vicus Esquilinus), is discussed by Stek 2018a: 289–90, noting, however, that communal colonial identities were not necessarily focused on Rome itself, and that colonial networks could also be configured around Latin identity. See also Bradley 2006.

other than temples.[7] Similarly, intensive research on the rural settlement in colonial territories has revealed a different form of territorial organization than the conventional model featuring individual farms regularly scattered across the centuriated landscape. The results demonstrate the existence of nucleated, clustered settlement made of village communities (*uici*) that enjoyed relatively autonomous status.[8] In sum, a much more variegated archaeological picture can be sketched for the Mid-Republican colonial enterprises, with significant repercussions for the study of later urban development in Roman Italy.

In light of these important theoretical insights, in this chapter I zoom out to the broader scale of analysis in order to characterize the distribution of building techniques at colonial sites that were either founded or resettled during the period in which cemented-rubble architecture made its first appearance at Rome and Pompeii (for the full list of sites see Appendix 5; see Figure 1.1 for the location). My overall objective in charting the early spread of lime-based structural mortar across these sites is not to reproduce the old diffusionist perspective, but to shift focus to how local sociopolitical institutions managed construction projects beyond the initial layout.

## BACKGROUND: THE MAKING OF MID-REPUBLICAN COLONIES

Although literary sources reconstruct a phase of Roman colonization during the Early Republic, the Roman practice of founding new towns developed substantially only in the aftermath of the Latin War in the years 338–334 BCE. The revival of the Latin colony, a political institution that originally involved the reorganization of existing settlements rather than the creation of new ones,[9] and whose legal status was strictly determined by geographical area, came with constitutional changes that made it possible to found self-supporting urban centers endowed with Latin rights in distant places.[10] Between 334 (the foundation date of Cales in Campania) and the late 3rd century BCE, twenty-three such sites were established,[11] many of them being constructed ex novo. This marked the beginning of a Roman tradition of town planning distinct from that of building small colonies of military character (*coloniae maritimae*), which lacked political architecture altogether.[12]

The best archaeological evidence for Latin colonies comes from settlements whose deduction falls within a period of two generations after start of the

---

[7] Summary of the evidence in Lackner 2008; Sewell 2010.

[8] Pelgrom 2008; Pelgrom 2014. On the *uici* as rural villages in a colonial network, see Stek 2009; Stek 2014. On the case of Alba Fucens, see Stek 2018b.

[9] Chiabà 2011. Material evidence shows that all known sites where Latin colonies from the 6th to the early 4th centuries BCE are reported were considerably older than the foundation date attributed by literary sources. See Lackner 2008: 232–33, 240; Termeer 2010; Attema *et al.* 2014.

[10] Cornell 1995: 347–52.

[11] Salmon 1969.

[12] Sommella 1988; Von Hesberg 1985.

colonization program. At Fregellae (328 BCE), Alba Fucens (303 BCE), Paestum, and Cosa (both founded in 273 BCE), construction techniques and settlement forms can be studied on the large scale. The topographical analysis reveals shared characteristics in both planning and architecture, which appear partly derived from contemporary Greek norms and partly from Roman, Etruscan, or Italic traditions predating the 4th century BCE.[13] Planners and architects operating in this early phase of Roman colonization were probably drawing from existing solutions to the practical problems they were being confronted with. This accounts for the physical resemblance of the plans, the articulation between constituent parts, and the design of both civic centers (with commercial infrastructure) and urban housing. Other communities in Italy were building fortified settlements with regularized layouts from the second half of the 4th century BCE onwards, reflecting a much broader context for the diffusion of architectural ideas.[14] What makes the Roman case stand out is the specific historical context that prompted the phenomenon. In order to function as nodes of the urban network supporting Rome's imperial agenda, Latin colonies required clearly demarcated public spaces for self-governing, and a system of housing based on a relatively standardized series of designs that would reflect property class, and by extension, materialize the range of social hierarchies operating in colonial contexts.

Stripping away later additions and modifications from the composite archaeological picture of the four better-known colonies, recurring formal features have been detected by comparing and contrasting their layouts.[15] The formal similarities in the relationship between the town's wall and the street grid, the proportions of the city blocks, the forum axiality and organization, and predesigned models for mass housing have been interpreted as evidence of the original plans, leading to the conclusion that shared concepts existed from the outset across these sites. How much of this pattern should be attributed directly to activities of the *tresuiri*, the Roman commissioners who administered colonial settlements, is a debated issue.[16] Polybius (3.40.9–10) and Livy (21.25.3–4) document the presence of commissioners at Placentia during the initial phases of the colonial enterprise in 218 BCE, describing them as being involved in the process of rural land division. Livy makes a reference to the existence or construction of town walls,[17] which may suggest that the *tresuiri*

---

[13] Sewell 2010.

[14] For Etruria: Paoletti 2005. For non-Greek South Italy: Osanna 2009. For a general synthesis, see Sewell 2016.

[15] Lackner 2008; Sewell 2010.

[16] Bispham 2006 (discussing the possible retrofitting of the literary sources); Coarelli 1988; Eckstein 1979; Gargola 1995: 71–87; Sewell 2010: 83–85.

[17] Upon being attacked by the Boii, the commissioners are said by Livy to have fled to Mutina because "they did not feel safe behind the walls" of Placentia. A plausible explanation is that the town's wall was still under construction. Labate *et al.* 2012 take this episode as a fixed point

also had oversight on how the new urban center ought to be planned. An inscription relating to the refoundation of the Latin colony of Aquileia (169 BCE) celebrates one of the commissioners for dedicating an *aedes* and for crafting the colony's political institutions (*legesq[ue] | composiuit deditque*).[18] It is entirely possible that the same Roman magistrate who devised the constitutional framework of the colony could be responsible for the configuring of the built environment in which it operated.[19] If so, the *tresuiri* (or their subordinates) probably came to the site of a future colony with some fixed concepts to define the template for the subsequent physical realization of the town.

Besides fortifications and temples, however, the public architecture of the first phase of the Mid-Republican colonies remains elusive. The case of the Latin *Comitia*, the main colonial assembly places, is the most emblematic. There is a consensus that the circular form attested across the four sites derives from the Curia-Comitium complex in Rome, even though the state of the archaeological data makes it impossible to reconstruct the actual shape of the supposed model.[20] The example at Fregellae, albeit found in poor conditions, has been assigned to the 3rd century BCE by taking as *terminus ante quem* the 2nd century BCE date of what appeared to be its substantial reconstruction.[21] At Alba Fucens, the excavator ascribed the structure to the late 3rd century BCE.[22] The date of the Comitium at Paestum is also disputed. Some considered the building as part of a single project carried out in the first years of the colonies to create the new forum in the sector southwest of the former agora. Both the Comitium and the *tabernae* lining it on the three excavated sides are built with ashlar masonry using the local limestone, which is the same technique that

---

for the chronology of Mutina's fired brick fortifications, with broader implications for the regional typology. See also Bonetto 2015. In his version of the story, Polybius calls Mutina a Roman *apoikia*, though the colony was only established in 183 BCE (Liv., 39.55.5–6; Vell. Pat., 1.15.2). He then refers to another fortified settlement at Vicus Tannetis, where another group of Romans fleeing the Gauls took refuge. Dyson (2014: 33) interprets these sites as part of a Roman line of defense along the southwest border of the Boii (identifies with Livy's Victumulae (21.57), an *emporium* southeast of Parma.

[18] *AE* 1996.685. On the inscription and the context of its dedication, see Zaccaria 2014 (with a date of 130–120 BCE for its composition).

[19] As noted by Sewell 2010: 84.

[20] Sewell 2010: 36–47; 62–63. The introduction of the circular shape in Rome has been variously dated: on or before 338 BCE (Lackner 2008: 260–65); between the 338 and the early 3rd century BCE (Humm 1999: 693); *c.* 318 BCE (Torelli 1999b: 26); *c.* 263 BCE (Coarelli 1998a: 138–39). Based on the analysis of the bedrock levels and the surviving remains, Amici 2004–05 concludes that the conventional major phases for the Republican Comitium and the Curia Hostilia should be rejected, and that the assembly place maintained its wedge shape throughout the period (followed in this by Davies 2017: 11, fig. 1.5; 31, fig. 1.28; 32–33, fig. 1.31; cf. Carafa 1998: 150–51).

[21] Coarelli 1998b: 56–68.

[22] Mertens 1988: 85.

characterizes the fortifications.[23] Stratigraphic finds from the construction layers of the building, however, may point to a slightly later date (second half of the 3rd century BCE).[24] The same can be said for the situation at Cosa (discussed in detail below). The overall pattern clearly indicates that political architecture came last in the monumentalization of colonial urban landscapes. In spite of the heterogeneous nature of the evidence, rows of stone-lined pits or pads attested at Latin colonial fora may betray that the practice of setting up temporary wooden features connected with *templa* and voting was common in the early period.[25]

The apparent paucity of 3rd century BCE domestic architecture in the colonies is equally puzzling. The genesis of both the canonical atrium house and of the more modest "row houses" with their sets of proportions has been linked with such needs arising from the post-338 BCE colonization program.[26] The application of modular designs for the mass construction of housing in newly urbanized contexts would have presented significant advantages, from aiding in effective resource management and financial planning prior to the beginning of building programs, to increasing the stability and structural integrity of city blocks in which houses shared the same load-bearing walls, to easing some of the social tensions that could arise at the time of property distribution, by providing the same predetermined set of building instructions (which in turn ensured that everyone had access to the same amount of building materials). It is also possible that standardized plans resulted from less centralized processes, such as joint or communal efforts organized by neighbors or neighborhoods.[27] At settlements with long-term occupation, the identification of original plot sizes and partitions is difficult due to continued building accompanied by boundary changes. At Paestum, for example, isolated fragments of ashlar architecture dating to the Republican period have been detected under the later remains investigated in the so-called north insula adjacent to the forum area. Only one house could be assigned with some confidence to the late 3rd or early 2nd century BCE, but its plan does not conform to the canonical Roman atrium design.[28] At Fregellae, the oldest

---

[23] Greco and Theodorescu (1987: 70) assign the Comitium to the second quarter of the 3rd century BCE. See also Torelli 1999b: 33.

[24] Brown *et al.* (1993: 253–95) publish the finds from the lowest stratum of a trench excavated by an American team in 1955 along the east side of the building at Paestum (unbeknownst to Greco and Theodorescu 1987).

[25] The state of the evidence and of the debate is thoroughly reviewed by Sewell 2010: 67–79. The pits at Fregellae have been dated to the 3rd century BCE or earlier by Coarelli 1998b: 56–61. At Paestum, stone pads are preserved on the Augustan pavement, but they are orientated on the axes of the 3rd century BCE *tabernae*, and thus may reflect similar arrangements existing in the Republican period. See Sewell 2010: 69.

[26] Sewell 2010: 87–136.

[27] For a model of this kind in the Greek context, see Cahill 2002 (Olynthus).

[28] Bragantini *et al.* 2008: 159–99.

atrium house from the lower habitation stratum has been tentatively dated to the middle of the 3rd century BCE, but the finds have not been fully published.[29] The excavators of Cosa found that the earliest lower-class houses documented were constructed at the end of the 3rd or early 2nd century BCE, suggesting, however, that there would have been predecessors.[30] More recent fieldwork places the atrium houses flanking the forum in the early 2nd century BCE, having recovered no structural evidence for the existence of earlier buildings.[31] The remains of Republican houses at Alba Fucens are also very limited.[32]

Although very small percentages of urban surface areas have been explored systematically, the conclusion seems to be that urban development at Mid-Republican colonies progressed in a piecemeal fashion, the initial focus being on defenses and religious architecture at the expense of political buildings, which initially must have been ephemeral in nature. Adding to the bleak picture, the city blocks were at best sparsely inhabited through most of the 3rd century BCE.[33] The insufficient size of colonial towns in proportion to the number of colonists they are reported or estimated to have received has already been noted, pointing to the fact that the vast majority of settlers resided in the countryside.[34] The absence of urban housing further supports this view, placing the emphasis on the establishment of the colony's rural base, at least for the first generations.

## THE URBAN DEVELOPMENT OF MID-REPUBLICAN COLONIES: NORBA AND FREGELLAE

After the Roman *tresuiri* had provided the formwork for the colonial urban projects, the completion of the plan depended mostly on the availability of

---

[29]  Battaglini and Diosono 2010: 224–25, n. 33 (Domus 7). The date ("not later than the mid-3rd century BCE") is based on the finds recovered from the leveling layers that obliterate the house. The structure was initially assigned by Pesando to either the late 4th century BCE (1999: 245–46) or the first half of the 3rd century BCE (2008: 160).

[30]  Bruno and Scott 1993, 27–30, 59–60.

[31]  Fentress *et al.* 2003.

[32]  Only a Late Republican atrium house has been fully excavated: Balty 1985. Traces of domestic architecture have been brought to light in the area of the forum under the Early Imperial basilica but are too fragmentary for an analysis. See Mertens 1969, 1: 63–65, fig. 11; Liberatore 2004: 136–38.

[33]  A picture of this kind is sketched by Crawford 2006 for Paestum.

[34]  Based on a notional population density of 120 persons per ha, Pelgrom (2008: 343) concludes that most Mid-Republican colonial towns could not hold more than 20 to 30 percent of the total population. Casarotto *et al.* 2016 show that site density in the territories of Mid-Republican colonies is not compatible with the expected number of sites based on ancient demographic accounts. At Cosa, small areas with high site density are found in the vicinity of the urban center, but the overall evidence suggests that a nucleated settlement strategy in villages farther away from the colony may have had an important role in early colonial societal organization.

resources to invest on the costly business of construction, and more generally on the economic conditions that allowed for members of the lower classes to reside in town. Thus, most building programs were only carried out decades or generations after the initial foundation, falling under the direct supervision of local magistrates who operated under the customary framework of the *locatio conductio operis*.[35] As M. Bolder-Boos puts it, therefore, the townscapes at colonial sites reflect the complex web of political, socioeconomic, symbolic, functional, and ideological activities at work within each community, thus leaving room for individual development.[36]

The relationship between economic intensification and urban infilling is particularly well documented for the Latin colony of Norba, where both the urban area and the countryside have been the object of intensive survey coupled with targeted excavation. The occupation history of Norba is different from the case studies discussed above (the colony was purportedly founded in 492 BCE within a settlement that goes back to the 7th century BCE), but its urban development seems to have been affected by the same trends characterizing the Mid-Republican colonization program. The first phase of fortification and town planning at the site has been dated to the 4th century BCE (more plausibly after 338 BCE),[37] but the distinct schemes and orientations betray subsequent interventions (Figure 6.1).[38] Most of the archaeology at the site belongs to the period between the 3rd and the early 1st centuries BCE.[39] The central open space bounded by the Acropoli Maggiore and the Acropoli Minore has been interpreted as the forum, but it seems to have remained devoid of any civic architecture until the latter part of the period. More information is available on the urban development of the south neighborhood. The thoroughfare generating the orthogonal street grid there connects in a straight line the west gate with the new monumental staircase leading to the so-called Acropoli Minore. Thus, the creation of the city blocks in this sector of town certainly postdates the reorganization of the terracing walls of the height, which has been assigned to between the late 3rd and the early 2nd century BCE. The retaining walls feature the same accurate kind of limestone polygonal masonry that was utilized for the town's wall, the terracing, the extraurban road infrastructure, and the rural platform sites, which document the prosperity of local colonial elites through the 3rd century BCE (*supra*, Chapter 4). However, the known examples of standardized atrium houses occupying the property lots at the foot of the

[35] E.g., the contract to rebuild the fortifications of the Latin colony of Luceria in the late 3rd or early 2nd centuries BCE was let by specially appointed *praefecti*. See Gregori and Nonnis 2013: 495 (with later comparanda for the practice).
[36] Bolder-Boos 2019: 122–24.
[37] Quilici and Quilici Gigli 2000.
[38] Quilici and Quilici Gigli 2018.
[39] Synthesis in Quilici Gigli 2003: 25–26. The town was destroyed in 81 BCE (App., *B Civ* 1.94) and never recovered after that major event.

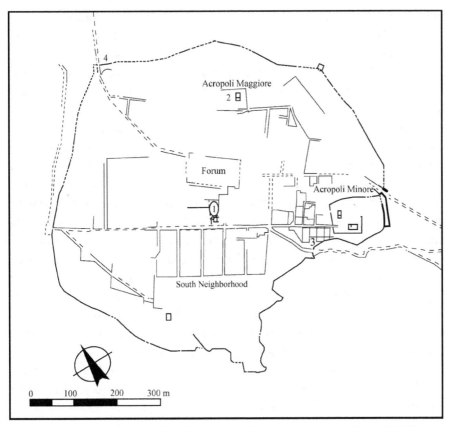

Figure 6.1 Schematic plan of Norba with location of the main monuments discussed in Chapter 6. Compiled from data in Quilici 2018. Key: 1=Terme Centrali; 2=Temple of Diana; 3=atrium houses; 4=Porta Signina. Drawing: M. Harder.

Acropoli Minore date to the 2nd century BCE.[40] While the façades of these private buildings are normally in polygonal masonry, non–load-bearing features located at the sides or at the back are made with the smaller and roughly squared blocks, finished with lime plaster. Party walls often include a stone footing made with small blocks of limestone, more or less accurately shaped, which support a superstructure of mud brick or pressed earth within formwork (but there are cases in which the walls are entirely built with clay). The choice of technique, however, does not seem to have a chronological value.[41]

Concrete architecture makes its appearance only toward the end of the 2nd century BCE, in the form of *opus incertum*. The use of the technique is attested primarily for cisterns and basins annexed to other structures (e.g., west slope of

---

[40] Carfora *et al.* 2010.
[41] Carfora *et al.* 2013: 95–101.

the Acropoli Minore; Porta Serrano di Bove; Porta Signina). Isolated terracing walls are also present in the west quarter and in the area of the forum.[42] The rebuilding of the sanctuary of Diana provides a well-dated, large-scale example. The new podium features a cemented-rubble grid and is associated with an *opus incertum* triporticus that abuts the preexisting podium.[43] The possibilities offered by the new building medium are exploited fully in the Terme Centrali, a bathing complex located on a lower terrace south of the forum, taken to be roughly contemporary with the Temple of Diana.[44] The building is centered on a large, rock-cut, open-air basin (29 × 32 m), oval in shape, and coated with hydraulic mortar, which functioned as the main water reservoir.[45] An annular vaulted corridor runs around the basin, leading to a set of rooms oriented toward the main thoroughfare. To the east is a rectangular room (a *frigidarium*?) covered with a wide concrete barrel vault spanning 7.10 m, and whose intrados consists of layers of flat and elongated rubble elements placed radially. A series of narrow vaulted ramps reached a second floor above the larger room. To the west is a round room (4.90 m in diameter) with an ogive dome, whose springing is marked by a course of bricks. Its heating system is not known in any detail because of the backfill, but an interpretation of the room as a sweat bath seems highly plausible.[46] In terms of building technique and typology, this was an innovative monument in the urban landscape of Norba. The *laconicum*, in particular, was clearly inspired by Greek prototypes that were first introduced in South Italy and Sicily in the 2nd century BCE. The insertion of the building in a prominent location within the regularly planned neighborhood must have represented a powerful statement about the cultural sophistication of the local patrons who donated it to the community.[47] The canonical atrium-type houses of the south neighborhood also stand out for their incorporation of *opus incertum* architecture. In House I, which is the best preserved of the pair, two parallel concrete vaulted substructures (each spanning 4 m) abutted the polygonal wall that delimited the rear of the house, thus creating an extension that filled the space previously occupied by a garden. The vaulting technique finds similarities with the Terme Centrali, confirming the late date of these concrete additions.

A similar trajectory can be sketched for the site of Fregellae. The town's orthogonal layout, whose main axis is represented by the urban stretch of the Via Latina, is believed to date to 313 BCE, when the site was refounded after suffering destruction by the Samnites

---

[42] Carfora *et al.* 2013: 94.
[43] Quilici Gigli 2003: 27. The dating is mostly based on the style of the surviving architectural decoration.
[44] Quilici Gigli and Quilici 1998.
[45] For a parallel from the acropolis of Signia, see Cifarelli 2003: 75.
[46] Trümper 2009: 169, table 7.
[47] As noted by Quilici and Quilici Gigli 1998: 80–82.

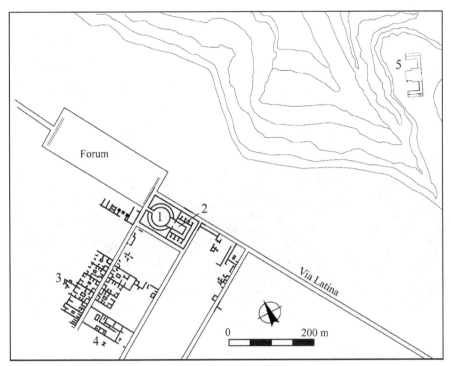

Figure 6.2 Schematic plan of Fregellae with locations of the main monuments discussed in Chapter 6. Key: 1=Comitium; 2=Curia; 3=Domus 7; 4=Baths; 5=Sanctuary of Asclepius. Compiled from data in Coarelli and Monti 1998. Drawing: M. Harder.

(Figure 6.2).[48] Having rebelled against the Romans in 125 BCE, the site was taken, razed to the ground, and never reoccupied on the same scale, being replaced by the new colony of Fabrateria Nova, located about 5 km to the southeast. Thus, the evidence gathered from the site presents the unique opportunity to trace back to the Mid-Republican period a number of important innovations in both the town-planning and the domestic spheres, as discussed previously. In an area adjacent to the Comitium, the excavations have exposed a series of city blocks on either side of the street departing from the short north side of the forum. The blocks are mostly occupied by private dwellings, though a multiphase public bath building has been identified at the east edge of the excavated area.

The stratigraphic sequence documented for one of the houses, Domus 7, corresponds well with what we know about the Comitium and the baths, both of which show construction episodes that are roughly contemporary with the two main phases of the house (3rd century BCE and early to mid

[48] Coarelli 1981; Coarelli 1998b, 31, 41–45, 55–56.

Figure 6.3 Fregellae. Domus 7, Phase 1 (3rd cent. BCE). Example of mortared-rubble founda-tion supporting a tile socle and pressed earth superstructure (Battaglini and Diosono 2010: 227, fig. 10; Archivio Progetto *Fregellae*; used by permission).

2nd century BCE, respectively).[49] In its earliest version, Domus 7 features almost exclusively walls whose lower portions consist of courses of broken tiles bonded with clay laid on top of limestone rubble foundations.[50] These footings support a superstructure consisting of pressed clay panels finished with lime plaster (Figure 6.3). Clay beds were abundant in the Sacco river valley bottom, where the plateau of Fregellae was located, at the confluence of the Liris. The site itself sat on an alluvial terrace that included layers of stratified limestone pebbles, so the building material was readily available. In the second phase, welded tuff (the Tufo Grigio outcropping close to the site on the left bank of the Liris) and travertine ashlar architecture was introduced on a larger scale.[51] The clay-based techniques that charac-terized the previous period were further developed at this stage. Party walls were built using a special type of tile with flanges on two sides, which was clearly manufactured for the purpose (i.e., not used for

[49]  Tsiolis 2013, 105 dates the first phase of the baths to the last three decades of the 3rd century BCE, and its abandonment sometime in the first quarter of the 2nd century BCE. Tsiolis 2008, 136 dates the second phase of the baths to 185–150 BCE. The supporting evidence, however, remains unpublished.

[50]  Battaglini and Diosono 2010: 227–29; Battaglini and Braconi 2019: 498, fig. 2.

[51]  Battaglini and Diosono (2010: 226) suggest the possibility that the travertine blocks may be *spolia* from the previous phase, given their different dimensions in comparison with the tuff blocks.

Figure 6.4 Fregellae. Domus 7, Phase 2 (early 2nd cent. BCE). Bottom section of a party wall built with modular brick elements laid on clay mortar, presumably with pressed earth superstructure (Battaglini and Braconi 2019: 500, fig. 4D; Archivio Progetto *Fregellae*; used by permission).

roofing).[52] These bricks were carefully placed in alternating courses of headers and stretchers, the gaps being filled with clay mortar and broken tiles (Figure 6.4). A similar, specialized use of terracotta elements is attested in the second phase of the baths. The vault spanning the *apodyterium/tepidarium* (6 m in width) is composed of a series of regularly spaced, parallel terracotta voussoir arches (or ribs), which supported a roof made with curved tiles joined by lead brackets. This represented a very costly, not to say heavy, vaulting system. The important implication seems to be that lime-based mortar had not yet been implemented on a large scale for structural purposes, although the technology was used in both the houses and the baths for floor revetment (load-bearing walls were built with *opus quadratum*). Only in the final phase of the houses (150–125 BCE, which has been described as a period of crisis for Fregellae) was the building medium exploited more extensively, particularly

[52] As suggested by Battaglini and Diosono 2010: 227. Battaglini and Braconi 2019: 504–05, with fig. 4 at 500. The technique was used in combination with *opus quadratum* for load-bearing walls.

in order to build water-related features (e.g., vats, channels, and drains).[53] Volcanic ash deposits were accessible in the area of Patrica-Supino, approximately 25 km upstream, but their exploitation for this period is not documented.

The only monumental context from Fregellae in which lime-based mortared rubble is attested is the extraurban sanctuary of Aesculapius.[54] The original construction date, initially assigned to the mid 2nd century BCE on epigraphic and stylistic grounds, has been subsequently revised to the early 3rd century BCE, thus coinciding with the first major phase of urban redevelopment.[55] The extant temple plan belongs to the second phase of the complex, whose associated terracotta decoration has been dated stylistically to the early 2nd century BCE (no stratigraphy is preserved at the site due to erosion).[56] A single fragmentary feature (measuring about 1 × 0.5 m) lies in the area occupied by the transverse cella, abutting the retaining wall of the podium; the mortar has been described as friable, but there is no scientific information regarding its actual composition.[57] Lippolis has interpreted the structure as part of a grid of concrete foundations, but the evidence is too scanty. Another possible interpretation is that the feature represented a minor repair of the podium foundations (of the kind documented for the Temple of Castor and Pollux in Rome, discussed in Chapter 3). The construction fills in the lower levels of the podium consist simply of clay layers, whereas all the main architectural features of the sanctuary, such as the triporticus that frames the temple and the terracing wall on the east side of the area, employ exclusively *opus quadratum*.

Most of the standing features built with mortared rubble at the long-lived sites of Alba Fucens and Paestum have been assigned to even later periods. Recent excavations in and around the forum area at Alba Fucens place its *opus incertum* architecture in the 1st century BCE (e.g., the *tabernae* flanking the square). The use of pressed earth or perishable materials in association with polygonal masonry for the main terracing walls is attested for the previous phase.[58] At Paestum, monuments of the early colonial period are built with ashlars, which are only occasionally of smaller dimensions (e.g., in the precinct wall of the so-called *heroön*). A local

---

[53]  Battaglini and Diosono 2010: 224. These features demonstrate that houses were converted into industrial buildings (probably *fullonicae*). This radical transformation of the site has been linked with the immigration of Samnite groups: Coarelli 1991; Coarelli 1995. Livy 41.8.8 reports that in 177 BCE 4,000 Samnite and Paelignan families moved to the colony of Fregellae and settled there. The event would be roughly contemporary with the redevelopment of the public baths, which does not seem to fit with the idea of crisis, as well as with the mass construction of housing.

[54]  Coarelli 1986a.

[55]  For the traditional chronology, see Lippolis 1986: 38–41. For the altar inscription, see Coarelli 1986b, 43 n. 1. Verzár-Bass 1986 presents a stylistic analysis of the architectural decoration. The revised dating is discussed by Lippolis 2009.

[56]  Känel 2015.

[57]  Lippolis 1986, 30. See also pl. XI, cross section 4–4; Lippolis 2009, 148–51.

[58]  For a synthesis of these results, see Di Cesare and Liberatore 2017; Di Cesare and Liberatore 2018.

variant of *opus uittatum* using blocks of heterogeneous size is not earlier than the 1st century BCE. Concrete walls described as rough *opus incertum* often overlay courses of ashlars, probably representing late restorations, since the house plans with which such walls are associated have been dated mostly to the Imperial period. In the absence of stratigraphic data, it is almost impossible to establish a typology and a chronology of wall facings for the site. The situation is complicated further by the problem of undocumented restorations and reconstructions from the 1950s, which often included repointing with mortar.[59]

In short, many of the better-known Mid-Republican colonies show multiple waves of urban development starting from the end of the 3rd or early 2nd century BCE. These building activities were the result of an euergetic urge that had little or no relationship with the activities of Roman magistrates.[60] Local elites responsible for these building projects relied at first on preexisting architectural traditions, as most evident in the case of Fregellae and Norba. At Norba, Alba Fucens, and Paestum, the introduction of concrete architecture can only be linked with the later stage of the phenomenon. The sudden abandonment of Fregellae in 125 BCE explains the dearth of structural mortar there. By contrast, Fabrateria Nova, which replaced Fregellae as the main center in the region in 124 BCE, was built predominantly with *opus incertum*.[61]

## THE EARLY DEVELOPMENT OF CONCRETE CONSTRUCTION AT COSA

Cosa represents a notable exception to the pattern just described for the better-known Mid-Republican colonies (Figure 6.5). The standing architecture at the site documents a significantly early use of mortared-rubble construction techniques. Because of the rich legacy data from Brown's excavations, the emergence of the technology at the site can be contextualized with some degree of resolution within the broader trajectory of urban development, by specific areas and building types.[62] Whereas the early researchers sketched the image of a fully developed Mid-Republican town, the results of more recent fieldwork projects have seriously questioned the existence of a substantial settlement within the fortification circuit of the colony for most if not all of the 3rd century BCE.[63] Unlike at Fregellae, Alba Fucens, and the sister colony of Paestum, the

[59] Bragantini *et al.* 2008: 21–24.
[60] David 1997: 99–119.
[61] Betori *et al.* 2013.
[62] Brown 1951 (on the fortifications); Brown *et al.* 1960 (on the temples of the Arx); McCann 1987 (on the port); Brown *et al.* 1993 (on the forum and its dependencies); Bruno and Scott 1993 (on atrium and lower-class houses). Adequate publication of the finds associated with these architectural remains, however, lagged generally behind, as it relied significantly on the final dissemination of Brown's stratigraphic analysis: Scott 2008 (Black Gloss pottery); Buttrey 1980 (coins). See the synthesis in Dyson 2013. For a revision of the evidence: Fentress 2003.
[63] Fentress *et al.* 2003: 14–28; Sewell 2005; Sewell 2010: 25–33.

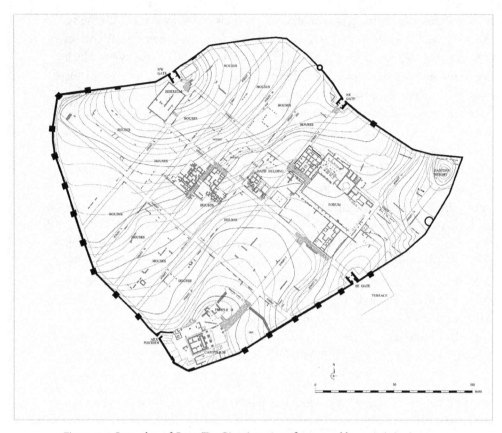

Figure 6.5  State plan of Cosa (De Giorgi 2018: 7, fig. 2; used by permission).

transformation of Cosa's urban fabric followed the arrival of a new contingent of
1,000 colonists in 197 BCE, who were sent out by Rome upon repeated requests
by the local community to counter its demographic decline (Liv., 33.24.8–9). The
remaking of the town, which spans the first half of the 2nd century BCE, can in
this case be linked with more complex processes unfolding at a time of social and
political crisis rather than prosperity.[64] The long-term success of the enterprise
would have been partly dependent on the strengthening of intergroup bonds of
solidarity and the fostering of a shared communal identity, which technological
practice and performance behind monumental construction could literally help
manufacture. Besides providing a privileged case study for reconstructing the
interplay between different regional building traditions, the economy of construction, and the supply of locally available building materials, Cosa represents an
ideal testing ground for exploring the relationship between technological innovation and stylistic behavior in the architecture of Roman Republican colonization.

[64] Mogetta 2019.

The main form of monumental building for the period predating the urban renovation at Cosa is represented by polygonal masonry (in combination with simple rubble fills). The technique is employed for the fortifications, whose blocks were quarried from the local dolomitic limestone deposits at multiple quarry faces very close to the walls themselves.[65] It is also documented for the cisterns located at the Northwestern Gate, at the intersection of Streets 4 and K, and of Streets 5 and O, highlighting the crucial role of water harvesting and storage at a waterless site.[66] Other structures securely dated to the initial phase of the colony of 273 BCE consist of simple rock-cut features.[67]

There is a general consensus that the final aspect of the forum materialized only in a piecemeal fashion (Figure 6.6). The excavators assigned the buildings that line the northeast side of the square – namely the voting structures (Comitium-Curia) with annexed ritual spaces (Templum Beta, a precursor to Temple B) and jail (Carcer) – to the first phase of occupation of the colony,[68] placing the progressive infilling and beautification of the remaining sides in the course of the 2nd century BCE.[69] The picture of gradual development has been challenged by Sewell, who has identified a series of anomalies in the planning of the excavated forum: the fact that the open square has no streets along its edges, as is normally the case for contemporary Mid-Republican colonial layouts; the irregular shape of the blocks on its northwest and southeast sides; the positioning of the Comitium/Curia complex in a lot that was not nearly wide enough, causing it to block Street 7 and encroach upon part of the adjoining plot.[70]

---

[65] For a recent reappraisal, see Benvenuti 2002. Poggesi and Pallecchi 2012 report the use of lime mortar for the single round tower inserted in the north stretch of the circuit, but according to Von Gerkan (1958b: 152) similar mortared-rubble additions on top of the projecting towers are to be understood as later restorations.

[66] As observed by De Giorgi 2018: 9.

[67] E.g., the so-called Auguraculum on the Arx (Brown et al. 1960: 11–13).

[68] Brown et al. (1993: 26) dated the Comitium to the 273–241 BCE period. Fentress and Perkins (2016: 381) recently revised the dating to the third quarter of the 3rd century BCE (between 240 and 220 BCE). For the Carcer: Brown et al. 1993: 38–39 (the identification is based on the presence of an underground chamber).

[69] The construction of the so-called Atrium Buildings (four on the long southwest side of the square, two on each of the short sides), which are best understood as elite domus (Sewell 2010: 137–65), would come first in the sequence, followed quickly by the addition of the Southwest Annex (an open-plan structure centered on the axis of the Comitium and Street P; Brown et al. 1993: 57–106), the colonnaded triporticus and monumental gateway (Brown et al. 1993: 107–38), and a small prostyle temple (Temple B, replacing Templum Beta; Brown et al. 1993: 142–53). The notable irregularities in the spacing of the columns of the forum portico as reconstructed by Brown, and the fact that the southeast stretch of the colonnade encroaches upon Street Q speak for a project that was the result of successive interventions. Brown's date of 175 BCE for the northwest gateway, which he assigns to either "before or right after construction of the portico" (Brown et al. 1993: 128) appears based primarily on comparanda known from literary sources for which we have no material correlate. The Basilica on the north corner was built in the second half of the 2nd century BCE (Brown et al. 1993: 207–27 gives a date of 150–140 BCE; on typological grounds, Gros 2011: 240 prefers a date of c. 120 BCE).

[70] Sewell 2005; Sewell 2010: 27–32.

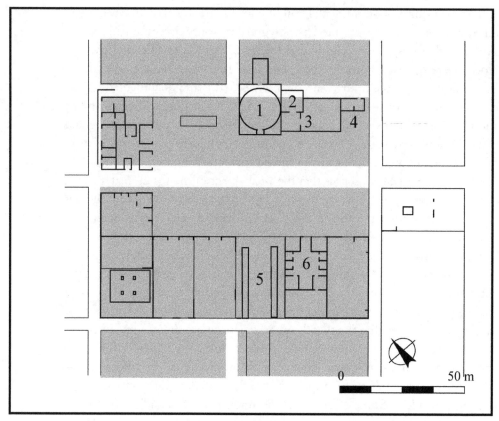

Figure 6.6 Reconstruction of the forum of Cosa, *c.* 180 BCE. Compiled from data in Fentress *et al.* (2003: 22, fig. 9). Key: 1=Comitium and Curia; 2=Templum Beta; 3=Forecourt; 4=Carcer; 5=Southwest Annex; 6=House of Diana. The shaded area indicates the position and extent of the 3rd century BCE forum and related blocks as hypothesized by Sewell (2005). The excavated features are in solid line. Drawing: M. Harder.

Despite the lack of direct archaeological evidence, an attractive explanation to account for these irregularities is to consider the existing forum as a later insertion into the preexisting layout (whether the original 3rd century BCE plan as reconstructed by Sewell was ever completed, however, remains debatable).[71] In terms of planning, the buildings on the northeast side of the forum – the Carcer, Templum Beta, and the back wall of the Comitium – share the same slightly odd angle generated by the axis of Street P, which stands out

[71] Sewell 2010: 29, fig. 10. According to Fentress and Perkins (2016: 380), a significant difference in height exists between Streets 5 and 7 (up to 3 m). A steep cut in the bedrock is still visible at the back of the House of Diana (one of the 2nd century BCE *domus* facing onto the southeast side of the square), i.e., where the southwest half of the original piazza would have stood, meaning that part of its surface would have remained unfinished until the creation of the domestic structure.

for having a different orientation to all other streets running from southwest to northeast.[72] Since it enters the redesigned forum exactly at its center, Street P was probably part of the same project, thus explaining the function of the Southwest Annex as a monumental entrance, directly opposite the Comitium. Given its axial position, the latter was probably the first to be built in the sequence.[73]

The series of building activities that produced the redevelopment of the forum must be compressed in a shorter period of time than previously assumed. The spike in public architecture may have provided the impetus for experimentation with new building methods in response to economic concerns, whereas earthen architecture (e.g., the first phase of the Curia; the water catchment E of the Comitium) or even polygonal masonry of smaller module (e.g., Temple B podium; later modifications of the Curia) can be found in combination with each other. All the components of the new forum ensemble feature exclusively lime-based mortar construction. By contrast, all the domestic buildings in Republican Cosa had a superstructure in *pisé de terre* (i.e., rammed earth laid on drystone footings or directly onto the cut bedrock).[74] The technique appears both in the elite houses close to the forum (e.g., the House of Diana)[75] and in the more modest dwellings investigated elsewhere (e.g., in the two city blocks bounded by Streets L, M, 4, and 5, and Streets M, N, 4, and 5).[76] In private dwellings, lime mortar was used sparingly for the bedding of voussoirs (e.g., in the vaults covering the cisterns, whose spans are usually less than 2 m wide), but thick coats of plaster of lime mixed with sand and crushed tile were also applied to the walls. Thus, the choice of using clay

[72] Mogetta 2019: 251–52, figs. 6–7. Assigning the Carcer to the later building phase does not pose problems. Brown *et al.* (1993: 40) dated it to the period between the First and Second Punic Wars (241–220 BCE) primarily on account of the odd alignment of the wall running from the south corner of Temple B to the north corner of the Carcer, contrasting the "random rubblework" and rusticated quoins of the Carcer's superstructure with the well-dressed and coursed facings of Temple B to confirm the earlier date of the former building. The vaulting technique (cemented-rubble laid directly on centering) does not have 3rd century BCE parallels. The method is also attested for the forum gate.

[73] The excavation of the deposits from the Comitium enclosure did not provide diagnostic materials to support its 3rd century BCE dating (Brown *et al.* 1993: 26; see also the discussion in Sewell 2005: 109–10). Indirect evidence is represented by the construction sequence of the adjoining buildings to the east (below Templum Beta) and associated ceramic finds, which are consistent with a date within the first half of the 2nd century BCE. See discussion in Mogetta 2019: 253–54, with fig. 8.

[74] On the technique, see Pesando 2012 (for Pompeii); Russell and Fentress 2016 (on Rome). At Cosa, it may have been already in use in the 3rd century BCE phase (e.g., for the superstructure of the square building under the cella of the so-called Capitolium on the Arx). See Brown 1960: 11; Taylor 2002: 78.

[75] Fentress *et al.* 2003: 19–21.

[76] Bruno and Scott 1993. Lime-base, mortared-rubble architecture surfaces only in the second phase of urban development, most notably in the lower houses occupying the W block, tentatively dated to *c.* 150 BCE. See Bruno and Scott 1993: 66–67, 71.

mortar for the main structural elements appears deliberate. Pockets of *terre rosse*, a reddish silty clay rich in ferrous oxides that results from the weathering of the local limestone, filled the depressions in the bedrock topography, and were easily accessible.

The building methods employed for the Comitium demonstrate which specific technological choices were made by the builders when structural mortar was first introduced at the site. A sounding on the northeast side near the north corner showed that the walls of the enclosure are laid on a foundation consisting of a single course of unworked limestone boulders laid directly on the bedrock, and leveled with rammed earth.[77] On the southwest side, a 0.35 m deep socle of mortared-rubble masonry was found resting directly on the crests of the bedrock. It, too, was found leveled by a layer of rammed clay, so the creation of a uniform foundation does not seem to have been a primary concern, which makes sense considering that the Comitium was unroofed and that the loads were not very heavy. The main structural function of the enclosure walls was to respond to the lateral thrusts from the fills it retained. Lime-based mortar was used for the bedding of bricklike slabs of the local calcareous sandstone (varying from 0.22 to 0.44 m in length and 3.5 to 6.5 cm in thickness), which are stacked in subhorizontal courses, to form thick walls (0.60 m) with two uniform faces and a core of smaller limestone rubble and tile fragments (Figure 6.7).[78]

The walls were built up using stone elements that could be handled by individual workmen without the need of complex lifting devices or form-works, and whose relatively flat dimensions allowed even the unskilled to stagger them in sections without much supervision: The layers and joints could be regularized by adjusting the thickness of the mortar beds.[79] The mortar used for both the southwest foundation and the superstructure of the Comitium contains a high proportion of local volcanic sands quarried from the dune beach and offshore bars south and east of the promontory of Cosa. Because of their alteration from weathering, the volcanic rock inclusions in these sands have inferior pozzolanic properties in comparison with the pyroclastic-flow and pyroclastic-fall deposits of the Vulsini district from which they originate, whose use is otherwise attested in structural mortars from Late Republican domestic contexts at Volsinii Novi.[80] Hydraulic mortars attested

---

[77] Brown *et al.* 1993: 14.

[78] Brown *et al.* 1993: 15.

[79] Only one leveling course has been identified across the four sides, 1.1 m from the reconstructed top of the precinct wall. Brown *et al.* 1993: 14.

[80] On the tuffs and pozzolans of the Vulsini district, see Marra and D'Ambrosio 2013. D'Ambrosio *et al.* (2015: 191) hint at the existence of an independent, early local tradition of concrete construction and of long-distance trade of the materials. At the Casa delle Pitture (first half of the 2nd century BCE), the walls of the original phase are in the local "checker-board" technique (from the Italian *opera a schacchiera*, French *mur en damier*), which does not

Figure 6.7  Cosa, Comitium Curia (Building C). Archival photo of SE Room. Level I. SW wall (American Academy in Rome, Photographic Archive: AAR.COSA.1954.16; used by permission).

across the site always include ground terracotta as a reactive agent, but are utilized primarily for revetments.[81] While bringing significant savings in labor costs due to ease of construction in comparison with polygonal masonry, however, the technological shift generated other production costs for the procurement of building materials. First, a lime industry or trade network had to be organized. As part of the building process, the quarrying and

feature lime-based mortar (Balland *et al.* 1971: 22; Gros 1981: 62; Stopponi 2006: 215–17, Type B; cf. Adam 1994: 119–24). The published sample (CP1; D'Ambrosio *et al.* 2015: 189, fig. 2d) must come from one of the *opus incertum* walls, which the excavators assigned to the Imperial phase of the house. The material from the Casa del Ninfeo, for which a late 2nd century BCE date is provided, was sampled from an *opus mixtum* wall (CP2; D'Ambrosio *et al.* 2015: 189 fig. 2e). This technique is typical of the late 1st century CE architecture at the site (Gros 1981: 56–59).

[81]  Gazda (2008) discusses the practice of mixing ceramic fragments as aggregates with mortars of lime and local sands with relation to the superstructures of the port and fishery of Cosa, where imported volcanic ash was selectively employed only for the submerged parts. Jackson *et al.* (2010) have inferred a provenance from Campania for the pumice in the mortars of the piers on the basis of the Zr/Y and Nb/Y ratios, though Marra and D'Ambrosio (2013: fig. 13a) show a compositional match with the 79 CE eruption of Mount Vesuvius, which is incompatible with the date assigned to the sample (60 BCE). Gazda (2008: 275–87) lays out the evidence for a possible even later date in the third quarter of the 1st century BCE (based on the 57 BCE–33 CE $^{14}$C date of a sample from Pier 1).

transportation of sands from the coastal dunes to the hilltop had to be arranged. Most notably, access to water supply from the storage system available on site needed to be regulated (there were no springs on the promontory, so the water collected in the rock-cut cisterns had to be shared for construction purposes).[82] The procurement of timber for scaffolding and centering probably relied on the broader supply for the shipbuilding industry that had developed locally in the 3rd century BCE.[83] This may perhaps explain the overall popularity of clay-based techniques using formworks at the site.

The type of construction just described for the Comitium and its annex is found at another major landmark at Cosa, the so-called Capitolium on the Arx, though in combination with more elaborate quoins. With the refoundation of the colony in the early 2nd century BCE, the citadel, too, became the focus of monumentalization and was the object of a new phase of temple building, which has been taken to be roughly contemporary with the construction activities in the forum (c. 175–150 BCE).[84] The Capitolium stands out not only for its plan and size (at 23.2 × 31.7 m, it is the largest temple of Cosa and the only one with tripartite cella), but also for its dominating position, with its front in a direct line of sight from the Comitium. Its original interpretation as a temple to the Capitoline triad has been rightly challenged.[85] However, it is likely that the cult activities relating to that temple had a prominent status in the colony's religious and cultural identity: The new temple stood on top of the first and only 3rd century BCE temple on the Arx, which was intentionally demolished to make room for it. Thus, we might suspect that the temple was dedicated to Cosa's tutelary deity, which expands the argument for its civic function despite the rejection of Brown's identification.[86]

The building process implemented for the main temple appears more complex than that of the Comitium, betraying an increased level of investment. Brick-shaped sandstone facing pieces were used selectively for the foundations and walls of the cella and its projecting antae.[87] Unlike in the Comitium, the mortar mix includes ground terracotta as an additive to increase hydraulicity. This technique is combined with high-status opus quadratum, which is employed for the corners of the antae (alternating headers and stretchers of

[82] A water catchment area adjacent to the SE corner of the Comitium was probably used while the site was under construction, only to be backfilled once the enclosure wall was completed. Significantly, the SW and SE walls of this annex were rebuilt to form the forecourt of Templum Beta, and extended to resemble the façade of the Comitium. See Mogetta 2019: 258, Figure 10.

[83] On the role of Cosa in ship construction for the Roman state, see Scott 2019: 24.

[84] Taylor 2002.

[85] On the identification as Capitolium, see Brown 1980: 53–56. Bispham (2006: 99–101) has pointed out that Capitolia at citizen colonies like Ostia, Tarracina, Minturnae, and Luna are normally located along the decumanus and near the forum.

[86] Bolder-Boos 2011: 27–28.

[87] Mogetta 2019: 259, fig. 11.

brecciated limestone), and for the exterior of the podium. The latter feature was purely formal in function (i.e., a revetment with no structural purpose, except beyond the *antae*, where it served to retain the fills of the pronaos).[88] In the front part of the long sides of the temple, it was founded on retaining walls made of unfinished limestone blocks laid up in clay, which maintained the base level of the pronaos. In its final plan, possibly Augustan in date, the complex terminated with a forecourt whose walls were built with polygonal masonry associated with concrete cores. In contrast with the *identitaire* character of polygonal masonry (its use at Latin colonies has often been taken to express both a symbolic link with Latium and an idea of Archaic solidity), the masonry style of the cella was in all likelihood not visible, so the specific choice has to be explained primarily in terms of construction process.

While the similarity between the precinct wall of the Comitium and the cella walls of the Capitolium may reflect a shorter time gap between the construction dates of the two monuments, the correlation with the main communal symbols of Cosa – the meeting place for the assembly of all male citizens, and the temple for the poliadic cult – may reveal other clues as to what prompted the technological change. Complex social dynamics were set in motion by the arrival of the new colonists with the 197 BCE *adscriptio*. The contingent, whose size corresponded to one third of the original colony, included participants from both Rome and Roman areas as well as other Italian allies who would have been given the opportunity to enlist. Local groups of *immixti* (resident aliens) could also have been recruited to fill the ranks.[89] Although colonies at this time were probably founded as hierarchical societies, with different classes of colonists receiving plots of different sizes (both at the urban and rural levels),[90] material practices could also serve as a mechanism to promote the growth of a stable community. The population of Cosa after 197 BCE was made up of groups that were largely unfamiliar to one another, so the initial emphasis on public projects, most notably on the political buildings, would have been instrumental in defining the new, common identity and purpose between the colonists and the previous town inhabitants. In this perspective, the building process devised for the main components of civic architecture, necessary for the functioning and self-governing of the town, could have been conceptualized and understood as a form of public engagement. They in turn gave both the designers and the colonists an opportunity to materially shape the collective identity of the colony – Varro, *Ling.* 5.179 appears to imply that

---

[88] The curved profile of the crown excludes the possibility that there was an ashlar revetment of the superstructure of the cella (for which, see Brown *et al.* 1960: 71, fig. 48).

[89] As suggested by Laffi 2017: 53–54 (interpreting Livy's specific reference to Cosa as evidence that the new colonists were recruited exclusively among Italian allies).

[90] On the idea that the residential areas of Cosa were allotted in accordance with the property class of the colonist, see Sewell 2010: 121–22; 137–41.

contributing such *munera* formed part of civic identity, whereby he defines the citizens (*municipes*) as those who must jointly perform a *munus*. The implementation of a building method based on the use of reasonably small, stackable elements and facing blocks may have represented a means for contractors to include larger pools of civic labor, drawing manpower from the new arrivals even if unskilled. While there are no contemporary textual sources for the direct participation of colonists in colonial public construction projects, it is fair to assume that at Cosa as elsewhere large amounts of unskilled settlers were involved in the construction of ashlar monuments like the early 3rd century BCE city walls.[91] The introduction of concrete construction in the 2nd century BCE probably lowered both overall costs and the ratio of skilled to unskilled builders within the workforce (for the laying of wall facings and cores, the generally accepted figure is one skilled to one unskilled laborer).[92]

In other words, the early form of Cosa's concrete construction would offer broader opportunities than ashlar masonry for unskilled colonial builders to be employed through the finishing stages of the building process, including the physical raising of walls, while at the same time ensuring efficient resource management. Furthermore, the cooperation of previous inhabitants and/or rural settlers, who had better knowledge of the local environment, must have been a crucial prerequisite for the selection of sources of building materials, especially the volcanic sands and the stratified sandstone. Under normal circumstances, the *tresuiri* would have been responsible for the assessment of the circumstances specific to the locality during initial development of colonies, including the characteristics of the surrounding territory.[93] The reorganization of Cosa, however, presented different tasks from those needed for new foundations, since building projects would have been managed directly by magistrates serving local institutions that were already in place by the time of the resettlement.

In contrast with polygonal masonry and *opus quadratum* facings, which were always left visible, the masonry style of the Comitium and the Capitolium

---

[91] Bernard (2018a: 108–14) discusses the role of *corvée* citizen labor for the 4th century BCE fortifications of Rome. The *Lex Ursonensis*, which contains explicit reference to *operae* for construction of *munitiones* (Crawford 1996, 1: 408, no. 25, ch. 98), makes it clear that some sort of labor was required from citizens for particular types of monuments (most notably fortifications and perhaps road infrastructure).

[92] See discussion in Chapter 1, and figures in DeLaine (2001: 234–45, with Appendix A). Tuff ashlar construction, which is made with a softer stone than the limestone available at Cosa, is on average two to four times more labor intensive than any form of concrete. Limestone can be two to three times harder to work than volcanic tuff. The labor structure for most operations (e.g., shaping, fine finishing, and squaring of the blocks, dressing of edges) would have been four skilled laborers to one unskilled. Larger amounts of unskilled labor were required for hauling, lifting, and placing blocks (ratio of three skilled to four unskilled for every ton of blocks).

[93] Sewell 2010: 85.

lacked symbolic value. What mattered most was the process of construction, not its finished aspect. The character of subsequent concrete architecture at the site is much more heterogeneous: from the random mortared rubble of the Carcer, to the polygonal masonry of smaller module in Temple B and Temple D on the Arx, to the *opus incertum* of parts of the Basilica and the monumental gateway of the forum.[94] A reason for this variation could be that the contracts for these monuments were let out to different firms. The mixed building techniques seen in the Basilica and the forum gate (whose bays feature cemented-rubble barrel vaults laid directly on centering) probably also betray their later date. Restrictions of locally available resources, commercial expediency, the need for structural strength, and fashions in aesthetic appearance probably influenced the pattern. But it is tempting to suggest that different variants of mortared architecture were specifically added to the repertoire for use in other structures that were not directly linked with the constitutive civic functions.

## COMPARATIVE EVIDENCE FROM ROMAN COLONIES (C. 200–150 BCE)

The resettlement and redevelopment of Cosa unfolded in the context of a broader phenomenon occurring during the first two decades of the 2nd century BCE, as a result of which the character of citizen colonies changed, too.[95] Mirroring the urbanization trajectory of the Mid-Republican Latin colonies, several of the old *coloniae maritimae* were enlarged at this time, taking on a much more recognizably urban character. A classic example is represented by Minturnae, first established as a small fort of approximately 2.25 ha in 296 BCE (Liv., 10.21.7–10), whose occupation expanded beyond the original area surrounded by the polygonal masonry fortifications to include a forum provided with *tabernae* (sometime before 191 BCE: Liv., 36.37.3).[96] In the aftermath of the Hannibalic war of 218–202 BCE, as many as twenty-six other Latin and Roman colonies in addition to Cosa were founded or reorganized – and on several occasions refounded after initial failure. The fast-paced sequence started with the dispatch of 300 colonists to the as yet unidentified Castrum (or Castra) in 199 BCE (Liv., 33.7.3; but confusion with Salernum is possible), and ended (temporarily) with the settlement of Luna in 177 BCE.[97] This juncture coincided with a phase of crucial developments in Roman architecture and urbanism, when important building types like the *basilica* and the *porticus* first materialized. Thus, the projects that we see reflected in the monumentalization

---

[94] See n. 740.

[95] Salmon 1982: 95 ("new model citizen colonies").

[96] On the urban development of Minturnae, see Bellini and Von Hesberg 2015. Sewell 2015 estimates that the surface area of Minturnae in the 2nd century BCE reached from a minimum of 17.2 ha to a maximum of 28 ha.

[97] A classic overview is presented in Salmon 1936. Settlement data are available in Sewell 2015 (excluding the Cisalpine region).

of Cosa might also be interpreted as a local response to global trends and ideas about how to build or reconfigure cities in contemporary Roman Italy.[98] To evaluate the degree to which shared designs and construction techniques could be received and adapted to local contexts, I turn to the archaeological evidence from this specific subset of colonial sites.

Even though chronologically the urban foundations in question are spread within a short period of time, it must be noted from the start that the pattern lacks uniformity. This surely reflects in part the different motivations and rationales behind the individual colonial settlements (military control; land distribution; economic integration of allied communities). In terms of size, the colonies of Roman citizens established early on in the series range from the 3 ha of Puteoli (Rione Terra), which conforms to the Mid-Republican template of the *coloniae maritimae*,[99] to the 18 ha of Salernum and Sipontum, which are larger than some of the Mid-Republican Latin colonies of the previous wave, including Cosa, in spite of the small-scale contingent they received (300 colonists: Liv., 34.45.1).[100] Thus, the inclusion of adequate space for future expansion of the urban population was in some cases planned from the beginning. Sipontum, however, was found deserted in 186 BCE and was effectively refounded as a result of this (Liv., 39.23.3–4, mentioning a similar fate for Buxentum). It is entirely possible that other sites in the list were unsuccessful at first. The example of Cales, a Mid-Republican Latin colony whose reinforcement sometime before 184 BCE is known only epigraphically (*InscrIt* 13.3.709), serves as a reminder.[101] Roman colonies founded

---

[98] Bolder-Boos 2019.

[99] Assuming that the old town was abandoned, the Roman colony of Croton has been located at the site of the sanctuary of Hera Lacinia (Capo Colonna). The 5.5 ha area of the promontory was surrounded by fortification on two sides, but recent stratigraphic investigations demonstrated that the walls date to the second half of the 1st century BCE or later. See Ruga 2014: 187–92. The identification is accepted by Sewell 2015.

[100] The case of Tempsa is disputed. Strabo (6.1.5) reports that the colony was placed within the territory of Hellenistic Temesa, whose site has been recently identified at the Piano della Tirena (24.2 ha): Cicala 2009. A Roman settlement is attested on the high part of the plateau, though it dates only from the late 2nd century BCE onwards, and its urban form is uncertain. The identification is rejected by Sewell 2015.

[101] [*P. Claudius Ap(pii) f(ilius) P(ubli) n(epos) Pulcher colono*]*s adscripsit Cales*. Nonnis (2014: 404–05) notes the discrepancy between the family names attested in the rich corpus of local pottery stamps for the 3rd century BCE and those known from the epigraphic record for the Late Republican and later periods. Livy (27.9.7) includes Cales in the group of twelve colonies that were unable to meet military obligations in 209 BCE (with Ardea, Nepet, Sutrium, Alba, Carseoli, Sora, Suessa, Circei, Setia, Cales, Narnia, and Interamna), testifying to the state of demographic and economic crisis. Cf. Tweedie (2011) argues that Livy does not give information about every supplement, but only provides routine notices about the establishment of boards for colonial foundations or viritane distributions. Coles (2017: 300) suggests that the supplementation of Cales may have been derived completely from the founder's initiative to strengthen his family's clientele in Campania. On the archaeology of Cales: Johannowsky 1961; Passaro 2009. Most of the architecture from the urban area dates to the 1st century BCE or later (with the possible exception of the *opus incertum* building under

on or after 184 BCE demonstrate the progression of the trend, as their urban areas vary in surface from the 18 ha of Potentia and Pisaurum to the 40 ha or so of Parma and Mutina (comparable to the 41 ha of Aquileia), with Graviscae clearly representing an outlier (6 ha).

The growth of Roman colonies is paralleled by the decline of Latin colonial foundations, in both number and popularity. Six of the ten Latin colonies known to have been sent during the period under discussion were established at preexisting sites (Placentia and Cremona, resettled in 190 BCE, had probably never been fully developed,[102] and thus should be considered as new foundations). Commissioners for the supplement of the Mid-Republican colonies of Venusia and Narnia were elected in 200 BCE (Liv., 31.49.6) and 199 BCE (Liv., 32.2.6–7), respectively. Vibo Valentia and Copia, formerly Greek and then Bruttian towns, saw few to no changes to their urban fabrics in the early Roman phase, so much so that their Latin colonial status has been interpreted as being just honorific, essentially representing a reward extended to the local pro-Roman factions for their loyalty during the Second Punic War.[103] The foundation of Bononia (189 BCE), which was planned within an extensive indigenous settlement,[104] was soon followed by the deduction of sizable Roman colonies in the same region. A similar situation is represented by the almost contemporary foundations of Luca (a Latin colony planned in 180 BCE) and Luna (a Roman colony settled in 177 BCE).[105] Given the wider

---

the Central Baths). The 2nd century BCE urban development of Carseoli features polygonal masonry terracing: Gatti and Onorati 1990.

[102] Both Placentia and Cremona were still controlled by the Romans in 217 BCE, since Scipio quartered his army in them after the battle of the Trebia (Polyb., 3.40.66; Liv., 21.56; App., *Hann.* 5.7). Placentia survived another attack in 207 BCE, but the following year both cities appealed to Rome, complaining that many of their colonists had been driven off by Gallic raiders (Liv., 28.11.10). The Gauls took Placentia in a surprise revolt in 200 BCE, plundering and burning the town and taking its inhabitants into captivity (Liv., 31.10).

[103] Because of the absence of cultural markers of Latin or west-central Italian origins such as anatomical votives and veiled heads from the known sanctuaries, and in light of the strong continuity of funerary customs at the main cemeteries, La Torre (2011: 146–47) suggests that the 3,700 *pedites* and 300 *equites* attested for Vibo (Liv., 34.53) were coopted from the native population. Given the lack of comparable archaeological data on Thurii, the same theory for Copia is based solely on literary evidence (App., *Hann.* 7.8.54, stating that the pro-Punic faction from Thurii was deported to the Roman colony of Croton). On the poor record for the first half of the 2nd century BCE at Copia, see Marino 2010: 111–20. Tweedie (2011: 463) considers Valentia and Copia as veteran colonies (the armies of Flamininus and Cato were both discharged in 194 BCE), linking the system of land allotments reported by Livy with the rank at which the colonists had already served.

[104] Malnati and Violante 1995: 106–08.

[105] The case of Luca is debated. The only reference to it is in Velleius's history of Roman colonial expansion (1.14–15), which presents problems. Salmon (1933: 30–35) notes the absence of Luna and thus a possible confusion between Luca and Luna. Livy (40.43.1) mentions the election of commissioners for an unnamed Latin colony in 180 BCE, whereas the status of Luna as a colony of Roman citizens is secure (Liv., 41.13.4). Gargola 1995: 69–70 accepts the attribution. On the value of Velleius as a source, see Tweedie 2011: 467–68 (with particular reference to the cases of Auximum and Heba).

geographical reach of the colonization program, the grant of Latin rights became unattractive to colonists, especially to Romans who would have had to relinquish citizenship in order to enlist. Not by chance, plots of 50 *iugera* of land had to be offered to recruit settlers for Aquileia (181 BCE), as opposed to the 10, 8, or 5 *iugera* allotted to colonists of Saturnia, Parma, and Mutina, who maintained Roman citizenship.[106] Even so, Aquileia struggled to get on its feet and had to be supplemented in 169 BCE (Liv., 43.17.1), when it finally received its constitution.

The layouts of the larger ex novo foundations show that new town-planning concepts were being tested throughout the period, regardless of the type of colony. Rectangular city blocks (with proportions of 2:3 or less) remained the most common design, but square or near-square insulae were also introduced for the first time (Placentia might represent the earliest example).[107] The use of ever-shorter city blocks was probably dictated by the desire to make communication between different sectors of the town easier and faster, since the design created more cross streets at the expense of the proportion of the town's surface area that would have been available to build.[108] However, the pace at which actual construction progressed does not appear to have been particularly sustained, as was the case for the Mid-Republican precedents. Thus, at both Potentia and Pisaurum (founded in 183 BCE), major urban elements were built only in 174 BCE (Liv., 41.27.11–12):

> One of the two [censors], Fulvius Flaccus – for Postumius had in fact announced that he would not let out contracts for anything which the Senate or the Roman people had not ordered – using the funds allotted to them let out contracts to build a temple of Jupiter at Pisaurum and Fundi and Potentia, where he also planned an aqueduct, and to pave with hard stone a road at Pisaurum, and at Sinuessa to extend the urban area (*scil.* beyond the earlier fortifications). In these places he gave contracts to lay out the sewer system, to encircle [the town] with a wall, to enclose the forum with colonnades and shops, and to build triple gateways. These public works were contracted out by the one censor [and completed] with great satisfaction of the colonists.[109]

---

[106] Based on census figures, Salmon (1936: 61–67) suggests that the cessation of the Latin colonization program was aimed at maintaining the number of Roman citizens in a period of demographic decline. See Brunt 1971: 190. Non-Romans were certainly admitted to the colonies of Potentia and Pisaurum in 184 BCE (Cic., *Balb.* 28). Inscribed boundary markers from Pisaurum suggest that most colonists came from west-central Italy. See Harvey 2006: 119–26. Cf. Erdkamp 2011.

[107] Conventi 2004: 201–05; Gros and Torelli 2014: 179–98.

[108] Sewell (2010: 34–35) notes how the development was probably influenced by contemporary Greek practice.

[109] *et alter ex iis Fuluius Flaccus++nam Postumius nihil nisi senatus Romani populiue iussu se locaturum <edixit>++ipsorum pecunia Iouis aedem Pisauri et Fundis et Potentiae etiam aquam adducendam, et Pisauri uiam silice sternendam, et Sinuessae maga<lia addenda> ⋆ auiariae, in his et clo<acas faciendas et mur>um circumducen<dum locauit> . . . et forum porticibus tabernisque claudendum et Ianos tris*

This passage provides the earliest evidence of building activities carried out on behalf of the Roman censors outside of Rome.[110] Colonial status, however, does not seem to have been a requirement. Whereas the *municipium* of Fundi had been granted full citizenship in 188 BCE (Liv., 38.36.7), and Sinuessa was a Mid-Republican *colonia maritima* (founded as a pair with Minturnae in 296 BCE), the same censors, acting together, built fortifications at Calatia and Auximum (Liv., 41.27.10), neither of which seems to have been a Roman colony at the time.[111] It is worth noting that two of the four towns that received the sole attention of Q. Fulvius Flaccus had ties with his family: The censor's brother, M. Fulvius Flaccus, was one of the commissioners in charge of the colonization program at both Pisaurum and Potentia (Liv., 39.44.10).[112] The circumstance might explain the opposition that Q. Fulvius Flaccus received from his colleague, and even reveal possible euergetic aims behind the scheme.[113]

In the case of Potentia, archaeological data gathered from recent geophysical surveys and targeted excavations supports the idea of protracted urban development (Figure 6.8).[114]Although the fragmentary state of Livy's testimony does not allow us to conclude that completion of the town's wall, beautification of the forum, and creation of the drainage and sewer system were part of the works initiated by Q. Fulvius Flaccus, the excavation of the west gate showed two major phases for the fortifications. The circuit consisted originally of a ditch, perhaps protected by a palisade, which was replaced by an ashlar fortification with *agger* in the second

---

*faciendos. haec ab uno censore opera locata cum magna gratia colonorum.* For the edited text, see Chaplin (2007: 310) who, however, does not translate the *in his* of 41.27.12. There are several instances in Livy where the expression means "in these (places)," and those places are the aforementioned ones (R. Marks, *pers. comm.*). In this passage it certainly must refer to Sinuessa and Pisaurum at least, but there is nothing that rules out its referring to all of the aforementioned places (i.e., Fundi and Potentia included). On the meaning of *magalia* as suburban quarters: Serv., *Aen* 1.421–22 (citing Cassius Hemina specifically on Sinuessa). Some manuscripts have *maga< . . . .>a* †*uiaria*†, so there might be reference to road infrastructure. Briscoe (2012: 145) takes "*in his*" to refer to *magalia*.

[110] Patterson 2006: 145–46.

[111] Velleius Paterculus (1.15) dates the foundation of the colony at Auximum to 157 BCE. Salmon (1969: 112–13) prefers 128 BCE based on *Lib. Colon.* 258L, but there are no reasons to doubt the earlier date.

[112] Broughton 1951: 391, n. 3.

[113] On the use of colonial commissions for aristocratic competition and the relevance of family connections, see Coles 2017 (but interpreting the text in question to mean that the projects were paid for with the communities' own funds: 300–01). Cf. the case of the *triumuir* T. Annius Luscus at Aquileia, who may have exploited his participation in the colonization program as a springboard to further his political career through the creation of a network of dependents. Discussion in Zaccaria 2014: 521–24. Laurence *et al.* (2011: 16), while recognizing that these projects individually enhanced the particular towns, take them collectively as a statement about urbanism as understood by the leaders of the Roman state (i.e., walls, temple of Jupiter, good water, and a forum surrounded with shops).

[114] Vermuelen 2014; Vermuelen and Verhoeven 2006.

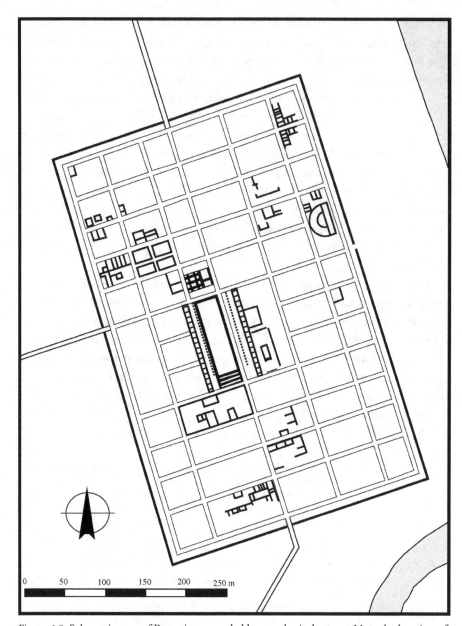

Figure 6.8 Schematic map of Potentia as revealed by geophysical survey. Note the location of the monuments attributed by Livy (41.27.11–12) to the Roman censor Q. Fulvius Flaccus, *c.* 174 BCE (forum; fortifications; podium temple on east side of the forum). Compiled from data in Vermuelen 2014. Drawing: M. Harder.

quarter of the 2nd century BCE.[115] The forum appears to have been fully developed by the second half of the 2nd century BCE at the latest, as revealed by the excavation of the podium temple on the east side of

[115] Vermuelen *et al.* 2011.

the square (featuring foundations in *petit appareil* of local calcareous sand-stone and a superstructure in fired bricks lined with *opus quadratum*).[116] Another possible temple structure has been detected on the short north side of the forum, for which a tentative identification with Livy's temple of Jupiter has been suggested (but its date and appearance remain uncertain).[117]

The distribution of concrete architecture across Roman colonial sites of the early 2nd century BCE is difficult to characterize due to the incomplete nature of the sample. Rarely has it been possible to test the deeper layers extensively, thus making the archaeological picture of the original urban form extremely fragmented (Buxentum, Puteoli, Salernum, Volturnum, Vibo, Cremona, Placentia, Bononia, Mutina, Parma, Pisaurum, Saturnia, and Luca are still occupied by modern towns). Like at Potentia and Pisaurum, for Sipontum, Mutina, and Luca the primary evidence on the first phase of the settlement is represented by the fortifications, none of which features lime-based construction techniques.[118] At Cales, Buxentum, Copia, and Saturnia, the circuit long predated the early 2nd century BCE colonial settlement; concrete repairs are attested, but cannot be unequivocally associated with the early 2nd century BCE historical dates.[119] As elsewhere, the peak in urban development has been referred to the late 2nd or 1st centuries BCE, though mostly on stylistic grounds.[120] Remains of the original circuit of Placentia and Bononia are seemingly not preserved. Fired brick buildings dating to the first phase of the colony are reported for Placentia,[121] where the earliest known stretches of the town's walls should be assigned to the second half of the 2nd century

---

[116] Percossi Serenelli 2012.

[117] Vermuelen 2014: 152.

[118] For Sipontum (*opus quadratum* of travertine/calcareous tufa): Tunzi *et al.* 2017. For Mutina (fired brick with clay mortar): Labate *et al.* 2012. On the building techniques of Republican Luca (*opus uittatum* with clay-based mortar), see Ciampoltrini and Rendini 2018, emphasizing the state of underdevelopment for most of the 2nd century BCE. Based on a reappraisal of the archaeological evidence and the results of recent excavations, Rendini (1999) dates the urban transformation of Saturnia to the post-89 BCE period, assigning the older polygonal masonry fortifications to the *praefectura* that the Romans would have established right after annexation in 273 BCE (Festus, *Gloss. Lat.* 233L).

[119] At Cales, the Mid-Republican ashlar fortifications feature stretches in *opus incertum* tentatively assigned by Johannowsky (1961: 259–60) to the 2nd century BCE based on style. The technique, however, is still used locally in the early Imperial period (Pedroni 2013), so typology has no chronological value. *Opus incertum* additions to the polygonal and ashlar fortifications of Buxentum are documented near the west gate, and have been assigned to the Augustan period. See Bencivenga Trillmich 1988: 708; Johannowsky 1992: 182. Stratigraphic evidence places the "Lungo Muro" at Copia (Casa Bianca site), which features a cemented-rubble core, in the early Imperial period: Greco *et al.* 2011.

[120] On the 1st century BCE building activities at Cales, see Johannowsky 1961: 260–62 (theater, with possible previous phase in *opus incertum*; baths). The evidence from Buxentum comes primarily from villa architecture of the mid 1st century BCE: Gualtieri and Fracchia 2014. On Copia's concrete houses from the so-called Insula del Teatro, see Malacrino 2011.

[121] Righini 1990: 278 (with an early 2nd century BCE date).

BCE.[122] Sizable 2nd century BCE wooden architecture is documented at Bononia below the 1st century BCE basilica. Because of its proximity to the forum, the complex has been interpreted as civic in nature.[123] Early fortifications at these sites probably consisted of a system of moats, earthworks, and palisades.[124] For Parma, the existence of fortifications prior to the Augustan period is inferred from an inscription commemorating, among other things, the beautification of the city gate by a *seuir* (*CIL* 11.1062), now corroborated by the excavation of a stretch featuring fired bricks bedded with clay mortar.[125] The only urban monument that has been tentatively assigned to the 2nd century BCE at the site is an ashlar podium on the west (long) side of the forum, possibly part of a temple.[126]

Occupation of the early Roman settlements at both Croton and Graviscae, on the other hand, is documented primarily through domestic architecture. At the Capo Colonna site, the area adjacent to the sanctuary of Hera Lacinia was taken over by industrial installations and private houses occupying the blocks of a grid generated by the Archaic Via Sacra, which provided the main alignment for two parallel thoroughfares crossed by a series of minor streets.[127] The quadrangular plots were progressively built up with "row houses" of medium and small size. The superstructure was in mudbrick, probably reinforced with wooden posts, and resting on footings made of rubble bound with simple clay

---

[122] On the fortifications, see Calvani Marini 1985: 266–67; Guarnieri 2000: 118 and 120 (cross section) raises the date to 190 BCE, using as *terminus ante quem* the materials recovered from the fills of a ditch that runs parallel to the fortifications on the interior side, which she suggests coexisted with the fired brick structure for some time without good reasons (a more likely explanation is that the ditch formed part of the original defensive system, and that it was obliterated for the construction of the wall). The brick size (the rectangular *sesquipedalis* of 0.45 × 0.30 m) differs from the formats attested at Ravenna (late 3rd or early 2nd century BCE) and Aquileia (mid 2nd century BCE), though it is found at Mutina (late 3rd century BCE?). On the metrology of early brick architecture, see Bonetto 2015 (with previous bibliography); Bonetto 2019: 319, fig. 1 (arguing for a Greek derivation of the rectangular type at 324).

[123] Lippolis 2000.

[124] These colonies are located atop fluvial terraces delimited by water features. On Placentia, see Dall'Aglio *et al.* 2007. For Parma, see Locatelli *et al.* 2013: 71–79. On the topography and pre-Roman fortification circuit of Felsina: Ortalli 2008.

[125] Marchi and Serchia 2019.

[126] Catarsi 2009: 425–29 (identified as a Capitolium based on location); Malnati and Marchi 2018. The monument is not included in the map of certain and likely Capitolia by Crawley Quinn and Wilson (2013: 134, fig. 4).

[127] Ruga 2014: 188, fig. 2 for the layout. The abandonment of the Greek sanctuary and the state of crisis of the settlement at Croton in the post-Hannibalic period seems demonstrated by the famous episode relating to the spoliation of the marble tiles from the temple by Q. Fulvius Flaccus in 174 BCE, to be repurposed in his Temple of Fortuna Equestris in Rome (Liv., 42.3.1–11). The looted material was returned to the original location due to opposition from the Senate in 173 BCE, but the contractors tasked with the project reported that as there was no one there with the required skills to replace the tiles, they had been left in the precinct of the temple.

mortar.[128] The technique continued to be used throughout the 2nd century BCE during the process of infilling, even for larger installations. The use of structural lime mortar is attested only in the first quarter of the 1st century BCE, for the original phase of a public building opening onto one of the thoroughfares (though only in combination with recycled ashlars).[129] As for Graviscae, Livy (41.16.12) provides reference to a gate as existing in 177 BCE, but the town's wall is not known archaeologically, and there is no evidence of other public infrastructure. Excavations showed that the Roman town was developed on top of a sequence of leveling layers (0.4–1.5 m thick), which covers the remains of the Etruscan site (whose structures had been razed to the ground).[130] Parts of three contiguous city blocks featuring multi-stratified remains of houses have been exposed. The earliest phase is represented by mortared-rubble foundations laid in deep trenches cutting into the dumps (Figure 6.9).[131] These support one or two courses of blocks, some of which may have been recycled from the demolition of the preexisting structures (which in fact consisted of shell-limestone, or *macco*, ashlars, and mudbrick walls). The fine *opus incertum* walls covering the ashlars' footings have been assigned by the excavators to the original phase and generically dated to the 2nd–1st century BCE. The concrete walls might just as well belong to later restorations of superstructures originally made with perishable materials (e.g., *pisé de terre*), mirroring the pattern seen at Paestum.[132] A destruction level containing 1st century CE pottery provides the *terminus ante quem* for the *opus incertum* walls, as well as a *terminus post quem* for the *opus reticulatum* phase that modified the houses.[133] Another masonry type featuring coursed clay-based mortared rubble is attested at the site and has been described as related to the preexisting local architectural tradition. A notable difference from the former technique is the sporadic use of ashlars (when present, blocks are employed for quoins), but in the absence of stratigraphic data and on the building types with which the technique is associated its chronology remains unclear.[134]

Perhaps unsurprisingly, the closest parallel for the Cosan evidence comes from coastal North Etruria. Two public building projects at Luna (Figure 6.10) made extensive use of structural mortar. The earliest monument is represented by the so-called Grande Tempio, which is located at the highest point on the north sector of

[128] Ruga 2014: 194.
[129] The building was subsequently transformed into public baths by the *duouiri* of the colony in the second quarter of the 1st century BCE. See Ruga 2014: 204–05; 239 (mosaic inscription commemorating the construction of the baths).
[130] Torelli 1972: 199 (Sector I).
[131] The foundations are described as "a sacco," but no information is provided as to the composition of the mortar.
[132] Torelli 1972: 209, Type A2.
[133] Torelli 1972: 209.
[134] Torelli 1972: 200, Type B1.

Figure 6.9 Graviscae. Remains of the Roman settlement, post-181 BCE. Archival photo showing the remains of mortared-rubble foundations. The fine *opus incertum* walls covering the ashlars' footing may have been added in a later phase (Torelli 1972: 209, fig. 13; used by permission).

town, aligned with one of the north–south streets (*cardines*), and probably func-tioned as the main polyadic temple.[135] Its design shares several features with the so-called Capitolium at Cosa (Figure 6.11): although smaller, at 16 × 20.5 m, the podium is characterized by the same basic proportions (3:4); the frontal staircase is flanked by projecting wings, and the deep tetrastyle pronaos has *antae* delimiting the second of two rows of columns; finally, the tripartite cella has narrow and elongated side rooms (these are subdivided into two noncommunicating spaces, the ones at the back being accessible only from the central cella).[136] The date of the

[135]  Bonghi Jovino 1973; Bonghi Jovino 1977. On its identification as polyadic temple dedicated to the goddess Luna, see Bolder-Boos 2014: 283–85.
[136]  Bonghi Jovino 1973: 686–87. *Contra* Gros 2011: 125–26 reconstructs a single central cella flanked by *alae*, giving less importance to the fact that its front wall continues across the entire width of the temple.

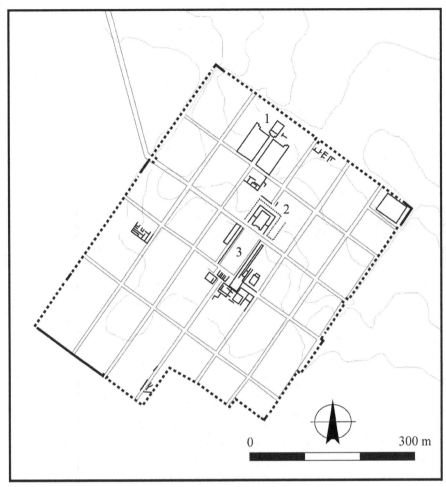

Figure 6.10 Schematic map of Luna with location of the main monuments discussed in Chapter 6. Compiled from data in Bolder-Boos 2019. Drawing: M. Harder.

temple is based on the stylistic analysis of its impressive terracotta decoration, whose quality surpasses other known examples from the region (e.g., at Cosa, Vulci, and Talamone). Despite the uncertainties surrounding the identification of the scenes, the group has been interpreted as the product of craftsmen from Rome, on account of the eclectic adaptation of iconographic models from Asia Minor, and placed within the second quarter of the 2nd century BCE.[137] A mosaic inscription (*AE* 1978.323) credits the colony's *duouiri* for letting the building

[137] Strazzulla 1992, 181–83 (160s BCE), linking the scenes with the Telephos saga. A different interpretation of the images is proposed by Pairault Massa 1992: 216–20, arguing for a direct connection with the building activities of M. Aemilius Lepidus in Rome. One of the *tresuiri* that founded the colony in 177 BCE (Liv., 41.13.4), Lepidus dedicated temples to Diana and Juno Regina *in Circo* during his censorship in 179 BCE. Both were vowed in a battle against the Ligurians in 187 BCE (Liv., 39.2.11; 40.52.1). On the broader interests of M. Aemilius

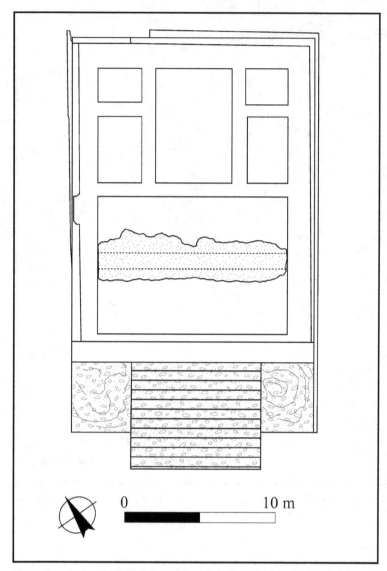

Figure 6.11 Luna. Simplified plan of the original phase of the podium of the "Grande Tempio" (2nd cent. BCE), based on data from Frova 1973. Drawing: M. Harder.

contract for the *cocciopesto* floor that decorates the pronaos, but its association with the original phase of the temple is uncertain (it could refer to a subphase).[138]

Lepidus in the colonization program in North Italy (he had served in the commissions founding Parma and Mutina): Coles 2017, 295–96; 298.

[138] *L(ucius) Folcinius L(uci) f(ilius) C(aius) Fabius [- f(ilius)] duomuirum | paui[m]en[tum faci]un[d]um dederun(t) eisd[emque probauerunt].* The inscription has been dated within the 2nd century BCE and variously assigned to the first temple or to subsequent repairs. See Frova 1984a: 35; Coarelli 1985–87: 31 (170s BCE); Nonnis 2003: 51, n. 202 (first half of the 2nd century BCE).

Figure 6.12 Luna, Grande Tempio. Archival photo of the mortared-rubble grid of the podium, viewed from the central space of the tripartite cella (Frova 1973, vol. 2: pl.179, fig. 5; by kind concession of the Soprintendenza Archeologia Belle Arti e Paesaggio per la città metropolitana di Genova e le province di Imperia, La Spezia e Savona; Archivio Fotografico Archeologia, Inv. no. L1523).

Local geology played a major role in the development of construction methods at the site. The original structure has foundations made with large sandstone pebbles sourced from the fluvial terrace on top of which the site was built, laid in lime mortar containing quartz sand and fragments of terracotta (presumably added to impart greater strength to the mortar).[139] The foundations support thick retaining walls consisting of two adjacent rings built with subhorizontal courses of mortared slabs of the local crystalline schist rock (Figure 6.12). The pieces were obtained by hammering larger fragments of the material, which tends to fracture along parallel planes, thus creating flat elements (the closest schist deposits outcropped on a promontory 3 km southwest of the town, on the other side of the Magra estuary). The slabs were laid one on top of the other with overlapping joints through the thickness of the wall without any distinction between faces and core, filling the gaps with smaller stones and chips (some of which resulted from the subsequent regularization of pointed edges). Preexisting Ligurian building traditions were exclusively based on the use of clay mortar, so the technology certainly represents an innovation (its use continued into the Imperial period).[140]

[139] Bonghi Jovino 1973: 662–63. See also Cagnana and Mannoni 1995: 139–42 (*opus incertum*); 155–59, fig. 18 (on the geology).
[140] Cagnana and Mannoni 1995: 144.

The other major sacred building at Luna, the temple dominating the north side of the forum and conventionally identified as the Capitolium, features a different building technique. Its original remains, dated to the mid 2nd century BCE, are in polygonal masonry of compact limestone (also known as Macigno; the Panchina stone, easier to work, is exploited for squared ashlar blocks).[141] The relative sequence between monumental ashlar construction and lime-based mortared-rubble architecture is difficult to determine. The two masonry styles appear juxtaposed in the tower and gate on the south front of the fortifications, with polygonal masonry at the bottom and the local form of concrete construction on top.[142] Based on the ceramic materials retrieved from associated stratigraphic deposits, the excavators have recently suggested that the lower courses of the fortification refer to the original circuit, dating the upper level to the second half of the 2nd century BCE. Further complicating the issue of chronology is the historical evidence for continued warfare in the region after the foundation of the colony: Livy (41.19) reports that both Luna and Pisae were ravaged by the Ligurians in 175 BCE, while the *Fasti Triumphales* record military campaigns in the area for 166, 158, and 155 BCE (the latter under M. Claudius Marcellus, who triumphed against both the Ligurians and the Apuani). Thus, the possibility that the completion or reconstruction of the fortifications as well as the final urban development of Luna postdate 155 BCE cannot be excluded. A dedicatory inscription carved on the plinth of a statue base honoring M. Claudius Marcellus was found in the forum (*CIL* 11.1389): It probably celebrated his triumph and may have been set up to mark the refurbishment of the square.[143] Excavations in the area south of the forum have in fact exposed an abandonment horizon covered with sterile soil, which separates the poorly preserved remains of structures made with pebble foundations (placed within the first half of the 2nd century BCE) and a more sizeable construction phase dated to the latter part of the 2nd century BCE (which, however, does not seem to feature lime mortar).[144]

## A TALE OF TWO CITIES: POZZOLANIC MORTARS AT PUTEOLI AND AQUILEIA

More systematic data on the early development and composition of the building medium comes from the sites of Puteoli and Aquileia, for which early dates have been recently reported. Although the survey above demonstrates that both would be rather exceptional cases, these contexts deserve a detailed

---

[141] D'Andria 1973.

[142] Durante and Landi 2012: 103–06, figs. 10–12 and n. 33 (on associated finds).

[143] See Frova 1984b: 8–10.

[144] Rossignani 1977: 12–31.

discussion, especially in light of the broader implications for our understanding of technological innovation and the spread of construction methods.

The harbor site of Puteoli was famous in antiquity for the supply of the *puluis* quarried from the Campi Flegrei volcanic district. The focus of ancient sources on the material from the area around Baiae and the northern coast of the Bay of Naples (Vitr., *De arch.* 2.6.1; 5.12.2; Sen., *QNat.* 3.20.3; Plin., *HN* 16.202; 35.166), the important socioeconomic role played by Puteoli since the mid 2nd century BCE (Polyb., 3.91.3–4, referring to it with the Greek name of its predecessor, Dicearchia), and the concentration of maritime villas in the area throughout the 2nd and 1st centuries BCE,[145] have been taken as a strong indication that the formula for hydraulic mortars originated in this region. While no concrete installations predating the late 1st century BCE are preserved in the harbor area,[146] the extensive use of the building medium for the urban development of the lower town is documented by the *Lex Puteolana parieti faciendo* (*CIL* 1$^2$.698 = 10.1781, 105 BCE), which records the building contract let by local magistrates for works in the area of the Temple of Serapis (as discussed more extensively in Chapter 1).[147] The text stipulates in great detail the structural requirements, including the ratio of ingredients in the binder (three parts of burnt lime for one part of volcanic sediments), the grade of rubble (as measured in weight after curing), and the size and species of timber (oak for doorposts, lintel, and corbel; fir for the components of the roof), thus demonstrating the consciousness of the commissioners for the quality of a diverse range of building materials.

Excavations on the hilltop site occupied by the earliest colonial settlement (the modern Rione Terra) have revealed a significant sample of Republican architecture, including both cemented-rubble and *opus incertum* architecture. The steeply sloped promontory, composed of Yellow Neapolitan Tuff (see Figure 5.11), was regularized by cutting artificial terraces into the bedrock and creating ashlar retaining walls (whose blocks were probably quarried in the process). The original layout is centered on an open square that occupies the highest terrace (Figure 6.13). This is bordered on the northern long side by an east–west street (*decumanus*) and features a temple in axial position (commonly referred to as a capitolium). Proportions and arrangement of the complex find a precise parallel with the layout of the forum of Liternum (one of the sister colonies of 194 BCE), whose earliest phase, however, is only partially known.[148] Two other *decumani* are attested, one farther to the north, and

---

[145] D'Arms 1970: 7–8; 17–38.

[146] Gianfrotta 1998.

[147] On the topography of Puteoli, see Gialanella 2003; Gialanella 2010. For the expansion of the settlement beyond the original fortified area in the 1st century BCE, see Sommella 1988: 217–19, figs. 65–66.

[148] The earliest feature detected in the forum at Liternum is the podium of the so-called Capitolium (identified as such on the analogy with the example of Puteoli), which is built

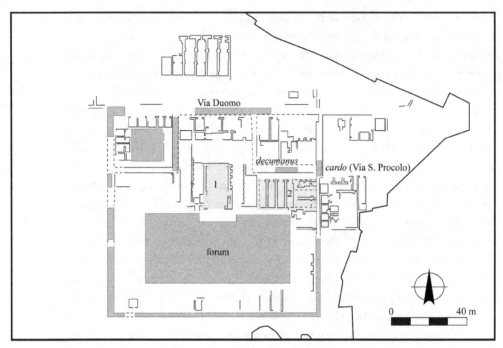

Figure 6.13  Puteoli. Schematic map of the colonial layout on the Rione Terra (paved surfaces in shaded gray). Compiled from data in Paternoster *et al.* 2007. Key: 1=Capitolium; 2="Criptoportici" complex. Drawing: M. Harder.

another south of the square, delimiting city blocks of less than 1 *actus* in width. A system of north–south axes (*cardines*) and ramps connecting the different terraces have also been mapped. Conforming to this plan is a rock-cut network of water features, including underground channels for drainage as well as cisterns for storage.[149]

With the possible exception of a semisubterranean room facing onto the Via Duomo *decumanus*,[150] the only monument that can be securely dated to the initial phase of the settlement is the forum temple. The original phase is represented by the high podium, partly carved in the bedrock and partly built up with ashlar masonry (the superstructure was rebuilt in the Augustan period).[151] Dug within the podium is a vaulted corridor paved with a decorated *cocciopesto* floor. These

with *opus quadratum* of local Tufo Grigio. An *opus uittatum* structure preserved on top of it on the south side cannot be dated with precision. The same technique is attested in the foundations of the Basilica (Room 1), whose *opus reticulatum* walls have been dated to the 1st century BCE: De Vincenzo 2018. Crawley Quinn and Wilson (2013: 141) reject the Capitolium identification at both Puteoli and Liternum.

[149] Gialanella 2010: 317–22.
[150] Proietti 2006: 519–20.
[151] Zevi and Grandi 2004.

structures do not employ any kind of mortar, as is also the case for the retaining walls that delimit the city blocks, all in *opus quadratum*. Republican-era occupation within the city blocks is attested by structures of two types: cemented rubble with large pieces (maximum 0.40 m) of Yellow Neapolitan Tuff (described as *opus incertum* by the excavators); and so-called *opus quasi reticulatum*, with smaller facing blocks of the same material and quoins in brick or ashlars of Piperno (a local grey welded tuff underlying the Yellow Neapolitan Tuff).[152] A third type, the so-called pseudo-polygonal masonry, has been categorized as a variant of the more common form of cemented rubble, even though lime mortar in it seems to have been used for pointing rather than bedding (in which case the technique should be classified as a type of drystone masonry).[153] The *opus quasi reticulatum* structures belong to multilevel buildings featuring concrete vaults and are associated with decorated floors that have been dated stylistically to the late 2nd and 1st centuries BCE.[154] By contrast, cemented rubble is used primarily for party walls in utilitarian structures whose load-bearing walls are normally in *opus quadratum*, as seen in the shops opening onto the Via Duomo *decumanus*, or in the first phase of the so-called Criptoportici complex (Figure 6.14). Located east of the forum, the latter is comprised of four parallel vaulted rooms oriented north–south (20 × 15 m), whose east side is abutted by three orthogonal vaulted rooms (about 10 × 15 m) opening onto the Via S. Procolo *cardo*. The extant building has been interpreted as a *horreum* or commercial space, but its original aspect was that of a semi-interred vaulted substructure, whose main function was to support a public monument facing the square.[155] The barrel vaults (spanning 4.50 m) are built with oblong wedge-shaped tuff blocks laid radially with some lime-based bedding mortar.

Given the lack of stratigraphic data, the dating of the cemented-rubble architecture of the Rione Terra is uncertain. The excavators assign it to the early years of the colony, but this interpretation seems contradicted by the fact that several cases are reported in which buildings made with cemented rubble destroy rock-cut water features created as part of the original orthogonal layout.[156] Thus, a date later in the 2nd century BCE is more probable.[157] The closest parallels for the vaulting system of the "Criptoportici" come from the Terme Centrali at Cumae, where a similar association with *opus quadratum* construction has been observed, and the Masseria Loreto terracing structures at Teanum. Both Anselmino (2006) and D'Alessio (2014) noted formal

---

[152] Paternoster *et al.* 2007: 25–35.

[153] Paternoster *et al.* 2007: 29–30.

[154] Proietti 2006: 518; 520–22.

[155] D'Alessio 2007b: 222–23, nn. 5–7; D'Alessio 2014: 19–20.

[156] Paternoster *et al.* 2007: 25. Zevi and Grandi 2004: 352 believe that the sector occupied by the "Criptoportici" was created by leveling a terrace along the course of the original fortifications.

[157] Cf. D'Alessio 2007b: 223–24, n. 10 ("a few decades after the foundation of the colony").

Figure 6.14 Puteoli, Rione Terra. Detail of the vaulting technique of the "Criptoportici" (Photo: M. Mogetta). Note the wedge-shaped oblong facing blocks laid radially along the intrados of the barrel vault. The vaulting ribs buttressing the vault belong to a later repair in *opus reticulatum*.

similarities with the terracing structures on the East Slopes of the Palatine in Rome, suggesting a possible connection between the two building sites.[158] It is reasonable to suppose that the local patrons in Puteoli looked first to the building industry existing at the largest centers in the neighboring region to draw skilled builders. A mid 2nd century BCE date for the monumentalization project would correspond well with the period of economic prosperity enjoyed by the site from 168 BCE onwards.

A series of lab tests conducted on a relatively small sample of standing architecture at the site suggests that cemented-rubble and *opus quasi reticulatum* masonry are closely related in terms of mortar composition, while a clear improvement in quality can only be observed with respect to structural remains of the Augustan and later periods.[159] Republican mortars are characterized by a high aggregate-to-binder ratio and contain higher proportions of extremely coarse volcanic sand. Because only the finer fraction reacted with hydrated lime, these mortars are characterized by lower pozzolanic properties. By contrast, the pozzolan in mortars of the Imperial period is well selected and is

[158] Anselmino 2006: 234–35; D'Alessio 2014: 19–20.
[159] Paternoster *et al.* 2007: 63–77.

mixed with a higher dose of lime.[160] The trace elements analysis shows
a relatively wide distribution, which perhaps indicates variation in the sourcing
of the aggregate (it is not entirely clear if this correlates with chronology, due to
the low number statistics). Samples from both periods appear well separated
from those collected from reference Vesuvian sites, though this cannot be taken
as incontrovertible evidence that only local materials were used.[161] To what
extent the *pulvis Puteolanus* quarried from the unconsolidated deposits of
Yellow Neapolitan Tuff was recognized as a superior material in the early
phase remains problematic, given that structural mortar at Puteoli is mostly
employed for walls of lesser load-bearing function.[162]

The case reported for the fortifications of Aquileia clearly demonstrates that
the judicious use of hydraulic mortars was widespread. The date of the layout of
the Latin colony, and therefore, of its fired-brick city walls is quite controversial
(Figure 6.15). Livy (43.1.5–7) records that an embassy was sent from Aquileia to
Rome in 171 BCE to complain about the unsafe state of the settlement
(*querentes coloniam suam nouam et infirmam necdum satis munitam inter infestas
nationes Histrorumet Illyriorum esse*). The reference makes it likely that the circuit
was completed only after the resettlement of the colony in 169 BCE, perhaps as
late as 153 BCE.[163] Concrete masses of irregular shape and undetermined size
have been found to fill the foundation trench of the southeast corner of the
fortifications, near the junction with one of the towers.[164] The precise extent
and depth of these features is unknown (Figure 6.16; Plate VIII.A), but the
excavators suggest that they were designed as part of the original project, with
the specific function of buttressing the town's wall at vulnerable locations.[165]
Vitruvius (*De arch.* 1.4.11) cites the case of Aquileia as a textbook example of

---

[160] Paternoster *et al.* 2007: 76, table IV.

[161] Paternoster *et al.* 2007 used Sr, Rb, and Zr, but the first two elements are not as stable as the latter, so the methodology is problematic for provenance study. See Lancaster *et al.* 2011 (recommending Nb, Zr, and Y).

[162] For scientific evidence on the continued use of the material at Baiae from the 2nd–1st century BCE onwards, see Rispoli *et al.* 2019 (with limited control on the chronology).

[163] Based on the formal incongruities in the layout, placement of the forum, and different modules of the city blocks, Lackner (2008: 31–34) has reconstructed three major phases of development: an early fort occupying a 10 ha area in the south sector of town (183–181 BCE); a first extension, reaching a total of 30 ha, with the forum occupying an axial position at the center of town (181 BCE); and a further expansion north of the Via Annia (169 or 153 BCE), which would have produced the final configuration of the Republican site (41 ha). Bertacchi (2003: 19–20) sees two phases corresponding to the early *castrum* and the final layout (which she assigns to 181 BCE and 169 BCE, respectively). Both theories have been rejected by Maselli Scotti *et al.* 2009: 243–46, who argue for a single original design planned in 181 BCE, whose construction would have been completed only after 169 BCE. Bonetto and Previato (2018: 328) suggest a 169 BCE date for the start of the construction project.

[164] Bonetto *et al.* 2016: 33–36.

[165] Bonetto *et al.* (2016: 32, n. 3) discuss the radiometric data derived from organic material associated with the foundation fills, which provides a *terminus post quem* of 380–170 BCE. On the dating, see also n. 171.

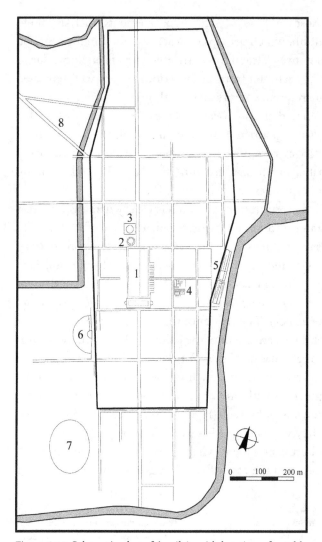

Figure 6.15 Schematic plan of Aquileia with location of notable monuments. Compiled from data in Bonetto and Previato 2018. Key: 1=Forum; 2=Comitium; 3=Macellum; 4=Domus of T. Macrus; 5=River Harbor; 6=Theater; 7=Amphitheater; 8=Via Annia. Drawing: M. Harder.

fortification building in waterlogged terrain. Initial testing revealed chemical phases identical to those that characterize pozzolanic mortars including volcanic ash, so the excavators first proposed that the mix included volcanic ash from the Campi Phlaegrei.[166] The material would have been imported to respond to the challenges posed by the environmental setting, allowing the concrete fills to

---

[166] See Bonetto et al. 2016: 36. The precise provenance had not been established, but based on the chemical signature the authors excluded the possibility that the volcanic rocks employed for the building medium came from sources north of the Apennines.

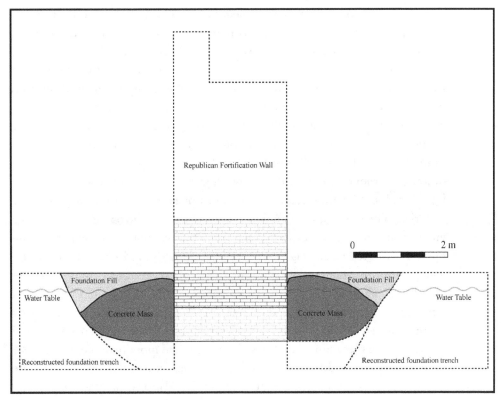

Figure 6.16 Aquileia. Southeast corner of the Republican fortifications. Restored cross section according to Bonetto *et al.* 2016. Rendered by M. Harder.

set in wet conditions and preventing any eventual infiltration of water.[167] In the northwest sector of the fortification circuit, which lies in an area affected by similar hydrology, a much different solution was adopted. The walls were built using ashlars of Istrian stone, an impermeable limestone whose quarries came probably under Roman control only after 177 BCE.[168] The choice of that material supports the idea of adaptive problem-solving based on the repurposing of resources available locally.[169] On the other hand, it would be a logical expectation to see imported volcanic ash being used on a large scale, since its high transportation costs made it economically viable only if used in bulk quantities, but this would be at odds with the contemporary pattern from central Italy, which consistently shows how early concrete construction was

[167] For a similar example of Roman overengineering, see Coletti *et al.* 2010 (final phase of the Temple of Venus in Pompeii, whose original podium was encased by a ring of blocks on top of deep concrete foundations).

[168] Previato 2015: 508–10 dates the structure to the second half of the 2nd century BCE.

[169] Bonetto and Previato (2018: 313–15) describe yet another system for the east side, where an artificial layer of gravel was deposited below the brick foundations across a stretch of 300 m.

based on the exploitation of local deposits.[170] The stratigraphic relationship between the fortification and the concrete masses, which abut the original foundation course, would be consistent with a later date for the project.

Subsequent scientific analysis of the binder has revealed that the burnt lime used for the mortar was obtained from an as-of-yet unprovenanced siliceous limestone (sources of which exist in the Southern Alps), capable of developing cementitious gels without adding volcanic ash to the mixture (chert aggregate fraction could have been another secondary activator of the pozzolanic reaction) (Plate VIII.B–C).[171] Thus, the technology employed to reinforce the southeast corner of the fortifications resulted from the expansion of an existing lime-based architectural tradition that did not rely on the use of pyroclastic materials. The Comitium, tentatively dated to the middle or second half of the 2nd century BCE, is the earliest Republican public building for which the use of lime is attested locally (again in combination with fired-brick architecture). The exterior retaining walls delimiting the stepped circular assembly space are built by juxtaposing two rows of small trapezoidal blocks of sandstone, laid in lime mortar to form horizontal courses with their flat quadrangular sides placed on the exterior.[172] The technique has been described as influenced by local practice, since these superstructures always measure more than the standard 1½ Roman feet in width. The same system was also employed for private buildings.[173] The use of cemented-rubble foundations, on the other hand, was implemented only during the 1st century BCE.[174] The most notable example is represented by the first phase of the river harbor site, which is located on the eastern side of town, running parallel to the fortifications. Given the context, the strategic use of hydraulic mortar is probable. Extensive poured concrete foundations also characterize the site's early Imperial monumentalization.[175] It is possible that these construction projects utilized

[170]  Evidence of maritime transport of volcanic materials is to date known from shipwrecks in the North Tyrrhenian Sea dating from the mid 1st century BCE onwards. The Madrague de Giens ship (*c.* 75–60 BCE; Liou and Pomey 1985: 559–68) is reported to have transported "volcanic sand" as ballast for Dressel 1B wine amphorae (from Tarracina?); in addition, amphorae of another series appeared sealed with "pozzolana" plugs (mortar? Liou and Pomay 1985: 562).

[171]  Dilaria 2020; Dilaria *et al.* 2019: 671–73. For the reinterpretation of the archaeological context: Bonetto forthcoming (dating the feature to *c.* 150 BCE).

[172]  Previato 2015: 280–85 and table 26 (Type IV.5). On the dating of the Comitium, see Previato 2015: 64–65, fig. 27.

[173]  Dilaria *et al.* 2019: 673–74. Lime mortars contain predominantly carbonate lithic aggregate, with secondary aliquots of chert and quartz and traces of sandstones, with binder/aggregate ratios of 1:2. The walls from the Republican *domus* of Titus Macrus show higher ratios of chert gravels.

[174]  Previato 2015: 251–53, with table 11 (Type III.1). On the diffusion and dating of mortared-rubble foundations, see Previato 2015: 256–59, with table 12 (Type III.4).

[175]  Summary in Previato 2015: 97, fig. 47. Unlike the later complex, these structures run parallel to the fortification.

imported pozzolana, since the material has been tentatively detected in the masonry of the theater (early 1st century CE).[176]

As evidence of an early trade of volcanic ash reaching the Cisalpine region in the context of fortification building, Bonetto *et al.* (2016) had recalled the case of Ravenna. The earliest fired-brick circuit at the site has been placed within the last quarter of the 3rd century BCE, linking its construction with Roman military interests in the region. Even though Ravenna was never refounded as a colony, the construction project has been described as a directly sponsored by Roman agents.[177] The dating is based on a small collection of pottery specimens retrieved from the construction fills of one of the towers, which consists of highly fragmented materials ranging from the first half to the end of the 3rd century BCE (the residuality of the sample suggests that the last quarter of the 3rd century should be taken as a *terminus post quem*).[178] At Ravenna, much like at Aquileia, Placentia, and Mutina, the bricks are laid across the entire thickness of the wall, though on thicker beds of lime mortar than at Aquileia (bedding clay mortar is used at Mutina).[179] Lab tests conducted on mortar samples have revealed the presence of augite, a mineral for which a provenance from central Italian volcanic deposits has been proposed,[180] overlooking that it also occurs in the products of the Euganean district.[181] Another aspect that the fortifications of Ravenna and Aquileia have in common is the adoption of Greek modules

---

[176] Bonetto *pers. comm.* Cf. Dilaria *et al.* 2019: 671 suggest that use of salt water in the preparation of the mixture could have determined a highly alkaline pH in the compounds, thus activating silica reaction of chert fragments.

[177] Malnati and Violante 1995: 116–17; Manzelli 2000.

[178] The materials are published by Malnati and Violante 1995: 114–16, and 121, fig. 12. The Greco-Italic amphora corresponds to the Vandermersch/Cibecchini Vc type (225/220–200 BCE; Cibecchini and Capelli 2013: 439–40). The Black Gloss specimens on fig. 13.2 and 13.3 can be referred to the forms Morel 2783 a1 (first half of the 3rd century BCE) and 2984 (late 3rd century BCE?), respectively. The styles of the *petites estampilles* vessels (with single central palmette at the bottom of the vase, Style G; and stamps surrounded by rouletting, Style H of the classification by Stanco 2009) can be assigned to the mid 3rd century BCE. The compact construction fills contained mostly fragments of bricks, but also river pebbles (indicating that soil was transported from elsewhere). See Bermond Montanari 1984–85: 30. *Contra* Manzelli 2000: 10, suggesting that the ceramics were being used and discarded by the masons while working at the site, taking the date proposed by Malnati and Violante 1995 as a *terminus ad quem*.

[179] As noted by Bonetto *et al.* 2016: 36 (describing the use of bedding lime mortar at Aquileia as "almost absent"). See also Previato 2015: 250 and table 10 (fired brick laid without lime mortar). Cf. Bonetto and Previato (2018: 322), who calculate that the amount of lime mortar needed to build the walls was 8,310 m³ (assuming that the composition of the fortification was 85 percent bricks and 15 percent mortar).

[180] Costa *et al.* 2000: 28.

[181] See Germinario *et al.* 2018: 427, fig. 9 for the distribution of Euganean Trachite artifacts in the region. Donati (2000) reports trachyte milestones placed along the Via Aemilia in the second half of the 2nd century BCE, which suggests that long-range trade of volcanic products from the Euganean region was already active during the early phase of Roman colonization in the area.

for the bricks (whereas at Mutina and Placentia the would-be standard rectangular *sesquipedalis* is employed).[182]

   This technical choice has been linked with the presence of Greek craftsmen, who would have been hired alongside workmen of Latin origins.[183] At Aquileia, Greek architects may in fact have been responsible for designing specific features such as the pentagonal towers and the circular gate court.[184] On the other hand, the suggestion that the construction project at Ravenna involved central Italian builders who had knowledge of pozzolanic mortars and could provide access to sources of the material, remains problematic.[185] Recently excavated evidence from the Roman theater at Padua (early 1st century BCE) points to the exploitation of rhyolitic sands from the Euganean district, which endow mortars with hydraulic properties.[186] The growing dataset from the Cisalpine region suggests that local independent developments may have played a bigger role. The announced new program of scientific testing on the mortar samples from Ravenna will hopefully clarify the issue. Based on the present state of the evidence, the possibility of a date closer to that of the fortifications of Aquileia cannot be excluded.

CONCLUSIONS

By contextualizing the available evidence on early concrete construction at colonial sites within the broader pattern of Mid-Republican urbanism, the nexus between the origins of the building medium, the emergence of monumentality, and Roman colonization can be revealed in all its complexity, avoiding the traps of cultural diffusionism. Because of the lack of any generalized trend in the archaeological phenomenon, the case studies presented above speak against essentialist views about the cultural meaning of Roman concrete and its relationship with Roman identity and ingenuity, moving the debate beyond impersonal mechanisms of technological transfer from core to periphery. Crucially, the comparison between Cosa and the other better-known colonies of Fregellae, Alba Fucens, and Paestum reveals that the development

---

[182] Ravenna: square bricks of 47–49 cm (*triemiplinthoi*), but often retouched to create rectangular elements of 47–49 × 30–32 cm). Aquileia: square bricks of 36–38 cm (*pentadoron*).

[183] On the problem, see most recently Bonetto 2015; Bonetto 2019. Latin alphabetical marks and numerals incised before the firing are attested on almost all the samples from Ravenna and have been interpreted as production marks: Manzelli 2000, 13–18. Some dubious cases have been interpreted as Greek marks (Manzelli 2000: 14–16; Bonetto *et al.* 2016: 38 n. 11).

[184] Bonetto 1998: 62–63; 78–79.

[185] Bonetto *et al.* 2016: 39, n. 17 hinedt to the Black Gloss pottery of Volterran and Latial production found at Ravenna to circumscribe the area of origins of the builders, but the circulation of ceramics could just as well be the result of independent trading networks in the region (both categories are attested at Ariminum even in the precolonial period: Malnati and Violante 1995: 109–14).

[186] Bonetto *et al.* forthcoming.

of lime-based construction at the site, which at present stands out as an isolated example, was implicated with the web of political, social, and economic negotiations that influenced the concerted efforts to resuscitate a town that had suffered substantial demographic decline in the latter part of the 3rd century BCE.[187]

The colonial supplementation of 197 BCE sets the case of Cosa apart from that of Fregellae, where an otherwise similar process of urban renewal is documented for the early 2nd century BCE. Despite the ready availability of both lime and volcanic ash in the surroundings, innovative building types at Fregellae were crafted by expanding on traditional materials and techniques (e.g., *opus quadratum* for the reconstruction of the Comitium and the Sanctuary of Aesculapius; fired bricks for vaulting in the baths). This suggests that environmental conditions alone were not sufficient to spark technological change. Were it not for the almost complete lack of parallels at contemporary Roman colonial foundations (with the problematic example of Ravenna representing the main anomaly), one might conclude from this fundamental contrast in the colonial makeup of the two Mid-Republican sites that the construction method first introduced at Cosa had exogenous origins. In order to interpret Roman colonial urbanism, the role of the *tresuiri coloniae deducendae* (and of their subordinates) in leading the colonists, organizing the space, and defining the civic institutions – in other words, in creating the conditions for city building by applying their own past experience and preference – must certainly be acknowledged. But so is the fact that the physical aspect of colonial settlements developed beyond the initial foundation through the continued interaction between colonists and locals. Successful completion of such costly enterprises could only be achieved through adaptation to local circumstances, relying on local knowledge for the survey and exploitation of available building materials, as well as efficient management of labor resources: The failed attempts at Buxentum and Sipontum, and the protracted development of Potentia and Pisaurum, where sufficient progress was the result of the direct intervention by a Roman censor acting as patron, demonstrate the high risks involved.

The main advantage of structural mortar as implemented at Cosa was that it allowed contractors to make greater use of unskilled manpower, recruiting laborers from within the colonial contingent while lowering overall construction costs in comparison with ashlar architecture. Thus, the building method

[187] On the broader context of population crisis at Latin colonies and Roman response to it, see Broadhead 2001: 87–89. In the case of Narnia, the first known case of colonial supplementation in 199 BCE (Liv., 32.2.6–7), the demographic problem was of a different nature: Delegates had reported to the Senate that colonists were not up to number, and that non-colonists had moved into the colony and were behaving as if they were colonists. The possible implications of the resettlement on the town planning are difficult to reconstruct due to limited knowledge of the early phases of the site: Monacchi *et al.* 1999.

responded primarily to economic concerns. As already discussed, however, the fact that the distinctive form was adopted for the creation of the main civic symbols might betray other possible motivations triggering the technological shift, such as the requirement for citizens of contributing *munera* in order to strengthen communal bonds, whereby structural mortar functioned as a social glue. At Aquileia, the only early feature in which a related masonry style is known to have been employed is the main political building, the Comitium. A variant of mortared-rubble architecture was added to the existing shelf, which included fired-brick architecture and ashlar masonry, incorporating elements of the preexisting local tradition (particularly on account of metrology). Perhaps not by chance, the innovation occurs in the aftermath of a colonial supplementation. Could this be interpreted, then, as another case in which we see an attempt to integrate local stakeholders in the process of identity construction through monumental building? At Luna, a Roman colony that did not require political buildings, the Grande Tempio provides a close parallel for the adoption of the new technique in the context of poliadic temple architecture, for which – whether one accepts the 160s BCE or post-155 BCE date – the larger but less nicely appointed Cosan monument may have actually represented the model, both in terms of design, construction process, and ideological aims.[188]

The evidence from both Cosa and Luna suggests that the building medium exploited exclusively local materials. Whereas at Cosa sands containing redeposited volcanic minerals were available, at Luna river sands of fluvial origin were employed. In both contexts, however, ground terracotta was used as an additive to impart hydraulic properties and mechanical strength. This is consistent with the pattern documented for contemporary Rome and Puteoli, where the fine aggregate in early lime mortars usually consists of smaller fragments of the tuffs employed as coarse aggregate mixed with the volcaniclastic sediments associated with those tuffs, and outcropping near the construction sites. The harbor sites linked with Cosa and Luna (the *Portus Lunae* had been playing a major military and commercial role for the Romans since the late 3rd century BCE)[189] did not feature any concrete installations for the period predating the late 1st century BCE, suggesting that the systematic use of select deposits from either the Roman or Campanian regions for marine-based architecture was a late development. Thus, further research on the exceptional cases of Aquileia and Ravenna is needed to clarify the issue: The state of the

---

[188] Based on her proposed identification of the iconography of the pedimental terracotta frieze, Strazzulla (1992: 181–83) suggests that the choice of the subject matter had the goal to foster the reconciliation between the neighboring communities of Luna and Pisae (which traced its mythical origins to Telephos), especially after a violent dispute concerning territorial boundaries had erupted in 168 BCE (Liv., 45.13.10).

[189] Mannoni 1985–87 dates the earliest submerged features to the Augustan period.

documentation does not make the reported early dates incontrovertible, and alternative explanations can be proposed to account for the introduction of imported material for mass-construction projects.

What the overall trajectory indicates, however, is that the early 2nd century urbanization program presented town-builders coming from the core regions of Italy with social, economic, and environmental challenges. These conditions provided the impetus for experimentation with construction methods, opening up new opportunities for the class of private entrepreneurs who, according to the standard Roman system of public building, we can assume were involved in the process. Far from being the outcome of a centrally regulated phenomenon, both the fired-brick architecture and the lime-based coursed masonry at Aquileia, which do not appear based on Roman modules, best reveal how Roman colonial sites materialized out of the close interaction between different architectural traditions.[190]

[190] Roselaar 2011 surveys the evidence for names from the Greek east, the Celtic world, Illyria, and southern Italy, concluding that Aquileia was a multiethnic community both before and after its colonization.

# SEVEN

# CONCLUSION

My intention in this study has been to retrace the formative steps of the technological innovation that lies at the root of Rome's architectural revolution: the invention of concrete construction. Commonly referred to as *opus caementicium*, cemented rubble has been traditionally conceptualized as the physical manifestation of *Romanitas*, or Romanness, partly reflecting the deeply seated belief that the Romans possessed unique practical abilities.[1] Scientific evidence from the Greek islands shows that the signature ingredient of Roman concrete, volcanic ash, was being added to create high-quality hydraulic compounds centuries before Italian builders exploited the materials available locally, so the discovery cannot be attributed to them. Rather, Roman architects should be credited for the implementation of that discovery for structural use. By reading the case studies presented in the previous chapters collectively, it finally becomes possible to elucidate the process of architectural change, contextualizing the diffusion and adaptation of the technology in the broader context of Italian urbanism, appreciating the crucial contribution of non-Roman craftsmen. Earlier models presented the introduction of structural mortar of superior quality as bound to happen, linking the subsequent dissemination to the agency of Roman sociopolitical institutions. The reassessment of the archaeological dataset from major urban centers across the

---

[1] For the essentialist view, see MacMullen 2011 (with direct reference to *opus caementicium* at 119–20). The author takes the "practical" to be one of the four salient features into which the true nature of the Roman personality can be broken down.

peninsula has demonstrated that, while relying on the economic integration of Roman Italy, the technology developed primarily as a result of independent processes that were set in motion by local circumstances and motivations.

I have introduced the book by examining the rich textual evidence available for Rome, where the innovation occurred in the midst of heated debates about excessive spending in architecture. The context allows us to tie cost-saving innovations in the organization of construction with the economic concerns of elite patrons, whether in their capacity as elected officials responsible for the letting of contracts and final inspection of public buildings or as private owners of urban mansions. As Davies (2017) remarks, successful conclusion of those projects could make or break political careers in the crowded arena of Roman politics. *Aedificare*, or to build, could be presented as a dangerous enterprise (Liv. 6.11.8: *res damnosissima*), but also as a source of *uirtus* (Sall., *Cat.* 2.7).

Recurring technological practice from both domestic and public contexts from the mid 2nd century BCE, especially the use of hydraulic mortars containing recycled waste material that enabled fast setting in airtight environments, strongly suggests that groups of builders with similar backgrounds were involved in these projects. Although the system of obligations and liabilities under contracts of the *locatio conductio operis* type was meant to protect those who had let the contract more than the contractors, I have argued that magistrates tasked with the completion of public works would have preferred to hire experts whose skills had been already put to the test. Ethnographic studies on the relationship between risk, innovation, and sociopolitical power suggest that, cross-culturally, new technologies often result from cooperation between an outsider innovator and a powerful person in a society, both of whom run fewer risks, although for different reasons.[2] The evidence from Rome places the context of innovation squarely at the top level of society. But it also suggests that the decisive stages of the initial development of concrete were achieved in a period whose politics were still dominated by corporate groups and traditional forms of patronage.[3] The important implication of my reconstruction is that it undermines the commonly accepted link between technological leaps and charismatic leaders or autocrats who could mobilize massive resources and labor. In fact, the use of pozzolanic mortar for constructional purposes, and especially its early employment for foundations, can be interpreted as an example of adaptation to the local environment. The empirical understanding and judicious selection of the natural resources available in the volcanic landscape of Rome and the Roman Campagna can be traced back

---

[2] E.g., Van der Leeuw and Torrence 1989, looking at a range of technologies such as herding, fishing, metal-casting, and pottery-making across different sociocultural systems, including precontact Hawai'i, the Inca conquest in the Andes, and Iron Age Scandinavia.

[3] Flower 2011: 59–117 describes the period between 180 and 139 BCE as one in which gradual change was achieved through paired competition and cooperation between the *nobiles*.

to the period of ashlar tuff masonry, when the technology of mixing different types of building stones first originated. The phenomenon, therefore, should be characterized as a form of local knowledge.

Archaeometry confirms that, throughout the latter part of the 2nd century BCE, the construction method was based on the use of materials quarried near the building site and processed in situ. This begs the question of what masons could easily learn, and what would be harder to discover, as they worked with new materials that were locally sourced. The use of simple lime would have made the hardening of mortared-rubble foundations and wall cores intolerably long and would have led to problems of compression in load-bearing structures that were not thick enough, causing them to collapse under their own weight. Some of the properties of hydraulic mortars would have been obvious at the time of construction, most especially the fact that such materials give water-proof characteristics and that they do not shrink on curing. Reliable curing is another feature of hydraulic cements that can be known to the masons without them knowing what else the material is good for. Previous experience with *cocciopesto*, commonly applied to prepare surfaces in bathing architecture (including in the domestic context) and for the bedding of pebble or tessellated decorations, could have offered the abstract conceptual link to switch from artificially fired clay to naturally baked earth, which is what Roman builders understood volcanic ash to be.

The social pressure of reshaping the plan and design of aristocratic houses to meet both cultural aspirations and the challenges of the political process – neatly reflected in the story about the relatively obscure Cn. Octavius succeeding in his bid to consulship in 165 BCE thanks to that practice – created the economic need to start exploiting a material that could be quarried in larger volumes and at a fraction of the production cost of ground terracotta, while achieving the same results for the required structural purpose.[4] The impetus for the extension of the technology to the public sphere probably came from failures such as those suffered by the censors of 169 BCE, who were unable to complete their ambitious building programs within the prescribed period of time. Mid-Republican ashlar architecture had already undergone significant developments, particularly in lifting technology. These advances were accompanied by an expansion of the labor market, in turn supported by the introduction of monetary instruments such as bronze coinage to satisfy the demand of free wage-laborers, both skilled and unskilled.[5] Technological change seems to have represented the only way for patrons of increasingly monumental building programs in Rome to overcome the restrictions imposed by senatorial over-sight in terms of time and resources. First developed for foundations supporting

---

[4] On the function of the elite Roman house as a locus of political activity and the relationship between *domus* and forum, see Sewell 2010: 149–59.

[5] See Bernard 2018a: 159–92.

ashlar walls and for fills between ashlars, pozzolanic mortar was implemented for structural walling and vaulting: The technology ultimately represented a formidable warranty against the loss of social and political capital. Its widespread application after 139 BCE, when secret ballots began to be carefully and intentionally introduced in Roman politics, may not come as a coincidence.

\*\*\*

The simultaneous occurrence of the building medium in the broader region around Rome undermines any core-periphery paradigm for the dissemination of the technology. Villa architecture in the *suburbium* underscores the correlation between the archaeological phenomenon and the underlying geology. Even though quarriable rubble and volcanic ash were readily available, elite buildings in the environs of Rome remained based on the old ashlar technology for a longer period of time, probably also because recycling demolition materials was rarely a factor there. By contrast, the buffer zone between the volcanic and limestone geology saw an early spike in lime-based mortared-rubble construction, but the impetus for the transition from polygonal masonry tradition came from the introduction of extra-large building types. Peer-to-peer interaction in the densely occupied countryside of Tibur may account for both the stark variation in building methods and rapid spread of designs, as picked up by reciprocal visits to the town houses and estates and further mediated by private entrepreneurs hired for – or even personally investing in – such projects.[6] The archaeological datum from Pompeii provides the strongest indication that comparable social and cultural processes were affecting the production of monumental architecture regardless of cultural boundaries.

The Pompeian evidence confirms that concrete construction could surface in different areas as a response to similar needs of elite self-presentation and competition. The use of cemented rubble can be traced back to the middle of the 2nd century BCE in the context of domestic architecture of the highest class. In the juxtaposition of expensive architectural refinements in imported stone and expedient concrete features in the Casa del Fauno or the Casa di Pansa, we can see another instance of the need to balance conspicuous consumption in the private sphere with the implementation of a building method that lowered the overall construction costs in terms of skilled labor and logistics. Greatly surpassing known contemporary examples from Rome as to the richness of designs, the luxury architecture seen in Pompeii speaks to the existence of exchange systems that operated independently from the metropolis. Sicily may have represented one of the main sources for the styles incorporated in the

---

[6] See Fentress 2013: 174, 177, with reference to such mechanism for the diffusion of *cocciopesto* in the Hellenistic west. On the role of contractors, see the discussion by Zevi (2013: 129) about the possible activities of businessmen like Sergius Orata in Latium (*c.* 100 BCE) and their connections to contemporary circles famous for architectural innovations.

new Pompeian houses.[7] The regional dissemination of the so-called *opus Africanum*, a limestone-framework walling technique utilized in Pompeii to build both canonical atrium-type dwellings and more modest "row houses" from the latter part of the 3rd century BCE onwards, demonstrates the link between the two regions.[8] What matters the most for our purposes, however, is that the introduction of concrete construction in Pompeii, roughly one generation later, represented a significant departure from the previous tradition, and that the shift correlated with status differentiation, since clay-based mortared-rubble construction continued to be used for some time in middle- and lower-class housing. Masons in Pompeii knew that lesser mortars clearly could be used to make walls stand up too but must have learned about the superior mechanical strength of hydraulic mortars by empirical observation, because they applied the material to both foundations and superstructures, including load-bearing walls.[9]

The same conditions that facilitated the early development of the technology in Rome were present in Pompeii. Pompeian builders drew their materials from a catchment area that was characterized by equally favorable environmental features, with volcanic and limestone geologies occurring side by side, and archaeometry demonstrates that Pompeii was linked to an extensive trade network around Vesuvius. The spread of *cocciopesto* in the region has also been documented for the 3rd century BCE. In short, the combined evidence tells us that the innovation could have just as well occurred independently. Moreover, epigraphic evidence shows that the organization of public building operating in Late-Samnite Pompeii mirrored the Roman system, whereby magistrates from the same wealthy families that were engaging in the beautification of the houses were also contracting and inspecting public projects. As demonstrated by the case of the Popidii family, who had direct links with the roof-tile industry, profits could also be made in the process by supplying building materials. The mechanism of transmission, therefore, corresponds well with the model I have outlined for Rome.

The extension of the technology to public building, however, lagged behind its first implementation in the domestic sphere, since the earliest safely datable

---

[7] See the example of the so-called Italo-Corinthian capitals: Lauter-Bufe 1987.

[8] The construction method was indeed common in east Sicily, where it probably came via the Punic sites of west Sicily and North Africa. It can be debated whether the dating evidence I presented for the limestone-framework architecture of Pompeii fits with the "prisoner of war" hypothesis, which Gaggiotti (1988) originally proposed to explain the diffusion of the *pauimenta punica* to central Italy – though one would expect the masonry technique to have spread to other sites of the limestone region that were being redeveloped at the turn of the century, such as Signia, Norba, or Setia, where the presence of Punic hostages and North African captives in the aftermath of the Hannibalic Wars is actually attested (Liv., 32.2; 32.26.5).

[9] Vaulting represents a notable exception, since the earliest attestations always feature oblong blocks laid radially at the intrados, a technique that derives from the vossouir technology, perhaps betraying an initial lack of confidence.

monuments can only be assigned to the period from around or after 130–120 BCE onwards. There is no need to attribute the pattern to direct Roman influence, since the phenomenon unfolded in the context of a generalized spike in the number of monumentalization projects being undertaken in the broader region of Campania and Samnium. As Maschek (2018) has noted with relation to religious architecture, this building boom in central Italy occurred at a critical juncture in which internal migration, land reforms, and disputes about the extension of Roman rights seriously threatened the power base of the ruling elites (the ill fate of Fregellae stood as a reminder). Thus, the trend can be read as the manifestation of a deliberate social strategy to avert potential crisis or collapse: By investing more resources and efforts in monumental construction that symbolized traditional authority, local aristocrats would have promoted effectively an image of internal stability.[10] Aside from temple architecture, other major building programs featuring early concrete monuments demonstrate a desire to bolster or revive existing forms of social organization. The local *uereiia*, an institution that has been interpreted as the Samnite equivalent of the Greek *ephebeia* and Latin *iuuentus*, was directly involved in some of the benefactions at both Pompeii and Cumae (respectively, the Samnite Palaestra adjacent to the Foro Triangolare, and the stadium and perhaps the Terme Centrali), whereas the Campanian *magistri* were involved in the urban renewal of Capua. Providing cities with building types that were related to the ideal of athleticism (baths with *palaestrae*; stadia) and cultural activities (especially theaters) would have certainly reinforced the message of prosperity in the face of insecurity.

The specifics of this process also meant that builders in Campania and Samnium generally had more opportunities to experiment with innovations for which contemporary Rome could not provide any prototype. The vaulted architecture associated with permanent entertainment structures provides the best example. The earliest occurrence of a freestanding *cauea* and of the use of the cross vault for the substructures at the temple-theater complex in Teanum testifies to the potential that local architects could achieve. Roman patrons were certainly letting contracts in the region in this period (the consul Ser. Fulvius Flaccus in 135 BCE used manubial funds for renovations at the sanctuary of Diana Tifatina), but were probably relying on the well-developed local industry. Increased Roman presence after the establishment of the *praefectura* in the late 3rd century BCE must have actually facilitated the creation of networks linking Roman elites and their agents with experts that likely operated on a regional scale.[11] In this perspective, the sharing of

[10]  Maschek 2018: 174–226. On the problem, see also Roselaar 2019 (especially ch. 5).
[11]  Flohr 2019 discusses the aggregate demand for decorative systems in the domestic contexts from Roman Pompeii, highlighting the role of regional markets in supporting the work of a relatively small number of specialized craftsmen working at multiple sites.

technology that must have been behind the diffusion of similar vaulting techniques between Cumae, Puteoli (Rione Terra), Teanum (Masseria Loreto), and Rome (East slopes of the Palatine; Testaccio Building) can be taken as indirect evidence of the quality of those client–patron relationships and personal contacts.[12]

***

When I first undertook this research, one of my main preoccupations was to disentangle the development and dissemination of building techniques from old arguments that associated the transmission of architectural models with the establishment of Roman hegemony in Italy, and inferred from the colonial pattern that the technology existed in some rudimentary form in Rome. Recent archaeological fieldwork at Mid-Republican colonial sites has made it abundantly clear that most monumental construction besides fortifications and temples should be assigned to the 2nd century BCE or even later, placing the phenomenon in the same phase in which concrete construction formed. These building activities were the result of an euergetic urge that was driven by the colonial elites, which managed the projects on behalf of the local socio-political institutions. By contrast, many of the early 2nd century citizen colonies resulted in failed attempts, requiring subsequent intervention on the part of the Roman state. The pace of construction in newly established colonial sites progressed more often than not in a piecemeal fashion. Even then, concrete was never regularly adopted. The most famous case is perhaps that of Potentia, one of the colonies that received contracts for monumental architecture through the direct initiative of a Roman censor in 174 BCE, for which traditional ashlar masonry, as archaeology shows, was the technique of choice.

As my survey of the evidence has ascertained, colonial encounters could have sparked technological change independently under favorable environmental conditions. Following the reinforcement of the colony, the urban transformation of Cosa focused on civic infrastructure: Structural mortar was first implemented to build the main civic symbols, but that didn't influence the construction methods in domestic architecture. While the evidence from Rome, Latium, and Campania allows us to elucidate the nexus between concrete technology and self-representation, whether at the level of individual actors (e.g., the owners of the aristocratic houses) or of corporate groups (e.g., the elites investing in communal projects on a scale never seen before), the building program at Cosa shows the same principle at work at the level of the civic body as a whole. Only those monuments which would have been

---

[12] On the patronage networks of Italian elites during and after the Roman conquest of Italy, see Patterson 2016; Terrenato 2019: 181–91; 208–11. For an example involving monumental construction, see Zevi 1997 (on the Sanctuary of Fortuna at Praeneste). For the prosopography approach, see also Cébeillac-Gervasoni 2002; 2008. On other mechanisms of interaction between Romans and Italians, see Roselaar 2019: 29–60.

instrumental in forging a sense of community – the assembly place for male citizens and the largest temple in town – were crafted using a new technique that enabled contractors to co-opt larger pools of unskilled civic labor all the way through the final stages of the construction process, while depending on native knowledge for the sourcing of the appropriate building materials – the brick-shaped sandstone pieces. Thus, colonial leaders gave both the designers and the colonists, old and new, an opportunity to materially shape the collective identity of the settlement, partly also to offset the risks of failure that colonial schemes notoriously presented.

The relevance of the distinctive Cosan technique to the broader phenomenon can be questioned. The evidence certainly confirms how the idea of building with cemented rubble could become caught up with social processes at different scales, and that technological experiments could happen at multiple points of origin under the right circumstances. At present, the development of Cosa's forum ensemble *c.* 180 BCE represents the earliest occurrence of construction with structural mortar. The immediate impact of those innovations, however, appears limited to coastal Etruria, and unrelated to the trend seen elsewhere in central Italy. The technique reemerges at Luna, a Roman colony located at the terminus of the Via Aurelia, the same interregional road that connected Rome with Cosa. The Grande Tempio, which has been identified as the poliadic temple at the site, shares building methods and elements of architectural design with the so-called Capitolium of Cosa and demonstrates how techniques could circulate within the region. Quite possibly, the same group of builders operated at both sites, executing projects characterized by stylistic and technical similarities. Through their personal networks, the patrons responsible for the monumentalization of the main temple at Luna could get access to a wide range of workshops, both regionally and from long distance.[13] When compared with regional parallels (Cosa included), the exceptional quality of the terracotta decoration associated with the Grande Tempio suggests that the locals reached out to artists of the highest caliber, possibly based in Rome, hiring them as part of the process.[14] Since transporting the heavy equipment necessary for terracotta production would not have been feasible, it is likely that these artisans were hosted in local coroplast workshops, which were in fact capable of producing different categories of objects using similar materials and techniques.[15]

---

[13] Cf. Downey 1995, who proposed a similar model to account for the diffusion of Archaic terracottas in Rome.

[14] On the political access and elite patronage connections enjoyed by ex novo colonial foundations vis-à-vis other Italian polities, see Terrenato 2019: 219–26 (especially 224–25).

[15] For the existence of kilns producing special-purpose terracotta elements in the environs of Luna, see Fabiani et al. 2019 (vaulting ribs of a type documented archaeologically at Fregellae).

The degree of mobility of workers in building trades is indeed a surprising aspect of early 2nd century BCE colonial urbanism. As Bernard (2019) aptly notes, while individual building projects could generate a large aggregate demand for skilled craftsmen depending on size, each particular skill was often required for a short time, as part of a schedule that progressed unevenly and sometimes unpredictably. Thus, the unstable nature of strictly local work compelled builders to travel frequently from site to site depending on job opportunities, and to rely on their own social networks to find customers.[16] We may refer to a process of this kind to account for the regional distribution of techniques as well as variation within sites (as seen at Cosa and Luna). At the broader level of analysis, this situation is neatly reflected in the epigraphic record from Hellenistic central Italy (assuming that it was more practical for artisans to move than for finished products): The signatures found on building elements (e.g., on stone blocks, wall paintings, or mosaics) demonstrate that skilled building workers other than coroplasts were predominantly of nonlocal origins.[17] While the presence of names of enslaved craftsmen or freedmen in the dossier suggests that the movements of skilled labor may have been determined to some extent by the social and economic links and interests of those who claimed them as property,[18] the activity of firms and entrepreneurs that could operate freely under the optimal setting brought about by the Roman conquest as well as of wage laborers of free status must also be accommodated.[19] Early brick architecture in the Cisalpine region, and especially its application to fortification-building, represents perhaps the best archaeological example in this sense. The metrology of the fired bricks and the methods of laying them across the entire thickness of the walls on top of stratified foundations betray a derivation from Greek practice of the late 4th and 3rd centuries BCE, indicating that both skilled and unskilled labor were involved in the process. Close comparanda can be found in mainland and northern Greece, Southern Italy, and Sicily (though the early attestations from Ravenna and Aquileia point to a preferential connection across the Adriatic).[20] Rome's urbanization program in the Po Plain, an area that was characterized by the lack of suitable stone deposits and by an abundance of clay sources, opened up unprecedented work opportunities for foreign craftsmen

[16] Harris 2015 holds the view that in most cities aggregate demand supported many highly specialized decorators.
[17] Bernard 2019: 503, table 4 (mostly datable from the later 2nd century BCE onwards).
[18] On the role of enslaved people as skilled labor, see Bernard 2016: 65–66.
[19] While the first overseas conquests certainly accelerated the phenomenon, the growth of slavery is now viewed in more gradualist terms, with increments spreading over a longer period of time: Scheidel 2011, table 14.2 (annual mean from c. 3,300 for 297–241 BCE, to c. 5,300 for 241–202 BCE, to c. 8,701 for the 202–167 BCE period). Nevertheless, the Mid-Republican building industry of Rome was not influenced by it.
[20] Bonetto 2019; Previato 2019.

that could offer extensive experience with clay-based building techniques, while the colonial contingents could supply the unskilled labor. Innovations first achieved in this context, such as brick-faced concrete, eventually trickled back to Rome, turning the core-periphery model on its head.

*** 

A recent provocative study by Scheidel (2019) has challenged the relationship between centralization and technological innovations, describing the collapse of the Roman Empire as a positive development for scientific and technological advances.[21] In his perspective, the fragmentation of Western Europe that followed Rome's demise brought that rich diversity which encourages creative breakthroughs.[22] In a much narrower scope, I have tried to argue that early Roman concrete architecture emerged out of the interactions occurring within the complex mosaic of polities that made up Roman Republican Italy, thus challenging from a different perspective the supposed "monolithic" properties of the building medium. Much like the early development of reinforced concrete in the 19th century, cemented rubble was invented "several times, in slightly different ways and in different places, [. . .] dispersed across a variety of different groups."[23] The social and cultural context of Rome's expansionism produced the ideal conditions for the widespread application of concrete to monumental architecture. Far from representing a key step in the path toward the disappearance of pre-Roman traits across the peninsula, however, its diffusion resulted from the dynamic exchange of practice between old and new elites, Roman generals and magistrates, entrepreneurs, local commoners and, to some extent, soldiers,[24] peaking paradoxically in the period of endemic instability, from the age of the Gracchi onwards. Contemporary developments in other spheres of cultural production should also be brought in to evaluate in full the significance of this crucial yet late phase for the emergence of Roman material culture.

Having established a reliable chronological framework for the main concrete building types and techniques of the Roman Republican period, this book will

---

[21] Scheidel 2019.

[22] Cf. Adams 1996: 42–46 considers the Roman engineering achievements of the Late Republican period as applications of previously existing knowledge rather than steps in some completely new technological direction. DeLaine 2006 examines the conflicting attitudes toward economic rationality in Roman construction, especially in the Imperial period.

[23] Forty 2012: 15–16. That the site of major use of a given technology is the site of its innovation has been recognized as a long-held assumption of modern nationalistic discourse: Edgerton 1999. As a general rule, modern countries make greater use of technology innovated abroad than of technology innovated at home (unless they also dominate industrial production), and no positive correlation is found between rates of innovation and rates of economic growth.

[24] On the role of the military in public construction of the Imperial period, see Lancaster 2015: 9. For the Republican period, see the discussion by Anderson 1997: 26–32 (on L. Cornelius, *praefectus fabrum*).

hopefully provide a useful reference tool for future studies that will apply geochemical methods for the characterization of the composition and physical properties of Roman-era mortars, demonstrating both the value of combining architectural analysis and scientific testing and the need to interpret the results against the bigger picture of the origins of concrete construction in Italy. The preliminary results of the systematic program of scientific analysis at Aquileia, where we now know that hydraulic mortars could be obtained by burning siliceous limestone, prompts us to acknowledge that builders outside the core region of Rome had other ways to create cementitious binders than adding volcanic ash, evidently unrelated to the contemporary realities at both Rome and Puteoli (where early mortars did not feature selected volcanic ash, exploiting predominantly the smaller fraction of the same material that was used as coarse aggregate). The composition of samples from easily accessible monuments at the key sites treated in my study, especially the *ager Tiburtinus*, Cosa, and Cumae, for which only macroscopic observations are currently available, will also merit systematic research. Experiments for the scientific dating of early Roman concrete have been conducted at several Late Republican sites in Latium (Praeneste, Tibur, Tarracina), particularly using $^{14}$C AMS analysis of mortars, but have so far produced inconsistent results.[25] It should be stressed that in most cases the implementation of lab protocols and the interpretation of ambiguous results depend on the comparison of the calibrated age profiles obtained in the tests with the estimated age of monuments. The continued refinement of the chronology based on archaeologically dated sites and monuments is, therefore, a precondition for future developments in this field.

Finally, the progress of work on the relative cost analysis of Late Republican architecture will put us in a better position to assess the economic scale of the phenomenon in relation to Imperial Rome.[26] One area that still awaits a comprehensive treatment to quantify the energetics of concrete construction is that of lime production. There is a limited number of excavated lime kiln sites in association with villa estates north of Rome, but their late date does not allow us to draw generalizations about the organization of the industry for the period under discussion. The systematic application of remote sensing techniques to low-visibility areas such as the forested slopes of the limestone region in combination with pedestrian survey could reveal the particulars and clarify the chronology in relation to the broader process of architectural change. The comparison in manpower requirements between imperially sponsored projects in Rome and well-documented Republican-era building programs in central Italy, such as the iconic Sanctuary of Fortuna at Praeneste (whose monumental

---

[25] See Ringbom *et al.* 2011: 204–06; Ringbom *et al.* 2014: 626–27. The calibration curve for C$^{14}$ in the period between the 2nd and 1st centuries BCE has a number of "loops," so even if this method worked well, there would still be a limit on the precision possible.

[26] For current perspectives on the main methodological issues, see DeLaine 2017.

development fits with the model outlined in this book) or the Pompeii forum ensemble, also merits further investigation. For too long the focus of much discussion has centered on aristocratic patrons and celebrated architects. Reconstructing the overall magnitude of the labor input and exploring its relationship to agricultural production will enable us, at last, to acknowledge the efforts of voiceless ordinary people who contributed with their work to one of the greatest cultural manifestations of Classical antiquity.

# APPENDIX

# CATALOG OF SITES

1   EARLY CONCRETE CONSTRUCTION IN ROME: EVIDENCE FROM
DATABLE PUBLIC MONUMENTS

| Monument | Building Technique | Type of Rubble | Vaulting Technique (Span) | Traditional Chronology | Stratigraphic Dating | Other Dating Evidence |
|---|---|---|---|---|---|---|
| Magna Mater (*Phase II*) [Figure 3.4.1] | CR; OI; OQR | TL; TGVT; Tr; P | CR on wooden centering (4.00–4.50 m); TL voussoirs | 204–191 | 150–100 | 102–101 (*locatio?*) |
| "Scalae Graecae" [Figure 3.4.2] | OI | TL | CR (2.80–5.00 m) with oblong wedge-shaped facing pieces laid radially (0.36 × 0.19 m; thickness: 0.08 m at the extrados, 0.06 m at the intrados) | *c.* 200–167? | n/a | 150–100? (cf. *Atrium Vestae*) |
| Atrium Vestae [Figure 3.4.3] | CR? | TGVT; TL; C | – | Late 3rd–mid 2nd cent. | 100–50 | Before 47 fire |
| Testaccio Building [Figure 3.4.4] | OI | TGVT or TGPP; C (lower parts); TL | CR (8.30 m) with oblong wedge-shaped facing pieces laid radially (max. 0.57 m long; 0.12 m at the extrados, 0.10 m at the intrados) | 192–174 (Porticus Aemilia) | n/a | *Naualia* (110–100?) |
| Via Consolazione (*Substructio super Aequimelium?*) [Figure 3.4.5] | OQ; OI | ? | – | 189 or 174 | n/a | n/a |
| Cliuus Capitolinus [Figure 3.4.6] | OI | C (core); TL (facing pieces) | CR (1.50 m) with oblong wedge-shaped TL facing pieces laid radially | 174 | n/a | Cf. Temple of Concord |
| Palatine East Slope (*Fortuna Respiciens?*) [Figure 3.4.7] | CR or OV? | TL (walls); TGVT (vaults) | CR (2.90–3.15 m) with oblong wedge-shaped facing pieces laid radially | 167–150 BCE or *c.* 146 | n/a | Via di S. Gregorio pediment? |

*(continued)*

(continued)

| Monument | Building Technique | Type of Rubble | Vaulting Technique (Span) | Traditional Chronology | Stratigraphic Dating | Other Dating Evidence |
|---|---|---|---|---|---|---|
| Castor and Pollux (*Phase I.A*) [Figure 3.4.8] | CR | C (frequent); TL, P | – | c. 164 (censorship of L. Aemilius Paullus) | n/a | Before 117 (Phase II); voting reforms 139–137? |
| Lacus Iuturnae (*Phase II.1*) [Figure 3.4.9] | OI; OQ | ? | – | c. 164 | n/a | After 117 (cf. *Castor and Pollux*); before 78–74 |
| Veiovis (*Phase II*) [Figure 3.4.10] | CR? | TGVT | – | c. 150 | 150–120? | CIL $1^2$.658 (122)? Before 80–70 (Phase III) |
| Porticus Metelli [Figure 3.4.11] | OI | TGVT; TL | – | c. 146 | n/a | 143–131 (*locatio?*) |
| Concord [Figure 3.4.12] | CR | TGVT | – | 121 | n/a | |
| Victoria (*Phase II*) [*Figure 3.4.13*] | CR | TGVT; TL; P (Italo-Corinthian capitals); T | – | n/a | 150–100 | After 111 fire |

**Key:** CR=cemented rubble; OQ=*opus quadratum*; OI=*opus incertum*; OQR= *opus quasi reticulatum*; OR=*opus reticulatum*; OV=*opus uittatum*; TL=Tufo Lionato; TGPP=Tufo Giallo di Prima Porta; TGVT=Tufo Giallo della Via Tiberina; Tr=Travertine; P=Peperino; C=Cappellaccio. All dates BCE.

2  EARLY CONCRETE CONSTRUCTION IN POMPEII: EVIDENCE
FROM DATABLE HOUSES

| House | Stratigraphic Dating | Type of Rubble |
|---|---|---|
| Casa del Fauno (VI.12) [Figure 5.4.1] | 175–150 or later | SL; CL (with NT façade) |
| Casa del Centauro (VI.9.3–5) [Figure 5.4.2] | After 175–150 | SL; CL |
| Casa di Sallustio (VI.2.4) [Figure 5.4.3] | 150–140 | SL |
| Casa dell'Ancora (VI.10.7–8) [Figure 5.4.6] | c. 140 BCE? Or 150–100 | SL; CL; Cemented-rubble barrel vaults? (max span 5.10 m) |
| Porta Vesuvio (VI.16.26–27) [Figure 5.4.8] | 140/130–110 | CL; SL (quoins); SL and Cr rubble in the back part of the house (remodeled at later stage?) |
| Casa delle Nozze di Ercole (VII.9.47) [Figure 5.4.9] | 125–100 | SL; CL (with NT pillars and SL quoins in the atrium) |

**Key:** SL=Sarno Limestone; CL=Compact Lava; Cr=*Cruma*; NT=Nocera Tuff. All dates BCE.

3  EARLY CONCRETE CONSTRUCTION IN POMPEII: EVIDENCE FROM
DATABLE PUBLIC MONUMENTS

| Site | Building Technique | Type of Rubble | Vaulting (Span) | Stratigraphic Dating | Other Dating Evidence |
|---|---|---|---|---|---|
| Stabian Baths [Figure 5.4.13] | CR; OI; OQ (NT quoins) | SL; CL | SL Vossoirs (north wing: 3.80 m); CR (east wing: 6–7 m) | Around or after 125 | Vetter 1953.12 |
| Temple of Apollo [Figure 5.4.14] | CR; OQ (SL and NT podium) | SL; CL | SL Voussoirs (cisterns: 1.35 m) | 150/125–100? (fill of ditch and destruction of *tabernae* on east side) | Vetter 1953.18 (cella mosaic); *CIL* 10.800 (altar; early colonial period) |
| Basilica [Figure 5.4.15] | OI | CL | CR (*tribunal*: 5.00 m) | Post-112 (Rhodian stamps) | *CIL* 10.794 (78) |
| Temple of Venus [Figure 5.4.18] | CR; OQR; OQ | SL; Cr | CR (cisterns: 2 m) | Mid/Late 1st cent. | Obliterates previous CR phase (domestic?) |

*(continued)*

*(continued)*

| Site | Building Technique | Type of Rubble | Vaulting (Span) | Stratigraphic Dating | Other Dating Evidence |
|---|---|---|---|---|---|
| Quadriporticus [Figure 5.4.20] | OI; OQ (NT) | SL (large pieces); CL (west terracing) | Vossoirs (SL) (northwest staircase: 1.20 m) | After 130 | Foro Triangolare (terracing wall); Samnite Palaestra (Vetter 1953.11; after 123?) |
| Fortifications (Porta Stabia) [Figure 5.4.24] | OI; OQ | SL; CL | CR (Gate: 4.00 m) | *c.* 100 | Vetter 1953.8 |

**Key**: CR=cemented rubble; OI=*opus incertum*; OQR=*opus quasi reticulatum*; OQ=*opus quadratum*; SL=Sarno Limestone; CL=Compact Lava; NT=Nocera Tuff; Cr=*Cruma*. All dates BCE.

## 4   EARLY CONCRETE CONSTRUCTION IN CAMPANIA: EVIDENCE FROM DATABLE PUBLIC MONUMENTS

| Monument | Building Techniques | Vaulting System | Stratigraphic Dating | Other Evidence |
|---|---|---|---|---|
| Cumae, Terme Centrali [Figure 1.1.14] | OQ (walls); CR (founda-tions); OI panels | Wedge-shaped oblong facing blocks laid radially at the intrados (7 m) | n/a | *uereiia* inscription |
| Cumae, Stadium [Figure 1.1.14] | OI | n/a | 150–100 | Late 2nd cent. (podium moldings); *uereiia* inscription |
| Capua, Temple and Sanctuary of Diana Tifatina [Figure 1.1.7] | OI? | n/a | n/a | 135 (*temenos*) 108 (cella floor) |
| Teanum, Masseria Loreto [Figure 1.1.46] | CR (foundations); OI? | Vaulted substructures (Terrace IV) | After 211 (coins) | 200–150? (Temples A–B); Corinthian order? |

**Key**: CR=cemented rubble; OI=*opus incertum*; OQ=*opus quadratum*; YNT=Yellow Neapolitan Tuff. All dates BCE.

## 5    EVIDENCE FROM COLONIAL SITES FOUNDED OR RESETTLED IN THE 2ND CENTURY BCE MENTIONED IN THE MAIN TEXT

| Site | Status | Foundation Date (Size) | Resettlement Date (Size) | Earliest Use of Structural Mortar |
|---|---|---|---|---|
| Alba Fucens [Figure 1.1.1] | L | 303 (32 ha) | n/a | Forum buildings (1st cent.) |
| Aquileia [Figure 1.1.2] | L | 181 (30 ha) | 169 (41 ha) | Fortifications (c. 150?); Comitium (150–100); in association with fired-brick architecture |
| Auximum [Figure 1.1.3] | R | 157 or 128 (13 ha) | n/a | n/a |
| Bononia [Figure 1.1.4] | L | 189 (36 ha) | n/a | n/a (wooden architecture) |
| Buxentum [Figure 1.1.5] | R | 194 (10.4 ha) | After 186 (10.4 ha) | Fortifications (concrete repairs); Villa sites (mid 1st cent.) |
| Cales [Figure 1.1.6] | L | 334 (64 ha) | Before 184 (64 ha) | Fortifications (2nd cent.?) |
| Copia [Figure 1.1.9] | R | 199 (50 ha?) | n/a | Houses at Insula del Teatro (late 2nd cent.) |
| Cosa [Figure 1.1.10] | L | 273 (13.5 ha) | 197 (14 ha) | Comitium (200–175); "Capitolium" (175–150); brick-shaped stone pieces (sandstone); boulders in foundations |
| Cremona [Figure 1.1.12] | L | 218 (?) | 190 (?) | n/a |
| Croton [Figure 1.1.13] | R | 194 (5.5 ha) | n/a | Capo Colonna, Baths (100–75) |
| Fabrateria Nova [Figure 1.1.15] | ? | 124 (37 ha) | n/a | Urban development |
| Fregellae [Figure 1.1.16] | L | 328–313 (82 ha) | n/a | Minor repairs of the podium foundations of Temple of Aesculapius (mid 2nd cent.?) |
| Grauiscae [Figure 1.1.19] | R | 181 (6 ha) | n/a | Houses at Sector I (2nd–1st cent.?) |
| Liternum [Figure 1.1.21] | R | 194 (13 ha) | n/a | Opus uittatum: "Capitolium" (2nd cent.?); Basilica (1st cent.) |
| Luca [Figure 1.1.22] | L | 180? (38 ha) | n/a | n/a (opus uittatum with clay-based mortar) |
| Luceria [Figure 1.1.23] | L | 314 (30 ha) | 200 (30 ha) | n/a (opus quadratum) |

(continued)

*(continued)*

| Site | Status | Foundation Date (Size) | Resettlement Date (Size) | Earliest Use of Structural Mortar |
|---|---|---|---|---|
| Luna [Figure 1.1.24] | R | 177 (24.6 ha?) | 155? (24.6 ha) | Grande Tempio (175–150); brick-shaped stone pieces (schist); pebble foundations |
| Minturnae [Figure 1.1.25] | R | 296 (2.25 ha) | Before 191? organic growth (28 ha) | Forum buildings (1st cent.) |
| Mutina [Figure 1.1.26] | R | End of 3rd cent. *apoikia* (?) | 183 (40 ha) | n/a (fired brick with clay mortar) |
| Narnia [Figure 1.1.27] | L | 299 (7 ha?) | 199 (max 12 ha?) | n/a (fired brick with clay mortar) |
| Norba [Figure 1.1.28] | L | Mid 4th cent.? (37 ha) | n/a | Terme Centrali (late 2nd or early 1st cent.); extension of *domus* (opus incertum) |
| Ostia [Figure 1.1.30] | R | c. 340 (2.4 ha) | 2nd–1st cent. growth (69 ha) | n/a (opus quadratum and mortared rubble); opus incertum temples (late 2nd cent.) |
| Paestum [Figure 1.1.31] | L | 273 (120 ha) | n/a | *Opus uittatum* (houses; not earlier than 1st cent.) |
| Parma [Figure 1.1.32] | R | 183 (40 ha) | n/a | n/a (fired brick with clay mortar) |
| Pisaurum [Figure 1.1.33] | R | 184 (18 ha) | n/a | n/a |
| Placentia [Figure 1.1.34] | R | 218 (?) | 190 (38.4 ha) | Fortifications (fired brick with lime mortar; *sesquipedales*) |
| Potentia [Figure 1.1.36] | R | 184 (18 ha) | 174 (18 ha) | n/a (opus quadratum fortifications; forum temple with *petit appareil* of local sandstone and superstructure in fired bricks lined with ashlars) |
| Puteoli [Figure 1.1.38] | R | 194 (3 ha) | Organic growth post-168? | Rione Terra "Criptoportici" (mid 2nd cent.?); cemented rubble (max. 0.40 m); barrel vaults with oblong wedge-shaped facing pieces laid radially at the intrados |
| Ravenna [Figure 1.1.39] | ? | Late 3rd cent.? (28.5 ha) | n/a | Fortifications (fired bricks with lime mortar) |
| Salernum [Figure 1.1.40] | R | 194 (18 ha) | n/a | n/a |
| Saturnia [Figure 1.1.41] | PR | 273 (P) (26 ha) | 183 (R) (26 ha) | Fortifications (concrete repairs); urban transformation post-82 |

*(continued)*

*(continued)*

| Site | Status | Foundation Date (Size) | Resettlement Date (Size) | Earliest Use of Structural Mortar |
|---|---|---|---|---|
| Sinuessa [Figure 1.1.44] | R | 296 (15.6 ha) | 174 (15.6 ha) | n/a |
| Sipontum [Figure 1.1.45] | R | 194 (18 ha) | After 186 (18 ha) | n/a (*opus quadratum* of travertine/calcareous tufa) |
| Tempsa [Figure 1.1.48] | R | 194 (24.2 ha) | n/a | Piano della Tirena (late 2nd cent.)? |
| Vibo Valentia [Figure 1.1.52] | R | 199 (200 ha?) | n/a | n/a |
| Volsinii Novi [Figure 1.1.53] | ? | 264 (65 ha) | n/a | Predominantly ashlar; *opus incertum*: Casa delle Pitture (Phase II, post 200–150?) |
| Volturnum [Figure 1.1.54] | R | 194 (7 ha?) | n/a | n/a |

**Key**: R=Roman colony; L=Latin colony; P=*Praefectura*. All dates BCE. Compiled from spatial data collected in Sewell 2015.

# GLOSSARY

**actus:**     A Roman land measurement (about 35 m in length or 120 Roman feet).

**aediles:**     From *aedes*, temple; in Rome and Roman municipal towns and colonies, a pair of elected magistrates responsible for the maintenance of public buildings and infrastructure.

**aggregate:**     Technical term used to refer to both fine and coarse materials (inert sand, gravel, or crushed stone) used in concrete. See also *caementa*.

**annular vault:**     As the name suggests, a vault arising from two or more walls arranged in a circle.

**apodyterium:**     The changing room in a Roman-style bath building. See *caldarium*, *frigidarium*, *laconicum*, and *tepidarium*.

**barrel vault:**     Vault whose shape approximates that of a semicylinder sitting atop two parallel walls.

**basilica:**     In Roman architecture, a multipurpose Roman building (usually used for legal proceedings). Basilicas are often a part of the forum. The fully developed type consists of a large rectangular hall forming a tall colonnaded central nave with upper galleries and clerestory windows.

**basis uillae:**     In classic villa architecture, a system of vaulted substructures creating an artificial platform occupied by the residential quarter.

**buttress:**     A projecting support of stone or brick built against a wall to sustain lateral thrust. See vault.

**caementa**     Latin word for stone rubble.

**caldarium:**     Hot water room in a Roman-style bath building. See *apodyterium*, *frigidarium*, *laconicum*, and *tepidarium*.

**cardo:**     A north–south road or axis in a Roman city, military camp (*castrum*), or land division schemes. See *decumanus*.

**cella:**     Inner, main chamber of a temple, containing the cult image (*naos* in Greek). The term is also used for rooms in tombs. See *pronaos*.

**censor:**     One of two Roman magistrates elected every eighteen months, whose duties included the administration of the finances of the state, under which was classed the erection of all new public works.

**centering:**     Wooden planking required to form and support concrete vaults during construction. Centering for the largest vaults depended on the principles of truss construction.

| | |
|---|---|
| *chalcidicum*: | In Roman architecture, the entrance vestibule of a public building, such as a *basilica*, that opens onto a forum (e.g., the Eumachia Building at Pompeii). |
| *cliuus*: | Latin word for slope; may refer to a road ascending a slope or hill. |
| *cocciopesto*: | An artificial compound with hydraulic properties, made of tiles broken up into very small pieces, mixed with mortar, and then beaten down with a rammer. Also known as *opus Signinum* (from Latin the town of Signia). Mainly used for waterproofing and pavements. |
| **concrete**: | A man-made Roman building material created by the mixture of stone fragments, and a high-quality mortar with high-quality hydraulic (i.e., pozzolanic) properties. See also aggregate, mortar. |
| *conductor*: | In Roman building, the contractor who has agreed to organize an architectural project on a fixed price. |
| **cross vault**: | A vault formed by the intersection at right angles of two barrel vaults. Also called a groin vault. |
| *cryptoporticus*: | Often used interchangeably with *basis uillae*, the term should only be applied to aboveground covered passageways enclosed by side walls provided with windows on one or both sides, as seen in villa architecture. |
| *cuniculus*: | A type of tunnel used for a cistern; a water channel. |
| *decumanus*: | An east–west road in a Roman city or military camp (*castrum*). See cardo. |
| **dipteral**: | Adjective denoting a building (usually a temple) surrounded by two rows of freestanding columns, instead of one. See also peripteral. |
| *domus*: | In Roman architecture, a high-status urban dwelling. |
| *emplekton*: | A Greek building technique where two parallel walls are constructed and the core between them is filled with rubble or other infill. The technique is singled out by Vitruvius (*De arch.* 2.8.7) for its excellent combination of building materials (hard stone) and of bonding blocks or rubble elements through the thickness of the wall. |
| *emporium*: | A Latin term for a trading station and/or market (town). |
| **engaged column**: | Column embedded in a wall and partly projecting from the surface of the wall, sometimes defined as semi- or three-quarter detached. |
| **entablature**: | A horizontal, continuous lintel supported by posts, columns, or a wall, comprising the architrave, frieze, and cornice. |
| **extrados**: | the upper or outer curve of an arch or vault. |
| *fauces*: | An architectural term given by Vitruvius (*De arch.* 6.3.6) to identify narrow passages that grant access to adjoining courts, the proportions of which are defined in relation to the width of the *tablinum*. In the literature on domestic architecture it usually refers to the entrance corridor. |

| | |
|---|---|
| **flange:** | A projecting rim or rib attached to an architectural element (e.g., tile), to lift or connect it with another. |
| *frigidarium:* | Cold water room in a Roman-style bath building. See also *apodyterium, caldarium, laconicum,* and *tepidarium.* |
| **header:** | In ashlar construction, a block placed with the longest end perpendicular to the face of the wall. |
| *horrea:* | A type of warehouse, public or private, used for the storage of different commodities. |
| *impluvium:* | Shallow basin in the atrium of a Roman house. It is normally connected with a cistern or tank, used for collecting rainwater that falls through the *compluvium.* |
| *insula:* | Latin word for island. In Roman town planning, a city block (i.e., a building area surrounded by four streets), or a type of apartment building that occupied an entire city block. |
| **intrados:** | The lower or inner curve of an arch or vault. |
| **isodomic masonry:** | A technique of wall construction with ashlars. It uses perfectly cut, completely regular squared stone blocks of equal height, and sometimes of the same length. The vertical joints between the blocks create a symmetrical pattern. |
| **Italo-Corinthian:** | Type of capital first developed in Hellenistic Sicily, in association with the classical Ionic columnar order. Compared to the normal Corinthian, the design is characterized by squatter proportions and a vegetation motif with two rings of acanthus leaves (the second of which is very tall). These have lobes with undulating margins and form projecting helices. The flower (or fleuron) on the abacus expands on the lower register. |
| **jamb:** | A post or surface lining a doorway, window, or other aperture in a building. |
| *laconicum:* | The dry sweating room in a Roman-style bath building, typically adjacent to the caldarium. See *apodyterium, caldarium, frigidarium,* and *tepidarium.* |
| **lapilli:** | Rock fragments falling out from a volcanic eruption (*tephra*), whose size is 2 to 64 mm in diameter. See also pyroclastic, scoria. |
| *lateres cocti:* | Latin for fired brick, produced to standardized size (*bessalis:* $^{2/3}$ Roman foot; *sesquipedalis:* 1 ½ feet; *bipedalis:* 2 feet). |
| *lateres crudi:* | Latin for sun-dried mudbrick. |
| **lime:** | A material derived from burning stones containing calcium carbonate ($CaCO_3$), usually limestone. The stones were burnt in a kiln at around 900–1000°C in order to release carbon dioxide. The reaction turned them into calcium oxide (CaO), or "quicklime," which was subsequently combined with water to produce calcium hydroxide ($Ca(OH)_2$), or "slaked lime." |

| | |
|---|---|
| *locatio conductio operis*: | The most common framework regulating architectural projects in Republican Roman architecture. In its basic form, the *locatio conductio operis* holds the contractor who has agreed to organize the job on a fixed price accountable for the correct execution of the work until final inspection and approval, normally by the same individual who let out the contract. See also *conductor*, *locator*, and *probatio*. |
| *locator*: | A private individual or magistrate letting a legally binding contract, for an architectural project. |
| **mortar**: | In Roman concrete construction, a mixture of lime, sand, and water. Simple lime mortar hardens by evaporation. Mortar containing volcanic ash reacts with water to form cementitious gels. See pozzolan. Mortars made with lime obtained from siliceous limestone are capable of developing cementitious gels without adding volcanic ash. |
| *munus*: | Latin for "service" or "duty" (plural *munera*); typically used in connection with Roman elites to describe charitable acts done for the benefit of the general Roman public. |
| *naualia*: | A military port that also included a naval dockyard; shipsheds. |
| *opus*: | Latin word meaning work, or masonry style. In Roman concrete construction, it is the conventional title used to describe walls in which thin bonding layers of core concrete are laid at the same time as different facing material that bonds in with the core. See *opus Africanum*, *opus caementicium*, *opus formaceum*, *opus incertum*, *opus quadratum*, *opus quasi reticulatum*, *opus reticulatum*, *opus testaceum*, and *opus uittatum*. |
| *opus Africanum*: | Walls in which ashlar blocks are laid horizontally (stretchers) and vertically (uprights) in alternation to build rows of load-bearing piers separated. The gaps, which may vary in width, are filled in with either flat blocks (in what can be described as an approximation of isodomic masonry) or mortared rubble. The term derives from the idea that the technique originated in Punic North Africa. In this book I refer to the variant attested at Pompeii and throughout Campania as "limestone-framework technique." See isodomic masonry, *opus*, stretchers, and uprights. |
| *opus caementicium*: | This term is generally used interchangeably with Roman concrete to describe any sort of rubble mixed with hydraulic mortar featuring volcanic additives. With relation to masonry styles, the term applies to layered concrete fabric with differentiated facing of any pattern, but the usage is often vague and inconsistent from author to author. Because of the lack of a precise parallel in the ancient lexicon, the term *opus caementicium* is not used in |

|  | this book. Instead, the hydraulic building medium is defined as "cemented rubble," while the nonhydraulic building medium is described as "mortared rubble," with distinctions between clay-based and lime-based mortar subtypes employed when necessary. |
|---|---|
| *opus formaceum*: | See *pisé de terre*. |
| *opus incertum*: | This term refers to walls in which facing pieces consisting of prisms with polygonal or oval outer surface of relatively uniform size create a smooth exterior that can be clearly distinguished from the core. |
| *opus quadratum*: | Ashlar; squared stones laid in regular, horizontal courses. |
| *opus quasi reticulatum*: | This modern term has been coined to describe a rough form of *opus reticulatum* that does not result in a regular grid. It has often been taken to correspond to an intermediate phase in the process of evolution from *opus incertum* to *opus reticulatum*. The term appears very subjective, since it has also been applied to *opus incertum* walls in which facing pieces are laid in orderly, nestled configuration. The title *opus quasi reticulatum* should be used with caution (i.e., only when facing pieces are cut to square or near-square shape fairly consistently, and then laid in place as easily as they will go, with a clear but also not rigorous netlike pattern). |
| *opus reticulatum*: | This term refers to walls whose facings feature pyramidal blocks cut in standardized shape and set in a diagonal grid pattern. |
| *opus testaceum*: | Also known as *opus latericium*, concrete masonry faced with fired bricks. The larger bricks were often cut into triangular pieces. See *lateres cocti*. |
| *opus uittatum*: | Commonly used term for concrete wall facings with courses of small, squared stones alternating with courses of brick. In this book it refers to a variant without bricks. |
| *pagus*: | Term of Roman administrative law used to refer to a subdivision of a territory or polity, typically a rural district. *Pagi* are characteristic of the pre-urban organization of the countryside. |
| *palaestra*: | Building (complex) for athletic training and education, characterized by a colonnaded court. Also known as *gymnasium*. |
| **peripteral**: | Having a continuous outer ring of columns, used often to refer to the temple type encircled by a freestanding ring of columns. |
| *peripteros sine postico*: | In Roman architecture, temple surrounded by a ring of columns on front and sides but not on the back. Some scholars suggest that the original term (Vitr., *De arch.* 3.2.5) may have been the equivalent of *opistodomos* in Greek temples (i.e., the rear room behind the cella). |

| | |
|---|---|
| *peristasis*: | The ring of columns surrounding all sides of a Greek temple. See peripteral. |
| **peristyle**: | An architectural space such as an interior court or porch that is surrounded or edged by a row of columns. |
| *petit appareil*: | French term for small cube-shaped masonry. Its Italian equivalent is *opera a blocchetti*, |
| **pier**: | A solid support (pillar) designed to sustain vertical pressure. |
| **pilaster**: | A rectangular column projecting from a wall. |
| *pisé de terre*: | French for rammed earth structures, made by compacting a damp mixture of soil (sand, gravel, or clay) and stabilizer into a an externally supported frame or mold. |
| **plinth**: | Square slab at the base (i.e., the foot) of a pedestal, podium, column (typically Ionic), or architrave. |
| **poliadic**: | Relating to the protecting, guardian, or patron deity of a city or state. |
| **polygonal masonry**: | Labor-intensive building technique frequently documented in the limestone region. Walls made of massive blocks of polygonal shape laid without mortar in a random pattern. The convention established by Lugli recognizes four styles based on the aspect of wall facings, progressing from the less accurate to the more accurate. |
| *porticus*: | A passageway defined by columns or piers on one side and a wall on the other; a colonnade. The term is used inconsistently to denote a building composed mainly of colonnaded or arcaded spaces, such as a warehouse (for example, Porticus Aemilia, in Rome). See also cryptoporticus, triporticus, quadriporticus, and stoa. |
| **pozzolan**: | The correct scientific word to describe materials with pozzolanic properties, that is, materials with properties similar to those of silica-rich volcanic ash (*pozzolana*) capable of chemically reacting with lime to form cementitious gels. As a category it includes fired clay and certain organic ashes in addition to volcanic ash. |
| *praefurnium*: | A furnace in a Roman-style bath building; heating room. |
| *probatio*: | The final inspection and approval of an architectural project, undertaken by the individual who let out the contract. See also *locatio conductio operis*, *locator*, and *conductor*. |
| *pronaos*: | The entrance porch in front of the *naos* (or "cella") of a temple; front porch, usually defined by columns. |
| *publicani*: | Contractors who accepted government contracts for public building works on behalf of Roman magistrates. |
| **pumice**: | A lightweight, vesicular igneous rock formed by the rapid solidification of magmas from a volcano. See also lapilli, pyroclastic, and scoria. |
| **pyroclastic**: | Adjective used to describe fragments of rock erupting from a volcano. See also lapilli, pumice, and scoria. |

| | |
|---|---|
| *quadriporticus*: | In Roman architecture, modern term identifying a porticus enclosing a quadrangular open area on all sides. See peristyle. |
| **quoin**: | An external angle of a wall or building. |
| *redemptor*: | In public contracts the role of the *conductor* is replaced by the *redemptor*. See *conductor*. |
| **row house**: | In Roman architecture, a lower-class dwelling, part of a series of houses connected by common sidewalls and forming a continuous group. |
| **scoria**: | A highly vesicular igneous rock formed by the rapid solidification of basaltic magmas. See also lapilli, pumice, and pyroclastic. |
| **shuttering**: | In concrete construction, two parallel wooden plank walls framed with vertical beams, used as a temporary structure to contain setting concrete. After the concrete mass had cured, the valuable wood was removed for reuse. The term may also be applied to formworks that support the sides of trenches. By extension, concrete wall facings are sometimes referred to as "lost shuttering." |
| **socle**: | Thicker foundation or footing made of unworked stone or tile, whose function was to protect superstructures of *pisé de terre*, mudbrick, or timber from the damp. |
| **spolia**: | From the Latin word for spoils, an architectural fragment that is taken out of its original context and reused or simply recycled as building material in a different context. |
| **stretcher**: | Also known as a horizontal. Blocks laid horizontally with their longest end parallel to the face of the wall. |
| *stipulatio*: | An older form of contract based on verbal agreements, which regulated architectural projects. See *locatio conductio operis*. |
| *stoa*: | Greek term for a long colonnaded building, typically used for shelter or general display in sanctuaries and *agorai*. Throughout the Roman era, the term continued in use in Asia Minor and the Greek East. The building type influenced the Roman porticus. See *porticus*. |
| *substructio*: | Latin word for semi-interred structure. See also terrace wall. |
| *suspensura*: | The architectural term given by Vitruvius (*De arch.* 5.10.2) to piers of square bricks (about 20 cm × 20 cm) that supported a suspended floor of a Roman bath covering a hypocaust cavity through which the hot air would flow. |
| *taberna*: | According to Isidorus (*Etym.* 15.2.43) *tabernae* are "the small buildings belonging to the common people, humble and simple neighborhood buildings that could be closed by planks and bar." The conventional title *taberna* generally describes outlets for food and drink, or simply a shop. |

| | |
|---|---|
| *tablinum*: | In the canonical Roman atrium house, a large, open reception room (office) opposite the main entrance. |
| **terrace wall**: | A type of retaining wall, for holding in place a mass of earth or the like, as at the edge of a terrace or excavation. |
| **testudinate**: | In Roman architecture, an adjective most often used to denote a roof with four sides converging at a point, or a ridge and points. It refers to a class of covered atria. |
| *tresuiri (coloniae deducendae)*: | Commission of three magistrates elected by the Senate to manage the foundation of a colonial settlement, responsible among other things for configuring the physical topography and urban fabric of colonies. They remained in office for three years (the last of which marks the colonial foundation date). |
| **tripartite**: | Adjective that denotes a building (typically a temple) divided into three parts. |
| **triporticus**: | In Roman architecture, modern term referring to a U-shaped porticus structure. It is often found in association with an axially placed temple. |
| **truss**: | Wooden structure of triangular shape, created by attaching the ends of horizontal ceiling joists ("tie beams") to those of the primary rafters. The lateral thrust of the tie beams kept the rafters in tension, thus supporting heavier loads. |
| **upright**: | Also known as a vertical. A pillar or column that stands upright and is used to support a structure. |
| **vault**: | a self-supporting arched form that spans a space (typically acting as a roof or ceiling), often made of masonry. |
| *uia tecta*: | Latin term for covered street or passageway, usually spanned by a continuous barrel vault. |
| *uicus*: | The smallest unit of ancient Roman municipal administration, consisting of a village or part of a town (street, quarter, or neighborhood). |
| **voussoir**: | A wedge-shaped or tapered stone used in the building of an arch. |
| *xystus*: | Greek architectural term for an elongated, covered colonnade attached to a *gymnasium*, and used for athletics during adverse weather. |

# BIBLIOGRAPHY AND ABBREVIATIONS

## ABBREVIATED WORKS

The abbreviated format I use to cite journals and series titles follows the conventions of the *American Journal of Archaeology* (www.ajaonline.org/submissions/abbr eviations). For ancient authors and corpora of ancient documents I refer to the *Oxford Classical Dictionary* (https://oxfo rdre.com/classics/page/ocdabbrevia tions/abbreviations). All translations are my own unless otherwise noted. Other works cited with frequency are abbreviated as follows:

*ArchLaz* = Archeologia Laziale: [Incontri di Studio]/Comitato per l'archeologia laziale. 1978–95. Rome: CNR

*Suburbium* I = Pergola, Ph., and R. Santangeli Valenzani, eds. 2003. *Suburbium: Il suburbio di Roma dalla crisi del sistema delle ville a Gregorio Magno.* CÉFR 323. Rome: École française de Rome.

*Suburbium* II = Jolivet, V., C. Pavolini, M. A. Tomei, and R. Volpe, eds. 2009. *Suburbium II. Il suburbio di Roma dalla fine dell'età monarchica alla nascita del sistema delle ville (V-II secolo a.C.).* CÉFR 419. Rome: École française de Rome.

*VAR* = De Franceschini, M. 2005. *Ville dell'agro romano.* Rome: L'Erma di Bretschneider.

## WORKS CITED

Abascal Palazón, J. M., and S. F. Ramallo Asensio. 1997. *La ciudad de Carthago Nova: la documentación epigráfica.* 2 vols. Murcia: Universidad de Murcia, Servicio de Publicaciones.

Adam, J.-P. 1983. *Dégradation et restauration de l'architecture pompéienne.* Paris: Éditions du CNRS.

——— 1994. *Roman Building: Materials and Techniques.* Translated by A. Mathews. Bloomington: Indiana University Press.

——— 2007. "Building Materials, Construction Techniques and Chronologies." In Dobbins and Foss, 98–113.

Adams, J.-N. 2003. *Bilingualism and the Latin Language.* Cambridge: Cambridge University Press.

Adams, R. McC. 1996. *Paths of Fire: An Anthropologist's Inquiry into Western Technology.* Princeton: Princeton University Press.

Aldrete, G. S. 2007. *Floods of the Tiber in Ancient Rome.* Baltimore: Johns Hopkins University Press.

Allen, J. 2006. *Hostages and Hostage-Taking in the Roman Empire.* Cambridge: Cambridge University Press.

Almagro Basch, M. 1958. "Excavaciones españolas en Gabii." *Italica* 10: 7–27.

Almagro Gorbea, M., ed. 1982. *El Santuario de Juno en Gabii.* Rome: Escuela Española de Historia y Arqueología en Roma.

Alvino, G., F. M. Cifarelli, and P. Innico. 2003. "Il complesso archeologico di Colle Noce a Segni. Le ultime novità." In *Lazio e Sabina, 1. Primo incontro di studi sul Lazio e la Sabina. Atti del convegno, Roma 28 – 30 gennaio 2002,* edited by R. Brandt, X. Dupré, and G. Ghini, 85–90. Rome: De Luca.

Amici, C. M. 2004–05. "Evoluzione architettonica del comizio a Roma." *RendPontAcc* 77: 351–79.

Anderson Jr., J. C. 1997. *Roman Architecture and Society*. Baltimore: Johns Hopkins University Press.

Anderson, M. A., and D. Robinson, eds. 2018a. *House of the Surgeon, Pompeii. Excavations in the Casa Del Chirurgo (IV, 1,9 – 10.23)*. Oxford: Oxbow.

2018b. "The Stratigraphic and Structural Sequence of the Casa Del Chirurgo." In Anderson and Robinson 2018a, 61–122.

Andreae, B., and H. Kyrieleis, ed. 1975. *Neue Forschungen in Pompeji und den anderen vom Vesuvausbruch 79 n.Chr. verschutteten Stadten*. Recklinghausen: Bongers.

Andreussi, M. 1981. "Stanziamenti agricoli e ville residenziali in alcune zone campione del Lazio. Sulla base degli studi pubblicati nella Forma Italia." In *Società romana e produzione schiavistica, 1. L'Italia. Insediamenti e forme economiche*, edited by A. Giardina and A. Schiavone, 349–70. Bari: Laterza.

Andrews, M. M. 2014. "A Domus in the Subura of Rome from Republic through Late Antiquity." *AJA* 118: 61–90.

Angelelli, C. 2010. *La basilica titolare di S. Pudenziana. Nuove ricerche*. Vatican City: Pontificio Istituto di Archeologia Cristiana.

Angelelli, C., C. Boscarini, and A. Lugari. 2012. "I rivestimenti marmorei del Foro di Gabii." In *Atti del XVII Colloquio dell'Associazione italiana per lo studio e la conservazione del mosaico: Teramo, 10–12 marzo 2011*, edited by F. Guidobaldi and G. Tozzi, 187–99. Tivoli: Scripta Manent.

Angelelli, C., and S. Musco. 2013. "Mosaici inediti da Gabii (Roma)." In *Atti del XVIII Colloquio dell'Associazione italiana per lo studio e la conservazione del mosaico (Cremona, 14–17 marzo 2012)*, edited by C. Angelelli, 727–38. Tivoli: Scripta Manent.

Angelelli, C., and F. Rinaldi, eds. 2008. *Atti del XIII Colloquio dell'Associazione italiana per lo studio e la conservazione del mosaico. Canosa di Puglia, 21–24 febbraio 2007*. Tivoli: Scripta Manent.

Anselmino, L. 2006. "Il versante orientale del Palatino dalla chiesa di S. Bonaventura alla Via di S. Gregorio." *ScAnt* 13: 219–47.

Anselmino, L., L. Ferrea, and M. J. Strazzulla. 1990. "Il frontone di Via di S. Gregorio ed il Tempio della Fortuna Respiciens sul Palatino: una nuova ipotesi." *RendPontAcc* 63: 193–262.

Arata, F. P., and E. Felici. 2011. "*Porticus Aemilia, navalia* o *horrea*? Ancora sui Frammenti 23 e 24b-d della Forma Urbis." *ArchCl* 62: 127–53.

Arthur, P. 1986. "Problems of the Urbanisation of Pompeii. Excavations 1980–1981." *AntJ* 66: 29–44.

Arvanitis, N., F. R. Paolillo, and F. Turchetta. 2010. "La stratigrafia." In *Il Santuario di Vesta. La casa delle Vestali ed il tempio di Vesta VIII sec. a. C.-64 d.C.*, edited by N. Arvanitis, 27–60. Pisa: F. Serra.

Attema, P. A. J. 2018. "Urban and Rural Landscapes of the Pontine Region (Central Italy) in the Late Republican Period, Economic Growth between Colonial Heritage and Elite Impetus." *BABesch* 93: 143–64.

Attema, P. A. J., G. J. L. M. Burgers, and P. M. Van Leusen. 2010. *Regional Pathways to Complexity. Settlement and Land-Use Dynamics in Early Italy from the Bronze Age to the Republican Period*. Amsterdam: Amsterdam University Press.

Attema, P. A. J., T. De Haas, and M. Termeer. 2014. "Early Colonization in the Pontine Region (Central Italy)." In Stek and Pelgrom 2014, 211–32.

Attema, P. A. J., T. C. A. De Haas, and G. W. Tol. 2013–14. "Villas and

Farmsteads in the Ager Setinus (Sezze, Italy)." *Palaeohistoria* 55–56:177–244.

Attema, P. A. J., and P. M. Van Leusen. 2004. "The Early Roman Colonization of South Lazio; a Survey of Three Landscapes." In *Centralization, Early Urbanization and Colonization in First Millennium BC Italy and Greece. Part 1: Italy*, edited by P. A. J. Attema, 157–95. Leuven/Paris/Dudley, MA: Peeters.

Attenni, L., and D. Baldassarre, eds. 2012. *Quarto seminario internazionale di studi sulle mura poligonali. Palazzo Conti Gentili 7–10 ottobre 2009. Atti del convegno.* Rome: Aracne.

Avagliano, A. 2013. "Il ginnasio di Vibio Adirano e la *vereiia*. Con una nota sulla domus publica di Pompei." In *Pompei/Messene: il Doriforo e il suo contesto*, edited by V. Franciosi and P. Thémelis, 67–123. Naples: Università degli Studi Suor Orsola Benincasa.

Avagliano, A., and R. Montalbano. 2018. "Greek Gymnasia for Non-Greek People. Archaeological and Epigraphic Evidence in Pre-Roman Italy." In Mania and Trümper 2018, 75–85.

Balasco, A. 2011. "Il teatro-santuario di Teano." In *Il teatro di Teanum Sidicinum. Dall'Antichità alla Madonna delle Grazie*, edited by F. Sirano, 71–86. Capua: Lavieri.

Ball, L. F., and J. J. Dobbins. 2013. "Forum Project. Current Thinking on the Pompeii Forum." *AJA* 117: 461–92.

———. 2017. "Pompeii Forum Project. Excavation and Urbanistic Reappraisals of the Sanctuary of Apollo, Basilica, and Via della Fortuna Neighborhood." *AJA* 121: 467–503.

Balland, A., A. Barbet, P. Gros, and G. Hallier. 1971. *Fouilles de l'École française de Rome à Bolsena (Poggio Moscini), 2. Les architectures,*

*1962–1967.* Rome/Paris: École française de Rome/Diff. De Boccard.

Balty, J.-Ch. 1985. "Une grande maison urbaine d'Alba Fucens. Contibution à l'étude de l'architecture domestique en Italie centrale." *ActaArchLov* 24: 19–31.

Barker, S. 2010. "Roman Builders. Pillagers or Salvagers? The Economics of Deconstruction and Reuse." In Camporeale *et al.* 2010, 127–42.

Barreda Pascual, A. 2009. "Pilemo Aleidi L.s. (*CIL* I³ 2271 = *CIL* II 3434). De Delos a Carthago Nova. El testimonio de un paralelo datado." *Faventia* 31: 25–47.

Bastien, J.-L. 2009. "Les temples votifs de la Rome républicaine. Monumentalisation et célébration des cérémonies du triomphe." In *Roma illustrata. Représentations de la ville*, edited by P. Fleury and O. Desbordes, 29–48. Caen: Presses universitaires de Caen.

Battaglini, G., and P. Braconi. 2019. "Dalla tegola al mattone: laterizi sperimentali a Fregellae." In Bonetto *et al.* 2019, 495–506.

Battaglini, G., and F. Diosono. 2010. "Le domus di Fregellae. Case aristocratiche di ambito coloniale." In Bentz and Reusser 2010, 217–31.

Battiloro, I., and M. Mogetta. forthcoming. "Il Santuario di Venere: Scavi 2017–2019." In *Studium erga populum. Studium erga sapientiam. In Ricordo di Enzo Lippolis. Tra Capitolium ed extra moenia: nuovi scavi e ricerche*, edited by M. Osanna. Rome: L'Erma di Bretschneider.

———. 2018. "New Investigations at the Sanctuary of Venus in Pompeii: Interim Report on the 2017 Season of the Venus Pompeiana Project." *Fasti On Line Documents & Research Italy* 425: 1–37.

Becker, J. A. 2007. "The Building Blocks of Empire: Civic Architecture, Central Italy, and the Roman Middle Republic." PhD diss., University of North Carolina at Chapel Hill.

———. 2012. "Polygonal Masonry and Republican Villas? The Problem of the Basis Villae." In Becker and Terrenato 2012, 111–28.

Becker, J. A., M. Mogetta, and N. Terrenato. 2009. "A New Plan for an Ancient Italian City: Gabii Revealed." *AJA* 113: 629–42.

Becker, J. A., and N. Terrenato, eds. 2012. *Roman Republican Villas: Architecture, Context, Ideology.* PAAR 32. Ann Arbor: University of Michigan Press.

Bedini, A. 1984. "Scavi al Torrino." *ArchLaz* 6: 84–90.

Bellini, G. R., and H. von Hesberg, eds. 2015. *Minturnae. Nuovi contributi alla conoscenza della Forma urbis. Giornata di studi sui lavori a Minturnae in collaborazione con la Seconda Università degli studi di Napoli, Facoltà di lettere e filosofia. Roma, 29 settembre 2011.* Rome: Quasar.

Bencivenga Trillmich, C. 1988. "Pyxous-Buxentum." *MÉFRA* 100: 701–29.

Bentz, M., and C. Reusser, eds. 2010. *Etruskisch-italische und römisch republikanische Häuser.* Wiesbaden: Reichert.

Benvenuti, V. 2002. "The Introduction of Artillery in the Roman World. Hypothesis for a Chronological Definition Based on the Cosa Town Wall." *MAAR* 47: 199–207.

Bergmann, B. 2010. "'What a Task for a Lady.' Marion Blake at Work." *Musiva & Sectilia* 7: 47–71.

Bermond Montanari, G. 1984. "Ravenna, 1980. Lo scavo della Banca popolare. Relazione preliminare, 1." *Felix Ravenna* 127–130: 21–34.

Bernard, S. 2016. "Workers in the Roman Imperial Building Industry." In *Work, Labour, and Professions in the Roman World,* edited by K. Verboven and C. Laes, 62–86. Leiden: Brill.

———. 2018a. *Building Mid-Republican Rome: Labor, Architecture and the Urban Economy.* New York: Oxford University Press.

———. 2018b. "*Aedificare, res damnosissima.* Building and Historiography in Livy, Books 5–6." In *Omnium annalium monumenta. Historical Writing and Historical Evidence in Republican Rome,* edited by K. Sandberg and C. Smith, 404–21. Leiden: Brill.

———. 2019. "The Status and Mobility of Coroplasts and Building Workers in the Epigraphy of Central Italy, 300–50 BC." In *Deliciae Fictiles V Networks and Workshops: Architectural Terracottas and Decorative Roof Systems in Italy and Beyond,* edited by P. Lulof, I. Manzini, and C. Rescigno, 499–507. Oxford, UK/ Havertown, PA: Oxbow.

Bernard, S.G. 2010. "Pentelic Marble in Architecture at Rome and the Republican Marble Trade." *JRA* 23: 35–54.

———. 2012. "Continuing the Debate on Rome's Earliest Circuit Walls." *PBSR* 80: 1–44.

Bertacchi, L. 2003. *Nuova pianta archeologica di Aquileia.* Udine: Edizioni del confine.

Betori, A., S. Marandola, and C. P. Venditti. 2013. "L'affermazione dell'opera cementizia nell'edilizia pubblica del Lazio meridionale interno. Novità dallo scavo del criptoportico repubblicano di Fabrateria Nova." In Cifarelli 2013, 71–78.

Bietti Sestieri, A. M., ed. 1985. *Roma. Archeologia nel centro, 1. L'area archeologica centrale.* Rome: De Luca

Billig, R. 1944. "Chronologische Probleme der römischen Konkretverkleidung." *OpArch* 3: 124–144.

Biscardi, A. 1960. "Il concetto romano di locatio nelle fonti epigrafiche." *Studi Senesi* 72: 409–47.

Bispham, E. 2006. "*Coloniam deducere*: How Roman was Roman Colonization during the Middle Republic?" In Bradley and Wilson 2006, 73–160.

2007. *From Asculum to Actium: The Municipalization of Italy from the Social War to Augustus*. Oxford: Oxford University Press.

Bizzarri, E. 1973. "Titolo mummiano da Fabrateria Nova." *Epigraphica* 35: 140–42.

Blackman, D. J. 2008. "Roman Shipsheds." In Hohlfelder 2008, 23–36.

Blake, M. E. 1947. *Ancient Roman Construction in Italy from the Prehistoric Period to Augustus: A Chronological Study Based in Part upon the Material Accumulated by the Late Dr. Esther Boise Van Deman*. Washington, DC: Carnegie Institute.

Bloy, D. 1998. "Greek War Booty at Luna and the Afterlife of Manius Acilius Glabrio." *MAAR* 43–44: 49–61.

Boëthius, A. 1939. "Vitruvius and the Roman Architecture of His Age." In *Dragma, Martino P. Nilsson, A.D. IV Id. Iul. Anno MCMXXXIX Dedicatum*, 114–43. Lund: C.W.K. Gleerup.

1978. *Etruscan and Early Roman Architecture*. Harmondsworth: Penguin Books.

Boëthius, A., and N. Carlgren. 1932. "Die spätrepublikanischen Warenhauser in Ferentino und Tivoli." *ActaArch* 3: 181–208.

Bolder-Boos, M. 2011. "In Excelsissimo Loco – an Approach to Poliadic Deities in Roman Colonies." In *TRAC 2010. Proceedings of the Twentieth Annual Theoretical Roman Archaeology Conference (Oxford 25–28 March 2010)*, edited by D. Mladenović and B. Russell, 18–31. Oxford: Oxbow.

2014. "Tutelary Deities in Roman Citizen Colonies." In Stek and Pelgrom 2014, 279–94.

2019. "Adorning the City. Urbanistic Trends in Republican Central Italy." In *Empire, Hegemony or Anarchy? Rome and Italy, 200–31 BCE*, edited by K.-J. Hölkeskamp, S. Karatas, and R. Roth, 107–29. Stuttgart: Franz Steiner Verlag.

Bonazzi, A., S. Santoro, and E. Mastrobattista. 2007. "Caratterizzazione archeometrica delle malte edegli intonaci dell'insula del Centenario." In *Pompei. Insula del Centenario (IX, 8), 1. Indagini diagnostiche, geofisiche e analisi archeometriche*, edited by S. Santoro, 93–128. Bologna: Ante Quem.

Bonetto, J. 1998. *Mura e città nella Transpadana romana*. Portogruaro: Fondazione A. Colluto.

2015. "Diffusione ed uso del mattone cotto nella Cisalpina romana tra ellenizzazione e romanizzazione." In *Il laterizio nei cantieri Imperiali. Atti del I workshop "Laterizio" (Rome, 27–28 Novembre 2014)*, edited by E. Bukowiecki, R. Volpe, and U. Wulf-Rheidt, 105–13. Florence: All'Insegna del Giglio.

2019. "Maestranze greche e laterizio cotto: alle origini dell'architettura della Cisalpina." In Bonetto *et al.* 2019, 317–34. Rome: Quasar.

forthcoming. "Le Mura Repubblicane." In *Aquileia. Fondi Cossar. 2.1 Lo scavo. Le fasi repubblicane e della prima età imperiale*, edited by J. Bonetto, G. Furlan, and C. Previato. Rome: Quasar.

Bonetto, J., G. Artioli, M. Secco, and A. Addis. 2016. "L'uso delle polveri pozzolaniche nei grandi cantieri della Gallia Cisalpina durante l'età romana repubblicana. I casi di Aquileia e Ravenna." In DeLaine *et al.* 2016, 29–44.

Bonetto, J., E. Bukowiecki, and R. Volpe, eds. 2019. *Alle origini del laterizio romano. Nascita e difusione del mattone cotto nel Mediterraneo tra IV e I secolo a. C. Atti del II Convegno Internazionale "Laterizio" (Padova, 26–28 Aprile 2016)*. Rome: Quasar.

Bonetto, J., E. Pettenò, C. Previato, F. Trevisonno, F. Veronese, and M. Volpin. forthcoming. "Il teatro romano di Padova. Contesto, costruzione, quadro storico." *Orizzonti: Rassegna di Archeologia*.

Bonetto, J., and C. Previato. 2018. "The Construction Process of the Republican City Walls of Aquileia (Northeastern Italy). A Case Study of the Quantitative Analysis on Ancient Buildings." In *Constructing Monuments, Perceiving Monumentality and the Economics of Building: Theoretical and Methodological Approaches to the Built Environment*, edited by A. Brysbaert, V. Klinkenberg, A. Gutiérrez Garcia, and I. Vikatoupp, 309–30. Leiden: Sidestone Press.

Bonghi Jovino, M. 1973. "Grande Tempio ed area adiacente." In Frova 1973, vol. 1: 653–92. Rome: L'Erma di Bretschneider.

1977. "Area del Grande Tempio." In Frova 1977, vol. 1: 413–52.

Boni, G. 1901. "Il sacrario di Juturna." *NSc*: 41–144.

Bradley, G. 2006. "Colonization and Identity in Republican Italy." In Bradley and Wilson 2006, 161–87.

Bradley, G., and J.-P. Wilson, eds. 2006. *Greek and Roman Colonization: Origins, Ideologies and Interactions*. Swansea: University of Wales Press.

Bragantini, I., R. De Bonis, A. Lemaire, and R. Robert. 2008. *Poseidonia Paestum V: les maisons romaines de l'Îlot Nord*. CÉFR 42/5. Rome: École française de Rome.

Bragantini, I., and F. Guidobaldi, eds. 1995. *Atti del II Colloquio dell'Associazione Italiana per lo Studio e la Conservazione del Mosaico (Roma, 5–7 dicembre 1994)*. Bordighera: Istituto Internazionale di Studi Liguri.

Brandon, C. J., R. L. Hohlfelder, M. D. Jackson, and L. Bottalico, eds.

2014. *Building for Eternity. The History and Technology of Roman Concrete Engineering in the Sea*. Oxford: Oxbow.

Briscoe, J. 2012. *A Commentary on Livy Books 41–45*. Oxford: Oxford University Press.

Broadhead, W. 2001. "Rome's Migration Policy and the So-Called *ius migrandi*." *Cahiers du Centre G. Glotz* 12: 69–89.

Broise, H., and X. Lafon. 2001. *La Villa Prato de Sperlonga*. CÉFR 285. Rome: École française de Rome.

Broughton, T. R. S. 1951. *The Magistrates of the Roman Republic*. 2 vols. New York: American Philological Association.

Brown, F. E. 1951. "Cosa I: History and Topography." *MAAR* 20: 1–113.

1980. *Cosa: The Making of a Roman Town*. Ann Arbor: University of Michigan Press.

Brown, F. E., E. H. Richardson, and L. Richardson Jr. 1960. "Cosa II: The Temples of the Arx." *MAAR* 26: 1–151.

Brown, F. E., L. Richardson Jr., and E. H. Richardson. 1993. "Cosa III: The Buildings of the Forum. Colony, Municipium, and Village." *MAAR* 37: 1–298.

Brun, J. P., and P. Munzi. 2011. "Cume (Italie). Les fouilles du Centre Jean-Bérard 2000–2010." *RA* 41: 147–72.

Bruno, V. J., and R. T. Scott. 1993. "Cosa IV: The Houses." *MAAR* 38: 1–211.

Brunt, P. A. 1971. *Italian Manpower, 225 B. C.–A.D. 14*. Oxford: Oxford University Press.

Bugini, R., C. D'Agostini, and A. Salvatori. 1993. "Tecnologia edilizia e indagini mineralogico-petrografiche di pavimenti in 'cocciopesto' di età classica in area romano-campana." In *Calcestruzzi antichi e moderni: storia, cultura e tecnologia (Atti del convegno di studi,*

*Bressanone 6–9 luglio 1993)*, edited by G. Biscontin and D. Mietto, 265–74. Padua: Libreria Progetto Editore.

Burgers, G.-J., A. Contino, L. D'Alessandro, V. De Leonardis, S. Della Ricca, R.-A. Kok Merlino, and R. Sebastiani. 2018. "The Afterlife of the Porticus Aemilia." *Fasti On Line Documents & Research Italy* 400: 1–17.

Buttrey, T. V. 1980. "Cosa: The Coins." *Memoirs of the American Academy in Rome* 34: 5–153.

Cagnana, A., and T. Mannoni. 1995. "Materiali e tecniche nelle strutture murarie di Luni. Risultati preliminari." *Quaderni di Studi Lunensi* n.s. 1: 137–64.

Cahill, N. 2002. *Household and City Organization at Olynthus*. New Haven, CT: Yale University Press.

Calvani Marini, M. 1985. "Piacenza in età romana." In *Cremona romana. Atti del Congresso storico archeologico per il 2200° anno di fondazione di Cremona, 30–31 maggio 1982*, edited by G. Pontiroli, 261–75. Cremona: Biblioteca statale e libreria civica di Cremona.

Camodeca, G. 2012. "L'iscrizione osca." In *Cuma. Le fortificazioni. 3. Lo scavo 2004–2006*, edited by B. d'Agostino and M. Giglio, 238–45. Naples: Direzione regionale per i Beni culturali e paesaggistici della Campania.

Camporeale, S. 2013. "*Opus africanum* e tecniche a telaio litico in Etruria e Campania [VII a.C.–VI d.C.]." *Archeologia dell'Architettura* 18: 192–209.

——— 2016. "Merging Technologies in North African Ancient Architecture. *Opus Quadratum* and *Opus Africanum* from the Phoenicians to the Romans." In *De Africa Romaque. Merging Cultures across North Africa. Proceedings of the International Conference Held at the University of Leicester (26–27 October 2013)*, edited by N. Mugnai, J. Nikolaus, and N. Ray, 57–71. London: The Society for Libyan Studies.

Camporeale, S., H. Dessales, and A. Pizzo (eds.). 2010. *Arqueología de la construcción II. Los procesos constructivos en el mundo romano: Italia y provincias orientales*. Anejos ArchEspArq 57. Mérida/Siena: Consejo Superior de Investigaciones Científicas, Instituto de Arqueología de Mérida/ Università di Siena.

Caputo, M. 1990–91. "La decorazione parietale di primo stile nel Lazio." *AnnPerugia* 1.28: 211–76.

Caputo, P. 1993. "Bacoli (Napoli). Cuma: indagini archeologiche all'anfiteatro." *Bollettino di Archeologia* 22: 130–32.

Carafa, P. 1998. *Il Comizio di Roma dalle origini all'età di Augusto*. Rome: L'Erma di Bretschneider.

——— 2011. "*Minervae et Marti et Herculi aedes doricae fient* (Vitr. 1.2.5). The monumental history of the sanctuary in the Triangular Forum." In Ellis 2011, 89–111.

Carafa, P., and M. T. D'Alessio. 1995. "Lo scavo nella Casa di Giuseppe II (VIII.2.38–39) e nel portico occidentale del Foro Triangolare a Pompei: Rapporto preliminare." *RStPomp* 7: 137–52.

Carandini, A. 1986. "Domus e insulae sulla pendice settentrionale del Palatino." *BullCom* 91: 263–78.

Carandini, A., D. Bruno, and F. Fraioli. 2010. *Le case del potere nell'antica Roma*. Rome: Laterza.

Carandini, A., and P. Carafa, eds. 1995. "Palatium e Sacra Via, 1. Prima delle mura, l'età delle mura e l'età delle case arcaiche." *Bollettino di Archeologia* 31–32: 1–326.

Carandini, A., P. Carafa, M. T. D'Alessio, and D. Filippi, eds. 2017. *Santuario di*

*Vesta, pendice del Palatino e Via Sacra. Scavi 1985–2016.* 2 vols. Rome: Quasar.

Carandini, A., M. T. D'Alessio, and H. Di Giuseppe, eds. 2007. *La fattoria e la villa dell'Auditorium nel quartiere Flaminio di Roma.* Rome: L'Erma di Bretschneider.

Carandini, A., and E. Papi, eds. 1999. "Palatium e Sacra Via, 2. L'età tardo repubblicana e la prima età imperiale." *Bollettino di Archeologia* 59–60: 3–327.

Carbonara, V. 2006. "Domus e tabernae lungo la via verso il foro." *ScAnt* 13: 15–35.

Carettoni, G. F. 1978–80. "La Domus Virginum Vestalium e la Domus Publica del periodo repubblicano." *RendPontAcc* 51–52: 325–55.

Carettoni, G., and L. Fabbrini. 1961. "Esplorazioni sotto la basilica Giulia al Foro Romano." *RendPontAcc* 8: 53–59.

Carfora, P., S. Ferrante, and S. Quilici Gigli. 2010. "Edilizia privata nell'urbanistica di Norba tra la fine del III e l'inizio del I secolo a.C." In Bentz and Reusser 2010, 233–42.

——— 2013. "Tecniche costruttive in epoca medio-tardo repubblicana. Il caso di Norba." In Cifarelli 2013, 93–102.

Carnabuci, E. 1991. "L'Angolo sud-orientale del Foro Romano nel manoscritto inedito di Giacomo Boni." *MemLinc* IX.1.4: 249–364.

Carrington, R. C. 1933. "Notes on the Building Materials of Pompeii." *JRS* 23: 125–38.

Carroll, M. 2010. "Exploring the Sanctuary of Venus and Its Sacred Grove. Politics, Cult and Identity in Roman Pompeii." *PBSR* 78: 63–106.

Carroll, M., and C. Godden. 2000. "The Sanctuary of Apollo at Pompeii: Reconsidering Chronologies and Excavation History." *AJA* 105: 743–54.

Casarotto, A., J. Pelgrom, and T. D. Stek. 2016. "Testing Settlement Models in the Early Roman Colonial Landscape of Venusia (291 B.C.), Cosa (273 B.C.) and Aesernia (263 B.C.)." *JFA* 41: 568–86.

Caspio, A., C. D'Agostini, C. Molari, S. Musco, D. Raiano, G. Rizzo, and F. Zabotti. 2009. "Riflessioni sul Suburbio orientale di Roma. I contesti tardo-repubblicani di viale della Serenissima e di Quarto del Cappello da Prete." In *Suburbium* II, 455–96.

Cassatella, A. 1985. "Il tratto orientale della Via Sacra." In Bietti Sestieri 1985, 99–105.

Cassetta, R., and C. Costantino. 2006. "La Casa del Naviglio (VI 10, 11) e le botteghe VI 10, 10 e VI 10, 12)." In Coarelli and Pesando 2006a, 243–336.

——— 2008. "Vivere sulle mura: il caso dell'Insula Occidentalis di Pompei." In Guzzo and Guidobaldi 2008, 197–208.

Cassieri, N. 2013. "Strutture in opera incerta nel territorio di Terracina e nel Lazio meridionale costiero." In Cifarelli 2013, 55–64.

Castagnoli, F. 1980. *Topografia di Roma Antica.* Turin: SEI.

Castrén, P. 1975. *Ordo populusque Pompeianorum: Polity and Society.* ActaInstRomFin 8. Rome: Bardi.

Catarsi, M. 2009. "Storia di Parma. Il contributo dell'archeologia." In *Storia di Parma, 2. Parma romana,* edited by D. Vera, 367–499. Parma: Monte Università Parma Editore.

Cébeillac-Gervasoni, M., ed. 1983. *Les "bourgeoisies" municipales italiennes aux IIe et Ier siècles av. J.-C. Centre Jean Bérard. Institut François de Naples, 7–10 décembre 1981.* Paris/Naples: CNRS/Centre Jean Bérard.

——— 1998. *Les magistrats des cités italiennes de la seconde guerre punique à Auguste. Le*

*Latium et la Campanie*, BÉFAR 299. Rome: École française de Rome.

———. 2002. "Note relative aux élites du Latium et de la Campanie et à leurs rapports avec la Méditerranée orientale." In *Les Italiens dans le monde grec, IIe siècle av. J.C. – Ier siècle ap. J.C. Circulation, activités, intégration. Actes de la table ronde, Paris 14 – 16 mai 1998*, edited by C. Müller and C. Hasenohr, 21–28. BCH Suppl. 14. Athens/Paris: École française d'Athènes/Diff. de Boccard.

———. 2008. "Les rapports entre les élites du Latium et de la Campanie et Rome (III s. av. J.-C. – I s. ap. J.-C.). L'apport d'une enquête prosopographique." In *Patria diversis gentibus una? Unità politica e identità etniche nell'Italia antica. Atti del convegno internazionale, Cividale del Friuli, 20–22 settembre 2007*, edited by G. Urso, 39–62. Pisa: ETS.

Chaplin, J. D. 2007. *Rome's Mediterranean Empire: Books Forty-one to Forty-five and the Periochae*. Oxford: Oxford University Press.

Chiabà, M. 2011. *Roma e le priscae Latinae coloniae: ricerche sulla colonializzazione del Lazio dalla costruzione della repubblica alla guerra latina*. Trieste: Edizioni Università Trieste.

———. ed. 2014. *HOC QVOQVE LABORIS PRAEMIVM. Scritti in onore di Gino Bandelli*. Trieste: Edizioni Università di Trieste.

Chiaramonte Treré, C. 1990. "Sull'origine e lo sviluppo dell'architettura residenziale di Pompei sannitica. Spunti di riflessione dagli scavi della Regio VI, 5." *Acme* 43: 5–34.

Christie, N., ed. 1995. *Settlement and Economy in Italy: 1500BC–AD 1500. Papers of the Fifth Conference of Italian Archaeology*. Oxford: Oxbow.

Ciampoltrini, G., and P. Rendini. 2018. "Pavimenti in cementizio e urbanizzazione di Lucca. Nuovi dati." In *Atti del XXIII Colloquio dell'Associazione italiana per lo studio e la conservazione del mosaico. Narni, 15–18 marzo 2017*, edited by C. Angelelli, C. Cecalupo, and M. E. Erba, 655–65. Rome: Quasar.

Ciancio Rossetto, P. 1995. "Indagini e restauri nel Campo Marzio meridionale: teatro di Marcello, portico d'Ottavia, circo Flaminio, porto Tiberino." *ArchLaz* 12: 93–101.

———. 1996. "Rinvenimenti e restauri al portico d'Ottavia e in piazza delle Cinque Scole." *BullCom* 97: 267–79.

———. 2009. "Portico d'Ottavia. Scavi, restauri, valorizzazioni." In *Arch.it.arch. Dialoghi di archeologia e architettura. Seminari 2005–2006*, edited by D. Manacorda, 62–77. Rome: Quasar.

Cibecchini, F., and C. Capelli. 2013. "Nuovi dati archeologici e archeometrici sulle anfore greco-italiche. I relitti di III secolo del Mediterraneo occidentale e la possibilità di una nuova classificazione." In *Itinéraires des vins romains en Gaule, IIIe -Ier siècles avant J.-C. Confrontation des faciès. Actes du colloque européen organisé par l'UMR 5140 du CNRS (Lattes, 30 janvier – 2 février 2007)*, edited by F. Olmer, 423–51. Lattes: Archéologie des Sociétés Méditerranéennes.

Cicala, L. 2009. "Nuovi dati sull'insediamento di Pian della Tirena a Nocera Terinese." In *Dall'Oliva al Savuto. Studi e ricerche sul territorio dell'antica Temesa. Atti del convegno, Campora San Giovanni (Amantea, CS), 15–16 settembre 2007*, edited by F. G. La Torre, 203–20. Rome: Serra.

Cifani, G. 2008. *Architettura romana arcaica: Edilizia e società tra monarchia e repubblica*. Rome: L'Erma di Bretschneider.

Cifarelli, F. M. 2003. *Il tempio di Giunone Moneta sull'Acropoli di Segni. Storia, topografia e decorazione architettonica*. Rome: L'Erma di Bretschneider.

2008. "Un complesso termale con mosaici a segni e l'opera vittata nel 'Lazio del calcare'." *Orizzonti: Rassegna di Archeologia* 9: 27–46.

2012. "Tecniche costruttive del tardo ellenismo a Segni: verso una sintesi." In Attenni and Baldassarre 2012, 295–301.

ed. 2013. *Tecniche costruttive del tardo ellenismo nel Lazio e in Campania. Atti del Convegno (Segni, 3 Dicembre 2011).* Rome: Espera.

2014. "The Bath-Sanctuary Complex of Colle Noce in the Territory of Signia. The Republican Phase." In Quilici and Quilici Gigli 2014, 215–24.

Cifarelli, F. M., F. Colaiacomo, S. Kay, L. Ceccarelli, and C. Smith. 2017. "Alle origini delle *signina opera*: la grande vasca di Prato Felici dagli scavi del Segni Project." In *Tecnica di idraulica antica: Atti del convegno nazionale, Roma, 18 Novembre 2016*, edited by A. Fiore, G. Gisotti, G. Lena, and L. Masciocco, 163–66. Rome: SIGEA.

Claridge, A. 2010. *Rome. An Oxford Archaeological Guide.* 2nd ed. Oxford: Oxford University Press.

Coarelli, F. 1977. "Public Building in Rome between the Second Punic War and Sulla." *PBSR* 45: 1–23.

1981. *Fregellae. La storia e gli scavi.* Rome: Quasar.

1982. "L'altare del tempio e la sua iscrizione." In Almagro Gorbea 1982, 125–30.

1985. "La fondazione di Luni. Problemi storici ed archeologici." In *Atti del Convegno: Studi lunensi e prospettive sull'Occidente romano*, 17–36. Quaderni di Studi Lunensi 10–12. Luni: Centro Studi Lunensi.

ed. 1986a. *Fregellae, 2. Il santuario di Esculapio.* Rome: Quasar.

1986b. "Le iscrizioni." In Coarelli 1986a, 43–44.

1987. *I santuari del Lazio in età repubblicana.* Rome: La Nuova Italia Scientifica.

1988. "Colonizzazione romana e viabilità." *DialArch* 6.2: 35–48.

1989. "La casa dell'aristocrazia romana secondo Vitruvio." In *Munus non ingratum. Proceedings of the International Symposium on Vitruvius' De Architectura and the Hellenistic and Republican Architecture, Leiden 20–23 January 1987*, edited by H. Geertman and J. de Jong, 178–87. Leiden: Stichting Bulletin Antieke Beschaving.

1991. "Sanniti a Fregellae." In *La Romanisation du Samnium aux IIe et Ier siècles av. J.-C. Actes du colloque, Naples, Centre Jean Bérard, 4–5 novembre 1988*, 177–85. Naples: Centre Jean Bérard.

1995. "Gli scavi di Fregellae e la cronologia dei pavimenti repubblicani." In Bragantini and Guidobaldi 1995, 17–30.

1996. *Revixit Ars: Arte e ideologia a Roma. Dai modelli ellenistici alla tradizione repubblicana.* Rome: Quasar.

1998a. "Comitium e Comitia: l'assemblea e il voto a Roma in età repubblicana." In *Venticinque secoli dopo l'invenzione della democrazia*, edited by E. Greco, 133–43. Paestum: Fondazione Paestum.

1998b. "La storia e lo scavo." In Coarelli and Monti 1998, 29–71. Rome: Quasar.

ed. 2002. *Pompei. La vita ritrovata.* Udine: Magnus.

2007. "Horrea Cornelia?" In *Res bene gestae. Ricerche di storia urbana su Roma antica in onore di Eva Margareta Steinby*, edited by A. Leone, D. Palombi, and S. Walker, 41–45. Rome: Quasar.

2012. *Palatium: Il Palatino dalle origini all'Impero.* Rome: Quasar.

Coarelli, F., and P. G. Monti, eds. 1998. *Fregellae: Le fonti, la storia, il territorio.* Rome: Quasar.

Coarelli, F., and H. Patterson. 2008. *Mercator Placidissimus. The Tiber Valley in Antiquity. New Research in the Upper and Middle River Valley.* Rome: Quasar.

Coarelli, F., and F. Pesando, eds. 2006a. *Rileggere Pompei I. L'insula 10 della Regio VI.* Rome: L'Erma di Bretschneider.

———. 2006b. "Introduction. Proposal for a Chronological Sequence of the Phases of Occupation of the Insula VI,10." In Coarelli and Pesando 2006a, 23–26.

———. 2011. "The Urban development of NW Pompeii. The Archaic Period to the 3rd c. B.C." In Ellis 2011, 37–58.

Coles, A. J. 2017. "Founding Colonies and Fostering Careers in the Middle Republic." *CJ* 112: 280–317.

Coletti, F., and G. Sterpa. 2008. "Resti pavimentali in cementizio, mosaico e sectile dall'area del tempio di Venere a Pompei. Dati di scavo." In Angelelli and Rinaldi 2008, 129–43.

Coletti, F., G. Sterpa, C. Prascina, and N. Witte. 2010. "Venus Pompeiana. Scelte progettuali e procedimenti tecnici per la realizzazione di un edificio sacro tra tarda repubblica e primo impero." In Camporeale *et al.* 2010, 189–211.

Colini, A. M. 1933. "Scoperte tra il Foro della Pace e l'Anfiteatro. Relazione preliminare." *BullCom* 61: 79–87.

———. 1940. "Notiziario." *BullCom* 68: 227–28.

———. 1942. "Aedes Veiovis inter Arcem et Capitolium." *BullCom* 70: 5–56.

Colini, A. M., and G. Matthiae. 1966. "Ricerche intorno a S. Pietro in Vincoli." *MemPontAcc* 9: 5–56.

Contino, A., and L. D'Alessandro. 2014. "Materiali ceramici dagli scavi della *Porticus Aemilia* (Testaccio, Roma). Campagne di scavo 2011–2012." *RCRFActa* 43: 323–34.

Conventi, M. 2004. *Città romane di fondazione.* StArch 130. Rome: L'Erma di Bretschneider.

Cooper, J. G., and J. J. Dobbins. 2015. "New Developments and New Dates within the Sanctuary of Apollo at Pompeii." *Fasti On Line Documents & Research Italy* 340: 1–7.

Cornell, T. 1995. *The Beginnings of Rome. Italy and Rome from the Bronze Age to the Punic Wars (c. 1000–264 BC).* London/New York: Routledge.

Costa, U., E. Gotti, and G. Tognon. 2000. "Nota tecnica: malte prelevate da mura antiche dallo scavo della Banca Popolare di Ravenna." In Quilici Gigli and Quilici 2000, 25–28.

Coutelas, A., ed. 2009. *Le mortier de chaux.* Paris: Errance.

Covolan, M. 2017. "*Venustius est reticulatum.* L'evoluzione dell'opera reticolata a Cuma." *REUDAR. European Journal of Roman architecture* 1: 7–24.

Cozza, L., and P. L. Tucci. 2006. "Navalia." *ArchCl* 57: 175–202.

Crawford, M. 2006. "From Poseidonia to Paestum via the Lucanians." In Bradley and Wilson 2006, 59–72.

Crawford, M. H., ed. 1996. *Roman Statutes.* 2 vols. BICS Suppl. 64. London: Institute of Classical Studies.

———. ed. 2011. *Imagines Italicae. A Corpus of Italic Inscriptions.* Vol. 2. BICS Suppl. 110. London: Institute of Classical Studies.

Crawley Quinn, J., and A. Wilson. 2013. "Capitolia." *JRS* 103: 117–73.

Cressedi, G. 1954. "Le fasi costruttive del portico di Ottavia." *Palladio* 4: 143–44.

Cullhed, M., T. Janson Borglund, and P. Reimers. 2008. "Trench B." In *The Temple of Castor and Pollux II.2: The Finds and Trenches*, edited by K. Slej and M. Cullhed, 327–32. Rome: L'Erma di Bretschneider.

Cuomo, S. 2016. "Tacit Knowledge in Vitruvius." *Arethusa* 49: 125–143.

Curti, E. 2008. "Il Tempio di Venere Fisica e il porto di Pompei." In Guzzo and Guidobaldi 2008, 47–60.

D'Alessio, A. 2006. "Il santuario della Magna Mater dalla fondazione all'età imperiale. Sviluppo architettonico, funzioni e paesaggio urbano." *ScAnt* 13: 429–54.

2007a. "L'avancorpo dell'"Acropoli" di Ferentino. Vecchi e nuovi dati per la lettura storica del monumento." *ArchCl* 58: 397–433.

2007b. "La diffusione degli impianti a sostruzione cava nell'architettura di età tardo-repubblicana. Considerazioni su due casi di Pozzuoli e Roma." In *Architetti, architettura e città nel Mediterraneo antico*, edited by C. G. Malacrino and E. Sorbo, 217–34. Milan: Mondadori.

2009. "Il rifacimento del Santuario della Magna Mater a Roma alla fine del II secolo a.C. Impianto architettonico, cronologia, techniche edilizie." In *Suburbium* II, 227–40.

2014. "L'edificio in opus incertum del Testaccio a Roma. Status quaestionis e prospettive di ricerca." In Quilici and Quilici Gigli 2014, 7–23.

2016. "Italic Sanctuaries and the Onset of the 'Total Architecture'. Some Observations on the Phenomenon." In *Orte Der Forschung, Orte Des Glaubens Neue Perspektiven Für Heiligtümer in Italien von Der Archaik Bis Zur Späten Republik: Akten Der Internationalen Tagung in Darmstadt Am 19. Und 20. Juli 2013*, edited by M. Bolder-Boos and D. Maschek, 149–63. Bonn: Verlag Dr. Rudolf Habelt.

D'Alessio, M. T. 2008. "La Casa delle Nozze di Ercole (VII,9,47): storia di un isolato presso il Foro alla luce dei nuovi dati ceramici." In Guzzo and Guidobaldi 2008, 275–82.

Dall'Aglio, P. L., G. Marchetti, K. Ferrari, and M. Daguati. 2007. "Geomorfologia e città di fondazione in pianura padana. Il caso di Placentia." In *Forme e tempi dell'urbanizzazione nella Cisalpina (II secolo a. C. – I secolo d.C.). Atti delle Giornate*

di studio, Torino 4–6 maggio 2006*, edited by L. Brecciaroli Taborelli, 91–96. Florence: All'Insegna del Giglio.

D'Ambrosio, E., F. Marra, A. Cavallo, M. Gaeta, and G. Ventura. 2015. "Provenance Materials for Vitruvius' Harenae Fossiciae and Pulvis Puteolanis: Geochemical Signature and Historical-Archaeological Implications." *JAS Reports* 2: 186–203.

D'Andria, F. 1973. "Lo scavo del Capitolium." In Frova 1973, vol. 1: 574–609.

D'Arms, J. H. 1970. *Romans on the Bay of Naples: A Social and Cultural Study of the Villas and Their Owners from 150 B. C. to A.D. 400*. Cambridge, MA: Harvard University Press.

Darsy, F. M. D. 1968. *Recherches Archéologiques à Sainte Sabine Sur l'Aventin*. Vatican City: Pontificio Istituto di Archeologia Cristiana.

David, J.-M. 1997. *The Roman Conquest of Italy*. Translated by A. Nevill. Oxford: Blackwell.

Davies, P. J. E. 2012. "On the Introduction of Stone Entablatures in Republican Temples in Rome." In *Monumentality in Etruscan and Early Roman Architecture. Ideology and Innovation*, edited by M. L. Thomas, G. E. Meyers, and I. E. M. Edlund-Berry, 139–65. Austin: University of Texas Press.

2014. "Rome and Her Neighbors: Greek Building Practices in Republican Rome." In *A Companion to Roman Architecture*, edited by R. B. Ulrich and C. K. Quenemoen, 27–44. Malden, MA: Wiley-Blackwell.

2017. *Architecture and Politics in Republican Rome*. New York: Cambridge University Press.

De Caprariis, F. 1988. "Le pendici settentrionali del Viminale ed il settore sud ovest del Quirinale." In *Topografia romana. Ricerche e discussioni*, 17–44. QITA 10. Rome: Olschki.

De Caro, D. 1986. *Saggi nell'area del tempio di Apollo a Pompei: scavi stratigrafici di A. Maiuri nel 1931–32 e 1942–43*. Naples: Istituto Universitario Orientale.

De Franciscis, A. 1956. *Templum Dianae Tifatinae*. Caserta: Società di Storia Patria di Terra di Lavoro.

De Giorgi, A. U. 2018. "Sustainable Practices? A Story from Roman Cosa (Central Italy)." *JMA* 31: 3–26.

De Haan, N., C. Peterse, and F. Schipper. 2005. "The Casa degli Scienziati (VI 14, 43). Elite architecture in fourth-century B.C. Pompeii." In Guzzo and Guidobaldi, 2005, 240–56.

De Haas, T. C. A., P. A. J. Attema, and G. W. Tol. 2011–12. "Polygonal Masonry Platform Sites in the Lepine Mountains (Pontine Region, Lazio, Italy)." *Palaeohistoria* 53–54: 195–282.

De Luca, R., D. Miriello, A. Pecci, S. Domínguez-Bella, D. Bernal-Casasola, D. Cottica, A. Bloise, and G. M. Crisci. 2015. "Archaeometric Study of Mortars from the Garum Shop at Pompeii, Campania, Italy." *Geoarchaeology* 30: 330–51.

De Spagnolis, M. 1982. "Ville rustiche e trasformazione agraria nel Lazio Meridionale." In *Il Lazio nell'antichita romana*, edited by R. Lefevre, 353–63. Rome: Gruppo culturale di Roma e del Lazio/Palombi.

De Vincenzo, S. 2018. "Indagini archeologiche nel foro della colonia romana di Liternum." *Fasti On Line Documents & Research Italy* 411: 1–25.

De Visscher, F., and F. De Ruyt. 1951. "Les Fouilles d'Alba Fucens (Italie Centrale) en 1949 et 1950." *AntCl* 20: 47–84.

Degrassi, A. 1967. "Epigraphica III: 13. La questura di Pompei. " In *MemLinc* VIII.13.1: 46–49.

1969. "Epigraphica IV: 1. Quando fu costruito il santuario della Fortuna Primigenia di Palestrina." In *MemLinc* VIII.13.2: 111–27.

DeLaine, J. 1989. "Some Observations on the Transition from Greek to Roman Baths in Hellenistic Italy." *MeditArch* 2: 111–25.

1995. "The Supply of Building Materials to the City of Rome." In Christie 1995, 555–62.

1997. *The Baths of Caracalla: A Study in the Design, Construction, and Economics of Large-Scale Building Projects in Imperial Rome*. JRA Suppl. 25. Portsmouth, RI: JRA.

2001. "Bricks and Mortar. Exploring the Economics of Building Techniques at Rome and Ostia." In *Economies beyond Agriculture in the Classical World*, edited by D. J. Mattingly and J. Salmon, 230–68. London/New York: Routledge.

2006. "The Cost of Creation. Technology at the Service of Construction." In Lo Cascio 2006, 237–52.

2017. "Quantifying Manpower and the Cost of Construction in Roman Building Projects. Research Perspectives." *Archeologia dell'Architettura* 22: 13–19.

DeLaine, J., S. Camporeale, and A. Pizzo (eds.). *Arqueología de la construcción V. Man-Made Materials, Engineering and Infrastructure. Proceedings of the 5th International Workshop on the Archaeology of Roman Construction, Oxford, April 11–12, 2015*. Anejos ArchEspArq 77. Madrid: Consejo Superior de Investigaciones Científicas.

Delbrück, R. 1912. *Hellenistische Bauten in Latium, 2: Baubeschreibungen, geschichtliche Erläuterungen*. Straßburg: Trübner.

Della Corte, M. 1922. "Case e abitanti a Pompei." *Rivista Indo-Greco-Italica* 6: 103–12.

DeRose Evans, J. ed. 2013. *A Companion to the Archaeology of the Roman Republic*. Chichester: Blackwell.

Dessales, H. 2011. "Les savoir-faire des maçons romains, entre connaissance technique et disponibilité des matériaux. Le cas pompéien." In *Les savoirs professionels des gens de métier*, edited by N. Monteix and N. Tran, 41–63. Naples/Paris: Centre Jean Bérard/Diff. de Boccard.

———. 2016. "La Lex parieti faciendo: de l'usage du vocabulaire de la construction à sa diffusion." In *Dire l'architecture dans l'Antiquité*, edited by R. Robert, 381–410. Aix-en-Provence: Karthala-MMHS.

Devore, G., and S. R. J. Ellis. 2008. "The Third Season of Excavations at VIII.7.1–15 and the Porta Stabia at Pompeii. Preliminary Report." *Fasti On Line Documents & Research Italy* 112: 1–15.

Di Cesare, R. 2010. "Frontone in terracotta di Via San Gregorio." In *I giorni di Roma. L'età della conquista*, edited by E. La Rocca and C. Parisi Presicce, 247–49. Milan: Skira.

Di Cesare, R., and D. Liberatore. 2017. "Le tabernae di Alba Fucens." *Fasti On Line Documents & Research Italy* 379: 1–26.

———. 2018. "Le trasformazioni del paesaggio urbano di una colonia latina. Il foro di Alba Fucens dalle fasi dell'impianto alle ultime frequentazioni." In *Storia e archeologia globale dei paesaggi rurali in Italia fra Tardoantico e Medioevo*, edited by R. Volpe, 505–18. Bari: Edipuglia.

Di Giuseppe, H. 2012. *Black-Gloss Ware in Italy: Production Management and Local Histories*. BAR-IS 2335. Oxford: BAR Publishing.

Di Luca, G., and A. Cristilli. 2011. "Origine ed evoluzione dell'opera a telaio. Le attestazioni campane." In *DHER. Domus Herculanensis rationes. Sito,*

*archivio, museo*, edited by A. Coralini, 455–78. Bologna: Ante Quem.

Dickmann, J. A. 1997. "The Peristyle and the Transformation of Domestic Space in Hellenistic Pompeii." In Wallace-Hadrill and Laurence 1997, 121–36.

———. 1999. *Domus frequentata. Anspruchsvolles Wohnen im pompejanischen Stadthaus*. München: F. Pfeil.

Dickmann, J. A., and F. Pirson. 2005. "Il progetto Casa dei Postumii. Un complesso architettonico a Pompei come esemplificazione della storia dell'insediamento, del suo sviluppo e delle sue concezioni urbanistiche." In Guzzo and Guidobaldi 2005, 156–69.

Dicus, K. 2014. "Resurrecting Refuse at Pompeii. The Use-Value of Urban Refuse and Its Implications for Interpreting Archaeological Assemblages." In *TRAC 2013. Proceedings of the Twenty-Third Annual Theoretical Roman Archaeology Conference Which Took Place at King's College London 4–6 April 2013*, edited by H. Platts, J. Pearce, C. Barron, J. Lundock, and J. Yoo, 65–73. Oxford: Oxbow.

Diffendale, D. P., F. Marra, M. Gaeta, and N. Terrenato. 2018. "Combining Geochemistry and Petrography to Provenance Lionato and Lapis Albanus Tuffs Used in Roman Temples at Sant'Omobono, Rome, Italy." *Geoarchaeology* 34: 187–99.

Dilaria, S., M. Secco, J. Bonetto, and G. Artioli. 2019. "Technical Analysis on Materials and Characteristics of Mortar-Based Compounds in Roman and Late Antique Aquileia (Udine, Italy). A Preliminary Report of the Results." In *Proceedings of the 5th Historic Mortars Conference (Pamplona 19–21 June 2019)*, edited by J. I. Álvarez, J. M. Fernández,

Í. Navarro, A. Durán, and R. Sirera, 665–79. Paris: RILEM.

2020. "Malte, calcestruzzi e intonaci dipinti in Aquileia romana. Un approccio archeometrico nello studio di miscele leganti impiegate nell'edilizia antica." PhD diss., University of Padua.

Dix, B. 1982. "The Manufacture of Lime and Its Uses in the Western Roman Provinces." *OJA* 1: 331–46.

Dobbins, J. J. 2007. "The Forum and Its Dependencies." In Dobbins and Foss 2007, 150–83.

Dobbins, J. J., L. F. Ball, J. G. Cooper, S. L. Gavel, and S. Hay. 1998. "Excavations in the Sanctuary of Apollo at Pompeii, 1997." *AJA* 102: 739–56.

Dobbins, J. J. and P. W. Foss (eds.). 2007. *The World of Pompeii*. London/ New York: Routledge.

Donati, A. 2000. "Scritture di Bologna romana: Alcune riflessioni." *Atti e memorie della Deputazione di storia patria per le province di Romagna* 51: 377–86.

Downey, S. B. 1995. *Architectural Terracottas from the Regia*. PAAR 30. Ann Arbor: University of Michigan Press.

Drerup, H. 1957. *Zum Ausstattungsluxus in der römischen Architektur*. Münster: Aschendörff.

Dunbabin, K. M. D. 1999. *Mosaics of the Greek and Roman World*. Cambridge, UK/New York: Cambridge University Press.

Durante, A. M., and S. Landi. 2012. "Il circuito delle mura della colonia romana di Luna." In Attenni and Baldassarre, 97–111.

Durm, J. 1905. *Handbuch der Architektur: die Baukunst der Etrusker, die Baukunst der Romer*. Stuttgart: Alfred Kroner.

Dyson, S. L. 2013. "Cosa." In DeRose Evans 2013, 472–84.

2014. *The Creation of the Roman Frontier*. Princeton: Princeton University Press.

Eckstein, A. M. 1979. "The Foundation Day of Roman Coloniae." *California Studies in Classical Antiquity* 12: 85–97.

Edgerton, P. 1999. "From Innovation to Use: Ten Eclectic Theses on the Historiography of Technology." *History and Technology* 16: 111–36.

Edwards, C. 1993. *The Politics of Immorality in Ancient Rome*. Cambridge: Cambridge University Press.

Ellis, S. R. J., ed. 2011. *The Making of Pompeii: Studies in the History and Urban Development of an Ancient Town*. JRA Suppl. 85. Portsmouth, RI: JRA.

2018. *The Roman Retail Revolution: The Socio-Economic World of the Taberna*. Oxford: Oxford University Press.

Erdkamp, P. 2011. "Soldiers, Roman Citizens, and Latin Colonists in Mid-Republican Italy." *Ancient Society* 41: 109–46.

Erhardt, Wolfgang. 2012. *Dekorations- und Wohnkontext: Beseitigung, Restaurierung, Verschmelzung und Konservierung von Wandbemalungen in den kampanischen Antikenstätten*. Wiesbaden: Reichert.

Ertel, C., and K. S. Freyeberger. 2007. "Nuove indagini sulla Basilica Emilia nel Foro Romano." *ArchCl* 58: 109–42.

Eschebach, H. 1975. "Feststellungen unter der Oberfläche des Jahres 79 n.Chr. im Bereich der Insula VII 1 (Stabianer Thermen) in Pompeji." In Andreae and Kyrieleis 1975, 179–90.

1979. *Die Stabianer Thermen in Pompeji*. Denkmäler antiker Architektur 13. Berlin: De Gruyter.

Esposito, D. 2007. "Silla, Pompei e la Villa dei Misteri." In *Villas, maisons, sanctuaires et tombeaux tardo-républicains. Découvertes et relectures récentes. Actes du colloque international de Saint-Romain-en-Gal en l'honneur d'Anna Gallina Zevi. Vienne, Saint-Romain-en-*

*Gal, 8–10 février 2007*, edited by B. Perrier, 441–65. Rome: Quasar.

Etani, H., ed. 2010. *Pompeii. Report of the Excavation at Porta Capua, 1993–2005*. Kyoto: The Paleological Association of Japan.

Evans, J. M., J. T. Samuels, L. Motta, M. Naglak, and M. D'Acri. 2019. "An Iron Age Settlement at Gabii: An Interim Report of the Gabii Project Excavations in Area D, 2012–2015." *EtrStud* 22: 1–33.

Fabbri, M. 2012. "Cerere, Libero e Libera a Gabii. Una Nuova Proposta Ricostruttiva Della Storia Edilizia Del Santuario Orientale." *Ostraka* 20: 13–38.

Fabbri, M., S. Musco, and M. Osanna. 2012. "Nuove indagini al santuario orientale di Gabii." In Marroni 2012, 229–42.

Faber, A., and A. Hoffmann. 2009. *Die Casa del Fauno in Pompeji (VI 12), 1. Bauhistorische Analyse*. Wiesbaden: Reichert.

Fabiani, F., E. Paribeni, and C. Rizzitelli. 2019. "Laterizi per la nuova colonia di Luni. Le fornaci di Massa." In Bonetto *et al.* 2019, 457–64.

Fagan, G. G. 2001. "The Genesis of the Roman Public Bath. Recent Approaches and Future Directions." *AJA* 105: 403–26.

Farr, J. 2014. *Lapis Gabinus: Tufo and the Economy of Urban Construction in Ancient Rome*. PhD diss., University of Michigan.

———. 2016. "Building Materials and Local Tufo." In Opitz *et. al.* 2016, 125–30.

Farr, J., F. Marra, and N. Terrenato. 2015. "Geochemical Identification Criteria for 'Peperino' Stones Employed in Ancient Roman Buildings: A Lapis Gabinus Case Study." *JAS Reports* 3: 41–51.

Favro, D. 2016. "Reverse Engineering Augustan Rome." *Maia* 68: 300–11.

Fentress, E. 2000. "Introduction. Frank Brown, Cosa, and the Idea of a Roman City." In *Romanization and the City. Creation, Transformations, and Failures. Proceedings of a Conference Held at the American Academy in Rome, 14 – 16* May 1998, 11–24. JRA Suppl. 38. Portsmouth, RI: JRA.

———. ed. 2003. *Cosa V: An Intermittent Town, Excavations 1993–1997*. MAAR Suppl. 2. Ann Arbor: University of Michigan Press.

———. 2013. "Strangers in the City: Élite Communication in the Hellenistic Central Mediterranean." In Prag and Crawley Quinn, 157–78.

Fentress, E., J. Bodel, A. Rabinowitz, and R. Taylor. 2003. "Cosa in the Republic and Early Empire." In Fentress 2003, 13–62.

Fentress, E., and P. Perkins. 2016. "Cosa and the Ager Cosanus." In *A Companion to Roman Italy*, edited by A. E. Cooley, 378–400. Oxford: Wiley-Blackwell.

Ferrandes, A. F., and R. Oriolo. 2019. "L'impiego del laterizio a Roma tra tecnologia, morfologia e contesti d'uso. Stratigrafie e strutture tra Palatino e Velia dall'età repubblicana alla prima età imperiale." In Bonetto *et al.* 2019, 531–37.

Ferrea, L. 2002. *Gli dei di terracotta: La ricomposizione del frontone da via di San Gregorio*. Rome: Electa.

Filippi, D. 1997. "Il percorso del Clivo Capitolino." *RendPontAcc* 70: 151–66.

Fincker, M., É. Letellier-Taillefer, and S. Zugmeyer. 2018. "Théâtres de Pompéi – Campagne 2016." *Chronique des activités archéologiques de l'École française de Rome [En ligne], Les cités vésuviennes, mis en ligne le 14 février 2018*. https://doi.org/10.4000/cefr.1853.

Finkielsztejn, G. 2001. *Chronologie détaillée et révisée des éponymes amphoriques rhodiens, de 270 à 108 av. J.-C. environ.*

*Premier bilan.* BAR-IS 990. Oxford: Archaeopress.

Fiorelli, G. 1873. *Gli scavi di Pompei dal 1861 al 1872: relazione al Ministro della istruzione pubblica.* Naples: Tipografia Italiana.

Fiorini, C. 1988. "Edificio di età repubblicana in via Sistina." In *Topografia Romana. Ricerche e Discussioni,* 45–57. QITA 10. Rome: Olschki.

Flohr, M. 2010. "Review of Andrea Faber – Adolf Hoffmann, Die Casa del Fauno in Pompeji (VI 12) 1. Stratigraphische Befunde der Ausgrabungen in den Jahren 1961 bis 1963 (von Andrea Faber). Bauhistorische Analyse (von Adolf Hoffmann nach Vorarbeiten von René von Schöfer und Arnold Tschira). Archäologische Forschungen Bd. 25. Wiesbaden: Reichert Verlag 2009." *Göttinger Forum für Altertumwissenschaft* 13: 1165–72.

——— 2016. "Innovation and Society in the Roman World." *Oxford Handbooks Online.* DOI: https://doi.org/10.1093/oxfordhb/9780199935390.013.85.

——— 2019. "Artisans and Markets. The Economics of Roman Domestic Decoration." *AJA* 123: 101–25.

Flower, H. I. 2011. *Roman Republics.* Princeton: Princeton University Press.

Fontana, S. 1995. "Un impianto per la produzione di calce presso Lucus Feroniae." In Christie 1995, 563–70.

Forni, G. M. 2012. "Extra portam Trigeminam." *Atlante Tematico di Topografia Antica* 22: 35–40.

Forty, A. 2012. *Concrete and Culture: A Material History.* London: Reaktion Books.

Franconi, T. V., C. M. Rice, D. Bloy, and G. D. Farney. 2019. "Excavations at the Roman Villa of Vacone (RI), Lazio by the Upper Sabina Tiberina

Project, 2012–2018." In *Oltre La Villa. Ricerche nei siti archeologici del territorio di Cottanello, Configni, Vacone e Montasola. Atti dell'incontro di studio. Cottanello 20 Ottobre 2018,* edited by C. Sfameni and M. Volpi, 109–36. Rome: Arbor sapientiae.

Frank, T. 1924. *Roman Buildings of the Republic: An Attempt to Date Them from Their Materials.* Rome: American Academy in Rome.

Frederiksen, M. W. 1959. "Republican Capua. A Social and Economic Study." *PBSR* 27: 80–130.

Freyberger, K. S., and C. Ertel. 2016. *Die Basilica Aemilia auf dem Forum Romanum in Rom: Bauphasen, Rekonstruktion, Funktion und Bedeutung.* Sonderschriften des Deutsches Archäologisches Institut Rom 17. Wiesbaden: Reichert.

Frizot, M. 1982. *Mortiers et enduit peints antiques: Étude technique et archéologique.* 2nd ed. Dijon: Université de Dijon.

Frova, A., ed. 1973. *Scavi di Luni I. Relazione preliminare delle campagne di scavo 1970–1971.* 3 vols. Rome: L'Erma di Bretschneider.

——— ed. 1977. *Scavi di Luni II. Relazione preliminare delle campagne di scavo 1972–1973–1974.* 3 vols. Rome: L'Erma di Bretschneider.

——— 1984a. "De statuarum basibus." *Quaderni di Studi Lunensi* 9: 5–34.

——— 1984b. "Nota sulle opere pubbliche a Luni." *Quaderni di Studi Lunensi* 9: 35–44.

Fulford, M., and A. Wallace-Hadrill. 1999. "Towards a history of Pre-Roman Pompeii. Excavations beneath the House of Amarantus (I 9, 11–12), 1995–98." *PBSR* 67: 37–144.

Fumadó Ortega, I., and S. Bouffier, eds. 2019. *Mortiers et hydraulique en Méditerranée antique.* Aix-en-Provence: Presses Universitaires de Provence.

Fusco, U. 2013. "Le ricerche dell'Università degli studi di Roma 'La Sapienza' a Veio, 4. Aspetti culturali e archeologici del sito di Campetti, area sud-ovest. Dall'età arcaica a quella imperiale." *RendPontAcc* 86: 309–45.

Gaba, E. 1972. "Urbanizzazione e rinnovamenti urbanistici nell'Italia centromeridionale del I sec. a.C." *Studi Classici e Orientali* 21: 73–112.

——— 1976. "Considerazioni politiche ed economiche sullo sviluppo urbano in Italia nei secoli II e I a.C." In Zanker 1976, 315–26.

Gaggiotti, M. 1988. "*Pavimenta poenica marmore Numidico constrata*." In *L'Africa romana. Atti del V Convegno di studio, Sassari 11–13 dicembre 1987*, edited by A. Mastino, 215–21. Sassari: Università degli Studi di Sassari.

Gallo, A. 2001. *Pompei: l'Insula 1 della regione IX: settore occidentale*. Rome: L'Erma di Bretschneider.

Gallone, A., and M. Mogetta. 2013. "Gabii in età repubblicana. I rivestimenti pavimentali di alcune unità abitative." In *Atti del XVIII Colloquio AISCOM, Cremona, Italy, 14–17 March 2012*, edited by C. Angelelli, 717–25. Tivoli: Scripta Manent.

Ganschow, T. 1989. *Untersuchungen zur Baugeschichte in Herculaneum*. Bonn: Habelt.

Gargola, D. J. 1995. *Lands, Laws, and Gods. Magistrates and Ceremony in the Regulation of Public Lands in Republican Rome*. Chapel Hill: The University of North Carolina Press.

Gasparri, C. 2009. "Il foro di Cumae. Un bilancio preliminare." In *Studi cumani, 2. Cuma. Indagini archeologiche e nuove scoperte*, edited by C. Gasparri and G. Greco, 131–47. Pozzuoli: Naus.

——— 2010. "Il foro di Cuma dal I sec. a. C. all'età bizantina." In *Cuma. Atti del quarantottesimo convegno di studi sulla Magna Grecia (Taranto 27 settembre – 1 ottobre 2008)*, 580–611. Taranto: Istituto per la storia e l'archeologia della Magna Grecia.

Gasparri, C., S. Adamo, and G. Greco. 1996. "Cuma (Napoli). Il foro. Campagne di scavo 1994, 1996–1997." *Bollettino di Archeologia* 39–40: 44–58.

Gatti, G. 1934. "*Saepta Iulia* e *Porticus Aemilia* nella Forma Severiana." *BullCom* 62: 123–49.

Gatti, S. 2013. "Tecniche costruttive tardo republicane a Praeneste." In Cifarelli 2013, 9–24.

Gatti, S., and M. T. Onorati. 1990. "Per una definizione dell'assetto urbano di Carsioli." *Xenia* 20: 41–64.

Gazda, E. K. 2001. "Cosa's Contribution to the Study of Roman Hydraulic Concrete: An Historiographic Commentary." In *New Light from Ancient Cosa. Classical Mediterranean Studies in Honor of Cleo Rickman Fitch*, edited by N. Wynick Goldman, 145–77. New York and Boston: P. Lang.

——— 2008. "Cosa's Hydraulic Concrete. Towards a Revised Chronology." In Hohlfelder 2008, 265–90.

Gerding, H. 2002. *The Tomb of Caecilia Metella. Tumulus, Tropaeum and Thymele*. Lund: Lund University.

Germinario, L., A. Zara, L. Maritan, J. Bonetto, J. M. Hanchar, R. Sassi, S. Siegesmund, and C. Mazzoli. 2018. "Tracking Trachyte on the Roman Routes: Provenance Study of Roman Infrastructure and Insights into Ancient Trades in Northern Italy." *Geoarchaeology* 33: 417–29.

Gialanella, C. 2003. "Nuovi dati sulla topografia di Puteoli alla luce degli scavi in corso sull'acropoli del Rione Terra." In *Da Puteoli a Pozzuoli. Scavi e ricerche sulla rocca del Rione Terra. Atti della giornata di studio, Istituto Germanico, Roma 27 aprile 2001*, edited by L. Crimaco, C. Gialanella, and F. Zevi, 21–34. Naples: Electa.

2010. "Appunti sulla topografia della colonia del 194 a.C. sul Rione Terra di Pozzuoli." In *Dall'immagine alla storia: studi per ricordare Stefania Adamo Muscettola*, edited by C. Gasparri, G. Greco, and R. Pierobon Benoit, 317–35. Naples: Naus.

Gianfrotta, P. A. 1998. "I porti dell'area flegrea." In *Porti, approdi e linee di rotta nel Mediterraneo antico. Atti del seminario di studi, Lecce 29 – 30 novembre 1996*, edited by G. Laudizi and C. Marangio, 153–76. Galatina: Congedo.

Giglio, M. 2010. "Lo stadio e le mura in età Repubblicana." In *Cuma. Atti del quarantottesimo convegno di studi sulla Magna Grecia (Taranto 27 settembre – 1 ottobre 2008)*, 623–42. Taranto: Istituto per la storia e l'archeologia della Magna Grecia.

———. 2014. "La casa pompeiana tra il III ed il I secolo a. C. Nuovi dati dagli scavi della regione IX, insula 7." In *Center and Periphery in the Ancient World: Proceedings of the XVIII International Congress of Classical Archaeology (Mérida, 13–17 mayo, 2013)*, edited by J. M. Alvarez Martínez, T. Nogales Basarrate, and I. Rodà de Llanza, 2: 1033–36. Mérida: Museo nacional de arte romano.

———. 2015. *Lo stadio di Cuma.* Naples: Università degli studi di Napoli.

———. 2017a. "Il primo impianto delle case e lo sviluppo tra il III ed il II sec. a.C." In Pesando and Giglio 2017, 243–53.

———. 2017b. "Edifici pubblici e complessi residenziali a sud del Foro. Nuove indagini e scoperte archeologiche nel quartiere di Championnet." In *Restauri a Pompei. Dalle case di Championnet alla domus dei Mosaici geometrici*, edited by C. Cicirelli, 39–44. Naples: Arte'm.

Ginouvès, R., and R. Martin, eds. 1985. *Dictionnaire méthodique de l'architecture grecque et romaine, 1: Matériaux, techniques de construction, techniques et formes du décor.* CÉFR 86. Athens/Rome: École française d'Athènes/École française de Rome.

Gioia, P., and R. Volpe, eds. 2004. *Centocelle, 1. Roma S.D.O. Le indagini archeologiche.* Soveria Mannelli: Rubettino.

Giuliani, C. F. 1970. *Tibur. Pars prima.* Forma Italiae, Regio I 7. Rome: De Luca.

———. 1973. "Contributi allo studio della tipologia dei cryptoportici." In *Les crypto-portiques dans l'architecture romaine. Rome, 19 – 23 avril 1972*, 79–98. CÉFR 14. Rome.

———. 1992. "*Opus signinum* e cocciopesto." In *Segni I*, edited by G. M. De Rossi, 89–94. Naples: Arte Tipograf.

———. 1998. "L'*opus caementicium* nell'edilizia Romana." In *Atti del seminario: Opus caementicium: il materiale e la tecnica costruttiva: Facoltà di Ingegneria, Sala del Chiostro, 11 giugno, 1997*, edited by C. F. Giuliani and A. Samuelli Ferretti, 49–62. Rome: L'Erma di Bretschneider.

———. 1998–99. "Il linguaggio di una grande architettura: Il santuario tiburtino di Ercole Vincitore." *RendPontAcc* 71: 53–110.

———. 2006. *L'edilizia nell'antichità.* 2nd ed. Rome: Carocci.

———. 2009. *Tivoli: Il Santuario di Ercole Vincitore.* 2nd ed. Tivoli: Tiburis artistica.

Giuliani, C. F., and A. Ten. 2016. "Santuario di Ercole Vincitore a Tivoli III. Le architetture." *BdA* VII.30: 1–50.

Giuliani, C. F., and P. Verduchi. 1987. *L'area centrale del Foro Romano.* Florence: Olschki.

Giustini, R. 1990. "Porticus Metelli. Nuove acquisizioni." *Bollettino di Archeologia* 4: 71–74.

Glisoni, S., S. Hasselin-Rous, and D. Roger. 2017. "Gabies. Campagne 2014 et 2016 du musée du Louvre et de la Surintendance de Rome." *Chronique Des Activités Archéologiques de l'École Française de Rome, Italie Centrale.* DOI: https://doi.org/10.4000/cefr.1644.

Goodchild, H., and R. Witcher. 2010. "Modelling the Agricultural Landscapes of Republican Italy." In *Agricoltura e scambi nell'Italia tardo repubblicana,* edited by J. Carlsen and E. Lo Cascio, 187–220. Rome and Bari: Edipuglia.

Graham, S. 2006. *Ex Figlinis. The Network Dynamics of the Tiber Valley Brick Industry in the Hinterland of Rome.* BAR-IS 1486. Oxford: Archaeopress.

Granino Cecere, M. G. 2014. "La presenza senatoria nei santuari del Latium attraverso le testimonianze epigrafiche." In *Epigrafia e ordine senatorio, 30 anni dopo,* edited by M. L. Caldelli and G. L. Gregori, 231–45. Rome: Quasar.

Greco, E., and D. Theodorescu. 1987. *Poseidonia-Paestum III, Forum Nord.* Collection de l'École Française de Rome, 42/3. Rome: École Française de Rome.

Greco, E., P. Vitti, and O. Voza. 2011. "Appunti sulla topografia di Casa Bianca." *ASAtene* 89: 305–19.

Greene, K. 1992. "How Was Technology Transferred in the Western Provinces?" In *Current Research on the Romanization of the Western Provinces,* edited by M. Wood and F. Queiroga, 101–05. BAR-IS 575. Oxford: Tempus reparatum.

——— 2004. "Archaeology and Technology." In *A Companion to Archaeology,* edited by J. L. Bintliff, 155–73. Malden, MA: Blackwell.

——— 2008. "Historiography and Theoretical Approaches." In Oleson 2008, 62–90.

Gregori, G. L., and D. Nonnis. 2013. "Il contributo dell'epigrafia allo studio delle cinte murarie dell'Italia repubblicana." *ScAnt* 19: 491–524.

——— 2017. "Culti pubblici a Pompei. L'epigrafia del sacro in età romana." In Lippolis *et al.* 2017, 243–72.

Grimaldi, M. 2011. "Charting the urban development of the Insula Occidentalis and the Casa di Marcus Fabius Rufus." In Ellis 2011, 138–57.

Groen-Vallinga, M. J., and L. E. Tacoma. 2016. "The Value of Labour. Diocletian's Prices Edict." In *Work, Labour, and Professions in the Roman World,* edited by K. Verboven and C. Laes, 104–32. Leiden: Brill.

Gros, P. 1973. "Hermodoros et Vitruve." *MÉFRA* 85: 137–65.

——— 1976. "Les premières générations d'architectes hellénistiques à Rome." In *L'Italie préromaine et la Rome républicaine: Mélanges offerts à Jacques Heurgon,* 387–409. CÉFR 27. Rome: École française de Rome.

——— 1978. "Le dossier vitruvien d'Hermogénès." *MÉFRA* 90: 687–703.

——— 1981. *Fouilles de l'École française de Rome à Bolsena (Poggio Moscini), 1. Bolsena. Guide des fouilles.* MÉFRA Suppl. 6. Rome: École française de Rome.

——— 2006. *L'Architecture Romaine: du début du IIIe siècle av. J.-C. à la fin du Haut-Empire 2. Maisons, palais, villas et tombeaux.* 2nd ed. Paris: Picard.

——— 2011. *L'Architecture Romaine: du début du IIIe siècle av. J.-C. à la fin du Haut-Empire 1. Les monuments publics.* 3rd rev. ed. Paris: Picard.

Gros, P., and M. Torelli. 2007. *Storia dell'urbanistica: Il mondo romano.* 2nd ed. Bari: Laterza.

Gruen, E. 1992. *Culture and National Identity in Republican Rome.* Ithaca, NY: Cornell University Press.

Gualandi, M. L., and E. Papi. 1999a. "Fase 10. La costruzione delle case." In Carandini and Papi 1999, 17–54.

——— 1999b. "Fase 13. Prime modifiche edilizie." In Carandini and Papi 1999, 101–17.

Gualtieri, M., and H. Fracchia. 2014. "Dal territorio di Roccagloriosa all'Ager Buxentinus." *MÉFRA* 127: 439–56.

Guarnieri, C. 2000. "Edilizia pubblica. Le mure urbiche." In *Aemilia. La cultura romana in Emilia Romagna dal III secolo a.C. all'età costantiniana*, edited by M. Marini Calvani, R. Curina, and E. Lippolis, 116–26. Venice: Marsilio.

Guilhembet, J.-P., and M. Royo. 2008. "L'aristocratie en ses quartiers (IIe s. avant J.-C.–IIe s. après J.-C.)." In *Rome des quartiers. Des vici aux rioni. Cadres institutionnels, pratiques sociales, et requalifications entre antiquité et époque modern. Actes du colloque international de la Sorbonne (20–21 mai 2005)*, edited by M. Royo, E. Hubert, and A. Bérenger, 193–227. Paris: De Boccard.

Guzzo, P. G., and M. P. Guidobaldi, eds. 2005. *Nuove ricerche archeologiche a Pompei ed Ercolano. Atti del convegno internazionale, Roma 28–30 novembre 2002*. Naples: Electa.

eds. 2008. *Nuove ricerche archeologiche nell'area vesuviana (scavi 2003–2006). Atti del Convegno Internazionale, Roma 1–3 febbraio 2007*. Rome: L'Erma di Bretschneider.

Habinek, T. N. 1998. *The Politics of Latin Literature: Writing, Identity, and Empire in Ancient Rome*. Princeton: Princeton University Press.

Hafner, H. 1984. "Aedes Concordiae und Basilica Opimia." *AA*: 591–96.

Harris, W. V. 2015. "Prolegomena to a Study of the Economics of Roman Art." *AJA* 119: 395–417.

Harvey Jr., P. B. 2006. "Religion and Memory at Pisaurum." In *Religion in Republican Italy*, edited by C. E. Schultz and P. B. Harvey Jr., 117–36. *Yale Classical Studies* 33. Cambridge: Cambridge University Press.

Helas, S. 2016. "Polygonalmauern in Mittelitalien und ihre Rezeption in mittel- und spätrepublikanischer Zeit." In *Focus on fortification. New research on fortifications in the ancient Mediterranean and the Near East*, edited by R. Frederiksen, S. Müth, P. I. Schneider, and M. Schnelle, 581–94. Oxford: Oxbow.

Henderson, T. K. 2014. "Constructing an Oscan Cityscape: Pompeii and the *Eítuns* Inscriptions." In *Urban Dreams and Realities in Antiquity: Remains and Representations of the Ancient City*, edited by A. Kemezis, 99–120. Mnemosyne Suppl 375. Leiden: Brill.

Hingley, R. 2005. *Globalizing Roman Culture: Unity, Diversity, Empire*. London: Routledge.

2010. "Cultural Diversity and Unity. Empire and Rome." In *Material Culture and Social Identities in the Ancient World*, edited by S. Hales and T. Hodos, 54–75. Cambridge: Cambridge University Press.

Hohlfelder, R. L., ed. 2008. *The Maritime World of Ancient Rome: Proceedings of "The Maritime World of Ancient Rome" Conference Held at the American Academy in Rome, 27–29 March 2003*. MAAR Suppl. 6. Ann Arbor: University of Michigan Press/ American Academy in Rome.

Holappa, M., and E.-M. Viitanen. 2011. "Topographic Conditions in the Urban Plan of Pompeii. The Urban Landscape in 3D." In Ellis 2011, 169–89.

Hölscher, T. 2008. "I Vincitori: Generale di Tivoli." In *Trionfi Romani (catalogo della mostra, Roma-Colosseo 5 marzo-14 settembre 2008)*, edited by E. La Rocca and S. Tortorella, 179. Milan: Electa.

Hopkins, J. N. 2017. *The Genesis of Roman Architecture*. New Haven: Yale University Press.

Horsfall, N. 1989. *Cornelius Nepos: A Selection, Including the Lives of Cato and Atticus*. Oxford: Clarendon Press.

Horster, M. 2014. "Urban Infrastructure and Euergetism Outside the City of

Rome." In *The Oxford Handbook of Roman Epigraphy*, edited by Ch. Bruun and J. Edmondson, 515–36. Oxford: Oxford University Press.

Humm, M. 1999. "Le comitium du forum romain." *MÉFRA* 111: 625–94.

Hurst, H. 2006. "The Scalae (Ex-Graecae) above the Nova Via." *PBSR* 74: 236–91.

——— 2010. "Exceptions Rather Than the Rule: The Shipshed Complexes of Carthage (Mainly) and Athens." In *Ricoveri per navi militari nei porti del Mediterraneo antico e medievale*, edited by D. J. Blackman and M. C. Lentini, 27–36. Bari: Edipuglia.

Hurst, H., and D. Cirone. 2003. "Excavation of the Pre-Neronian Nova Via, Rome." *PBSR* 71: 17–84.

Iacopi, I. 1997. *La decorazione pittorica dell'Aula Isiaca*. Milan: Electa.

Jackson, M., D. Deocampo, F. Marra, and B. Sheetz. 2010. "Mid-Pleistocene Pozzolanic Ash in Ancient Roman Concretes." *Geoarchaeology* 25: 36–74.

Jackson, M., and F. Marra. 2006. "Roman Stone Masonry: Volcanic Foundations of the Ancient City." *AJA* 110: 403–36.

Jackson, M., F. Marra, D. Deocampo, A. Vella, C. Koss, and R. Hay. 2007. "Geological Observations of Excavated Sand (*harenae fossiciae*) Used as Fine Aggregate in Roman Pozzolanic Mortars." *JRA* 20: 25–53.

Jackson, M. D. 2014. "Sea-Water Concretes and Their Material Characteristics." In Brandon *et al.* 2014, 141–87.

Jackson, M. D., and C. K. Kosso. 2013. "*Scientia* in Republican Stone and Concrete Masonry." In DeRose Evans 2013, 268–84.

Johannowsky, W. 1961. "Relazione preliminare sugli scavi di Cales." *BdA* 46: 258–68.

——— 1963. "Relazione preliminare sugli scavi di Teano." *BdA* 48: 131–65.

——— 1976. "La situazione in Campania." In Zanker 1976, 267–88.

——— 1989. *Capua antica*. Naples: Banco di Napoli.

——— 1992. "Appunti su Pyxous-Buxentum." *AttiMGrecia* 3: 173–83.

Johnston, A. C. 2017. *The Sons of Remus: Identity in Roman Gaul and Spain*. Cambridge, MA: Harvard University Press.

Johnston, A. C., and M. Mogetta. 2020. "Debating Early Republican Urbanism in Latium Vetus: The Town Planning of Gabii, between Archaeology and History." *JRS* 110: 91–121.

Johnston, A. C., M. Mogetta, L. Banducci, E. Casagrande Cicci, J. Farr, A. Gallone, R. Opitz, and N. Terrenato. 2018. "A Monumental Mid-Republican Building Complex at Gabii." *PBSR* 86: 1–35.

Jolivet, V. 2011. *Tristes portiques. Sur le plan canonique de la maison étrusque et romaine des origines au principat d'Auguste (VIe – Ier siècles av. J.-C.)*. BÉFAR 342. Rome: Écoles française de Rome.

Jones, G. D. B. 1962. "Capena and the Ager Capenas." *PBSR* 30: 116–207.

——— 1963. "Capena and the Ager Capenas: Part II." *PBSR* 31: 100–58.

Jouffroy, H. 1986. *La construction publique en Italie et dans l'Afrique romaine*. Strasbourg: AECR.

Känel, R. 2015. "Das Aesculapius-Heiligtum in Fregellae und sein Bauschmuck aus Terrakotta." In Stek and Burgers 2015, 67–96.

Kastenmeier, P., G. Di Maio, G. Balassone, M. Boni, M. Joachimski, and N. Mondillo. 2010. "The Source of Stone Building Materials from the Pompeii Archaeological Area and Its Surroundings." *Periodico di Mineralogia* 79 (Special Issue): 39–58.

Kawamoto T., and Y. Tatsumi. 1992. "Classification and Regional Distribution of Lava Blocks in

Pompeii." *Opuscola Pompeiana* 2: 92–97.

Kay, Ph. 2014. *Rome's Economic Revolution.* Oxford: Oxford University Press.

Keay, S., G. Earl, F. Felici, P. Copeland, R. Cascino, S. Kay, C. Triantafillou, and A. Pellegrino. 2012. "Interim Report on an Enigmatic New Trajanic Building at Portus." *JRA* 25: 487–512.

Keay, S., and N. Terrenato, eds. 2001. *Italy and the West: Comparative Issues in Romanization.* Oxford: Oxbow.

Kirsch, J. H. I. 1993. *Villa dei Misteri. Bauaufnahme, Bautechnik, Baugeschichte.* Freiburg: IuK Rieth GmbH.

Kloppenborg, J. S., and R. S. Ascough. 2011. *Greco-Roman Associations. Texts, Translations, and Commentary, 1. Attica, Central Greece, Macedonia, Thrace.* Berlin: De Gruyter.

Kockel, V. 2008. "Forschungen im Südteil des Forums von Pompeji. Ein Vorbericht über die Arbeitskampagnen 2007 und 2008." *RM* 114: 271–303.

Kosmopoulos, D. 2012. "Il tempio presso S. Salvatore in Campo: lo stato della questione." *BullCom* 113: 7–42.

Koui, M., and C. Ftikos. 1998. "The Ancient Kamirian Water Storage Tank: A Proof of Concrete Technology and Durability for Three Millenniums." *Materials and Structures* 31: 623–27.

La Rocca, E. 1993. "Riflessi di Roma a Pompei: alcuni aspetti della colonizzazione." In *Riscoprire Pompei (Catalogo Mostra Roma, 13 novembre 1993 – 12 febbraio 1994),* edited by L. Franchi Dall'Orto and A. Varone, 26–49. Rome: L'Erma di Bretschneider.

——— 2011. "La forza della tradizione. L'architettura sacra a Roma tra II e I secolo a.C." In *Tradizione e innovazione. L'elaborazione del linguaggio ellenistico nell'architettura romana e italica di età tardo-repubblicana,* edited by E. La Rocca and A. D'Alessio, 1–24. StMisc 35. Rome: L'Erma di Bretschneider.

La Torre, F. G. 2011. "Reflections on the Lucanians and Bruttians in Calabria between Hannibal and the Principate. *Coloniae, civitates foederatae, municipia.*" In *Local Cultures of South Italy and Sicily in the Late Republican Period: Between Hellenism and Rome,* edited by F. Colivicchi, 139–59. JRA Suppl. 83. Portsmouth, RI: JRA.

Labate, D., L. Malnati, and S. Pellegrini. 2012. "Le mure repubblicane di Mutina. Gli scavi di piazza Roma (2006–2007)." In *Atlante Tematico di Topografia Antica* 22: 7–20.

Lackner, E.-M. 2008. *Republikanische Fora.* München: Biering and Brinkmann.

Laffi, U. 2017. "Italici in colonie Latine e Latini in colonie Romane." In *Itinerari di storia: In ricordo di Mario Pani,* edited by M. Chelotti, M. Silvestrini, and E. Todisco, 51–61. Bari: Edipuglia.

Lafon, X. 2001. *Villa maritima. Recherches sur les villas littorales de l'Italie romaine. IIIe siècle av. J.C. – IIIe siècle ap. J.C.* BÉFAR 307. Paris: Boccard.

Laidlaw, A., and M. S. Stella, eds. 2014. *The House of Sallust in Pompeii (VI 2, 4).* JRA Suppl. 98. Portsmouth, RI: JRA.

Lamboglia, N. 1958. "Opus Certum." *RStLig* 24: 158–70.

Lamprecht, Heinz-Otto. 1987. *Opus caementitium: Bautechnik der Römer.* Düsseldorf: Beton-Verlag.

Lancaster, L. C. 2005. *Concrete Vaulted Construction in Imperial Rome: Innovations in Context.* Cambridge, UK/New York: Cambridge University Press.

——— 2008. "Roman Engineering and Construction." In Oleson 2008, 256–84.

2009. "Auguste Choisy and the Economics of Roman Construction." In *Auguste Choisy (1841–1909) l'architecture et l'art de Batir (Actas del Simposio Internacional celebrado en Madrid, November 19–20, 2009)*, edited by J. Giron and S. Huerta, 307–28. Madrid: Instituto Juan de Herrera.

2015. *Innovative Vaulting in Architecture of the Roman Empire: 1st to 4th Centuries CE.* Cambridge: Cambridge University Press.

Lancaster, L. C., G. Sottili, F. Marra, and G. Ventura. 2011. "Provenancing of Lightweight Volcanic Stones Used in Ancient Roman Concrete Vaulting: Evidence from Rome." *Archaeometry* 53: 707–27.

Laurence, R., S. Esmond Cleary, and G. Sears. 2011. *The City in the Roman West, c. 250 BC – c. AD 250.* Cambridge: Cambridge University Press.

Lauter, H. 1975. "Zur Siedlungsstruktur Pompejis in samnitischer Zeit." In Andreae and Kyrieleis 1975, 147–52.

1976. "Die hellenistischen Theater der Samniten und Latiner in ihrer Beziehung zur Theaterarchitektur der Griechen." In Zanker 1976, 413–22.

1979. "Zur späthellenistische Baukunst in Mittelitalien." *JdI* 94: 390–457.

1980. "Porticus Metelli – Porticus Octaviae. Die bauliche Reste." *BullCom* 87: 37–46.

2009. *Die Fassade des Hauses IX, 1, 20 in Pompeji. Gestalt und Bedeutung.* Mainz am Rhein: Von Zabern.

Lauter-Bufe, H. 1987. *Die Geschichte des sikeliotisch-korinthischen Kapitells. Der sogenannte italisch-republikanische Typus.* Mainz am Rhein: Von Zabern.

Lea, F. M. 1970. *The Chemistry of Cement and Concrete.* London: Edward Arnold.

Leach, E. W. 2004. *The Social Life of Painting in Ancient Rome and on the Bay of Naples.* Cambridge: Cambridge University Press.

Leander Touati, A.-M. 2008. "Shared Structures-Common Constraints. Urbanisation of Insula V 1." In Guzzo and Guidobaldi 2008, 117–24.

Lechtman, H. N., and L. W. Hobbs. 1987. "Roman Concrete and the Roman Architectural Revolution." *Ceramics and Civilization* 3: 81–128.

Lepone, A., and C. M. Marchetti. 2018. "Il Capitolium." Paper presented at *Studium erga populum. Studium erga sapientiam. In Ricordo di Enzo Lippolis. Tra Capitolium ed extra moenia: nuovi scavi e ricerche*, Pompeii, July 13, 2018.

Liberatore, D. 2004. *Alba Fucens: studi di storia e di topografia.* Bari: Edipuglia.

Linderski, J. 1984. "*Si vis pacem, para bellum.* Concepts of Defensive Imperialism." In *The Imperialism of Mid-Republican Rome. The Proceedings of a Conference Held at the American Academy in Rome, November 5–6, 1982*, edited by W. V. Harris, 133–64. PAAR 29. Rome: American Academy in Rome.

Ling, R. 1991. *Roman Painting.* Cambridge: Cambridge University Press.

Liou, B., and P. Pomey. 1985. "Informations archéologiques. Direction des recherches sous-marines." *Gallia* 43: 547–76.

Lippolis, E. 1986. "L'architettura." In Coarelli 1986a, 29–41.

2000. "Edilizia pubblica. Fora e basiliche." In *Aemilia. La cultura romana in Emilia Romagna dal III secolo a.C. all'età costantiniana*, edited by M. Marini Calvani, R. Curina, and E. Lippolis, 106–15. Venice: Marsilio.

2004. "Triumphata Corintho. La preda bellica e i doni di Lucio Mummio Achaico." *ArchCl* 55: 25–81.

2009. "L'Asklepieion di Fregellae. Architettura, esigenze rituali e forme di ricezione del culto ellenistico in ambito centro-italico." In *Il culto di Asclepio nell'area mediterranea. Atti del convegno internazionale, Agrigento 20–22 novembre 2005*, edited by V. Calì, G. Sfameni Gasparro, and R. De Miro, 145–57. Rome: Gangemi.

2017. "Il Capitolium." In Lippolis *et al.* 2017, 111–48.

Lippolis, E., M. Osanna, and A. Lepone, eds. 2017. *I pompeiani e i loro dei. Culti, rituali e funzioni sociali a Pompei*. ScAnt 22.3. Rome: Quasar.

Lo Cascio, E., ed. 2006. *Innovazione tecnica e progresso economico nel mondo romano. Atti degli incontri capresi di storia dell'economia antica (Capri 13–16 Aprile 2003)*. Bari: Edipuglia.

Locatelli, D., L. Malnati, and D. F. Maras, eds. 2013. *Storie della prima Parma: Etruschi, Galli, Romani: le origini della città alla luce delle nuove scoperte archeologiche : mostra al Museo Archeologico Nazionale di Parma, Palazzo della Pilotta, (12 gennaio – 2 giugno 2013)*. Rome: L'Erma di Bretschneider.

Lomas, K. 1993. *Rome and the Western Greeks, 350 BC–AD 200: Conquest and Acculturation in Southern Italy*. London and New York: Routledge.

Loustaud, J. P. 1983. "Cuves à chaux gallo-romaines en Haut-Limousin." *Aquitania* 1: 143–54.

Lugli, G. 1923. "Note topografiche intorno alle antiche ville suburbane." *Bull Com* 51: 3–62.

1926. *Anxur-Tarracina. Forma Italiae I.2*. Rome: De Luca.

1928. *Circeii. Forma Italiae I.1*. Rome: Danesi.

1956. "L'opus caementicium in Vitruvio." *ClMed* 17: 99–108.

1957. *La tecnica edilizia romana. Con particolare riguardo a Roma e Lazio*. 2 vols. Rome: Bardi.

MacDonald, W. L. 1982. *The Architecture of the Roman Empire. Vol. 1, An Introductory Study*. 2nd ed. New Haven/London: Yale University Press.

MacKendrick, P. L. 1954. "Roman Colonization." *Phoenix* 64: 139–46.

MacMullen, R. 2000. *Romanization in the Time of Augustus*. New Haven: Yale University Press.

2011. *The Earliest Romans: A Character Sketch*. Ann Arbor: University of Michigan Press.

Maggi, S. 1996. "Opera a blocchetti semplice e mista nella Cisalpina e nelle Gallie dal I secolo a.C. al I secolo d. C. (e oltre): certezze e problemi." *Latomus* 55: 368–80.

Maiuri, A. 1947. *La Villa dei Misteri*. 2nd ed. Rome: Libreria dello Stato.

1973. *Alla ricerca di Pompei preromana: saggi stratigrafici*. Naples: Società Editrice Napoletana.

Malacrino, C. 2010. *Constructing the Ancient World: Architectural Techniques of the Greeks and Romans*. Los Angeles: J. Paul Getty Museum.

Malacrino, C. G. 2006. "*Ex his venustius est reticulatum*. Diffusione e significato dell'opera reticolata a Nicopoli d'Epiro." *Polis. ΠΟΛΙΣ. Studi interdisciplinari sul mondo antico* 2: 137–56.

2011. "Pavimenti in cementizio dall'Insula del teatro di Copia." In *Atti del XVI Colloquio dell'Associazione Italiana per lo Studio e la Conservazione del Mosaico (Palermo Piazza Armerina, 17–20 marzo 2010)*, edited by C. Angelelli, 215–28. Tivoli: Scripta Manent.

Malnati, L., and A. R. Marchi. 2018. "Le origini della colonia di Parma alla luce degli scavi. The Origins of the Colony of Parma in the Light of Excavations." In *Fondare e ri-fondare. Parma, Reggio e Modena lungo la via Emilia romana. Founding and refounding Parma, Reggio and Modena along the Roman Via Aemilia. [Atti del simposio internazionale. International Symposium Proceedings. Parma, Palazzo del*

*Governatore, 12 e 13 dicembre 2017]*, edited by A. Morigi and C. Quintelli, 97–111. Padua: Il Poligrafo.

Malnati, L., and A. Violante. 1995. "Il sistema urbano di IV e III secolo in Emilia-Romagna tra Etruschi e Celti (Plut. *Vita Cam.* 16, 3)." In *Europe celtique du Ve au IIIe siècle avant J.C. Contacts, échanges et mouvements de populations. Actes du Deuxième symposium international d'Hautvillers 8 – 10 octobre 1992*, edited by J. J. Charpy, 97–123. Sceaux: Kronos B. Y.

Mania, U., and M. Trümper, eds. 2018. *Development of Gymnasia and Graeco-Roman Cityscapes*. Berlin: Edition Topoi.

Mannoni, T. 1985. "Primi probabili impieghi del marmo lunense e il Portus Lunae." In *Atti del Convegno: Studi lunensi e prospettive sull'Occidente romano*, 395–403. Quaderni di Studi Lunensi 10–12. Luni: Centro Studi Lunensi.

Manzelli, V. 2000. "Le mura di Ravenna repubblicana." In Quilici Gigli and Quilici 2000, 7–28.

Maravelaki-Kalaitzaki, P., A. Bakolas, and A. Moropoulou. 2003. "Physico-Chemical Study of Cretan Ancient Mortars." *Cement and Concrete Research* 33: 651–61.

Marchi, A. R., and I. Serchia. 2019. "Parma, via del Conservatorio: la scoperta di un tratto delle mura difensive di età repubblicana." In Bonetto *et al.* 2019, 383–92.

Mari, Z. 1983. *Tibur. Pars tertia (Forma Italiae, Regio I, 17)*. Florence: Olschki.

——— 1991. *Tibur. Pars quarta (Forma Italiae, Regio I, 35)*. Florence: Olschki.

——— 1992. "Una cava romana all'Acquoria (Tivoli)." *AnalRom* 20: 31–42.

——— 2003. "Substructiones." In *Subterraneae domus. Ambienti residenziali e di servizio nell'edilizia privata romana*, edited by P. Basso and F. Ghedini, 65–112. Verona: Cierre.

——— 2005. "La villa romana di età repubblicana nell'ager Tiburtinus e Sabinus. Tra fonti letterarie e documentazione archeologica." In *Roman Villas around the Urbs. Interaction with Landscape and Environment. Proceedings of a Conference at the Swedish Institute in Rome, September 17–18, 2004*, edited by B. S. Frizell and A. Klynne, 75–95. Rome: Swedish Institute of Rome.

——— 2012a. "Il santuario di Ercole Vincitore a Tivoli. Considerazioni sulle fasi tardo-repubblicana e augustea." In Marroni 2012, 255–79.

——— 2012b. "Terrazzamenti in opera poligonale delle ville dell'agro Tiburtino e Sabino." In Attenni and Baldassarre 2012, 327–33.

——— 2013. "Tecniche murarie a Tibur e nell'area tiburtina in epoca tardo-repubblicana." In Cifarelli 2013, 25–32.

——— 2017. "Il c.d. 'Mercato coperto' a Tivoli." *Atti e Memorie della Società Tiburtina di Storia e d'Arte* 90: 119–40.

Marino, S. 2010. *Copia-Thurii. Aspetti topografici e urbanistici di una città romana della Magna Grecia*. Tekmeria 14. Paestum: Pandemos.

Marra, F., and E. D'Ambrosio. 2013. "Trace Element Classification Diagrams of Pyroclastic Rocks from the Volcanic Districts of Central Italy. The Case Study of the Ancient Roman Ships of Pisa." *Archaeometry* 55: 993–1019.

Marra, F., E. D'Ambrosio, M. Gaeta, and M. Mattei. 2016. "Petrochemical Identification and Insights on Chronological Employment of the Volcanic Aggregates Used in Ancient Roman Mortars." *Archaeometry* 58: 177–200.

——— 2018. "The Geochemical Fingerprint of Tufo Lionato Blocks from the Area Sacra di Largo Argentina: Implications for the Chronology of

Volcanic Building Stones in Ancient Rome." *Archaeometry* 60: 641–59.

Marra, F., A. Danti, and M. Gaeta. 2015. "The Volcanic Aggregate of Ancient Roman Mortars from the Capitoline Hill: Petrographic Criteria for Identification of Rome's 'Pozzolans' and Historical Implications." *Journal of Volcanology and Geothermal Research* 308: 113–26.

Marra, F., D. Deocampo, M. D. Jackson, and G. Ventura. 2011. "The Alban Hills and Monti Sabatini Volcanic Products Used in Ancient Roman Masonry (Italy): An Integrated Stratigraphic, Archeological, Environmental and Geochemical Approach." *Earth-Science Reviews* 108: 115–36.

Marroni, E., ed. 2012. *Sacra nominis latini: i santuari del Lazio arcaico e repubblicano : atti del convegno internazionale, Roma, Palazzo Massimo, 19–21 febbraio 2009.* Ostraka, Volume Speciale 2012. Naples: Loffredo.

Martelli, A. 2002. "Per una nuova lettura dell'iscrizione Vetter 61 nel contesto del santuario di Apollo a Pompei." *Eutopia* 2: 71–81.

2005. "Titolo mummiano nel tempio di Apollo a Pompei: l'iscrizione Vetter 61." In Guzzo and Guidobaldi 2005, 383.

Martin, S. D. 1989. *The Roman Jurists and the Organization of Private Building in the Late Republic and Early Empire.* Brussels: Latomus.

Marzano, A. 2007. *Roman Villas in Central Italy. A Social and Economic History.* Leiden: Brill.

Maschek, D. 2012. *Rationes Decoris: Aufkommen und Verbreitung dorischer Friese in der mittelitalischen Architektur des 2. Und 1. Jahrhunderts v. Chr.* Wien: Phoibos Verlag.

2013. Review of *Die republikanischen Otiumvillen von Tivoli. Palilia 25.* Wiesbaden: Reichert Verlag, 2012, by Martin Tombrägel. *Göttinger Forum für Altertumswissenschaft* 16: 1129–45.

2014. "Der Tempel neue Kleider? Rezeptionsästhetische und semantische Aspekte von Bauornamentik im spätrepublikanischen Mittelitalien." In *Antike Bauornamentik. Grenzen und Möglichkeiten ihrer Erforschung*, edited by J. Lipps and D. Maschek, 181–202. Wiesbaden: Reichert.

2016. "Quantifying Monumentality in a Time of Crisis. Building Materials, Labour Force and Building Costs in Late Republican Central Italy." In DeLaine *et al.* 2016, 317–29.

2018. *Die römischen Bürgerkriege. Archäologie und Geschichte einer Krisenzeit.* Mainz: Von Zabern.

Maselli Scotti, F., L. Mandruzzato, and C. Tiussi. 2009. "Primo impianto coloniario di Aquileia: l'area tra foro e macellum." In *Forme e tempi dell'urbanizzazione nella Cisalpina (II secolo a. C. – I secolo d.C.). Atti delle Giornate di studio, Torino 4–6 maggio 2006*, edited by L. Brecciaroli Taborelli, 235–77. Florence: All'Insegna del Giglio.

Mau, A. 1908. *Pompeji in Leben und Kunst.* Revised 2nd ed. Leipzig: Engelmann.

Mau, A., and F. W. Kelsey. 1907. *Pompeii; Its Life and Art.* 2nd ed. New York/ London: Macmillan.

McAlpine, L. 2015. "Heirlooms on the Walls. Republican Paintings and Imperial Viewers in Pompeii." In *Beyond Iconography. Material, Methods, and Meaning in Ancient Surface Decoration*, edited by S. Lepinski and S. McFadden, 167–86. Boston: Archaeological Institute of America.

McCann, A. M., ed. 1987. *The Roman Port and Fishery at Cosa.* Princeton: Princeton University Press.

McDonald, K. 2012. "The Testament of Vibius Adiranus." *JRS* 102: 40–55.

Medri, M. 1999. "Fase 12. Le ricostruzioni delle case." In Carandini and Papi 1999, 63–100.

2001. "La diffusione dell'opera reticolata: considerazioni a partire dal caso di Olimpia." In *Constructions publiques et programmes édilitaires en Grèce entre le IIe siècle av. J.-C. et le Ier siècle ap. J.-C.: actes du colloque organisé par l'École Française d'Athènes et le CNRS, Athènes 14–17 mai 1995*, edited by J. Y. Marc and J. Ch. Moretti, 15–40. BCH Suppl. 39. Athens: École française d'Athènes.

Melillo Faenza, L. 2012. "Riflessioni e approfondimenti sullo scavo del 1993 del tempio di Diana Tifatina." In *Carta archeologica e ricerche in Campania, 6. Ricerche intorno al santuario di Diana Tifatina*, edited by S. Quilici-Gigli, 6: 193–204. Rome: L'Erma di Bretschneider.

Mertens, J. 1969. *Alba Fucens: Rapports et études*. 2 vols. Bruxelles: Institut historique belge de Rome.

Mertens, J. 1988. "Alba Fucens." *DialArch* 6.2: 87–104.

Middleton, J. H. 1892. *The Remains of Ancient Rome*. 2 vols. London/Edinburgh: A. and C. Black.

Mielsch, H. 1987. *Die römische Villa: Arkitechtur und Lebensform*. München: Beck.

Miriello, D., D. Barca, A. Bloise, A. Ciarallo, G. Crisci, T. Rose, C. Gattuso, F. Gazineo, and M. La Russa. 2010. "Characterisation of Archaeological Mortars from Pompeii (Campania, Italy) and Identification of Construction Phases by Compositional Data Analysis." *JAS* 37: 2207–39.

Misiani, A. 1999. "Le tecniche edilizie." In Carandini and Papi 1999, 179–96.

Mogetta, M. 2015. "A New Date for Concrete in Rome." *JRS* 105: 1–40.

2016. "The Early Development of Concrete in the Domestic Architecture of Pre-Roman Pompeii." *JRA* 29: 43–72.

2019. "Monumentality, Technological Innovation, and Identity Construction in Roman Republican Architecture: The Remaking of Cosa, Post-197 BCE." In *Size Matters – Understanding Monumentality across Ancient Civilizations*, edited by F. Buccellati, S. Hageneuer, S. van der Heyden, and F. Levenson, 241–68. Bielefeld: Transcript.

Mogetta, M., and J. A. Becker. 2014. "Archaeological Research at Gabii, Italy: The Gabii Project Excavations 2009–2011." *AJA* 118: 171–88.

Mommsen, T. 1854–56. *Römische Geschichte*. 3 vols. Leipzig: Weidmann.

Monacchi, D., R. Nini, and S. Zampolini Faustini. 1999. "Forma e urbanistica di Narni romana." *Rivista di Topografia Antica* 9: 237–98.

Monteix, N. 2010. *Les lieux de métier: Boutiques et ateliers d'Herculanum*. BÉFAR 344. Rome: École française de Rome.

Moorman, E. M. 2011. *Divine Interiors: Mural Paintings in Greek and Roman Sanctuaries*. Amsterdam: Amsterdam University Press.

Morel, J.-P. 1981. *Céramique campanienne: les formes*. BÉFAR 244. Rome.

2008. "Early Rome and Italy." In *The Cambridge Economic History of the Greco-Roman World*, edited by W. Scheidel, I. Morris, and R. P. Saller, 485–510. Cambridge: Cambridge University Press.

Morgan, M. G. 1971. "The Porticus of Metellus. A Reconsideration." *Hermes* 99: 480–505.

1973. "Villa Publica and Magna Mater: Two Notes on Manubial Building at the Close of the Second Century B.C." *Klio* 55: 215–45.

Morricone, M. L. 1980. *Scutulata pavimenta. I pavimenti con inserti di marmo o di pietra trovati a Roma e nei dintorni*. Rome: L'Erma di Bretschneider.

Morricone Matini, M. L. 1967. *Mosaici antichi in Italia. Regione prima. Roma. Regio X, Palatium.* Rome: Istituto Poligrafico dello Stato.

1971. *Pavimenti di signino repubblicani di Roma e dintorni.* Rome: Istituto Poligrafico dello Stato.

Munzi, P. 2019. "Forme di autorappresentazione nella necropoli osca di Cuma tra il II e il I secolo a.C." In *Dialoghi sull'archeologia della Magna Grecia e del Mediterraneo. Atti del III Convegno internazionale di studi. Paestum, 16–18 novembre* 2018, edited by M. Cipriani, E. Greco, A. Pontrandolfo, and M. Scafuro, vol. 1: 109–22. Paestum: Pandemos.

Muzzioli, M. P. 2009. "Fonti per la topografia di Roma antica tra novità e vecchi problemi." *Rivista di Topografia Antica* 19: 21–40.

Nappo, S. C. 1997. "Urban Transformation at Pompeii in the Late 3rd and Early 2nd Centuries B. C." In Wallace-Hadrill and Laurence 1997, 91–120.

Neutsch, B. 1956. "Archäologische Grabungen und Funde im Bereich der unteritalischen Soprintendenzen von Tarent, Reggio di Calabria und Salerno, 1949–1955." *AA*: 193–450.

Nichols, M. F. 2017. *Author and Audience in Vitruvius' De Architectura.* Cambridge: Cambridge University Press.

Nicotera, P. 1950. "Sulle rocce laviche adoperate nell'antica Pompei." In *Pompeiana. Raccolta di studi per il secondo Centenario degli scavi di Pompei,* edited by A. Maiuri, 396–424. Naples: Macchiaroli.

Nielsen, I. 1992. "The Metellan Temple." In Nielsen and Poulsen 1992, 87–117.

Nielsen, I., and B. Poulsen, eds. 1992a. *The Temple of Castor and Pollux I: The Pre-Augustan Temple Phases with Related Decorative Elements.* LSA 17. Rome: De Luca.

1992b. "The Rebuilding of the First Temple (Temple IA)." In Nielsen and Poulsen, 80–86.

Noack, F., and K. Lehmann-Hartleben. 1936. *Baugeschichtliche Untersuchungen am Stadtrand von Pompeji.* Berlin/Leipzig: De Gruyter.

Nonnis, D. 1999. "Attività imprenditoriali e classi dirigenti nell'età repubblicana. Tre città campione." *Cahiers du Centre G. Glotz* 10: 71–109.

2003. "Dotazioni funzionali e di arredo in luoghi di culto dell'Italia repubblicana. L'apporto della documentazione epigrafica." In *Sanctuaires et sources: Les sources documentaires et leurs limites dans la description des lieux de culte,* edited by O. De Cazanove and J. Scheid, 25–54. Naples: Publications du Centre Jean Bérard.

2014. "A proposito del 'monumento dei Calpurnii' a Cales: una nuova proposta interpretativa." In Chiabà 2014, 391–414.

2015. *Produzione e distribuzione nell'Italia repubblicana: uno studio prosopografico.* Rome: Quasar.

Nünnerich-Asmus, A. 1994. *Basilika und Portikus: die Architektur der Säulenhallen als Ausdruck gewandelter Urbanität in später Republik und früher Kaiserzeit.* Cologne: Böhlau.

Ohr, K. 1991. *Die Basilica in Pompeji.* Berlin: De Gruyter.

Oleson, J. P., ed. 2008. *The Oxford Handbook of Technology and Engineering in the Classical World.* Oxford: Oxford University Press.

2014. "Ancient Literary Sources Concerned with Roman Concrete Technology." In Brandon *et al.* 2014, 11–36.

Oleson, J. P., C. Brandon, S. M. Cramer, R. Cucitore, E. Gotti, and R. Hohlfelder. 2004. "The ROMACONS Project: A Contribution to the Historical and Engineering Analysis of Hydraulic

Concrete in Roman Maritime Structures." *International Journal of Nautical Archaeology* 33: 199–229.

Onorato, O. 1951. "Pompei Municipium e Colonia Romana." *RendNap* 26: 115–56.

Opitz, R., M. Mogetta, and N. Terrenato, eds. 2016. *A Mid-Republican House from Gabii*, edited by R. Opitz, M. Mogetta, and N. Terrenato. Ann Arbor: University of Michigan Press. DOI: https://doi.org/10.3998/mpub .9231782.

Ortalli, J. 2008. "La prima Felsina e la sua cinta." In *La città murata in Etruria. Atti del XXV Convegno di studi etruschi ed italici. Chianciano Terme, Sarteano, Chiusi. 30 marzo – 3 aprile 2005. In memoria di Massimo Pallottino*, 492–506. Pisa: Serra.

Osanna, M., ed. 2009. *Verso la città. Forme insediative in Lucania e nel mondo italico fra IV e III sec. a.C. Atti delle Giornate di studio, Venosa, 13–14 maggio 2006*. Venosa: Osanna Edizioni.

———. 2015. "Sanctuaries and Cults in Pre-Roman Pompeii." In *Greek Colonisation: New Data, Current Approaches.*, edited by P. Adan-Velene and D. Tsagari, 73–91. Athens: Alpha Bank/Archaeological Museum of Thessaloniki.

———. 2017. "Nuove ricerche nei santuari Pompeiani." In Lippolis *et al.* 2017, 71–88.

Osanna, M., and C. Rescigno. 2018. "Nuove indagini nel foro e nel santuario di Apollo." Paper presented at *Studium erga populum. Studium erga sapientiam. In Ricordo di Enzo Lippolis. Tra Capitolium ed extra moenia: nuovi scavi e ricerche*, Pompeii, July 13, 2018.

Pairault Massa, F.-H. 1992. *Iconologia e politica nell'italia antica: Roma, Lazio, Etruria dal VII al I Secolo a.C.* Milan: Longanesi.

Palmer, R. E. A. 1990. "A New Fragment of Livy Throws Light on the Roman Postumii and Latin Gabii." *Athaeneum* 78: 5–18.

Palombi, D. 2015. "Gabii, Giunone, e i Cornelii Cethegi." *ArchCl* 66: 253–87.

Panariti, D. 2018. "Il santuario del Monte San Nicola a Pietravairano (CE). Modelli architettonici e aspetti metrologici." In *Il ruolo del culto nelle comunità dell'Italia antica tra IV e I sec. a. C. Strutture, funzioni e interazioni culturali (ricerca PRIN 2008)*, edited by E. Lippolis and R. Sassu, 375–96. Rome: Quasar.

Panciera, S. 1997. "L'evergetismo civico nelle iscrizioni latine d'età repubblicana." In *Actes du Xe Congrès international d'épigraphie grecque et latine, Nîmes 4–9 octobre 1992*, edited by M. Christol and O. Masson, 249–90. Paris: Publications de la Sorbonne.

———. 2000. "L. Arrunti Stellae sub officio ad calcem." In *Epigraphai. Miscellanea epigrafica in onore di Lidio Gasperini*, 671–84. Tivoli: Editrice Tipigraf.

Panella, C. 1990. "La valle del Colosseo nell'antichità." *Bollettino di Archeologia* 1–2: 35–88.

———. 2006. "Il Palatino nord-orientale. Nuove conoscenze, nuove riflessioni." *ScAnt* 13: 265–99.

———. 2010. "Roma, il suburbio e l'Italia in età medio- e tardo-repubblicana. Cultura materiale, territori, economie." *Facta* 4: 11–123.

Panella, C., A. F. Ferrandes, G. Iacomelli, and G. Soranna. 2019. "Curiae Veteres. Nuovi dati sulla frequentazione del santuario in età tardo-repubblicana." *ScAnt* 25: 41–71.

Panella, C., S. Zeggio, and A. F. Ferrandes. 2014. "Lo scavo delle pendici nord-orientali del Palatino tra dati acquisiti e nuove evidenze." *ScAnt* 20: 159–210.

Paoletti, O., ed. 2005. *Dinamiche di sviluppo delle città nell'Etruria meridionale: Veio, Caere, Tarquinia, Vulci: atti del XXIII*

*Convegno di studi etruschi ed italici, Roma, Veio, Cerveteri/ Pyrgi, Tarquinia, Tuscania, Vulci, Viterbo: 1–6 ottobre 2001*. Pisa: Istituti editoriali e poligrafici internazionali.

Papi, E. 1995. "I pavimenti delle domus della pendice settentrionale del Palatino (VI–II secolo a.C.)." In Bragantini and Guidobaldi 1995, 337–52.

1998. "*Domus est quae nulli villarum mearum cedat* (Cic. *Fam.* 6, 18, 5). Osservazioni sulle residenze del Palatino alla metà del I secolo a.C." In *Horti romani. Atti del convegno internazionale, Roma 4–6 maggio 1995*, edited by M. Cima and E. La Rocca, 45–70. Rome: L'Erma di Bretschneider.

Parmegiani, N., and A. Pronti. 2004. *S. Cecilia in Trastevere. Nuovi scavi e ricerche*. Vatican City: Pontificio Istituto di Archeologia Cristiana.

Passaro, C. 2009. *Cales. Dalla Cittadella medievale alla città antica. Recenti scavi e acquisizioni*. Sparanise: Grafiche Mincione.

Paternoster, G., L. M. Proietti, and A. Vitale. 2007. *Malte e tecniche edilizie del Rione Terra di Pozzuoli: L'età romana*. Naples: Giannini Editore.

Patterson, J. R. 1992. "The City of Rome: From Republic to Empire." *JRS* 82: 186–215.

2006. "The Relationship of the Italian Ruling Classes with Rome. Friendship, Family Relations and Their Consequences." In *Herrschaft ohne Integration? Rom und Italien in Republikanischer Zeit*, edited by M. Jehne and R. Pfeilschifter, 139–53. Frankfurt am Mein: Verlag Antike.

2016. "Elite Networks in Pre-Social War Italy." In *E pluribus unum? L'Italie, de la diversité préromaine à l'unité augustéenne, Vol. II. L'Italia centrale e la creazione di una koiné culturale? I percorsi della "Romanizzazione,"*

edited by M. Aberson, M. C. Biella, and M. Di Fazio, 43–55. Bern: Peter Lang.

Pedroni, L. 2011. "Excavations in the History of Pompeii's Urban Development in the Area North of the So-Called 'Altstadt'." In Ellis 2011, 158–68.

2013. "Il tempio romano di Cales." *Fasti On Line Documents & Research Italy* 326: 1–11.

Pelgrom, J. 2008. "Settlement Organization and Land Distribution in Latin Colonies before the Second Punic War." In *People, Land, and Politics: Demographic Developments and the Transformation of Roman Italy 300 BC–AD 14*, edited by L. de Ligt and S. Northwood, 333–72. Mnemosyne Suppl. 303. Leiden/ Boston: Brill.

2014. "Roman Colonization and the City-State Model." In Stek and Pelgrom 2014, 73–86.

Pensabene, P. 1978. "Saggi di scavo sul tempio della Magna Mater del Palatino." *ArchLaz* 1: 67–71.

1980. "La zona sud-occidentale del Palatino." *ArchLaz* 3: 65–81.

1985. "Area sud-occidentale del Palatino." In Bietti Sestieri 1985, 179–212.

1991. "Il Tempio della Vittoria sul Palatino." *Bollettino di Archeologia* 11: 11–51.

2017a. *Scavi del Palatino, 2. Culti, architettura e decorazioni. Tomo 1, Gli edifici arcaici e repubblicani, i templi della Vittoria e della Magna Mater, i rinvenimenti votivi a "torre," le iscrizioni*. StMisc 39. Rome: L'Erma di Bretschneider.

2017b. *Scavi del Palatino, 2. Culti, architettura e decorazioni. Tomo 2, La "Casa dei Grifi," la casa di Ottaviano-Augusto e il tempio di Apollo*. StMisc 39. Rome: L'Erma di Bretschneider.

Pensabene, P., P. Battistelli, and L. Borrello. 1993. "Campagne di scavo 1988–1991 nell'area sud-ovest del Palatino." *ArchLaz* 11: 19–37.

Pensabene, P., and A. D'Alessio. 2006. "L'immaginario urbano. Spazio sacro sul Palatino tardo-repubblicano." In *Imaging Ancient Rome. Documentation, Visualization, Imagination. Proceedings of the Third Williams Symposium on Classical Architecture Held at the American Academy in Rome, the British School at Rome and the Deutsches Archäologisches Institut, Rome, on May 20–23, 2004*, edited by L. Haselberger and J. Humphrey, 30–49. JRA Suppl. 61. Portsmouth, RI: JRA.

Percossi Serenelli, E. 2012. "Le fasi repubblicane di Potentia." In *I processi formativi ed evolutivi della città in area adriatica*, edited by G. De Marinis, G. M. Fabrini, and G. Paci, 309–30. BAR-IS 2419. Oxford: Archaeopress.

Pesando, F. 1999. "Forme abitative e controllo sociale. La documentazione archeologica delle colonie latine in età repubblicana." In *Habitat et société. XIXe rencontres internationales d'archéologie et d'histoire d'Antibes. Actes des rencontres 22–23–24 octobre 1998*, edited by F. Braemer, S. Cleuziou, and A. Coudart, 237–54. Antibes: APDCA.

2002–03. "Le terme repubblicane di Pompei. Cronologia e funzione." *AION* 9–10: 221–43.

2005. "Il progetto Regio VI. Le campagne di scavo 2001–2002 nelle Insulae 9 e 10." In Guzzo and Guidobaldi 2005, 73–96.

2006. "Il secolo d'oro di Pompei. Aspetti dell'architettura pubblica e privata nel II secolo a.C." In *Sicilia ellenistica, consuetudo italica. Alle origini dell'architettura ellenistica d'Occidente. Spoleto, Complesso monumentale di S. Nicolò, 5–7 novembre 2004*, edited by M. Osanna and M. Torelli, 227–41. Roma: Edizioni dell'Ateneo.

2008. "Case di età medio-sannitica nella Regio VI. Tipologia edilizia e apparati decorativi." In Guzzo and Guidobaldi 2008, 159–72.

ed. 2010a. *Rileggere Pompei III. Ricerche sulla Pompei Sannitica. Campagne di scavo 2006–2008*. Rome: Bardi.

2010b. "La domus pompeiana in età sannitica. Nuove acquisizioni dalla Regio VI." In Bentz and Reusser 2010, 243–53.

2011. "L'*ars struendi* nella precettistica catoniana (*Agr.*, 14)." In *L'insegnamento delle technai nelle culture antiche. Atti del convegno, Ercolano, 23–24 marzo 2009*, edited by A. Roselli and R. Velardi, 85–94. Annali dell'Università degli studi di Napoli "L'Orientale" Quaderni 15. Pisa: Serra.

2012. "*Fundamenta sub terra*. Breve nota sulle fondazioni murarie pompeiane durante l'età sannitica." *Vesuviana* 4: 69–85.

2013. "Pompei in età sannitica. Tipologia, uso e cronologia delle tecniche edilizie." In Cifarelli 2013, 117–26.

Pesando, F., D. Cannavina, F. Freda, A. Grassi, R. Tilotta, and E. Tommasino. 2006. "La Casa dell'Ancora (VI 10, 7)." In Coarelli and Pesando 2006a, 161–242.

Pesando, F., and M. Giglio, eds. 2017. *Rileggere Pompei V. L'insula 7 della Regio IX*. Rome: L'Erma di Bretschneider.

Pesando, F., and M. P. Guidobaldi. 2004. *Gli ozi di Ercole. Residenze di lusso a Pompei ed Ercolano*. Rome: L'Erma di Bretschneider.

Petacco, L., and C. Rescigno. 2007. "I saggi sul Capitolium e il settore occidentale della piazza forense." In *Cuma. Il foro. Scavi dell'Università di Napoli Federico II, 2000–2001*, edited by C. Gasparri and G. Greco, 77–117. Pozzuoli: Naus.

Peterse, C. 2007. "Select Residences in Regions V and IX: Early Anonymous Domestic Architecture." In Dobbins and Foss 2007, 373–88.

Peterse, C. L. J. 1985. "Notes on the Design of the House of Pansa (VI, 6, 1) in Pompeii." *Meded* 46: 35–55.

Peterse, K. 1999. *Steinfachwerk in Pompeji. Bautechnik und Architektur*. Circumvesuviana 3. Amsterdam: Gieben.

Pfanner, Michael. 1989. "Über das Herstellen von Porträts." *Jahrbuch des Deutschen Archäologischen Instituts* 104: 157–257.

Pietilä-Castrén, L. 1978. "Some Aspects of the Life of Lucius Mummius Achaicus." *Arctos* 12: 115–23.

Piovesan, R., E. Curti, C. Grifa, L. Maritan, and C. Mazzoli. 2009. "Petrographic and Microstratigraphic Analysis of Mortar-Based Building Materials from the Temple of Venus, Pompeii." In *Interpreting Silent Artefacts. Petrographic Approaches to Archaeological Ceramics*, edited by P. S. Quinn, 65–79. Oxford.

Piranomonte, M., and G. Ricci. 2009. "L'edificio rustico di viale Tiziano e la fonte di Anna Perenna. Nuovi dati per la topografia dell'area Flaminia in epoca repubblicana." In *Suburbium* II, 413–35.

Pobjoy, M. 1997. "A New Reading of the Mosaic Inscription in the Temple of Diana Tifatina." *PBSR* 65: 59–88.

2000. "Building Inscriptions in Republican Italy. Euergetism, Responsibility, and Civic Virtue." In *The Epigraphic Landscape of Roman Italy*, edited by A. Cooley, 77–92. BICS Suppl. 73. London: Institute of Classical Studies.

Poccetti, P. 1981. *Nuovi documenti italici a complemento del Manuale di E. Vetter*. Pisa: Giardini.

Poehler, E. E. 2012. "The Drainage System at Pompeii. Mechanisms, Operation and Design." *JRA* 25: 95–120.

2017. *The Traffic Systems of Pompeii*. Oxford: Oxford University Press.

Poehler, E. E., and B. M. Crowther. 2018. "Paving Pompeii. The Archaeology of Stone-Paved Streets." *AJA* 122: 579–609.

Poehler, E. E., and S. R. J. Ellis. 2011. "The 2010 Season of the Pompeii Quadriporticus Project. The Western Side." *Fasti On Line Documents & Research Italy* 218: 1–10.

2012. "The 2011 Season of the Pompeii Quadriporticus Project. The Southern and Northern Sides." *Fasti On Line Documents & Research Italy* 249: 1–12.

2013. "The Pompeii Quadriporticus Project. The Eastern Side and Colonnade." *Fasti On Line Documents & Research Italy* 284: 1–14.

2014. "The 2013 Season of the Pompeii Quadriporticus Project. Final Fieldwork and Preliminary Results." *Fasti On Line Documents & Research Italy* 321: 1–10.

Poggesi, G., and P. Pallecchi. 2012. "La cinta muraria di Cosa (GR)." In Attenni and D. Baldassarre, 161–68.

Prag, J. R. W. and J. Crawley Quinn, eds. 2013. *The Hellenistic West: Rethinking the Ancient Mediterranean*. Cambridge: Cambridge University Press.

Previato, C. 2015. *Aquileia. Materiali, forme e sistemi costruttivi dall'età repubblicana alla tarda età imperiale*. Padua: Padua University Press.

2019. "Modi d'uso e sistemi di messa in opera del laterizio in Italia settentrionale in età repubblicana." In Bonetto et al. 2019, 369–81.

Prigent, D. 2009. "Les traités." In *Le mortier de chaux*, edited by A. Coutelas, 21–32. Collection "Archeologiques." Paris: Editions Errance.

Proietti, L.M. 2006. "I pavimenti del Rione Terra di Pozzuoli. Un aggiornamento." In *Atti dell'XI Colloquio dell'Associazione italiana per lo studio e la conservazione del mosaico. Ancona, 16–19 febbraio 2005*, edited by C. Angelelli, 517–27. Tivoli: Scripta Manent.

Pucci, G. 1973. "La produzione della ceramica aretina. Note sull'"industria" nella prima età imperiale romana." *DialArch* 7: 255–93.

Purcell, N. 2017. "'Such Is Rome . . .' Strabo on the 'Imperial Metropolis'." In *The Routledge Companion to Strabo*, edited by D. Dueck, 22–34. London: Routledge.

Quilici, L. 1974. *Collatia (Forma Italiae, Regio I 10)*. Rome: De Luca.

—— 1986. "Il Tevere e l'Aniene come vie d'acqua a monte di Roma in età imperiale." In *ArchLaz*, 7: 198–217.

—— 1987. "La posterula di Vigna Casali nella pianificazione urbanistica dell'Aventino e sul possibile prospetto del Tempio di Diana." In *L' urbs. Espace urbain et histoire (Ier siècle av. J.-C. – IIIe siècle ap. J.-C.). Actes du colloque international Rome, 8–12 mai 1985*, 713–45. CÉFR 98. Rome: École française de Rome.

—— 1995. "Interventi di incentivazione agraria in un fundus visto da Varrone lungo la Via Salaria." In *Interventi di bonifica agraria nell'Italia Romana*, edited by L. Quilici and S. Quilici Gigli, 157–81. Rome: L'Erma di Bretschneider.

Quilici, L., and S. Quilici Gigli. 2000. "Sulle mura di Norba." In Quilici Gigli and Quilici 2000, 181–244. Rome: L'Erma di Bretschneider.

—— eds. 2014. *Roma, Città Romane, Assetto del Territorio*. Rome: L'Erma di Bretschneider.

—— 2018. "Aggiornamento della pianta di Norba." In *Norba. Scavi e ricerche*, edited by S. Quilici Gigli, 195–98. Rome: L'Erma di Bretschneider.

Quilici Gigli, S. 2003. "Trasformazioni urbanistiche ed attività edilizia in epoca repubblicana. Il caso di Norba." *Orizzonti: Rassegna di Archeologia* 4: 23–32.

—— 2008. "Strutturazione e monumentalizzazione dello spazio pubblico a Capua. Il criptoportico lungo la Via Appia." In *Spazi, forme e infrastrutture dell'abitare*, edited by L. Quilici and S. Quilici Gigli, 93–118. Rome: L'Erma di Bretschneider.

—— 2009. "Organizzazione e aspetti dello spazio sacro. Appunti sul santuario capuano di Diana alle falde del Tifata." *Atlante Tematico di Topografia Antica* 19: 123–47.

Quilici Gigli, S., and L. Quilici. 1998. "Interventi tardo-repubblicani nella pianificazione di Norba. Le terme centrali." In *Architettura e pianificazione urbana nell'Italia antica*, 63–82. Rome: L'Erma di Bretschneider.

—— eds. 2000. *Fortificazioni antiche in Italia. Età Repubblicana*. Rome: L'Erma di Bretschneider.

Rakob, F. 1976. "Hellenismus in Mittelitalien: Bautypen und Bautechnik." In Zanker 1976, vol. 2: 366–88.

—— 1983. "*Opus caementicium* und die Folgen." *RM* 90: 359–72.

Ramieri. 1980. "Roma, Regio VI. Via Cimarra. Resti di edifici monumentali del I sec. a.C. sulle pendici del Viminale." *NSc* 34: 25–49.

Rankov, B. 2013. "Roman Shipsheds." In *Shipsheds of the Ancient Mediterranean*, by D. J. Blackman, B. Rankov, K. Baika, H. Gerding, and J. Pakkanen, 30–54. Cambridge: Cambridge University Press.

Rapp, G. 2009. *Archaeomineralogy*. Berlin/Heidelberg: Springer Verlag.

Rawson, E. 1975. "Architecture and Sculpture. The Activities of the Cossutii." *PBSR* 43: 36–47.

1976. "The Ciceronian Aristocracy and Its Properties." In *Studies in Roman Property*, edited by M. I. Finley, 85–102. Cambridge: Cambridge University Press.

Reitz-Joosse, B. 2016. "The City and the Text in Vitruvius's *de Architectura*." *Arethusa* 49: 183–197.

Rendini, P. 1999. "L'urbanistica di Saturnia. Un aggiornamento." In *Città e monumenti nell'Italia antica*, edited by L. Quilici and S. Quilici Gigli, 97–118. Rome: L'Erma di Bretschneider.

Rescigno, C. 2017. "Il santuario di Apollo tra vecchie acquisizioni e nuove prospettive di ricerca." In Lippolis *et al.* 2017, 37–69.

Rescigno, C., and F. Senatore. 2009. "Le città della piana campana tra IV e III sec. a.C. Dati storici e topografici." In *Verso la città. Forme insediative in Lucania e nel mondo italico fra IV e III sec. a.C. Atti delle Giornate di studio, Venosa, 13–14 maggio 2006*, edited by M. Osanna. Venosa: Osanna Edizioni.

Richardson Jr., L. 1976. "The Evolution of the *Porticus Octaviae*." *AJA* 80: 57–64.

1988. *Pompeii: An Architectural History*. Baltimore/London: Johns Hopkins University Press.

Righini, V. 1990. "Materiali e tecniche da costruzione in età preromana e romana." In *Storia di Ravenna, 1: l'evo antico*, edited by D. Berardi and G. Susini, 257–96. Venice: Marsilio.

Rihll, T. E. 2013. "Depreciation in Vitruvius." *CQ* 63: 893–97.

Ringbom, Å., J. Heinemeier, A. Lindroos, and F. Brock. 2011. "Mortar Dating and Roman Pozzolana, Results and Interpretations." In *Building Roma Aeterna. Current Research on Roman Mortar and Concrete*, edited by Å. Ringbom, R. L. Hohlfelder, P. Sjöberg, and P. Sonck-Koota, 187–208. Helsinki: Societas Scientiarum Fennica.

Ringbom, Å., A. Lindroos, J. Heinemeier, and P. Sonck-Koota. 2014. "19 Years of Mortar Dating: Learning from Experience." *Radiocarbon* 56: 619–35.

Rispoli, C., A. De Bonis, V. Guarino, S. F. Graziano, C. Di Benedetto, R. Esposito, V. Morra, and V. Cappelletti. 2019. "The Ancient Pozzolanic Mortars of the Thermal Complex of Baia (Campi Flegrei, Italy)." *Journal of Cultural Heritage* 40: 143–54.

Rodríguez Almeida, E. 1981. *Forma Urbis marmorea: aggiornamento generale*. Rome: Quasar.

Romanelli, P. 1963. "Lo scavo al tempio della Magna Mater sul Palatino e nelle sue adiacenze." *MonAnt* 46: 201–330.

Romano, E. 1994. "Dal *De officiis* a Vitruvio, da Vitruvio a Orazio: il dibattito sul lusso edilizio." In *Le projet de Vitruve: objet, destinataires et réception du De architectura: actes du colloque international organisé par l'École française de Rome, l'Institut de recherche sur l'architecture antique du CNRS et la Scuola normale superiore de Pise (Rome, 26–27 mars 1993)*, 63–73. CÉFR 192. Rome/Paris: École française de Rome/De Boccard.

Romizzi, L. 2001. *Ville d'otium dell'Italia antica. II secolo a.C. – I secolo d.C.* Naples: Edizioni scientifiche italiane.

Roselaar, S. T. 2011. "Colonies and Processes of Integration in the Roman Republic." *MÉFRA* 123: 527–55.

2019. *Italy's Economic Revolution: Integration and Economy in Republican Italy*. Oxford: Oxford University Press.

Rossi, F. M. 2009. "Indagini nel temenos del tempio della Magna Mater sul Palatino. Strutture murarie, materiali e cronologia." In *Suburbium* II, 213–25.

Rossignani, M. P. 1977. "Saggio della piazza E2." In Frova 1977, 9–23.

Rostovtzeff, M. I. 1953. *The Social and Economic History of the Hellenistic World.* 3 vols. Oxford: Clarendon Press.

Roth, R. 2007. *Styling Romanisation: Pottery and Society in Central Italy.* Cambridge: Cambridge University Press.

Rous, B. D. 2010. *Triumphs of Compromise: An Analysis of the Monumentalisation of Sanctuaries in Latium in the Late Republican Period (Second and First Centuries BC).* PhD diss., University of Amsterdam.

Rowland, I. D., and T. N. Howe. 1999. *Vitruvius: Ten Books on Architecture.* New York: Cambridge University Press.

Royo, M. 1999. *Domus imperatoriae. Topographie, formation et imaginaire des palais impériaux du Palatin IIe siècle av. J.C.–Ier siècle ap. J.C.* BÉFAR 303. Rome: École française de Rome.

Ruga, A. 2014. "Crotone romana. Dal promontorio lacinio al sito 'acheo'." In *Kroton: Studi e ricerche sulla polis Achea e il suo territorio*, edited by R. Spadea, 181–272. AttiMGrecia 5. Rome: L'Erma di Bretschneider.

Russell, A. 2015. "Domestic and Civic Basilicas. Between Public and Private Space." In *Public and Private in the Roman House and Society*, edited by K. Tuori and L. Nissin, 49–56. JRA Suppl. 102. Portsmouth, RI: JRA.

Russell, B., and E. Fentress. 2016. "Mud Brick and *pisé de terre* between Punic and Roman." In DeLaine *et al.* 2016, 131–43.

Russo Tagliente, A., G. Ghini, and L. Caretta, eds. 2017. *Lucus Feroniae. Il santuario, la città, il territorio.* Rome: Scienze e Lettere.

Säflund, G. 1932. *Le mura di Roma repubblicana.* ActaRom 1. Uppsala: Gleerup.

Salmon, E. T. 1933. "The Last Latin Colony." *CQ* 27: 30–35.

——— 1936. "Roman Colonisation from the Second Punic War to the Gracchi." *JRS* 26: 47–67.

——— 1969. *Roman Colonization under the Republic.* London: Cornell University Press.

——— 1982. *The Making of Roman Italy. Aspects of Greek and Roman Life.* London: Cornell University Press.

Sampaolo, V. 2010. "Il quartiere degli anfiteatri. L'espansione di Capua fuori le mura occidental." In *Il Mediterraneo e la storia: epigrafia e archeologia in Campania: letture storiche. Atti dell'incontro internazionale di studio, Napoli, 4–5 dicembre 2008*, edited by L. Chioffi, 73–94. Naples: Luciano Edizioni.

Sanguinetti, F. 1958. "Il mosaico del ninfeo ed altre recenti scoperte nella Domus Aurea." *BCSSA* 12: 35–46.

Santangeli Valenzani, R., and R. Volpe. 1986. "Ambienti tra Via Nova e Clivo Palatino." *BullCom* 91: 411–22

Santangelo, F. 2012. "From Pompeii to Ameria: Patrimonies and Institutions in the Age of Sulla." In *Gérer Les Territoires, Les Patrimoines, et Les Crises*, edited by L. Lamoine, C. Berrendonner, and M. Cébeillac-Gervasoni, 417–31. Clermont-Ferrand: Presses Universitaires Blaise-Pascal.

Santoro, S., and D. Scagliarini Corlàita. 2005. "Progetto Insula del centenario (IX, 8). Saggi di scavo 1999–2004." *RstPomp* 16: 211–56.

Savi Scarponi, A. 2013. "Fornaci da calce di epoca romana e medievale in territorio capenate." *Fasti On Line Documents & Research Italy* 301: 1–18.

Scheidel, W. 2009. "In Search of Roman Economic Growth." *JRA* 22: 46–70.

——— 2011. "The Roman Slave Supply." In *The Cambridge World History of Slavery, 1. The Ancient Mediterranean World*, edited by K. Bradley and P. Cartledge, 287–310. Cambridge: Cambridge University Press.

——— 2019. *Escape from Rome: The Failure of Empire and the Road to Prosperity.* Princeton: Princeton University Press.

Schingo, G. 1996. "Indice topografico delle strutture anteriori all'incendio del 64 d.C. rinvenute nella valle del Colosseo e nelle sue adiacenze." In *Meta Sudans I. Un'area sacra in Palatio e la valle del Colosseo prima e dopo Nerone*, edited by C. Panella, 145–58. Rome: Istituto poligrafico e Zecca dello Stato.

Scott, A. R. 2008. *Cosa: The Black-Glaze Pottery, 2.* MAAR Suppl. 5. Ann Arbor: University of Michigan Press.

Scott, R. T. 2009. *Excavations in the Area Sacra of Vesta (1987–1996).* MAAR Suppl. 8. Ann Arbor: University of Michigan Press.

——— 2019. "Cosa: How Perfect! How Come?" In *Cosa and the Colonial Landscape of Republican Italy (Third and Second Centuries BCE)*, edited by A. U. De Giorgi, 21–29. Ann Arbor: University of Michigan Press.

Sear, F. 2006. *Roman Theatres: An Architectural Study.* Oxford: Oxford University Press.

Secco, M., C. Previato, A. Addis, G. Zago, A. Kamsteeg, S. Dilaria, C. Canovaro, G. Artioli, and J. Bonetto. 2019. "Mineralogical Clustering of the Structural Mortars from the Sarno Baths, Pompeii: A Tool to Interpret Construction Techniques and Relative Chronologies." *Journal of Cultural Heritage* 40: 265–73.

Seiler, F., H. Beste, C. Piraino, and D. Esposito. 2005. "La Regio VI Insula 16 e la zona della Porta Vesuvio." In Guzzo and Guidobaldi, 216–34. Naples: Electa.

Serlorenzi, M. 2010. "La costruzione di un complesso horreario a Testaccio. Primi indizi per delineare l'organizzazione del cantiere edilizio." In Camporeale *et al.* 2010, 105–26.

——— 2014. "Cave di pozzolana in 'Urbe'." In *Arqueología de la construcción IV. Las canteras en el mundo antiguo: sistemas de explotacion y procesos productivos (Actas del Congreso de Padova, 22–24 de noviembre de 2012)*, edited by J. Bonetto, S. Camporeale, and A. Pizzo, 87–103. Anejos ArchEspArq 69. Mérida: Instituto de Arqueología de Mérida.

Sewell, J. 2005. "Trading Places? A Reappraisal of the Fora at Cosa." *Ostraka* 14: 91–114.

——— 2010. *The Formation of Roman Urbanism, 338–200 B.C.: Between Contemporary Foreign Influence and Roman Tradition.* JRA Suppl. 79. Portsmouth, RI: JRA.

——— 2014. "Gellius, Philip II and a Proposed End to the 'Model-Replica' Debate." In Stek and Pelgrom 2014, 125–39.

——— 2015. *ROMURBITAL – an Archaeological Database of Higher-Order Settlements on the Italian Peninsula (350 BCE to 300 CE) [Data-Set].* York: Archaeology Data Service. DOI: https://doi.org/10.5284/1031492.

——— 2016. "Higher-Order Settlements in Early Hellenistic Italy. A Quantitative Analysis of a New Archaeological Database." *AJA* 120: 603–30.

Sgobbo, I. 1977. "Il maggior tempio del Foro di Cuma e la munificenza degli Heii cumani in epoca sannitica." *RendNap* 52: 231–64.

Sirano, F. 2007. "Teano. La scoperta del tempio di Iuno Puplona." In *In Itinere: Ricerche di archeologia in Campania*, edited by F. Sirano. S. Angelo in Formis: Lavieri.

ed. 2011. *Il teatro di Teanum Sidicinum: dall'antichità alla Madonna delle Grazie.* Caserta: Lavieri.

2013. "Novità dal territorio Campano." In Cifarelli 2013, 103–15.

2015. "La 'romanizzazione' dei luoghi di culto della Campania settentrionale. Proposte di lettura del dato archeologico tra ager Falernus, area aurunca e sidicina." In Stek and Burgers 2015, 199–237.

2017. "Architettura ellenistica nel III secolo a.C. Il contributi dei centri della Campania settentrionale interna." In *L'architettura greca in Occidente nel III secolo a.C. Atti del convegno di studi, Pompei-Napoli 20–22 maggio 2015*, edited by L. M. Caliò, J. des Courtils, and F. Leoni, 83–94. Rome: Quasar.

Sommella, P. 1988. *Italia antica. L'urbanistica romana.* Rome: Jouvence.

Specchio, P. 2011. "L'insula della Salita del Grillo all'interno dei Mercati di Traiano a Roma." In *Il futuro nell'archeologia. Il contributo dei giovani ricercatori. Atti del IV convegno nazionale dei giovani archeologi, Tuscania (VT), 12–15 Maggio 2011*, edited by G. Guarducci and S. Valentini, 349–58. Rome: Scienze e Lettere.

Stanco, E. A. 2009. "La seriazione cronologica della ceramica a vernice nera etrusco-laziale nell'ambito del III secolo a.C." In *Suburbium* II, 157–93.

Steinby, E. M. 1985. "Lacus Iuturnae, 1982–1983." In Bietti Sestieri 1985, 73–92.

1987. "Il lato orientale del Foro Romano. Proposte di lettura." *Arctos* 21: 139–84.

1988. "Il lato orientale del Foro Romano." *ArchLaz* 9: 32–36.

1993. "Sulla funzione della rampa situata fra l'area di Giuturna e l'atrium Vestae." In *Eius virtutis studiosi: Classical and Postclassical Studies in Honor of Frank Edward Brown (1908–1988)*, edited by R. T. Scott and A. Reynolds Scott, 149–59. Washington, DC: National Gallery of Art.

2011. "The Arch Meets the Orders." *Atlante Tematico di Topografia Antica* 21: 7–13.

2012a. *Edilizia pubblica e potere politico nella Roma repubblicana.* Milan/Rome: Jaca Book/Unione internazionale degli Istituti di archeologia, storia e storia dell'arte in Roma.

2012b. *Lacus Iuturnae, 2. Saggi degli anni 1982–85. 1. Relazioni di scavo e conclusioni.* ActaInstRomFin 38. Rome: De Luca.

Stek, T. D. 2009. *Cult Places and Cultural Change in Republican Italy: A Contextual Approach to Religious Aspects of Rural Society after Roman Conquest.* Amsterdam: Amsterdam University Press.

2014. "The City-State Model and Roman Republican Colonization: Sacred Landscapes as a Proxy for Colonial Socio-Political Organisation." In Stek and Pelgrom 2014, 87–105.

2018a. "The Impact of Roman Expansion and Colonization on Ancient Italy in the Republican Period. From Diffusionism to Networks of Opportunity." In *The Peoples of Ancient Italy*, edited by G. D. Farney and G. Bradley, 269–94. Berlin: De Gruyter.

2018b. "Early Roman Colonisation beyond the Romanising Agrotown." In *The Archaeology of Imperial Landscapes: A Comparative Study of Empires in the Ancient Near East and Mediterranean World*, edited by B. S. Düring and T. D. Stek, 145–72. Cambridge: Cambridge University Press.

Stek, T. D., and G.-J. Burgers, eds. 2015. *The Impact of Rome on Cult Places and Religious Practices in Ancient Italy.* BICS

Suppl.132. London: Institute of Classical Studies.

Stek, T. D., and J. Pelgrom, eds. 2014. *Roman Republican Colonization: New Perspectives from Archaeology and Ancient History*. Rome: Palombi.

Stopponi, S. 2006. "Tecniche edilizie di tipo misto a Orvieto." In *Tarquinia e le civiltà del Mediterraneo. Convegno internazionale, Milano, 22–24 giugno 2004*, edited by M. Bonghi Iovino. Milan: Cisalpino.

Strazzulla, M. J. 1992. "Le terrecotte architattoniche frontonali di Luni nel problema della coroplastica templare nelle colonie in territorio etrusco." In *La coroplastica templare etrusca fra il IV e il II sec. a.C., Atti del XVI Convegno di Studi Etruschi e Italici, Orbetello 25–29 Aprile 1988*, 161–83. Florence: Olschki.

—— 1993. "Fortuna etrusca e Fortuna romana. Due cicli decorativi a confronto. Roma, via S. Gregorio e Bolsena." *Ostraka* 2: 317–49.

—— 2010. "L'architettura religiosa di Roma tra tradizione e innovazione." In *I giorni di Roma: L'età della conquista*, edited by E. La Rocca and C. Parisi Presicce, 83–94. Milan: Skira.

Tamm, B. 1963. *Auditorium and Palatium*. Stockholm: Almqvist and Wiksell.

Tang, B. 2006. "Towards a Typology and Terminology of Ancient Pavements." *AnalRom* 32: 93–104.

Taylor, R. 2002. "Temples and Terracottas at Cosa." *AJA* 106: 59–83.

Ten, A. 2010. "Santuario di Ercole Vincitore. La fase precedente al teatro." *Atti e memorie della Società tiburtina di storia e d'arte* 83: 7–22.

Termeer, M. K. 2010. "Early Colonies in Latium (ca 534–338 BC): A Reconsideration of Current Images and the Archaeological Evidence." *BABesch* 85: 43–58.

Terrenato, N. 1998. "*Tam Firmum Municipium*: The Romanization of Volaterrae and Its Cultural Implications." *JRS* 88: 94–114.

—— 2001a. "Ancestor Cults: The Perception of Ancient Rome in Italian Culture." In *Images of Rome: Perceptions of Ancient Rome in Europe and the United States in the Modern Age*, edited by R. Hingley, 71–89. JRA Suppl. 44. Portsmouth, RI: JRA.

—— 2001b. "The Auditorium Site and the Origins of the Villa." *JRA* 14: 5–32.

—— 2008. "The Cultural Implications of the Roman Conquest." In *The Short Oxford History of Europe. Roman Europe*, edited by E. Bispham, 234–64. Oxford: Oxford University Press.

—— 2012. "The Enigma of the 'Catonian' Villas: The *De Agri Cultura* in the Context of Second-Century BC Italian Architecture." In Becker and Terrenato 2012, 69–93.

—— 2019. *The Early Roman Expansion into Italy: Elite Negotiation and Family Agendas*. Cambridge: Cambridge University Press.

Terrenato, N., and J. A. Becker. 2009. "Il sito del Monte delle Grotte sulla via Flaminia e lo sviluppo della villa nel suburbio di Roma." In *Suburbium* II, 393–401.

Tölle-Kastenbein, R. 1994. *Das Olympieion in Athen*. Weimar/Wien: Böhlau.

Tombrägel, M. 2012. *Die republikanischen Otiumvillen von Tivoli*. Wiesbaden: Reichert.

—— 2013. "Considerazioni sulle origini dell'*opus incertum*: il caso delle ville repubblicane di Tivoli." In Cifarelli 2013, 33–42.

Tomlinson, R. A. 1961. "Emplekton Masonry and Greek Structura." *JHS* 81: 133–40.

Torelli, M. 1972. "Gravisca (Tarquinia). Scavi nella città etrusca e romana. Campagne 1969 e 1970." *NSc* 25: 195–241.

1973. "Feronia e Lucus Feroniae in due iscrizioni latine." *ArchCl* 25–26: 741–50.

1980a. "Innovazioni nelle tecniche edilizie romane tra il I sec. a.C. e il I sec. d.C." In *Tecnologia, economia e società nel mondo romano. Atti del convegno di Como 27 – 29 settembre 1979*, 139–61. Como: Banca Popolare Commercio e Industria.

1980b. "Industria estrattiva, lavoro artigianale, interessi economici. Qualche appunto." In *The Seaborne Commerce of Ancient Rome: Studies in Archaeology and History*, 313–23. MAAR 36. Rome: American Academy in Rome.

1983. "Edilizia pubblica in Italia centrale tra guerra sociale ed età augustea. Ideologia e classi sociali." In Cébeillac-Gervasoni 1983, 241–50.

1999a. *Paestum Romana*. Paestum: Soprintendenza per i beni archeologici delle Province di Salerno, Avellino e Benevento.

1999b. *Tota Italia: Essays in the Cultural Formation of Roman Italy*. Oxford: Oxford University Press.

2012. "The Early Villa. Roman Contributions to the Development of a Greek Prototype." In Becker and Terrenato 2012, 8–31.

Torelli, M., and F. Marcattili. 2010. "La decorazione parietale domestica romano-italica tra fase medio-repubblicana e cultura della *luxuria*." *Bollettino di Archeologia Online* 1, Edizione Speciale D.6.5: 40–55.

Tortorici, E. 1988. "Il tempio presso S. Salvatore in Campo. V. Vespignani ed Ermodoro di Salamina." In *Topografia romana. Ricerche e discussioni*, 59–75. QITA 10. Rome: Olschki.

1991. *Argiletum. Commercio, speculazione edilizia e lotta politica dall'analisi topografica di un quartiere di Roma di età repubblicana*. Rome: L'Erma di Bretschneider.

Traini, L. 2013. *La lavorazione della calce dall'antichità al medioevo: Roma e le province dell'Impero*. Rome: Scienze e Lettere.

Trümper, M. 2009. "Complex Public Bath Buildings of the Hellenistic Period. A Case Study in Regional Differences." In *Le bain collectif en Égypte. Balaneia, Thermae*, edited by M. F. Boussac, T. Fournet, and B. Redon, 139–79. Cairo: Institut français d'archéologie orientale.

2010. "Bathing Culture in Hellenistic Domestic Architecture." In *Städtisches Wohnen im östlichen Mittelmeerraum 4.Jh. v.Chr. – 1.Jh. n. Chr. Akten des Internationalen Kolloquiums vom 24. – 27. Oktober 2007 an der Österreichischen Akademie der Wissenschaften*, edited by S. Ladstätter and V. Scheibelreiter, 534–42. Wien: Verlag der Österreichischen Akademie der Wissenschaften.

2018. "Gymnasium, Palaestra, Campus and Bathing in Late Hellenistic Pompeii: A Reassessment of the Urban Context of the Republican Baths (VIII 5, 36)." In Mania and Trümper 2018, 87–113.

Trümper, M., C. Brünenberg, J. A. Dickmann, D. Esposito, A. F. Ferrandes, G. Pardini, A. Pegurri, M. Robinson, and C. Rummel. 2019. "Stabian Baths in Pompeii. New Research on the Development of Ancient Bathing Culture." *RM* 125: 103–59.

Tsiolis, V. 2008. "Modelli di convivenza urbana. Fregellae e la questione dell'introduzione delle pratiche termali nel Lazio meridionale." In *Dalle sorgenti alla foce. Il bacino del Liri-Garigliano nell'antichità. Culture, contatti, scambi. Atti del convegno, Frosinone – Formia, 10 – 12 novembre*, edited by C. Corsi and E. Polito, 133–43. Rome: Quasar.

2013. "The Baths at Fregellae and the Transition from Balaneion to Balneum." In *Greek Bath and Bathing Culture. New Discoveries and Approaches*, edited by S. K. Lucore and M. Trümper, 89–111. Leuven: Peeters.

Tucci, P. L. 2012. "La controversa storia della 'porticus Aemilia'." *ArchCl* 63: 575–91.

2018. *The Temple of Peace in Rome*. Cambridge: Cambridge University Press.

2019. "Living on the Capitoline Hill. The *domus* of the Aracoeli and Its Sculptural and Painted Decoration." *PBSR* 87: 71–144.

Tuck, S. L. 2000. "A New Identification for the Porticus Aemilia." *JRA* 13: 175–82.

Tunzi, A. M., R. Cassano, and F. M. Martino. 2017. "La vicenda urbana di Siponto ridisegnata dalle recenti indagini." In *Dialoghi sull'archeologia della Magna Grecia e del Mediterraneo: atti del I. convegno internazionale di studi, Paestum, 7–9 settembre 2016*, edited by A. Pontrandolfo Greco and M. Scafuro, 503–10. Paestum: Pandemos.

Tweedie, F. C. 2011. "The Case of the Missing Veterans. Roman Colonisation and Veteran Settlement in the Second Century B.C." *Historia* 60: 458–73.

Uroz Sáez, J. 2008. "Fundiary Property and Brick Production in the High Tiber Valley." In Coarelli and Patterson, 123–42.

Valenti, M. 2003. *Forma Italiae, 41. Ager Tusculanus (IGM 150 III NE – II NO)*. Florence: Olschki.

Van Balen, K. 2003. "Understanding the Lime Cycle and Its Influence on Historical Construction Practice." In *Proceedings of the First International Congress on Construction History. Madrid, 20th – 24th January 2003*, edited by S. Huerta, 2041–54. Madrid: Instituto Juan de Herrera.

Van Deman, E. B. 1912a. "Methods of Determining the Date of Roman Concrete Monuments (First Paper)." *AJA* 16: 230–51.

1912b. "Methods of Determining the Date of Roman Concrete Monuments (Second Paper)." *AJA* 16: 387–432.

1922. "The Sullan Forum." *JRS* 12: 1–31.

Van der Graaff, I. 2019. *The Fortifications of Pompeii and Ancient Italy*. Abingdon/ New York/Oxon: Routledge.

Van der Leeuw, S. E., and R. Torrence, eds. 1989. *What's New? A Closer Look at the Process of Innovation*. One World Archaeology, 14. London/Boston: Unwin Hyman.

Van Dommelen, P., and N. Terrenato. 2007. *Articulating Local Cultures. Power and Identity under the Expanding Roman Republic*. JRA Suppl. 63. Portsmouth, RI: JRA.

Van Oyen, A. 2015. "Deconstructing and Reassembling the Romanization Debate through the Lens of Postcolonial Theory: From Global to Local and Back?" *Terra Incognita* 5: 205–26.

Van Oyen, A., and M. Pitts, eds. 2017. *Materialising Roman Histories*. Oxford/Philadelphia: Oxbow.

Varriale, I. 2010. "I cicli decorativi di età tardo-ellenistica dal tempio di Venere a Pompei." In *Atti del X Congresso internazionale dell'AIPMA (Association internationale pour la peinture murale antique). Napoli, 17–21 settembre 2007*, edited by I. Bragantini, 375–86. Naples: Università degli studi di Napoli "L'Orientale."

Vassal, V. 2006. *Les pavements d'opus signinum: technique, décor, function architecturale*. BAR-IS 1472. Oxford: Archaeopress.

Veal, R. 2018. "Fuel and Timber in the Casa del Chirurgo." In Anderson and Robinson 2018a, 516–24.

Vecchi, C. 2013. "Tivoli. Ricerche nell'area archeologica del criptoportico di Piazza D. Tani." *ScAnt* 19: 271–89.

Venditti, C. P. 2011. *Le villae del Latium adiectum. Aspetti residenziali delle proprietà rurali.* Bologna: Ante quem.

Vermuelen, F. 2014. "Republican Colonization and Early Urbanization in Central Adriatic Italy: The Valley of the River Flosis." In Stek and Pelgrom 2014, 141–59.

Vermuelen, F., M. Destro, M. Monsieur, F. Carboni, S. Dralans, and D. Van Limbergen. 2011. "Scavi presso la porta occidentale di Potentia. Notizia preliminare." *Picus* 31: 169–205.

Vermuelen, F., and G. Verhoeven. 2006. "An Integrated Survey of Roman Urbanization at Potentia, Central Italy." *JFA* 31: 395–409.

Verzár-Bass, M. 1986. "Elementi lapidei del tempio e della porticus." In Coarelli 1986, 45–49.

Verzár-Bass, M., and F. Oriolo. 2009. "Lo sviluppo architettonico dell'insula VI, 13." In *Rileggere Pompei II. L'Insula 13 della Regio VI*, edited by M. Verzár-Bass and F. Oriolo, 495–97. Studi della Soprintendenza archeologica di Pompei 30. Rome: L'Erma di Bretschneider.

Verzár-Bass, M., F. Oriolo, and F. Zanini. 2008. "L'Insula VI, 13 di Pompei alla luce delle recenti indagini." In Guzzo and Guidobaldi 2008, 189–96.

Vetter, E. 1953. *Handbuch der italischen Dialekte.* Heidelberg: Winter.

Veyne, P. 1979. "The Hellenization of Rome and the Question of Acculturations." *Diogenes* 27: 1–27.

Vincenti, V. 2008. "Pavimenti dalla prima fase delle terme di Fregellae (FR). Cenni preliminari." In Angelelli and Rinaldi 2008, 407–18.

Vlad Borrelli, L. 1967. "Il restauro dell'Aula Isiaca." *Bollettino dell'Istituto Centrale del Restauro*, 23–36.

Vogel, S., M. Märker, D. Esposito, and F. Seiler. 2016. "The Ancient Rural Settlement Structure in the Hinterland of Pompeii Inferred from Spatial Analysis and Predictive Modeling of *Villae Rusticae*." *Geoarchaeology* 31: 121–39.

Volpe, R. 2012. "Republican Villas in the Suburbium of Rome." In Becker and Terrenato 2012, 94–110.

Volpicella, D. 2006. "Cuma. Le terme centrali. Un preliminare inquadramento cronologico delle fasi edilizie." *AION* 13–14: 197–220.

Von Gerkan, A. 1958a. "Rez. zu Giuseppe Lugli, La tecnica edilizia Romana, con particolare riferimento a Roma e Lazio. G. Bardi, Roma 1957." *GGA* 212: 178–97.

———. 1958b. "Zur Datierung der Kolonie Cosa." In *Scritti in onore di Guido Libertini*, edited by P. E. Arias, 149–56. Florence: Olschki.

Von Hesberg, H. 1985. "Zur Plangestaltung der Coloniae maritimae." *RM* 92: 127–50.

———. 2005. *Römische Baukunst.* München: Beck.

Waelkens, M. 1987. "The Adoption of Roman Building Techniques in the Architecture of Asia Minor." In *Roman Architecture in the Greek World*, edited by S. Macready and F. H. Thompson, 94–105. London: Society of Antiquaries.

Wallace-Hadrill, A. 2007. "The Development of the Campanian House." In Dobbins and Foss 2007, 269–78.

———. 2008. *Rome's Cultural Revolution.* Cambridge: Cambridge University Press.

———. 2013. "Hellenistic Pompeii: Oscan, Greek, Roman and Punic." In Prag and Crawley Quinn, 35–43.

Wallace-Hadrill, A., and R. Laurence, eds. 1997. *Domestic Space in the Roman World. Pompeii and Beyond.* JRA Suppl. 22. Portsmouth, RI: JRA.

Ward-Perkins, J. B. 1970. "From Republic to Empire. Reflections on the Early Provincial Architecture of the Roman West." *JRS* 60: 1–19.

——— 1979. "Taste, Tradition and Technology. Some Aspects of the Architecture of Late Republican and Early Imperial Central Italy." In *Studies in Classical Art and Archaeology. A Tribute to Peter Heinrich von Blanckenhagen*, edited by G. Kopcke and M. B. Moore, 197–204. Locust Valley, NY: J. J. Austin.

——— 1981. *Roman Imperial Architecture.* Harmondsworth/New York: Penguin.

Weber, M. 1904. *Die protestantische Ethik und der "Geist" des Kapitalismus.* Tübingen: Mohr.

Welch, K. E. 2006. "*Domi militiaeque.* Roman Domestic Aesthetics and War Booty in the Republic." In *Representations of War in Ancient Rome*, edited by S. Dillon and K. E. Welch, 91–161. Cambridge: Cambridge University Press.

Westgate, R. 2000. "*Pavimenta atque emblemata vermiculata*: Regional Styles in Hellenistic Mosaic and the First Mosaics at Pompeii." *AJA* 104: 255–75.

Widrig, W. M. 1987. "Land Use at the Via Gabina Villas." In *Ancient Roman Villa Gardens. Dumbarton Oaks Colloquium on the History of Landscape Architecture, 10. [Held in May 1984]*, edited by E. B. McDougall, 223–60. Washington, DC: Dumbarton Oaks Research Library and Collection/ Trustees for Harvard University.

Wilson, A. 2006. "The Economic Impact of Technological Advances in the Roman Construction Industry." In Lo Cascio 2006, 225–36.

Wiseman, T. P. 1993. "Rome and the Resplendent Aemilii." In *Tria Lustra: Essays and Notes Presented to John Pinsent, Founder and Editor of Liverpool Classical Monthly, by Some of Its Contributors on the Occasion of Its 150th Issue*, edited by H. D. Jocelyn and H. Hunt, 181–92. Liverpool: Liverpool Classical Monthly.

Wootton, W. 2016. "A Portrait of the Artist as a Mosaicist under the Roman Empire." In *Beyond Boundaries. Connecting Visual Cultures in the Provinces of Ancient Rome*, edited by S. E. Alcock, M. Egri, and J. F. D. Frakes, 62–83. Los Angeles: Getty Publications.

Wright, G. R. H. 2005. *Ancient Building Technology, 2: Materials.* Leiden/ Boston: Brill.

Yegül, F., and D. Favro. 2019. *Roman Architecture and Urbanism: From the Origins to Late Antiquity.* New York: Cambridge University Press.

Zaccaria, C. 2014. "*T. Annius T. f. tri(um) vir e le prime fasi della colonia latina di Aquileia.* Bilancio storiografico e problemi aperti." In Chiabà 2014, 519–52.

Zaccheo, L., and F. Pasquali. 1972. *Sezze dalla preistoria all'eta romana.* Sezze: A cura dell'Amministrazione comunale.

Zampetti, M. 2006. "La casa VI 10, 3–4 e la bottega VI 10, 5." In Coarelli and Pesando 2006a, 75–118.

Zanker, P., ed. 1976. *Hellenismus in Mittelitalien. Kolloquium in Göttingen vom 5. bis 9. Juni 1974.* 2 vols. Göttingen: Vandenhoeck and Ruprecht.

——— 1998. *Pompeii: Public and Private Life.* Translated by D. L. Schneider. Cambridge, MA/London: Harvard University Press.

Zarmakoupi, M. 2011. "Porticus and Cryptoporticus in Roman Luxury Villas: Architectural Design and Cultural Implications." In *Art, Industry and Infrastructure in Roman Pompeii*, edited by E. Poehler, M. Flohr, and K. Cole, 50–61. Oxford: Oxbow.

2014. *Designing for Luxury on the Bay of Naples*. Oxford: Oxford University Press.

Zeggio, S. 2006. "Dall'indagine alla città. Un settore del centro monumentale e la sua viabilità dale origini all'età neroniana." *ScAnt* 13: 61–122.

Zevi, F. 1991. "La città sannitica. L'edilizia privata e la Casa del Fauno." In *Pompei 1*, edited by F. Zevi, 47–74. Naples: Banco di Napoli.

1996. "Pompei dalla città sannitica alla colonia sillana. Per un'interpretazione dei dati archeologici." In *Les élites municipales de l'Italie péninsulaire des Gracques à Néron. Actes de la table ronde de Clermont-Ferrand, 28 – 30 novembre 1991*, edited by M. Cébeillac-Gervasoni, 125–38. Naples: Centre Jean Bérard.

1997. "Considerazioni vecchie e nuove sul santuario della Fortuna Primigenia. L'organizzazione del santuario, i Mucii Scaevolae e l'architettura mariana." In *Le Fortune dell'età arcaica nel Lazio ed in Italia e loro posterità. Atti del 3° Convegno di studi archeologici, Palestrina 15 – 16 ottobre 1994*, 137–83. Palestrina: Comune di Palestrina, Assessorato alla cultura.

2003. "L'ellenismo a Roma nel tempo della colonizzazione in Italia." In *Il fenomeno coloniale dall'antichità ad oggi. Giornate dell'antichità. Roma, 19 e 20 marzo 2002*, 53–104. Rome: Accademia nazionale dei Lincei.

2013. "Brevi appunti in chiusura." In Cifarelli 2013, 127–31.

Zevi, F., and M. Grandi. 2004. "Il pavimento del Capitolium di Pozzuoli." In *Atti del IX Colloquio dell'Associazione Italiana per lo Studio e la Conservazione del Mosaico, Aosta, 20–22 febbraio 2003*, edited by C. Angelelli, 351–60. Ravenna: Edizioni del Girasole.

Zimmer, G. 1982. *Römische Berufsdarstellungen*. Berlin: Mann.

Zink, S. 2015. "The Palatine Sanctuary of Apollo. The Site and Its Development, 6th to 1st c. B.C." *JRA* 28: 358–70.

# INDEX

CPSIA information can be obtained
at www.ICGtesting.com
Printed in the USA
LVHW062346190621
690667LV00005B/215

9 781108 845687